SOCIAL SCIENCE
EDUCATIONAL POLICY
AND THE SEARCH FOR STANDARDS

INDETERMINACY IN EDUCATION

EDITED BY

John E. McDermott

Western Center on Law and Poverty

McCutchan Publishing Corporation
2526 Grove Street
Berkeley, California 94704

©1976 by McCutchan Publishing Corporation
All rights reserved

Library of Congress Catalog Card Number 76-2987
ISBN 0-8211-1251-1

Printed in the United States of America

—To Harold W. Horowitz for his dedication to egalitarian ideals, his compassion for children, and his inspiration to me—

Acknowledgments

This book was prepared with the support of a grant from the Ford Foundation. The grant is but one example of the extensive support given by the Ford Foundation in recent years to the study of educational policy. Much of this support is due to Dr. James A. Kelly, Jr., a program officer at Ford, whose contributions to the field of educational policy are widely recognized. At the same time, it should be noted that the views expressed in this book are those of the authors, and do not necessarily represent the views of the Ford Foundation or its program officers.

Special credit is also due to Dr. Harold W. Horowitz, a law professor at UCLA School of Law and now Vice Chancellor at UCLA. Dr. Horowitz, who has written extensively about equal educational opportunity and the law, was a principal legal theorist for the *Serrano v. Priest* case challenging the constitutionality of the California school finance system because of interdistrict per pupil spending disparities. A major issue in that trial, in which I was privileged to serve as trial counsel, was the existence, if any, of a relationship between school spending levels and student achievement patterns, and the role of social science research in examining that relationship. Out of our discussions of this issue during the trial came the idea for this volume of essays. Dr. Horowitz assisted in the planning and structuring of the volume, and reviewed and evaluated the manuscript. For all of his efforts in support of this volume, I am especially grateful.

I would also like to thank my wife Linda for her help in the preparation and typing of the manuscript, and for her encouragement during those moments when my impatience and frustration with the inevitable delays involved in publishing any book seemed to get an upper hand.

Foreword

"Educational policymaking is now in a state of indeterminacy," we are told by John E. McDermott and the other contributors to this volume. By this McDermott and his colleagues mean that there does not exist a social science knowledge base to guide educational policymaking. A decade or two ago this conclusion was so obvious that it would not be drawn. To be sure psychologists and other social scientists have long struggled to understand the educational *process*. However, during the last decade or two there has been an unprecedented attempt to use social science in educational policymaking. Educational policymakers have turned to social science in an effort to reduce indeterminacy.* Their hope was to reduce the need to develop policy in the absence of knowledge about the condition of education or about the consequences of proposed actions. Social scientists responded with increasingly sophisticated analyses and with the promise—some would say overpromise—that their analyses would reduce indeterminacy. That neither the policymakers nor the social

---

*The parallel between "decisionmaking under uncertainty" and "policymaking under indeterminacy" seems obvious; why a concern for "policymaking" has replaced the concern for "decisionmaking" is less obvious.

scientists were satisfied by the intense activity of the last decade is the clear message of this book. The rediscovery of indeterminacy becomes then a new conclusion.

Most of the contributors to this volume use the term "indeterminacy" to refer to the lack of scientifically validated guidelines for policymaking. Gregory S. Kavka uses the term to refer to the lack of a consensus on the aims of education. Agreement on the aims of education is necessary before scientifically validated guidelines can, in principle, operate. The search for consensus on the aims of education is a moral, political, and legal process. "Indeterminacy" is also used in its general sense meaning a state of being "not fixed," "not clear," "not established," or "not settled." However, there is an additional and more specific meaning of the term which the reader may wish to ponder. An equation is said to be "indeterminate" when it can be satisfied by more than one value for each unknown. Is the search to reduce technical indeterminacy in education a search for equations which can be satisfied by only one value for each unknown?

Educational policy development is the creation of a set of imperatives to govern an educational system. A policy is based upon a vision of what the educational system is to accomplish and a "theory of instruction."* Policy then consists of a statement of aims which are not, even in principle, scientifically derivable.[†] And policy consists of a theory of instruction which includes hypotheses formally or, more likely, informally drawn. In other words, the policy is a set of imperatives which, if based upon correct hypotheses, will achieve the desired aim. To what sources of authority do policymakers turn? For the aims of education they must obviously turn to other than scientific authority. But where to turn for a theory of instruction—for a set of hypotheses which will allow the prediction of consequences?

One set of sources may be moral philosophy, ethics, and religions which contain not only a vision of society but also ideas about how individuals need to behave in order to achieve the vision of society. A second set of sources may be history, tradition, and precedent which, to the extent that the vision of society is constant, contain ideas

---

*An understanding of the needs of the child *vis a vis* the aims of education is part of "a theory of instruction."

[†]Scientific surveys of people's values do not render the collective opinion scientific.

about how to implement the vision. A third set of sources may be constitutional, statutory, and case law which embody a concept of society as well as rules for behavior. A fourth set of sources may be common sense and professional lore which are constituted of uncodified and codified ideas about education. A fifth source might be the exercise of discretion—individual or group—which, too, may reveal not only a vision of the purposes of education but also a theory of instruction.*

The problem with these sources of authority is that their hypotheses may not be correct. In fact, in late twentieth century America many are not even regarded as sources of authority. Thus, policymakers often turn to the authority of science. Science is the source of confirmed or confirmable hypotheses and is thus seen as a way to reduce indeterminacy. Science itself generates hypotheses and provides the means to test hypotheses generated by other sources of authority. Under what circumstances is a policymaker likely to turn to the authority of social science?

Formal educational policy is developed at the national, state, and local levels of government. Indeed, at the local level, educational policy is developed at the district, school, and classroom levels. Policy development at each of these levels may be assumed to proceed differently. Educational policy is developed legislatively, administratively, and judicially. Policy development in each of these arenas may also be assumed to proceed differently. How does social science impact upon educational policy development at different levels of government and in the legislative, administrative, and judicial arenas?

It may be supposed that some policymakers feel greater need to reduce indeterminacy. Three factors which may influence policymakers are (1) the scope of impact of the policy, (2) the ease with which the policy can be rescinded if it is found to be incorrect, and (3) the degree of flexibility in the application of the policy.

Policies are made for the classroom, the school, the district, the state, and the nation. The consequences of an ill-formulated policy are more disastrous the higher the level of government because of the larger number of persons affected. Lower-level policymakers also have the option of "experimentally" introducing a policy into only

---

*The political and the legislative process includes the exercise of group discretion.

some sub-units so that the impact of a policy can be assessed before it is applied generally. Thus, higher-level policymakers may be more inclined to turn to social science guidance.

Policies vary in the degree to which they can easily be rescinded, depending upon whether they are administrative, legislative, or judicial in origin. If a policy is found to have undesired consequences, then efforts may be made to rescind that policy. Thus, it may be supposed that the greater the anticipated difficulty of rescission, the more likely a policymaker is to turn to social science to attempt to reduce the likelihood of undesired consequences. It appears easier for an administrator to rescind a policy than for a legislature to rescind a policy and easier for a legislature to rescind a policy than for the courts to rescind a policy. If this impression is correct, then it may help to account for courts having been quick to embrace social science.

Akin to ease of rescission is flexibility in the application of the policy. Judicial standards of desegregation and equalization must, in principle, be implemented more rigorously and rigidly than a policy of a school to increase individualized instruction. As well, a judicial policy must be stated in more precise terms, leaving little discretion at lower levels where the policy is to be implemented. Thus, the courts may be more likely to try to reduce indeterminacy through the use of social science.

The traditional purpose of the social sciences has been to increase our understanding of naturally occurring social phenomena.* To this end each of the social sciences has pursued disciplined inquiry into individual and social behavior. More recently we have come to expect the social sciences to increase our understanding of social inventions. To this end the sub-disciplines known collectively as "evaluation" have developed to study formal interventions in the social system. Most recently we have come to use the social sciences in an engineering or application mode. In other words, the theories, concepts, methods, and findings of the social sciences are expected to help us design and redesign our institutions. This book, while dealing with all three expectations for social science, focuses upon the last.

Over the years, the full range of social sciences has been brought

---

*Of course, experiments may be conducted to help illuminate naturally occurring events.

to bear on the study of education. While psychology with its many sub-disciplines and hybrids has been dominant for most of this century, the last two decades have seen the other social sciences turning to the study of education. Most of the appropriate concepts and methods of the social science disciplines have been employed to study the learner, the teacher, and the institution of education.

As the essays in this book make clear, however, the public policy debate in education over the last decade has fixed upon one line of research—the school-effectiveness studies. The Coleman Report and its progeny have been the nearly exclusive source of social science input into educational policy deliberations.* The preoccupation with this line of research no doubt has been due primarily to an overwhelming desire to justify the efficacy of schooling in policy-relevant terms. Thus, research which does not deal with education in "input-output" terms is ignored. And research which aggregates data below the level of the school is largely ignored as is most research which fails to define output as scores on reading and mathematics achievement tests. It is important to note that while the school-effectiveness studies have been the most visible educational research of the last decade, they represent only a small fraction of educationally relevant research.

The Coleman Report and its progeny have created the parameters of policy debates in education. Originally, of course, the objective was to find hard data to determine whether there was equality of educational opportunity. The impressionistic approach and the input approach to equality of educational opportunity were abandoned; in their place came the output—meaning achievement test score—approach. The statistical models used in this research and the underlying educational models assumed surely have been worthy of development and scientific testing. However, the scientific debate—replete with methodological arguments—has framed the policy debate. Thus, policy reforms such as desegregation, finance equalization, compensatory education, accountability, decentralization, and community control are evaluated against an incomplete model of schooling. These reforms—when they are found to lack an effect upon achieve-

---

*James S. Coleman *et al.*, *Equality of Educational Opportunity*, Office of Education, National Center for Educational Statistics, OE 38001 (Washington, D.C.: Government Printing Office, 1966).

ment scores—are challenged. In the process the objectives of these reforms are redefined; the aims of education are redefined; and the goals of society are redefined.*

The Coleman Study and its numerous subsequent reanalyses may in fact be a commentary on the limited investment in social science research which our nation is willing to make. The first, necessarily crude, and hastily gathered data became for years the only data source for dozens of educational researchers and the only source for policy-relevant analyses. As each succeeding reanalysis was published, it was greeted as a new study which confirmed the increasingly familiar "no school effects" conclusion. As policymakers sought guidance over the years there was nowhere else to turn. What was an excellent research model which should have given rise to a new generation of research instead became the source of a pessimistic refrain in the policy arena. In the quest to reduce indeterminacy, a partial model of educational reality became the complete framework for the debate. The model of education, which social scientists are forced to assume because of their problem (school effectiveness), available research designs, and statistical models force a narrow view of education. This narrow view is necessary to abstract reality for *research* purposes; it does not follow that policy should be developed on the basis of this narrow view of education.

As I suggested at the outset, indeterminacy in education is not new. Some will not have noticed the temporary passing and return of indeterminacy for they have never believed in the potential of social science. But those, like the contributors to this volume, who have been active in efforts to reform educational policy through the use of social science must turn to other sources of authority.

Consider school *finance reform* which, if one looks at the current policy debate, has become synonymous with *educational reform*. In less sophisticated times, school finance disputes were settled on the basis of political authority perhaps with a touch of fairness. Then ensued the effort to redistribute financial resources based upon the authority of constitutional law. Along the way that effort became transformed by the use of social science into an educational reform effort. As the school-effectiveness question is raised, it has appeared that school finance reform cannot proceed unless educational reform

---

*See generally chapter 5.

is guaranteed. But the question is for the present indeterminate, leading McDermott to return to constitutional authority: "For purposes of educational inequality litigation, social science output research arguably can even be deemed legally irrelevant. Under the equal protection clause, the concern is with whether government treats people equally. . . . Equal protection decisions have never required proof of the *effects* of unequal government treatment." The circle is complete.

The indeterminacy conclusion is a sobering one; social science has not yielded guidance for educational policy. Traditional beliefs have been challenged but not necessarily destroyed by social science; a substitute for traditional beliefs has yet to be created. The social sciences need to mature in order to overcome indeterminacy; educational policymakers need to have courage in order to make policy in the face of indeterminacy.

Arthur E. Wise

Visiting Scholar
Education Policy Research Institute
Educational Testing Service

Contributors

Arthur E. Wise (Ph.D., Chicago, 1967; B.A., Harvard 1963) is currently a Visiting Scholar at Education Policy Research Institute, an affiliate of Educational Testing Service (ETS). Dr. Wise was an Associate Director of the National Institute of Education and directed its Office of Research and its Basic Skills Group from 1973 to 1975. He is the author of *Rich Schools, Poor Schools: The Promise of Equal Educational Opportunity* (Chicago: University of Chicago Press, 1968), a book which played a major role in stimulating school finance reform.

Alexander M. Mood (Ph.D., Princeton, 1940; B.A., Texas, 1934) was Assistant U.S. Commissioner of Education and Director of the National Center for Educational Statistics from 1964 to 1967, and supervised the Equality of Educational Opportunity study (Coleman Report). Since 1967, Dr. Mood has been Professor of Administration at the University of California at Irvine.

Stephen P. Klein (Ph.D., Purdue, 1965; B.A., Tufts, 1960) is currently a researcher at the RAND Corporation in Santa Monica and a member of the teaching faculty in the Department of Education at UCLA. Dr. Klein has been a research psychologist at ETS and a project director at the UCLA Center for the Study of Evaluation.

Donald R. Winkler (Ph.D., Berkeley, 1972; B.A., Wisconsin, 1966) is Assistant Professor of Economics and Education at the University of California at Santa Barbara.

Audrey James Schwartz (Ph.D., UCLA, 1967; B.S., Pennsylvania, 1947) is an Associate Professor of Education at the University of Southern California, and the author of *The Schools and Socialization* (New York: Harper and Row, 1975).

Henry M. Levin (Ph.D., Rutgers, 1967; B.S., New York, 1960) is Professor of Education and Economics at Stanford University.

Theodore M. Hesburgh, C.S.C., is President of the University of Notre Dame and former Chairman of the United States Commission on Civil Rights.

Gregory S. Kavka (Ph.D., Michigan, 1973; B.A., Princeton, 1968) is Assistant Professor of Philosophy at UCLA.

James W. Guthrie (Ph.D., Stanford, 1968; B.A., Stanford, 1958) is Associate Professor of Education at the University of California at Berkeley and a member of the Board of Education of the Berkeley Unified School District.

David W. O'Shea (Ph.D., Chicago, 1971) is Associate Professor of Education at UCLA.

Contents

Foreword   ix
    Arthur E. Wise

        Introduction: Indeterminacy in Education   1
        John E. McDermott

**PART ONE: THE STATE OF THE ART OF
            EDUCATIONAL RESEARCH**

    1.   The State of the Art of Educational Evaluation   17
         Alexander M. Mood

    2.   Cost-Quality Research Limitations:
         The Problem of Poor Indices   33
         Stephen P. Klein

    3.   The Policy Implications of Research in
         Educational Production   51
         Donald R. Winkler

    4.   Social Science Evidence and the Objectives
         of School Desegregation   73
         Audrey James Schwartz

PART TWO: THE PUBLIC POLICY IMPLICATIONS OF EDUCATIONAL RESEARCH

5. Education, Life Chances, and the Courts:
    The Role of Social Science Evidence   117
    Henry M. Levin

6. Public Policy, Desegregation, and the Limits
    of Social Science Research   149
    Theodore M. Hesburgh, C.S.C.

7. The Cost-Quality Debate in School Finance
    Litigation   169
    John E. McDermott

8. Equal Educational Opportunity and the
    Distribution of Educational Expenditures   189
    Henry M. Levin

9. Equality in Education   211
    Gregory S. Kavka

10. Social Science, Accountability, and the Political
    Economy of School Productivity   253
    James W. Guthrie

11. Social Science and School Decentralization   309
    David W. O'Shea

Introduction: Indeterminacy in Education

JOHN E. McDERMOTT

Educational policymaking is now in a state of indeterminacy. No satisfactory criteria exist by which to make important decisions regarding school desegregation, school financing, compensatory education, accountability, decentralization, and community control.

The origin of this condition is recent social science research evidence which challenges the traditional American notion that schools engender social mobility. Eminent social scientists assert that differences in schooling do not matter much in terms of student outcomes, at least as measured by pupil performance on standardized achievement tests. Home background and socioeconomic status are what account for variations in pupil achievement, not inequalities in schools. One policy or spending level or teacher, then, is as good as any other, so far as student achievement is concerned. Even if schooling could equalize cognitive outcomes, that would not significantly reduce adult income inequality, according to Christopher Jencks. Thus, a seemingly irrefutable array of statistics and data obtained through the most sophisticated social science research techniques leads to the conclusion that differences in schooling have little impact on student school outcomes or adult life chances.

1

Defenders of education vigorously dispute not only the soundness of these pronouncements, but the whole enterprise of social science research as well. Much evidence exists to suggest that social science research, given the present state of the art, is simply inadequate as a basis for making public policy decisions about education. Thus, while American society may have been naive in its belief that the power of schooling could alter life outcomes, the traditional importance attached to schooling in America should not be discarded quite yet.

The public policy implications of this uncertainty about the importance of schooling, of this lack of satisfactory criteria with which to make important decisions, are profound. How, for example, can a judge formulate judicial standards to compare the quality of educational opportunities from district to district or school to school? On what basis can legislators attempt to hold schools accountable for the way money is spent or to decide how much money is enough to provide a quality education? And how do local school officials decide how to allocate their resources to obtain the highest yield on their investment, or how do they resolve complex issues like decentralization and community control? Do social science research findings provide any significant help in establishing viable standards on which to make these important policy decisions? If not, are other criteria available on which to base such decisions?

This collection of essays examines the public policy implications of social science research on education and the lack of qualitative standards for defining and evaluating educational opportunities. The implications of inadequate evaluative criteria are explored in the following contexts: (1) the determination of equality of educational opportunity for purposes of school desegregation and school financing, (2) the development of viable standards needed to hold schools accountable for their performance and effectiveness, and (3) the availability of useful criteria by which school officials can make decisions about other important policy matters such as decentralization and community control. There is particular emphasis on the usefulness of recent social science research efforts to evaluate educational opportunities in terms of student outcomes, as measured by student performance on standardized achievement tests, and whether the conclusions of such research provide viable standards for concerned public policymakers.

While social science research findings have received considerable public exposure, little attention has been given to the emphasis of this volume—the practical implications of the limited usefulness of social science research for determining public policy. This requires an overview of the research and its limitations, then a look at the implications for educational policymaking of the lack of satisfactory criteria for evaluation, and finally some general observations on the significance of the state of indeterminacy in educational policymaking.

AN OVERVIEW OF THE RESEARCH
AND ITS LIMITATIONS

Any review of social science research on the effectiveness of our nation's public school system must begin in 1966 with the publication of *Equality of Educational Opportunity Report* (EEOR),[1] better known as the Coleman Report after its principal author, Dr. James S. Coleman of Johns Hopkins University. The Civil Rights Act of 1964 contained a mandate from Congress to the U.S. Office of Education to conduct a survey "concerning the lack of availability of equal educational opportunities for individuals by reason of race, color, religion, or national origin in public educational institutions . . ." (Civil Rights Act of 1964, §402, 42 U.S.C. §2000 c-1 (1970)). Conducted in 1965, the Equality of Educational Opportunity Survey (EEOS) collected extensive data from a sample of 4,000 schools across the country, containing almost 600,000 students and 60,000 teachers. Data were obtained through questionnaires given to students, teachers, and administrators and through verbal achievement tests given to students and teachers. Several aspects of school inequality were investigated: (1) inequality in tangible school inputs (expenditures, facilities, etc.); (2) degree of racial segregation; (3) inequality in intangible school inputs (e.g., teacher expectations); (4) inequality in school outputs as measured by pupil performance on standardized achievement tests relative to non-school factors; and (5) inequality of school output as measured by pupil performance on standardized achievement tests without regard to non-school factors.[2]

The Coleman Report reached the following conclusions:

1. The nation's public schools were heavily segregated, in the North as well as in the South.

2. Despite widespread segregation, tangible school inputs were relatively equal between black and white schools.

3. Minority children score lower on standardized achievement tests on the average than do white children.

4. The gap in achievement between the average minority child and the average white child gets larger over the school years.

5. Family background and socioeconomic status have a powerful effect upon student achievement, an effect which does *not* diminish over the years of schooling.

6. Only a relatively small amount of school-to-school variation in student achievement is not accounted for by differences in family background, indicating the small independent effect of variations in school facilities, curriculum, and staff upon achievement.

7. Given the fact that no school resources account for much variation in achievement, the school resources that most influence achievement and attitudes are, first, the social composition of the student body and, second, the quality of the teaching personnel.

8. A pupil's sense of confidence that through his own actions he can exercise control over his environment is highly related to achievement, but appears to be little influenced by variations in school characteristics.[3]

The Report's most important and controversial finding dealt with the relatively insignificant effect that differential school resources had on school outcomes independent of other factors such as home background:

Taking all these results together, one implication stands out above all: that schools bring little influence to bear on a child's achievement that is independent of his background and general social context; and that this very lack of an independent effect means that the inequalities imposed on children by their home, neighborhood, and peer environment are carried along to become the inequalities with which they confront adult life at the end of school. For equality of educational opportunity through the schools must imply a strong effect of schools that is independent of the child's immediate social environment, and that strong independent effect is not present in American schools.[4]

After an initial period of silent reaction, which some have regarded as conspiratorial,[5] this major and startling finding generated a rising crescendo of scientific and public debate. One writer described the

Report's conclusion as "literally of revolutionary significance. . . . [U]ntil these findings are clarified by further research they stand like a spear pointed at the heart of the cherished American belief that equality of educational opportunity will increase the equality of educational achievement."[6] Moynihan termed the Report "the most powerful empirical critique of the myths . . . of American education ever produced."[7]

The Report also met with intense criticism of its data and methodology, primarily from economists who challenged the Report's usefulness as an instrument for public policymaking. In the most celebrated attack, Bowles and Levin charged that: (1) the EEOS data was deficient because of poor sample response, particularly from large urban school districts, and a large nonresponse rate on particular questionnaire items; (2) the measures of school resources were inadequate because data was averaged over an entire school district, thus ignoring school-to-school differences within a district; (3) the statistical procedures used significantly understated the effect of school resources on student achievement; and (4) the Report failed to consider the effects of past influences of school resources on student achievement.[8]

As a result of the Report, new school effectiveness studies were conducted, some of which found positive relationships between specific school inputs and student achievement. Several studies reanalyzed EEOS data, compensating for the Report's statistical and methodological weaknesses. Bowles and Levin, in a study of 12th-grade black and white students, found teachers' salaries, science laboratories, and teacher verbal ability significantly related to student achievement.[9] Hanushek, using EEOS data on Northern sixth graders, found positive effects for teacher verbal ability and teacher experience.[10] Perhaps the most comprehensive study, described in *Schools and Inequality,* took place in Michigan, based partly on EEOS data and partly on data about Michigan schools from another source.[11] Students were grouped into deciles by socioeconomic status to control for its influence. Within each decile the relationship between school inputs and achievement was examined. Teacher verbal ability, teacher experience, and to a degree teacher salary were found to relate consistently with student achievement. The authors also described 17 other studies demonstrating a relationship between school resources and achievement.

The Coleman Report had been criticized for failing to consider the effects of school resources on achievement over time. At least two longitudinal evaluations have been conducted since the Coleman Report and both show significant student input-output relationships. Hanushek studied third-grade students in a California school district using achievement and school input data for these students for the first, second, and third grades. He classified the students ethnically and by socioeconomic status (based on occupation of the father). For white manual-occupation students, he found teacher verbal ability and recentness of teacher educational experience significantly related to achievement; for white non-manual occupation students, he found recentness of teacher education and teacher experience to be so related.[12] Winkler, in a study described elsewhere in this volume, studied eighth-grade students in a California school district and found important effects for teacher verbal ability, teacher experience, and teacher salary.

In 1972, however, Daniel Moynihan and Frederick Mosteller published *On Equality of Educational Opportunity*, a collection of essays reflecting an intensive reanalysis of EEOS data conducted during a three-year Harvard faculty seminar sponsored by the Carnegie Corporation and in general confirming the Coleman Report's major conclusions.[13] That same year, the Rand Corporation conducted a review of research on educational effectiveness for the President's Commission on School Finance. That report entitled *How Effective is Schooling?*[14] concluded, "Research has not identified a variant of the existing system that is consistently related to students' educational outcomes."[15] Finally, in 1972 Christopher Jencks asserted that not only schooling differences, but cognitive inequalities as well, have little impact on adult income and job status. In other words, equalizing school outcomes is not likely to reduce adult inequality.[16]

Part One of this volume examines the usefulness of such research in establishing practicable standards for educational policymaking. Dr. Alexander Mood, former Assistant Commissioner of Educational Statistics of the U.S. Office of Education, one of the authors of the Coleman Report, and one of the country's most respected educational researchers, examines educational evaluation and its primary limitations, including (1) entanglement of influences, (2) limited domain of measurement, (3) hidden biases in tests, (4) disconnection with process, (5) failure to detect deplorable outcomes, (6) the mass production mold of current evaluation technology, and (7) the absence of integrated educational theory. Because of these limitations, Dr. Mood concludes that current evaluation efforts are too primitive to serve as an adequate basis on which to make public policy decisions about education.

Research examining the impact of differential school resources on achievement must employ valid indices of both student achievement and school spending levels to reflect accurately how much students really learn, and how much and for what purpose money is actually spent. Indeed, the legitimacy of the entire analysis procedure rests on the validity of these indices. Dr. Stephen Klein examines the indices typically used in research efforts, considering such problems as test content validity, poor overlap between test objectives and school program content, cultural bias, and the difficulty in matching school inputs with specific program outcomes. He concludes that both the indices for student achievement and school spending levels are severely inadequate.

Much of the research on educational production, the Coleman Report included, is cross-sectional, conducted at one point in time, rather than longitudinal, which considers the cumulative effects of schooling over time. Dr. Donald Winkler asserts that any model of the educational process that ignores the cumulative impacts of school resources not only is defective in its description of the educational process, but also imparts a serious downward bias to the importance of school resources as determinants of student achievement. Instead, he advocates longitudinal studies and describes the methodology and findings of the study he conducted.

Finally, Dr. Audrey Schwartz critically reviews the existing research literature on the effectiveness of our national desegregation policy, considering the extent desegregation has achieved three principal objectives: (1) fostering individual social mobility, (2) desegregating the adult community, and (3) improving minority achievement. She concludes that data on each of these objectives is sparse, beset with methodological difficulties, and often leads to conflicting conclusions. Although she is hopeful that desegregation can accomplish these objectives, it is doubtful that integration policy decisions can be based on social science evidence.

PUBLIC POLICY IMPLICATIONS OF THE
RESEARCH AND ITS LIMITATIONS

Our review of social science research on education and its limitations prompts us to conclude that such research, given the current state of the art, is simply inadequate as a basis upon which to make important educational policy decisions. Part Two of this volume examines the consequences of inadequate standards from three public policy perspectives—equality, accountability, and decentralization.

In the last two decades courts, legislators, and educators have struggled to construct viable standards for determining equality of educational opportunity for purposes of school integration and school financing. From the beginning of this struggle in *Brown v. Board of Education*,[17] in which the U.S. Supreme Court declared state-imposed school segregation unconstitutional, social science evidence has played a visible but not always illuminating role. As one commentator has observed, "Social science begins by attempting to simplify human affairs in order that they can be more easily explained, but it often ends by making them even more complex than originally supposed."[18] Social science has indeed made specification of equality of educational opportunity more problematical. Without hard evidence that desegregation improves student achievement, enhances social mobility, or alleviates racial hostility, equality is more an ephemeral abstraction than an achievable reality. Similarly, if differences in schooling do not matter, then financial disparities from district to district or school to school do not result in unequal educational opportunities afforded schoolchildren. But valid scientific criteria with which to implement these policies so as to assure equality of educational opportunity are not available.

Dr. Henry Levin evaluates the role of social science evidence in the evolution of law and public policy on school segregation and school financing. Because social science evidence cannot produce conclusive results to support a particular educational strategy to improve the life attainments of students from low-income and minority families, Levin speculates that the advocacy of particular educational policies, and the selection of social science evidence supporting those policies, is based not on standards of scientific acceptability but on preexisting policy commitments of researchers, policymakers, and laymen who consider these matters. He warns that such misuse of social science evidence has tended to reframe the issues of school integration and school financing in terms of whether such policies improve the test scores of poor and minority children. Those issues should be resolved on the basis of higher moral and human considerations.

Father Theodore Hesburgh, President of Notre Dame and former head of the U.S. Civil Rights Commission, examines the usefulness of social science evidence in deciding matters of desegregation policy. After reviewing the raging social science debate over integration, and describing the competing intellectual traditions which underlie the controversy, he warns against relying on social science evidence alone as a basis for decisionmaking. He argues that social science is not objectively neutral and value-free, but is inherently political, and that desegregation policy decisions involve fundamental ethical judgments that cannot be resolved by social science alone. History and morality provide essential perspectives from which social science evidence must be evaluated.

John McDermott focuses upon the appropriateness of using the judicial process as a forum for resolving the cost-quality debate in school finance litigation. He examines existing judicial standards for achieving equalization of educational opportunity through the allocation of resources in an attempt to discover some manageable standard which at once permits the judicial machinery to function and avoids settling the scientific dispute. Particular emphasis is given to the use of pupil performance on standardized achievement tests as the measure of equality, a measure which is rejected because of substantial methodological weaknesses. Rather, resort is made to the history and purpose of the equal protection clause of the Fourteenth Amendment to the U.S. Constitution, which evinces a concern for equality in the way government treats people, not with making people equal or producing equal results, for the latter are beyond the capacity of government and schools to control. Thus, a standard is chosen that is concerned with whether schools are equal, not with whether children are made equal.

Indeterminacy in education also affects the allocation of educational resources. If socioeconomic status is the most powerful influence on student achievement, then neither reallocating existing resources nor increasing those resources holds much promise for improving the quality of education. Dr. Henry Levin, reconsidering the role of equal educational opportunity in achieving equal occupational opportunity, concludes that schools alone cannot do the job; there must be large scale compensatory programs for disadvantaged children which seek to equalize their human capital embodiment with that of other children, a task which requires a far greater commitment to non-instructional services such as nutrition, health, shelter, etc.

Dr. Gregory S. Kavka, a philosopher, examines in an educational context the application of principles of distributive and compensatory justice and the meaning of equality. He disputes Jencks' concern for adult income equality, asserting that equal educational opportunity does not aim for equal results, but presupposes unequal results. He also reasons that there is no way to determine equality in education without specifying the aims and purposes of our educational institutions. Yet conflicting views on the purposes of our educational institutions exist, and moral philosophy provides no solution to this problem of indeterminacy. Even if the agreed aim of education was equal occupational opportunity through equal educational opportunity, there remains the problem of how to achieve equality in education, given the indeterminate state of social science technology. Equality, it would appear, is an abstraction that may not be a desirable social goal at all. Nevertheless, traditional efforts to achieve equality through desegregation and equalization of financial resources should proceed because they may be an essential, if not sufficient, part of the solution to inequality in education, and because the symbolic importance of equality in a just society demands that we move in what we believe is the right direction.

The failure of social science research to provide viable standards to evaluate educational opportunities has profound implications for efforts to hold schools accountable for their performance and effectiveness. Without adequate criteria for measuring whether one program or expenditure level or teacher or teaching strategy is better than another, accountability appears to be a dubious enterprise at best. Dr. James Guthrie reviews the political and economic roots of the renewed school evaluation movement, and examines in some detail those inherent characteristics of schooling that resist scientific measurement techniques. After describing the consequences of indeterminacy for school evaluation efforts, he sets forth an elaborate plan for assessing school effectiveness that (1) attempts to adjust for the vast scientific vacuum regarding educational processes, (2) embraces both state and local district interests, and (3) subjects school policy determinations to lay control yet protects the professional prerogatives of educators.

Another recent development in educational policymaking is the rising demand for community control and decentralization of schools. Although low achievement in urban, usually minority, schools caused that demand, social science research provides no hope that local control will enhance student learning. What basis exists, then, for allowing parents to interfere with professional judgment in educational matters? Dr. David O'Shea writes that pressure for organizational change is continuing because minority communities believe that achievement or other important schooling outcomes can be improved, at least where community control is not simply an attempt to increase the effectiveness of existing education, but rather an effort to create a different kind of education relevant to minority children and minority cultures. Even if achievement patterns cannot be altered, decentralization produces other desirable outcomes, such as resources for community development and increased public participation in decisionmaking, that provide a basis for its adoption.

CONCLUSION

Educational policymaking, then, is in a state of indeterminacy. There exist no satisfactory scientific criteria with which to make important policy decisions about education.

What, then, is the solution to the problem of indeterminacy? How and on what basis do school administrators make decisions? How can decisions about compensatory education or integration or innovative programs be justified? What assurance is there that such programs or decisions will improve the quality of education? How can we know how to properly allocate resources or spend money wisely?

One response is that, without standards, administrators are forced to rely on their own judgment, common sense, experience, observation, history, morality, values, etc. Henry Levin, for example, directs us to morality rather than social science, while Father Hesburgh resorts to both history and morality. The editor also refers to the history and purpose of the equal protection clause in the narrowly circumscribed context of judicial decisionmaking.

These bases for decisionmaking, moreover, have been too much disregarded and even maligned in our demand for quantification of human behavior. Scientific criteria are not the exclusive bases for decisionmaking. Two reasons caution against overreliance on scientific proof. First, education is a process that may be unquantifiable, serve goals unmeasurable. Second, reliance on current research like the Coleman Report would end efforts at improvement. Even given their limitations and inadequacies, it might be wiser to rely on the experience, observations, and good judgment of administrators and teachers that certain things do work (even if not confirmed by the measurement apparatus). At least that is an affirmative choice, an option for improvement, a belief that schools do matter.

This response, however, raises a troublesome question. Whose morality are we to rely on? Whose common sense? Whose experience? Whose judgment? Whose values? And how are we to choose between competing notions of the purposes of our educational institutions? As Dr. Kavka points out, without consensus on the aims of education, moral considerations provide little guidance in policymaking. No such consensus now exists. As a result, educational policymaking is in a state of double indeterminacy—on the one hand without satisfactory scientific criteria to guide policymaking, and on the other hand without the consensus on the aims of education necessary for the application of moral considerations. This scientific and moral indeterminacy constitutes the central dilemma in any attempt to improve the quality of education.

Given the absence of adequate moral and social science standards, we are, in the final analysis, remitted at least in part to the political process for a sometimes arbitrary resolution of matters of educational policy. We are remitted to the political process, with all its inevitable compromises, because school policy decisions must be made now and cannot await development of adequate standards and because the political process is the only resort left to us to resolve disputes, although to a limited extent the judicial process may serve that function too.

NOTES

1. James S. Coleman *et al.*, *Equality of Educational Opportunity*, Office of Education, National Center for Educational Statistics, OE 38001 (Washington, D.C.: Government Printing Office, 1966). Hereafter cited as the Coleman Report.

2. James S. Coleman, "The Concept of Equality of Educational Opportunity," *Harvard Educational Review* 38(1968), 7.

3. Coleman Report, 8-23.

4. *Ibid.*, 325.

5. Daniel P. Moynihan, "Sources of Resistance to the Coleman Report," *Harvard Educational Review* 38(1968), 23.

6. D. Nichols, "Schools and the Disadvantaged," *Science* 153 (No. 3754, Dec. 9, 1966), 1314.

7. Daniel P. Moynihan and Frederick Mosteller, "A Pathbreaking Report," in F. Mosteller and D. Moynihan (eds.), *On Equality of Educational Opportunity* (New York: Random House, 1972), 5.

8. Samuel Bowles and Henry M. Levin, "The Determinants of Scholastic Achievement—An Appraisal of Some Recent Evidence," *Journal of Human Resources* 3(Winter 1968), 3.

9. Samuel Bowles and Henry M. Levin, "More on Multicollinearity and the Effectiveness of Schools," *Journal of Human Resources* 3(Winter 1968), 393.

10. Eric A. Hanushek, "The Production of Education, Teacher Quality, and Efficiency," in *Do Teachers Make a Difference?* U.S. Department of Health, Education and Welfare (Washington, D.C.: Government Printing Office, 1970), 79.

11. James Guthrie *et al.*, *Schools and Inequality* (Cambridge, Mass.: MIT Press, 1971).

12. Hanushek, *op. cit.*

13. Moynihan and Mosteller, *op. cit.*

14. Harvey A. Averch *et al.*, *How Effective Is Schooling? A Critical Review and Synthesis of Research Findings* (Santa Monica, Cal.: RAND, 1972).

15. *Ibid.*, 154.

16. Christopher Jencks *et al.*, *Inequality* (New York: Basic Books, 1972).

17. *Brown v. Board of Education*, 347 U.S. 483 (1954).

18. Alan Wilson, "On Pettigrew and Armor: An Afterword," *Public Interest* 30(Winter 1973), 134.

PART ONE

The State of the Art of Educational Research

1. The State of the Art of Educational Evaluation

ALEXANDER M. MOOD

Educational evaluation is being called upon to bear very heavy burdens in both accountability and policymaking. Lessinger[1] provides an excellent survey of the accountability problem which increases in every state and school district as educational budgets escalate seemingly without limit. Citizens are demanding to know what they are buying with their education tax dollars, what extras they are buying with the additional tax dollars that schools seem to need each year, what might be cut out of school programs without significantly impairing the fundamental education of children, whether or not schools are operated efficiently, and why so many high school graduates are so poorly equipped to enter employment. These demands have become so widespread that many state legislatures have embarked on programs to increase accountability in education. For example, the California Legislature has a Joint Committee on Educational Goals and Evaluation,[2] which is developing a massive program to involve citizen advisory committees in decisions about goals and evaluation in every school attendance area in the state.

All this hue and cry has forced state legislators, governors, Congress, the U.S. Office of Education, the courts, and other federal agencies to deal with a variety of policy issues that heretofore have been left to local school boards. At the same time, the egalitarian revolution has raised numerous complicated and troublesome policy questions having to do with school segregation and school financing. Decisionmakers who must deal with these policy questions need valid information about the likely outcomes of various choices available to them—information that can only come through good evaluation.

Unfortunately, evaluation is in no condition to shoulder the burden being thrust on it. To describe the state of the art of educational evaluation in a single word, the most appropriate one might be *primitive*. This chapter will elaborate on and substantiate that characterization.

ENTANGLEMENT OF INFLUENCES

Evaluation refers to the appraisal of the effectiveness of an educational process or policy. Usually, the appraisal is done in terms of the policy's impact on student learning as measured by a standardized test. To determine the unique or independent effect of a policy or program on learning, however, it is essential that non-school (extraneous) factors that affect achievement, such as innate ability, family background, peer group composition, and motivation be disentangled from school effects. Yet to single out and precisely isolate the unique effect of school policies or educational methods on achievement is an awesome task.

To give an example, a professor of education devises a new curriculum for teaching reading. Several elementary schools cooperate in an experiment to try out the new curriculum. Some schools use the new curriculum while others use a standard curriculum—probably the one they already were using. At the end of the experimental period all students take a standardized test and the proposed new curriculum is evaluated in terms of the success on the test of students enrolled in the standard curriculum.

Evaluation of the new curriculum, however, is seriously hindered by the fact that student test performance depends on many factors other than the new curriculum one is trying to evaluate. Some obvious occurrences that might intervene to contaminate a straightforward evaluation of this sort are: (1) students in one group may be more able or better prepared than those in the other group and may score higher on the test for those reasons rather than for any reason related to the new curriculum; (2) teachers in one group may be more able than those in the other group; (3) curricular materials may be better in one case than in the other; (4) teachers of the new curriculum may resent having to abandon the curriculum of their choice and hence execute the new curriculum rather poorly; and (5) teachers of the new curriculum may become very enthusiastic about participation in the development of a new curriculum and execute it much more energetically than the average teacher would in ordinary circumstances.

To get around this difficulty, evaluators use more elaborate evaluations that attempt to measure not only the effect of the variable under study (the new curriculum), but also the effects of all other important extraneous factors that may contaminate the results. In this way, the effects of such extraneous factors can be controlled so as to determine the independent effect of the factor of primary interest (the new curriculum).

Practical constraints usually prevent the effective use of these sophisticated techniques (formal experimental designs and randomization procedures) for disentangling the effects of educational factors from non-educational factors. These procedures sometimes work well at a technical level in dealing with teaching processes when the extraneous factors can be manipulated to some extent. They do not work well in evaluation of policy matters because one cannot manipulate those extraneous factors that frequently are naturally related in the population in a way that does not permit assessment of their independent effects. These extraneous factors are inextricably intertwined with each other and with the effects of educational policies. (In technical language, they are collinear.)

The problem of entanglement of influences is so critical to effective evaluation that further explanation is in order. A child learns from parents, siblings, peers, neighbors, teachers, numerous members of the community, television, radio, movies, newspapers, magazines, libraries, and so on. Of course the relative importance of these agencies varies enormously from child to child. Some parents spend a great deal of time drilling their children from a very early age in the alphabet, spelling simple words, explaining concepts associated with words, counting, addition and subtraction, and the like. In this case, the family may be a much stronger educational force than the school. Other parents who speak little or no English cannot give their children much help in becoming acquainted with English. For these children, the school may be a much stronger educational force than the family although sometimes older brothers and sisters may make the family as a whole a stronger educational force than the school.

If children were given a general vocabulary test in first grade, one would find a range of vocabulary. The mere numerical estimate of the size of a child's vocabulary would obviously give no clue as to how much of the vocabulary should be attributed to each of the many educational forces acting on the child. Even a complete audio-visual record of the child's entire life from the moment of birth would not indicate what specific educational force or collection of experiences added the word *cat* to the child's vocabulary. The abstraction, *cat,* in the child's mind changes as the child grows from the babbling stage to the first grade. Clues to *cat* are supplied by various encounters—some are insightful, others contribute little, and still others are downright misleading. But how can we identify the insightful ones? Somehow out of the totality of their experiences most children arrive at the first grade with a reasonably satisfactory *cat* in their vocabularies. It will continue to change over the years, perhaps at school, perhaps at cathouses, but whatever it becomes, there is no way to disentangle the school's contribution from all the other contributions.

Now let us turn to something that is surely learned in school and nowhere else—determination of the density of a cat. As everyone who has been to school knows, one plunges the cat into a graduated tub of water and then divides the volume of water displaced by the cat into the cat's weight. Simple enough. But can that bit of knowledge be entirely ascribed to schooling? Not at all. The concept of *density* rests on an elaborate structure of other concepts such as weight, mass, measurement of mass, units of mass, gravitational force, scales, springs, volume, three-dimensional bodies, two-dimensional surfaces, dimension, units of linear measure, units of surface measure, units of volume, cylinders, volume of cylinders, areas of circles, pi, algebraic symbols, geometric points, lines, and curves. Each has its own substructure of concepts. All these concepts are supported by one's experience with light and heavy objects, the nature of water, the use of scales and rulers, the drawing of diagrams with pencil and paper, and so on. All these concepts and experiences are interlaced with the symbols and abstractions of language; these symbols grow with and at the same time illuminate new concepts and experiences to make them more understandable and better related to one's existing stock of knowledge. Every small bit of knowledge is an element of a highly complex structure in which one bit supports a large number of other bits and in turn is itself supported by a large number of other bits. The whole structure is synthesized out of one's whole life experience.

A person's knowledge structure is not a rigid structure like a building; it is amorphous, flexible, partly organized, and partly disorganized. A small new addition may bring about substantial rearrangement of a segment of the structure; an insightful new synthesis may rearrange the whole structure and perhaps bring a little order into some relatively disorganized parts of the structure. It is a constantly changing, shifting, growing thing. The rate of growth depends somewhat on its size for a knowledge structure is a huge collection of tools useful for adding to the structure and for capitalizing on experience. A child who enters school with a vocabulary of 1,000 words is severely disadvantaged relative to the child who enters with a vocabulary of 2,000 words. The child with the smaller vocabulary often falls farther behind as the years go by because the second child has a larger set of learning tools and hence a greater rate of learning. This advantage applies not only to school studies but to all experiences so that if the two were tested on matters entirely outside the school curriculum the second child would normally score higher.

When a child takes a test, his or her whole knowledge structure is involved. Whatever the test claims to be getting at, it is really appraising the knowledge structure in toto. That is evident when a great variety of tests are given the same children; those who score high on one test normally score high on all tests and those who score low on one normally score low on all the rest. There is no sense trying to cut up a child's intellectual power into arithmetic, English, science, verbal aptitude, history, general information, and so on. That intellectual power is a single integrated entity not to be confused with the arbitrary way schools happen to divide up curricula.

Attempts to attribute a child's intellectual power to one or another educational influence have been largely unsuccessful. Perhaps the most elaborate analysis of this kind has been carried out by Mayeske and others[3] using data obtained by the massive educational opportunity survey described in Coleman.[4] Several tests were taken by a nationwide sample of some 650,000 students and a great deal of information about their family backgrounds and schools was obtained. Using an index A of achievement, which was a combination of several test scores, and an Index F of items indicating educational quality of home environment (education of parents, father's occupation, books and magazines in the home, and so on), Mayeske found that roughly 90 percent of the variance* between children's achievement scores in index A could be removed by adjusting them for differences in F. Therefore, the ability of a child to cope with achievement tests can be almost entirely attributed to the educational quality of the home. This finding (of extremely high correlation between school achievement and family background) has been confirmed by every piece of research that has explored the relationship. See, for example, Jencks.[5]

At the same time achievement can be attributed to the quality of the school. Mayeske developed an index S of school quality using items such as teacher verbal ability, teacher experience, education and experience of other school staff, quality of curricula, quality of school facilities, and so on. When the average school achievement index is adjusted using the school quality index S, some 50 to 80 percent or more (depending on grade level and ethnic group) of the variance in achievement between schools is removed. On this basis one might reasonably conclude that the school is primarily responsible for children's ability to cope with achievement tests.

The effect of the adjustment is larger for higher grades than for lower grades indicating that the relative influence of schools increases with years of attendance. For example, Mayeske finds that adjustment for school quality can remove 56 percent of the variance of achievement scores of all students in the third grade and 86 percent in the 12th grade.[6]

At the same time achievement can be attributed to the educational quality of a child's peers. Mayeske's analysis using an index P of the educational quality of a child's fellow students found that 80 percent

---

*The *variance* of a set of scores is a measure of their scatter about their average. If all scores are identical, then there is no scatter and the variance is zero. The more widely scores are scattered above and below their average, the larger the variance.

and more (depending on grade level) of the variance between achievement scores A could be removed by adjusting them for P. Evidently a child's ability to cope with achievement tests depends mostly on his or her associates at school.

Although I know of no proof, I am willing to give heavy odds that a similar adjustment using an index of the educational quality of the families in a child's neighborhood would produce the same result. That is, the great bulk of the child's intellectual power could be attributed to the neighbors.

The generally accepted explanation of these results of statistical studies of student achievement is as follows: children with educated parents get a better start on vocabulary and intellectual concepts than children with poorly educated parents; they tend to live in better neighborhoods with neighbors who are educated and hence with peers who are richer in vocabulary and intellectual concepts; these educated people tend to insist on better schools and, simultaneously, better teachers gravitate toward schools in those neighborhoods where good teaching is appreciated. Thus all the major educational influences in a child's life tend to be interrelated so that if one is high the rest are likely to be high and vice versa. Hence a child's intellectual competence will correlate strongly with any one of these influences on a statistical basis. *Since there is no way to disentangle the unique effect of each of these influences, there is no way to estimate how much effect schooling has on intellectual competence independent of these other influences.*

There is some evidence that family background may have a little larger influence on achievement for white students than for black students and, correspondingly, that school quality may have a little larger influence on achievement of black students than that of white students. Smith[7], for example, finds that of the 92 percent of variance of achievement within schools in scores of 12th-grade white students in the Northeast (the other 8 percent lies between schools), 19 percent can be removed by adjusting for home background. Of the 89 percent of the variance of achievement within schools in scores of 12th-grade black students in the Northeast, only 8 percent can be removed by adjusting for home background. Turning to school characteristics, of which teacher quality is the most important, Smith finds that of the 8 percent of variance of 12th-grade white students in the Northeast, 4 percent (that is, one-half—not 4 percent of 8 percent) can be removed by adjusting for teacher quality; of the 11 percent of variance of 12th-grade black students in the Northeast, 6 percent can be removed by adjusting for teacher quality.

But it is not correct to conclude from these statistical studies that schools make little contribution. They make a substantial contribution on purely cognitive matters as can be seen by examining children who do not go to school. The most dramatic experiment of this kind was brought about in Prince Edward County, Virginia, by a racist board of supervisors that closed down the public schools entirely for four years (1959-63) in order to circumvent court desegregation orders. White children attended a specially organized private school while black children and their parents were left to fend for themselves. The following account is taken from Green et al.[8]

Most black families in the professional category (primarily school teachers) moved out of the county, as did a large number of other families mostly in the upper part of the socioeconomic scale; this exodus may have removed 15 to 20 percent of the black population. Roughly a third of the remaining families arranged for their children to get formal schooling by either commuting to schools in neighboring counties or by going to live with friends or relatives outside the county. However, on the average, these children received only two years of formal schooling because in the first year of the shutdown most parents believed schools would reopen shortly. The remaining children received no formal schooling during the four years but their education was not totally neglected. Several black churches in Farmville, Virginia, operated training programs that were more in the nature of caretaking than educational endeavors. More importantly, the Virginia Teachers Association operated a summer school in Farmville during three of the four summers. But since the majority of the black population is rural, only 20 to 30 percent of the children took part in any of these training or summer programs. In addition to these two programs, some 30 percent of parents and 60 percent of older siblings made some effort to teach children in the home.

After the Prince Edward County schools had been closed for four years, the Stanford Achievement Test (Form N) was given to a sample of 154 children who had received no regular education, 125 children who had received some regular education (2 years, on the average) outside the county, and 338 black children in a nearby county with a comparable largely rural black population. Older students (age

17) who had no regular schooling for four years fell back exactly four years in educational achievement (as measured by the test) while those receiving some schooling fell back two years in achievement. The younger children (age 11) receiving no schooling fell back somewhat less (2.7 years in educational achievement), possibly as a result of some success on the part of parents and older siblings in teaching basic skills.

LIMITED DOMAIN OF MEASUREMENT

The Prince Edward County disaster may not have been quite as serious as it first appeared because the domain measured by standard achievement tests may be a relatively small part of the whole domain of human development. For example, the following educational goals were adopted recently by many California school districts:

1. Understand and practice the skills of family living.
2. Learn how to be a good manager of time, money, and property.
3. Gain a general education.
4. Develop good character and self-respect.
5. Develop skills in reading, writing, speaking, and listening.
6. Learn and understand the changes that take place in the world.
7. Learn how to examine and use information.
8. Develop a desire for learning now and in the future.
9. Develop pride in one's work and a feeling of self-worth.
10. Prepare to enter the world of work.
11. Practice and understand the ideas of health and safety.
12. Learn to respect and get along with people who think, dress, and act differently from oneself.
13. Understand and practice democratic ideas and ideals.
14. Learn to respect and get along with those with whom we work and live.
15. Learn how to use leisure time.
16. Learn how to be a good citizen.
17. Develop the ability to make job selections.
18. Learn to appreciate culture and beauty.

Testing technology does not deal with most of the domain covered by the list: The third goal has good coverage but not complete coverage by any means; a few other goals are partly covered but most goals are touched very little or not at all.

The great gaps in testing technology indicated by this list of goals are often minimized by pointing out that the third goal is usually regarded as much more important than the other seventeen. However, even that defense is losing its force because the trend of many communities is to place personal development goals higher on the priorities list than the traditional academic goals. Personal development goals include the following:

Social competence
Sense of responsibility
Creativeness and inventiveness
Confidence
Integrity
Ambition
Ability to concentrate
Common sense and judgment
Ability to reason and rationalize
Being observant
Enthusiasm
Humanity
Curiosity
Self-discipline
Conviction
Self-esteem

In a highly organized society, interpersonal skills may be at least as important as reading, writing, and arithmetic. Some California school districts have put a few of these goals ahead of reading, writing, and arithmetic; it is a reasonable expectation that more will do so in the near future. Yet not one of these goals has received more than passing attention from test developers and most have received no attention at all.

It is surprising that measurement of personal development has been so neglected. Schools often claim that personal development is a very important segment of education. Thus, when some agency attempts to use conventional achievement test data to evaluate schools, the most resounding defense offered by educators is that cognitive things are the lesser half of the business of schooling; the larger half, they say, has to do with socializing their charges. It is an excellent defense, but apparently it is not offered seriously because educators have given almost no attention to developing programs for pursuing personal development goals or to developing instruments for measuring progress toward them.

Evaluation technology is confined to the simpler cognitive aspects of education, which are easy to measure; it does not deal with large segments of the cognitive domain, in particular, the completeness, validity, and consistency of a person's knowledge structure. Evaluation techniques have hardly begun to scratch the surface of the affective domain.

The most damaging effect of the narrowness of evaluation technology is not inability to measure important educational outcomes but the enormous distortion it inevitably brings about in the entire educational program. Those things that are easy to measure attract excessive time and resources because everyone dislikes low measurements. Although low measurements can be improved or insured against, schools overlook other educational dimensions that cannot be measured.

HIDDEN BIASES IN TESTS

It is increasingly apparent that many standard evaluation instruments possess one or both of two handicaps for certain categories of students. One is an assumption of a level of familiarity with the English language that is not warranted for children whose parents do not speak English or have a limited knowledge of English. The other is an assumption of familiarity with the white middle-class American background that is not warranted for most minority children and many disadvantaged white children.

While these two defects do considerable damage to the test's precision for the narrow purpose for which they were designed, they are less significant when the tests are viewed (as all should be) as appraisals of total intellectual competence. Intellectual competence in the U.S. requires some familiarity with the dominant language and the dominant culture of our society.

In another sense, these defects do a disservice to white middle-class children by exaggerating their intellectual competence. Intellectual competence in the U.S. requires some familiarity with the languages and cultures of the large minorities that constitute a substantial fraction of our society. But the advantage that middle-class white children receive over others in certification standing far outweighs the disservice. Certification standing carries immense practical benefits in access to higher education and access to employment.

DISCONNECTION WITH PROCESS

The primary purpose of educational evaluation is improvement of educational programs. Existing instruments, by focusing on outcomes, do not serve that purpose except incidentally by identifying programs that produce poor outcomes. No clue is provided as to why the outcomes are poor and hence no basis is provided for improving the programs. It is almost fair to state that so far as improving education is concerned the whole technology of educational evaluation is worthless.

As an example, consider the policy of racial integration in the public schools. A number of major studies have found that integration may improve the performance of black children on achievement tests somewhat but the evidence is not overwhelming and, in any case, the improvement is not large.[9] Following Katz[10] we may infer that these statistical investigations are averaging achievement data over a wide spectrum of process situations. In some schools, black children are made to feel entirely welcome and accepted; the school programs deal with them equitably; they are not dumped into low-achiever tracks; the integration is successful in practice as well as in label. At the other end of the spectrum the black children sit in the back row and rarely participate in classroom or any other school activities; they are essentially segregated despite being members of an "integrated" school. Is it surprising that integration does not seem to accomplish much when data are aggregated over such a spectrum?

Obviously it is impossible to do any kind of sensible evaluation of an integration program by merely examining cognitive outcomes. One must look at the process in some detail, at the teacher-student interactions, at the black student-white student interactions, at the attitudes of all the participants in the integration program. The same is true of any other educational program; outcomes alone cannot tell us what is good and what is bad about a program. We must connect the outcome of individual students with the treatment they receive during the course of the program. But current evaluation technology is far from enabling us to do that.

A particularly sad consequence of the fact that evaluation is wholly restricted to outcomes is the implicit whitewashing of process. Poor outcomes appear solely the responsibility of the student; the possibility of a faulty process is never even raised. Thus faulty process victimizes students doubly and ineffectual evaluation technology permits this year after year.

FAILURE TO DETECT DEPLORABLE OUTCOMES

Even in the limited arena of cognitive outcome measurement, current evaluation technology is seriously defective in not detecting positive harm done to children. For example, many plodding teachers convince gifted children, especially minority and disadvantaged children, that they cannot write by attaching great importance to minor mechanics of writing such as spelling, grammar, punctuation, and legibility while attaching little importance to valuable attributes of writing such as imagination, imagery, wit, style, insight, suspense, and entertainment.

Another common crime is teaching children that mathematics is mysterious and unfathomable. Of course, there is no more logical discipline but, by pulling answers out of the air instead of building them up logically from first principles, inept teachers annually convince great numbers of children that they will never learn mathematics. Naturally, traditional mathematics tests find that these children do not do mathematics very well; what they do not reveal is that the children have specifically been taught that they cannot do mathematics.

Current evaluation technology gives no hint of the kind and quantity of these disastrous outcomes of schooling.

THE MASS PRODUCTION MOLD

Current evaluation technology is worthless for evaluating an individual student's progress because it does not take into account the student's own personal value system, the family's value system, or the student's talents. Students are people with perfectly legitimate aspirations and preferences. In fact, so far as the future is concerned (and they are preparing themselves for the future), their viewpoints and values may be more legitimate than those of adults because a time will come when their values will prevail.

A process for evaluating progress toward district goals is a system for evaluating school programs, not a system for evaluating individuals. Thus, if a school district chose the eighteen goals listed earlier in this chapter, it would make no sense to evaluate a student by measuring his or her progress toward each of those eighteen goals. The student has different goals and, even when some of a student's goals coincide with some of the district goals, the importance attached to them will be different. Students are pursuing their own goals as best they can within the limits available in the local school. A superior educational system would provide a unique education for each student especially related to his or her talents and interests. Society cannot afford that; it can only afford a mass production system. But that does not mean the products should be identical.

Students must be evaluated on the basis of their progress toward their own personal goals. Of course, schools and parents have a responsibility to try to persuade each student to select a set of goals appropriate to his or her own talents and interests that at the same time will give the student a reasonable prospect of a satisfying life. But identity with the district goals is not a test of the validity of a student's goals. The wide diversity of goals from district to district is proof enough that a student's goals need not be identical to district goals, but the wide diversity of people in the world makes any proof unnecessary.

EDUCATIONAL THEORY LACKING

Science develops knowledge by creating models and theories that are continually tested and improved as research workers devise experiments to clarify the theory and then analyze the data resulting from those experiments. We shall not have a satisfactory knowledge foundation on which to base policy decisions until educational research develops a theory comprised of soundly constructed quantitative models of learning that are mutually self-consistent and reinforcing. At present only the most rudimentary models are available.[11]

Despite decades of data gathering on a gigantic scale (every student is tested over and over), the models remain in an embryonic state because of the inattention to process. We know what goes into schools and what comes out but we have precious little information about what goes on inside. As a result, any model maker who attempts to relate outputs to inputs is reduced to pure speculation about what mechanisms transform inputs into outputs. These speculations naturally vary from person to person and since no hard data exists to appraise them, it is impossible to develop any generally accepted theory.

Data and analyses of data do not comprise a scientific basis for making policy decisions. Any single analysis illuminates only a microscopic facet of an extremely complicated business; the same is true of any simple model. These bits and pieces need to be organized into a structure that gives us a fair representation of the whole complicated business. But there are not enough of those bits and pieces to make the attempt now. Meanwhile policymakers have no choice but to put a great deal of reliance on their own judgment.

SUMMARY

While policymakers wish to get all the information they can out of educational evaluation, they must keep in mind all the shortcomings that inevitably accompany any evaluation of such a complex human activity as education. The principal shortcomings are: (1) many of the forces that strongly influence a child's learning are inextricably entangled and there is no way at present to disentangle their effects (it is probably impossible to assess the efficacy of a policy that affects one of those forces); (2) evaluation ignores large domains of learning that are difficult to measure while concentrating all its energy on things that are easy to measure; (3) current evaluation technology is not competent to deal fairly with children outside the dominant white middle-class American culture; (4) current evaluation technology, by focusing on outcomes, cannot contribute effectively to improvement of educational processes; (5) current evaluation technology does not detect harm done to students by faulty teaching; (6) the technology takes no account of legitimate personal educational goals of students; and (7) there exists no satisfactory fundamental theory of education and hence no solid foundation for evaluation.

Therefore policymakers must view all educational evaluation with considerable skepticism and be prepared to reject any particular instance of it on the basis of their own judgment of its plausibility.

NOTES

1. L. M. Lessinger, "Issues and Insights into Accountability in Education," in J. E. Bruno (ed.), *Emerging Issues in Education* (Lexington, Mass.: D. C. Heath and Co., 1971).

2. California Legislature, Joint Committee on Goals and Evaluation, *Education for the People*. Vols. 1, 2 (Sacramento, Cal.: State Printing Office, 1972).

3. G. W. Mayeske *et al.*, *A Study of Our Nation's Schools*, U.S. Department of Health, Education, and Welfare (Washington, D.C.: Government Printing Office, 1972); *A Study of the Achievement of Our Nation's Students*, U.S. Department of Health, Education, and Welfare (Washington, D.C.: Government Printing Office, 1973); *A Study of the Attitude Toward Life of Our Nation's Students*, U.S. Department of Health, Education, and Welfare (Washington, D.C.: Government Printing Office, 1973).

4. James S. Coleman *et al.*, *Equality of Educational Opportunity*, Office of Education, National Center for Educational Statistics, OE 38001 (Washington, D.C.: Government Printing Office, 1966). Hereafter cited as Coleman Report.

5. C. Jencks *et al.*, *Inequality* (New York: Basic Books, 1972).

6. G. W. Mayeske *et al.*, *A Study of Our Nation's Schools*, *op. cit.*, 45.

7. Marshall S. Smith, "Equality of Educational Opportunity: The Basic Findings Reconsidered," in F. Mosteller and D. Moynihan (eds.), *On Equality of Educational Opportunity* (New York: Random House, 1972).

8. R. L. Green *et al.*, *The Educational Status of Children in a District Without Public Schools*, Bureau of Educational Research, Michigan State University (East Lansing, Mich.: The Bureau, 1964).

9. See, for example, Coleman Report; J. McPartland, *The Desegregated Negro Student in Segregated High Schools*, Center for the Study of the Social Organization of Schools, Johns Hopkins University (Baltimore, Md.: The Center, 1968); David J. Armor, "School and Family Effects on Black and White Achievement," in F. Mosteller and D. Moynihan (eds.), *op. cit.*; and D. K. Cohen, T. F. Pettigrew, and R. T. Riley, "Race and the Outcomes of Schooling," in F. Mosteller and D. Moynihan, *op. cit.*

10. I. Katz, "Review of Evidence Relating to Effects of Desegregation on the Intellectual Performance of Negroes," *American Psychologist* 19(1964), 381-99.

11. See H. M. Levin, "A New Model of School Effectiveness," in *Do Teachers Make a Difference?*, U.S. Department of Health, Education, and Welfare (Washington, D.C.: Government Printing Office, 1970), S. Michelson, "Equal School Resource Allocation," *Journal of Human Resources* 7(1971), 283-306, or A. M. Mood, "Partitioning Variance in Multiple Regression Analyses as a Tool for Developing Learning Models," *American Educational Research Journal* 8(1971), 191-202.

2. Cost-Quality Research Limitations: The Problem of Poor Indices

STEPHEN P. KLEIN

Recent social science research in education has challenged the traditional importance attached to schooling in America. The Coleman Report[1] and similar research conclude that there is no statistically significant relationship between the amount of money spent on education and the quality of education, as measured by pupil performance on standardized achievement tests. The measure of achievement typically used is the average score of all children in a school district, as expressed in a percentile ranking in the state, while the expenditure measure is typically the average expenditure per pupil in a district's instructional program. These two variables, expenditures and achievement, are compared with each other to determine the frequency with which higher expenditures occur together with higher achievement scores. The question, in other words, is whether higher spending districts have higher achievement scores on the average than

Adapted, with permission, from John E. McDermott and Stephen P. Klein, "The Cost-Quality Debate in School Finance Litigation: Do Dollars Make A Difference?" which appeared in a symposium on Future Directions for School Finance Reform in *Law and Contemporary Problems* 38(No. 3, Winter-Spring 1974), published by Duke University School of Law, Durham, North Carolina. Copyright, 1974, by Duke University.

lower spending districts, or put still another way, will increased expenditures raise achievement? The Coleman team reasoned that if differential levels of per pupil expenditures do make a difference in the quality of education provided, then a strong relationship should exist between spending and student achievement.

The approach described above appears on the surface to be a fair and legitimate means for determining whether the quality of education is influenced by the amount of money spent on education. The procedure takes into consideration both how much is spent and whether this expenditure has corresponding dividends in terms of student performance. There is, however, an important premise on which this entire analysis procedure rests: that the *indices* used to assess the degree of student achievement and to measure the level of per pupil expenditures accurately reflect both how much students really learn, and how much and for what purpose money is actually spent. Before the results of the Coleman Report and similar research are accepted for purposes of deciding matters of public policy, that premise deserves to be examined carefully. This chapter explores the validity of the *indices* that have been employed and concludes that both indices are severely inadequate.

STUDENT ACHIEVEMENT AS AN
INDEX OF EDUCATIONAL OUTPUT

An assumption that is implicit in any method of analyzing the relationship between expenditures and achievement is that pupil performance on standardized achievement tests provides a satisfactory index of educational output that is useful for comparisons of educational opportunity among school districts. Clearly, any method of evaluating program and expenditure effectiveness based on student outcomes must employ a valid system of assessing student performance. There are other educational output measures, such as school drop-out rates, later life income, job status, and delinquency rates, but all the prominent social science output research relies on student test scores.

Standardized achievement tests have come to be recognized as the best indicators of the effectiveness of educational programs. Such tests appear to be fair (certainly all students take the same test when comparisons are made), they are usually developed by reputable and well-established companies, and they offer a relatively inexpensive means for gathering a great deal of potentially important information about student performance.

Yet standardized achievement tests are not necessarily adequate measuring devices for the purpose of assessing the effectiveness of school programs. There are a range of problems in using test scores to measure school effectiveness; these problems stem from certain faults inherent in the tests themselves or arise from how tests are used. Not all tests suffer from these deficiencies to the same degree, but tests usually are deficient in one or more of the ways described below.

Limited Measurement of School Outcomes

One problem in using achievement scores to compare inter-district school effectiveness is that achievement tests measure only a few outcomes of the instructional process, typically in reading and mathematics. The cognitive academic domain is usually the only area tested, and within that domain many subject areas and goals are not tested. Only occasionally do statewide testing programs include assessment of social studies, science, language, arts, and other areas of concern. Moreover, researchers seldom test the "psychomotor" domain, which relates to physical skills used in physical education and vocational education, or in the "affective" domain, which includes educational goals such as citizenship, self-concept, political socialization, attitudes toward school, maturity, and interpersonal skills. These goals have been ignored in assessing school effectiveness largely because of the paucity of good measures and the impracticality of measuring everything schools try to do.

Standardized tests, then, do not measure many of the goals emphasized by the educational process. For districts that have goals other than those tested, as all districts do, test scores on reading and mathematics alone do not provide a complete or accurate index of how well that district is achieving its goals.

Poor Overlap

A second and more important problem in using standardized achievement tests to evaluate program effectiveness among districts is that achievement tests commonly do not overlap well with the program objectives of schools even within the cognitive domain purportedly being tested. An achievement test in a particular subject, for example, may cover areas not taught in a particular school, while, on the other hand, a school may cover areas within a subject that are not covered by the test. As a result, the degree of overlap will vary from school to school and district to district. A test that may be consistent with the educational objectives of one school may be inconsistent with those of another. Although one of the arguments for the fairness of using tests to measure school effectiveness is that all schools use the same test, that argument is vitiated by the overlap problem. Because of poor overlap, a test instrument may not be especially sensitive to the effects of instruction, and therefore not measure very accurately what the student knows with respect to what he or she has been taught.

The problem of poor overlap between test objectives and program objectives is magnified by the fact that the degree of importance attached to certain content objectives in standardized achievement tests may vary considerably from the degree of emphasis placed on the same items within any school. As illustrated in Table 1, a commonly used first-grade mathematics test covers eight content objectives, yet 44 out of the 55 test items are devoted to four of the areas, while the other four areas are measured by only 11 items. As a result, the test does not measure all eight objectives equally well.

Even more disconcerting is the variation in the average difficulty of the items among different content objectives. On the first-grade mathematics test referred to above, two content areas containing 23 items are comparatively easy, while two other areas totaling 21 items

TABLE 2-1

Analysis of the Mathematics Achievement Test (Form 12a)
of the Cooperative Tests of Primary Mental Abilities

Content area	Number of items	Average proportion passing
Number	17	.73
Symbolism	6	.66
Operation	13	.55
Function and Relation	3	.59
Approximation	1	.32
Measurement	8	.54
Estimation	1	.65
Geometry	6	.75

are comparatively difficult. Only a total score for all eight content objectives is reported as the pupil's performance on that test. The test, then, does not really measure how well a student does at mathematics; it measures how well he or she can answer easy items in two of the other content areas.

A related aspect of the problem is that, even though a test is administered to all students at a particular grade level, schools do not place the same emphasis on each learning objective for all children at that grade level. Schools have different programs for different children—programs that vary in the amount of instructional time, staff, and funds devoted to any particular school objective. Because of these problems of poor overlap between test objectives and program objectives, it is very difficult to interpret what a test score means and, as a result, a test result may bear little or no relationship to the effectiveness of a program.

The importance of a good overlap between test objectives and an educational program's objectives cannot be minimized. It would be unfair to assess the effectiveness of a science program by giving students a history test. It would be unfair to measure a child's knowledge of the meaning of certain words when that child never had the opportunity to learn them. Similarly, it would be unfair to evaluate a school's relative effectiveness in developing certain skills (or knowledge) when the achievement test used to measure that effectiveness overlaps the skills only slightly in coverage and emphasis.

Validity

The most serious problem in using test scores as an index of educational output is validity, that is, whether a test score accurately reflects what the test purports to measure. If the title of a test says "Reading," one presumes that the test requires the student to demonstrate his ability to read and comprehend the meaning of words, sentences, paragraphs, poems, etc. All too often, however, the title of a test is misleading. Tests frequently include items that require skills and knowledge that go well beyond what is implied by the test's title and description. The following questions from a typical first-grade "reading" test* illustrate this problem:

---

*The name of the tests on which this and all subsequent items mentioned herein appear have been deliberately omitted. The intention here is not to criti-

READ THIS

A GAME

You say "box"   You say "bean"

I say "animal"   I say "girl"

You say "fox"   You say "Jean"

#3   You say "men"

I say "number"

You say . . . . . . four   hen   ten

#4   You say "head"

I say "food"

You say . . . . . . bread   cake   red

It is evident that reasoning ability as well as reading ability is required to answer the questions correctly. Items measuring reasoning ability are heavily influenced by non-school factors, such as home background and innate ability. These items should appear on a general intelligence test, not on a test that purports to assess "reading" if the "reading" test is to be used to compare the quality of instruction in reading among districts.

Because of the validity problem, it is difficult, if not impossible, to interpret what a test score means. For example, two children receive a score of 27 on a reading test, but one child answers 20 reading items correctly and 7 reasoning items, while the other child answers correctly only 12 reading items but correctly answers 15 reasoning items. Because the two children behave quite differently, their scores of 27 mean very different things, and it is therefore very difficult to evaluate the effects of instruction on these children by referring to the total test score.

The problem is magnified even further when the test scores of all children in a school district are averaged together to compute an average score for the entire district and then compared with the results obtained in other districts. The failure of the test score to

---

cize a particular test or test item, but rather to illustrate the kinds of limitations typically present in tests when used for the purpose of evaluating school effectiveness.

disclose whether the result reflects the effects of instruction or of reasoning ability or of some combination of the two makes it impossible to compare the relative effectiveness of reading programs in different districts.

Test publishers, moreover, often deliberately select items measuring reasoning ability in order to spread students out so as to have variation in test scores. Items that are sensitive to instruction but do not produce test score variations are often rejected for inclusion in the tests.

Achievement tests, to the extent that they are really intelligence tests measuring non-school factors over which the school has no control, are often not valid instruments for the purpose of assessing the outcomes of instruction because the characteristics these tests measure are not necessarily the outcomes of instruction. Researchers claim that there is a strong statistical relationship between family background and achievement, while school expenditures have little relationship to student outcomes as measured by standardized achievement tests. Because standardized achievement tests are not very sensitive to instruction and measure general intellectual ability, which is affected by non-school factors such as family background, it should not be surprising that family background should correlate so much more highly with achievement scores than school expenditures. Validity defects, therefore, can make pupil performance on standardized achievement tests an inappropriate index of educational output.

Cellar and Ceiling Effects

Some tests may be too hard for students at one school but too easy for students at another school. When this situation occurs, it is generally inappropriate to compare the relative effectiveness of the two schools. The reason for this is illustrated by the following examples:

A track coach set the high jump bar at six feet and then had 100 10th-graders in the school try to jump over it. None of the students could do it. He then instructed them in the fine points of high jumping for several weeks and again tested them in the same manner. Now 3 students could jump over the six-foot level. The coach concluded that his instructional program was not very successful.

A second track coach also tested these same students before and after they received the instruction, but the testing was done in a different manner; namely, the coach measured the highest level each student could jump both before and after instruction. This coach found that the average height on the pretest was four feet and the average height on the posttest was five feet. This coach concluded that the instructional program was very successful.

The moral of these examples is that if one wants to know the level at which students are performing, then one must use a test that is geared to their general range of ability. If the test is too easy to too hard (as was the case with the first coach), then actual gains in student performance levels are understated while non-school factors are exaggerated. Only when the test does not have an artificially high "cellar" or low "ceiling" (as was the case with the second coach) can there be an accurate assessment of performance.

Standardized tests often exhibit this difficulty because at the extreme ends of the score only a few items answered correctly (or incorrectly) can make a big difference in the interpretation of the score obtained. For example, a score of 47 versus 48 out of 50 points might correspond to a grade equivalent difference of six months; but a difference between 26 and 29 points on this same test might correspond only to a grade equivalent difference of one month. Thus, small differences in performance near a test's "cellar" or "ceiling" may have a profound and unwarranted influence on the interpretation of the test's scores and impair its usefulness for comparative evaluation purposes.

Format

The use of test scores to measure educational output is further complicated by problems in test format, that is, how the test questions (items) are presented to the student and how that student marks or otherwise indicates his answer to the questions. Questions administered orally, such as typical spelling tests, are open to a host of extraneous influences ranging from the particular pronunciation patterns of the test administrator to the acoustics of the room in which the test is given. The formats of some measures are so difficult to comprehend (especially for early primary pupils not used to standardized tests) that one wonders whether the test assesses the ability listed in its title or simply test-taking skills per se. Several well-known reading tests for first graders, for example, have two columns of items on each page with eight or more items per column, and four choices per item plus the item stem or stimulus (*e.g.,* a picture). This complexity is frequently compounded by small print, poor and ambiguous drawings, and by how the student has to mark his choice —in very small boxes next to the item or even on separate answer sheets. This might be acceptable for upper elementary pupils, but clearly inappropriate for first graders not used to taking tests. One example of this response format problem is illustrated by a frequently used first-grade reading vocabulary test in which the first grader is presented with a set of eight pictures and four words. His task is to draw a line from a small star in front of each word to the star in the box with the picture that goes best with this word. Not only is this task complicated for the first grader, its difficulty is increased by the fact that as he draws lines (with his extra thick, first-grade pencil) he crosses out parts of words and pictures. Thus, in answering one question, he reduces the legibility of the next question and the possible answers to it. These problems in format increase the influence of extraneous, non-school factors on student test score results.

Directions and Standardization of Procedures

One of the important assumptions necessary for comparing test results across schools is that the students at each school really take the same "test." This means that not only the same test booklets must be used, but that the directions and testing conditions must also be the same at each school. As noted above, a test administrator may slur the pronunciation of words and/or directions at one school while at another school the directions may be read clearly. This fact would most likely influence student scores in ways not related to the quality of each school's educational program. Further, some test directions are so long and complicated that they place demands on the short-term memory span and linguistic capabilities of students far beyond what one should reasonably expect of the full range of students taking the test. In other words, a student's score can be influenced by his ability to understand unusual and difficult syntax and to follow complex directions rather than just by his ability to answer the questions.

Instructions to teachers (or paraprofessionals) who give these instruments are equally confusing and often quite vague as to what should be done. The instructions for a test given to every first grader as part of a large western state's mandated testing program illustrate the common problems with such directions:

> Now look at the first row of boxes on the page.
>
> Read the word in the arrow. Which box goes best with it?
>
> See how the box with the bird has been marked. The word is fly. The picture of the bird goes best with it.
>
> Now look at the second row of boxes on the page.
>
> Read the sentence in the arrow. Then make a big X on the box that goes best with it.
>
> Did you mark the picture of the car? The arrow says I went for a ride. The box with the car goes best with it. (Make sure every child marked the box correctly.)

What happens if the students did not mark correctly the boxes to these sample items? There are no instructions in the manual telling the teacher what to do. When this situation happens, as it often does among students with marginal test-taking and/or English skills, test administrators must either rely on their own abilities to explain the sample items further or proceed as if the students really did get the sample items correct. In any event, the so-called "standardization" of the test has been broken. If this were not enough to make normative data provided by this measure difficult to interpret, the publishers added the following directions: "Allow enough time, in your mind, for all the children to finish the test." It appears that the publishers assume that there is unlimited class time or that there are no pressures (either for or against) giving students more or less time to complete the test.

Compare the instructions above with Anastasi's comments regarding standardized tests: "Standardization implies uniformity of procedures in administering and scoring tests. If the scores obtained by different individuals are to be comparable, testing conditions must obviously be the same for all."[2] Many so-called "standardized" tests do not meet the requirements of standardization and, as a result, the influence of non-school factors on student test performance is increased.

Bias

The usefulness of test scores for comparative purposes is also impaired by cultural bias. On a very simple level, tests are culturally biased in that items on the tests may refer to things that are not present in the cultural experience and background of many children taking the test. Test items dealing with snow and sleds are not particularly relevant for students in Southern California while those dealing with orange trees are not especially appropriate for students in Maine. As long as a test is balanced with respect to such cultural influences, there is no problem with bias. But it is rare to find a test that is equally balanced for all students.

More significantly, however, standardized achievement tests are norm-referenced in that the test scores of children or school districts are compared with scores of a national or state sample of the normative or typical student population. As a result, standardized tests reflect the cultural characteristics of generally white middle-class suburban students, partly because large urban school districts with heavy concentrations of low income and minority students often decline to be included in the reference sample, as happened in the Coleman Report. Thus, tests may not be as appropriate for certain minority or cultural groups as they are for the main body of white students because the normative sample may not truly reflect the student population.

Another serious problem is that the content of the tests reflects the cultural biases of the item writers, who are also white middle-class people. An item that assumes knowledge of a sled, for example, may produce variations in test scores that reflect differences in cultural backgrounds, not differences in the instruction provided to the children who take the test.

The most egregious type of cultural bias in tests occurs when the scores of children with English language disabilities are compared with students whose primary language is English. This is due both to the language disability and to the fact that test administrators must translate the English directions and items on a test, often losing much in the translation. When that occurs, the test is no longer standardized and is a qualitatively and quantitatively different test for different groups of children, based upon their proficiency in English. Use of test scores to measure the relative effectiveness of school programs in districts that contain large numbers of bilingual children is a hazardous undertaking.

Tests Are Often Inadequate Indices

As noted above, extraneous, systematic, and chance factors influence test scores in that such factors have little or nothing to do with measuring the relative effectiveness of educational programs. In all fairness to the test publishers, the tests used in the Coleman Report were never developed nor intended to be used for measuring program effects. Rather, the tests were designed for counseling, placing, and selecting students. Further, many publishers are now marketing tests specifically geared to be sensitive to program effects.

When test scores are subject to severe and/or several extraneous influences, however, it is impossible to interpret what such scores mean. The lay public often holds the misconception that such factors balance out. That is not the case. Loaded dice do not follow the same laws of probability as dice that have not been tampered with. Each extraneous factor influencing student test performance reduces and dulls that test's ability to make appropriate and precise discriminations between different levels of student proficiency. Thus, test scores are meaningless if they have been unduly influenced by poor formatting, directions, standardization, validity, objectives matching, biasing factors, or any combination of these faults. Moreover, there is no adequate method for correcting such deficiencies once the scores are obtained.[3] As a result, standardized achievement tests that are used in social science research on school effectiveness are often inadequate as indices of educational output.

PER PUPIL EXPENDITURE AS AN INDEX OF EDUCATIONAL INPUT

The determination of the degree of relationship between school effectiveness and money spent on education requires a comparison between two indices; namely, student scores on achievement tests and per pupil expenditures. The first portion of this chapter described the plethora of faults commonly associated with the test scores that have rendered them inadequate for the purpose of providing a good index of school effectiveness. On the other hand, the index of how much money a school spends on education, "per pupil expenditure," would seem to be free of contaminating factors. There is no confusion as to what a dollar means.

Yet there is some concern as to what the expenditure index actually represents when it is used as the metric against which school expenditures for education are assessed.[4] In much of the research that has been conducted, for example, expenditures for specific programs are often not matched with the student test scores that are supposed to measure their effectiveness. Typically, the attempt is made to correlate among school districts the average *instructional* expenditure per child with the average test score on a particular achievement test in each district. A sixth-grade reading test, however, is not appropriate for measuring all of the programs and expenditures that are included in the average instructional expenditure per child for a school district. Obviously, one does not use a reading test to evaluate the effectiveness of expenditures relating to the mathematics curriculum. Yet the instructional expenditure per child includes salaries for principals and vice-principals, supervisors, consultants, classroom teachers including substitutes, counselors, librarians, psychologists, instructional aides, secretaries and clerks, as well as expenditures for reading instruction. The instructional expense per child, in other words, includes expenses for all the educational programs and goals of a school district, the effectiveness of which a reading test was never designed to and cannot possibly evaluate. A reading test can measure, if it can do even that, only the results obtained for those resources devoted by a district to its reading program. The present battery of tests in the composite does not measure whole areas in which a school expends its money. To correlate performance on a reading test with expenditures for a whole host of programs, goals, services, and materials that have nothing to do with reading is clearly an inappropriate use of the tests for purposes for which they were never designed. The expenditure indices used by researchers, then, are often inadequate because they fail to adequately match specific inputs with the specific outputs being measured.

Another serious problem in using average district instructional expenditures as an index of educational input is that such a measure assumes either that every district spends its money in the same manner or, conversely, that, no matter how differently districts spend their money, the same expenditure level will have the same effect on test scores. Neither assumption is justifiable. School districts do spend their money in very different ways depending on the needs and costs peculiar to each district. The same expenditure level, then, must be assumed to have the same effect on test scores, and any violation of this assumption will reduce the potential size of the correlation between student test scores and per pupil expenditures. No matter how differently schools spend their funds, they must get the same educational value per dollar in order to make a legitimate comparison between funds expended and student scores. Thus, if a school spends $1,000 on security guards or on in-service training for teachers or on replacing used student workbooks, the effect on student test scores for all these options must be the same in order to use per pupil expenditures as an appropriate index of educational input. The fact that one school spends its dollars more wisely than another is not considered, nor is the fact that one school because of economies of size or geographic location can obtain more per dollar expended. The assumption of equal educational value, then, is never met, thereby introducing further inaccuracy and foreordaining unpromising correlation results.

A related problem with the expenditure index is that the instructional expenditure per child is the average amount spent on pupils within a district. Yet the amount spent per child varies widely from school to school within a district and from classroom to classroom within a school. Even within a school, more money is spent on some children than others because of higher costs at the high school level than the elementary level, tracking, special education programs, compensatory programs, etc. The expenditure index, then, ignores these intradistrict and intraschool variations. When district average expenditure data are correlated with district average achievement scores, input-output relationships may thus be masked because of the grossness of the data. It is impossible to use the individual student as the unit of analysis or to match specific school inputs to the individual student, and, as a consequence, there can be little precision in any conclusions drawn from the social science research about the impact of school inputs on student achievement. This was one of the major defects of the Coleman Report.

A final problem with the expenditure index is what it does not measure. Some schools, because of their location and facilities, can attract better teachers than others for the same salary. Some schools can take advantage of existing facilities and resources, such as volunteer forest rangers to teach segments of a biology course, whereas other schools must spend their educational dollars for this general purpose. Some schools have a high transient population and require special and expensive programs that are not needed at other schools. And the list goes on. The expenditure index, in other words, does not adequately reflect how much and in what way money is really spent on achieving educational goals.

ANALYSIS OF THE RELATIONSHIP BETWEEN EXPENDITURES AND TEST SCORES

The correlation coefficient has been used as the criterion for measuring the relationship between cost and quality because it supposedly indicates the degree of relationship between expenditures and student performance. If expenditures and student performance were perfectly related to one another in "the real world," then at least two conditions must prevail in order for researchers to obtain a positive 1.00 correlation coefficient (any deviation from these assumptions would lower the correlation coefficient): (1) reliable and valid indices of expenditure and student performance, with no chance or systematic errors in the recording of these data prior to or during the correlation analyses; and (2) a perfect linear relationship between the indices of expenditures and achievement (*e.g.*, for every $3 spent on education there is a corresponding increase in achievement of exactly 2 points). If either or both of these assumptions is not fully met, then the correlation coefficient between the two indices of these variables necessarily will be less than 1.00.

This chapter so far has focused on the invalidity of the first assumption. As demonstrated above, the indices of both expenditures and achievement are severely inadequate. The result of poor indices is to bias downward any correlation coefficient and to undermine the validity of the entire analysis procedure. The situation is analogous to one that occurred during World War II. At that time, the Army Air Corps tried to find a battery of tests to predict good bombardiers.[5] A "good" bombardier was determined by how closely he dropped a practice bomb to the center of a target. The tests used to predict this score seemed relevant, such as eye-hand coordination, but no relationship was found between successful bombardiers and the index of bombardier accuracy. Later it was discovered that this failure in prediction was caused by inadequacies in the measure of bombardier success. For example, how close the bomb fell to the target was overly influenced by such extraneous factors as the skill of the pilot who flew the plane, the wind conditions on the day the practice bomb was dropped, the precision of the bomb sight used, etc. In short, whether or not the bomb fell near the center of the target had little to do with the bombardier's skill per se. On the other hand, if a *good* index of bombardier skill had been used rather than a faulty one, then many of the psychological tests that were discarded might actually have done an excellent job in predicting this skill.

By the same logic, one should not expect that the indices of student test scores and per pupil expenditures will be highly correlated with one another simply because neither of them accurately assesses the variables they are supposed to represent, i.e., the effectiveness of school programs and the amount of money spent on achieving effectiveness. The more inadequate the index, the lower the possible relationship. Even if just one of the two indices is inadequate, the chances of finding a significant relationship between them is severely curtailed.

Another problem that reduces the possibility of finding a strong relationship between expenditures and achievement is the nonlinearity of both measures. Although social science research assumes that for each additional dollar spent there will be a corresponding increase in test scores, actually there are serious discontinuities in the scale of measurement on both indices. Thus, the difference in temperature between $76°$ and $78°$ is the same as between $82°$ and $84°$. Yet no test publisher would claim that a difference of two points means the same thing throughout an entire distribution of test scores. It may take far more instructional time to move a student from a score of 48 to 50 than from a score of 46 to 48 or from a score of 40 to 42. Cellar and ceiling effects previously discussed only heighten this problem.

The index of per pupil expenditure also exhibits scale inconsistencies, but in a more subtle manner. Providing one more dollar per student may not be sufficient to make an appreciable difference in test scores. Several dollars may be needed and the kind of educational program (including teacher training and materials) necessary to improve scores of low-ability students may be far more costly than what is needed to improve the scores of average-ability students. The importance of such discontinuities is that the statistical techniques used to examine the relationship between test scores and expenditures *require* that no such anomalies exist in either index. To the extent that they are present, it will lower the magnitude of possible relationships that can be obtained between them.

CONCLUSION

The first section of this chapter described the problems associated in using standardized achievement tests as the index of educational output. The problems ranged from the choice of measures used to how the measures were administered. The second portion of the chapter examined the inadequacies of per pupil expenditures as an index of educational input. These two indices are seriously inadequate, so serious that one cannot interpret the results of social science research studies on school effectiveness with any degree of confidence that the results truly reflect the relationship between expenditures and achievement. Indeed, to use such fallible indices to evaluate school effectiveness is a venture in correlating the mysterious with the unknown.

NOTES

1. James S. Coleman *et al.*, *Equality of Educational Opportunity*, Office of Education, National Center for Educational Statistics, OE 38001 (Washington, D.C.: Government Printing Office, 1966). Hereafter cited as the Coleman Report.

2. A. Anastasi, *Psychological Testing* (3rd ed.) (New York: Macmillan, 1968).

3. E. O'Connor and S. P. Klein, "A critique of the report by Garfinkel and Gramlich entitled 'A Statistical Analysis of the OEO Experiment in Performance Contracting'." Paper presented at the American Educational Research Association Convention, New Orleans, 1973.

4. C. Blaschke, "Performance Contracting Costs, Management Reform, and John Q. Citizen," *Phi Delta Kappan* 53(No. 4, 1971), 245-47.

5. R. L. Thorndike, *Personnel Selection* (New York: John Wiley and Sons, 1961).

3. The Policy Implications of Research in Educational Production

DONALD R. WINKLER

Almost a decade has passed since the Coleman Report[1] concluded that school resources are only weakly related to measures of student learning. That Report, like much of the research done in educational production to date, was strictly cross-sectional in nature. Cross-sectional research is conducted at one point in time, that is, the relationship between expenditures and achievement is examined using data from one particular school year, rather than considering the cumulative effects over time that the educational process may have on student achievement. Problems associated with cross-sectional research have often resulted in a downward bias to the estimated importance of the school as an input to the learning process. In spite of this downward bias, cross-sectional research findings have shown statistically significant relationships between school inputs and measures of student achievement, and these findings suggest that increased school budgets, if allocated wisely, *can* result in increased student achievement. Unfortunately, the findings do not precisely indicate *how* dollars should be allocated to maximize achievement.

Some problems associated with cross-sectional research can be avoided through the use of "longitudinal" data in measuring school inputs and outputs. Longitudinal studies measure the achievement level of students at two points in time and match specific input received by a pupil over a period of years with that pupil's growth in achievement over the same period. The estimated productivities of school inputs that result are more likely to be true and unbiased, but longitudinal research can be subject to other problems that also plague strictly cross-sectional research.

The general policy limitations of research in educational production are discussed in this chapter, followed by an evaluation of the model and findings of cross-sectional research. Longitudinal research in educational production is also evaluated, and I report in detail my study of changes in black and white student achievement scores over an eight-year period in a large urban school district. The results indicate that, if blacks had the school environment, including peer-group composition, that whites have, and vice versa, over an eight-year period, the achievement gap between blacks and whites in the district studied would have been significantly reduced by the time students reached the eighth grade. The policy implications of cross-sectional and longitudinal research are discussed at length, and some new directions for research on schools and learning are proposed. A caveat about applying existing research findings to educational practice is issued.

GENERAL POLICY LIMITATIONS OF RESEARCH IN EDUCATIONAL PRODUCTION

While studies in educational production have shown that there are important relationships between student achievement and factors in the school environment, the policy implications of such findings are strictly limited. In some instances the variables used to measure the school environment are difficult to interpret. For example, does teacher verbal score reflect ability, which cannot be easily altered by public policy, or does it reflect communication skills, which might be amenable to change? In other cases, statistically insignificant results cannot be interpreted as meaning that the variable in question is unimportant in terms of producing other outputs of the school. For example, class size may not be important in determining student verbal achievement, but it may have an important effect on the student dropout rate. Policy conclusions, in other words, vary greatly with alternative interpretations of the school variables.

Recent discussion of school finance inequities has also introduced the question: "What minimal level of spending provides an adequate educational program?" In other words, at what point do we find zero marginal returns from a small increase in educational expenditures? The production function literature provides no answer to this question. Researchers have not even shown that marginal returns diminish with increased expenditures, much less the point at which they reach zero.

Determining policy according to the results of educational production research is hindered by still another factor. Research in educational production is based on certain assumptions about the way the educational process operates, which is to say that the researcher employs a hypothetical model of how the process operates. If the model is seriously defective, then the research results are of little use in setting policy. The models of the educational process that have been used by researchers can fairly be described as crude. For example, while a general theoretical model of the process can be expected to provide information concerning the productivity of home and school inputs, the same model provides no information as to which technology is most efficient. The theory is that of the "black box" type, which states that there is a relationship between inputs and outputs but it does not reveal the process by which inputs affect outputs. Unfortunately, there is no accepted learning theory to state what the process is or should be.

CROSS-SECTIONAL RESEARCH IN EDUCATIONAL PRODUCTION

The Model

A rather commonsense theory underlying most researchers' models of the educational production process is that student achievement is a function of the genetic potential of the child and the home and school environments to which the child has been exposed. Strictly cross-sectional research assumes a general theoretical model which states that achievement at time t is a function of the student's genetic potential, variables that characterize the home environment at time t, variables that characterize the school environment at time t, and measures of student attitudes at time t. The general model is restated:

$$EA_{it} = f(GP_i, HE_{it}, SE_{it}, A_{it}, EA_{i,t-1})$$

where:

EA_{it} = level of educational achievement at time t

GP_i = genetic potential of the ith student

HE_{it} = home environment of the ith student in time period t

SE_{it} = school environment of ith student in time period t

A_{it} = attitudes of ith student in time period t

$EA_{i,t-1}$ = level of educational achievement at time $t-1$.

The measures of educational achievement most frequently used are scores on achievement tests and IQ tests, which should be properly regarded as generalized verbal achievement tests. While pupil performance on standardized achievement tests is the best output measure available, it is clearly unsatisfactory. The test score is a purely ordinal measure, and different tests can produce different rankings. Furthermore, achievement test scores may represent culturally biased estimates of learning, although not necessarily biased predictions of future economic success. Another problem with using test scores as the output measure is the implicit assumption that schools are interested in maximizing just that one output measure. If schools have other objectives as well, the parameters of the estimated production function are not easily interpreted.

Genetic potential, of course, cannot be directly measured by testing instruments. However, an indirect proxy for genetic potential is the IQ of the child upon entering school, although data on entering IQ is often unavailable. Since the child has received only a minute amount of school input at that time, one can assume that the sole determinants of the entering achievement level are genetic potential and the preschool home environment.

The other variables in the model are more easily defined and measured. The home environment is defined by characteristics of the student's home and neighborhood, especially the racial and socioeconomic status of the family and the neighborhood peers. The school environment is defined by characteristics of the facilities and curriculum, the teachers, the administrators, the textbooks and supplies, and the peers of the student's school. The kinds of student attitudes often considered relevant to scholastic achievement are motivation to achieve, control over one's own fate, and future time orientation.

Cross-sectional studies of educational production, depending on the nature of the data used, may employ the student, the classroom, the school, or the school district as the unit of observation. If the unit of observation is not the individual student, the above general model can be rephrased in terms of the average child; that is, one can talk about the mean genetic potential of students in school or district, the average school environment surrounding students in school or district, and so forth. The unit of observation used in a study determines how much of the variation in achievement among individual students can be explained. A cross section of individual students is the most desirable category because variation in achievement can be divided into variation within schools or districts and variation between schools or districts. Cross sections of schools or districts, on the other hand, can be expected to explain only variation in achievement between schools or districts, which is small (say, 20 percent of total variance in individual achievement), compared to variation within schools (say, 80 percent). Educational production studies of variation between schools are limited as to the kinds of questions that can be answered. For example, a study using observations on schools or districts cannot determine whether students in college preparatory and vocational tracks receive different amounts of school resources, or whether it is differences in school resources between the tracks that produce achievement differences between the two groups of students.

An effort can be made, by utilizing the above model, to discover the statistical relationship between student test scores and school inputs in order to determine the amount of variation in achievement that can be statistically explained by variations in inputs or expenditure levels. The strength of statistical association between two variables is expressed in a correlation coefficient. The correlation may range from -1.0, a perfect negative correlation (meaning that as one variable increases, the other decreases), to $+1.0$, a perfect positive correlation (meaning that as one variable increases, so does the other). A zero correlation would indicate no relationship at all between two variables. From the simple correlation coefficient one can then determine the amount of variance in one variable explained by a second variable by squaring that coefficient (expressed as a "coefficient of determination"). Because other variables not considered may affect the variable being studied, more sophisticated statistical procedures such as "regression analysis" are employed in an effort to separate out the confounding effect other factors may have on the variable being studied. It should also be noted that a correlation coefficient or a regression coefficient represents only a *statistical* relationship between two variables, not necessarily a *causal* relationship in the real world. A positive correlation between expenditures and achievement, for example, means only that, as expenditures vary upward or downward, so also do achievement scores. That higher expenditures in fact *cause* higher achievement scores is not implied and does not necessarily follow from a positive correlation.

Cross-Sectional Findings

Much cross-sectional research, most notably the Coleman Report, has been the focus of publicity and critical attention because of no-school-effect findings. The Coleman Report has severely understated school effects for several reasons, among them the quality of the data, the nature of the data, and the statistical methodology.[2] These and other faults are common to much of the research in educational production, longitudinal as well as cross-sectional. For example, many studies attempt to explain variations in *individual* student achievement by looking at variations in *average* school or school district inputs. At most one could expect school inputs so measured to explain only that variation in student achievement that lies between schools and school districts. Because the largest part of the variation in student achievement lies within the same school and not between schools, variation in school inputs could potentially explain only a small proportion of total variance in achievement, precisely what the Coleman Report discovered. Failure to match specific school inputs with specific school outputs is an important limitation of much research in educational production.

Another fault common to research in educational production is the inclusion of an endogenous variable, student attitudes, in the regression equation.[3] Student attitudes are a function of not only home and school environments but also past and present scholastic achievement:

$$A_{it} = f(HE_{it}, SE_{it}, EA_{i0}, \ldots, EA_{it}).$$

Treating attitudes as exogenous variables will result in biased estimates of the productivities of school inputs. If our interest is in the total impact of changes in school inputs on student achievement, attitudes should be omitted from the model. If, for some reason, we are specifically interested in the indirect effect of school inputs on achievement via changes in attitudes, a simultaneous equation estimation method is required.

A shortcoming of many cross-sectional studies is omission from the model of $EA_{i,t-1}$, the achievement level of the student at the beginning of the schooling period under study. Controlling for achievement at the beginning of the period permits us to examine the effects of school resources upon changes in achievement or the "educational value added" during the time period. Omission of $EA_{i,t-1}$ means, in effect, that we are attempting to determine the effects of school resources for one period, say one year, upon the *level* of achievement at the current grade level. Since current school resources cannot logically be expected to "explain" growth in achievement in the preschool or school years prior to the period studied, however, this latter model is likely to result in biased estimates of the productivities of school inputs.

Cross-sectional studies also typically relate achievement to school resources received at one grade level only. For example, the eighth-grade achievement level or the change in achievement between grades one and eight may be regressed on school resources received in grade eight only. This procedure implicitly assumes that the amount of resources received in prior years are the same as that received in the current year or, alternatively, that any differences in inputs received in prior years did not have any impact on the output measured in the year of testing. When a model of the educational process ignores the school resources received by a student prior to the year of testing, not only is it defective in its description of the way the educational process operates, but it can also seriously distort the resulting estimates of school effects.

Despite errors that often impart a downward bias to the importance of school resources as determinants of student achievement, cross-sectional studies have found statistically significant relationships between school inputs and achievement, some of which are consistently strong. Four major findings are revealed by the literature. First, there is a strong, positive relationship between teacher quality as measured by verbal test score and student achievement.[4] Second, there is a positive relationship between teacher experience and achievement.[5] Third, there is a positive relationship between average teacher salary or starting teacher salary and achievement.[6] This finding, however, does not imply that increasing the salaries of teachers presently in a school system will improve teaching performance and thereby increase student achievement. Rather, it probably indicates that school districts paying higher starting salaries attract higher-quality teachers. Fourth, there is no statistically significant relationship between class size or student-teacher ratio and student achievement.[7]

LONGITUDINAL RESEARCH IN
EDUCATIONAL PRODUCTION

Most research in educational production to date has attempted to ascertain the relationship between a current level of achievement and current measures of the home and school environments. Implicit assumptions that lie behind this general cross-sectional model are either that prior measures of home and school environments are unrelated to current achievement or that prior measures are perfectly correlated with current measures of resources received by the pupil.

The first of these assumptions implies that students should not be given resources until the current year since resources received earlier do not affect achievement. If this assumption is true, programs like Head Start are doomed to failure. The second assumption is somewhat more realistic. The home environment, especially, may not change much over time. Parental education levels, attitudes, and other factors are likely to remain constant over time. On the other hand, family income, number of siblings, and the neighborhood in which the family resides are likely to change over time.

The school environment, however, may exhibit considerably more variability from year to year than the home environment. Teachers, especially, may vary from grade to grade or even from class to class in terms of characteristics and teaching styles. We know, furthermore, that expenditures per pupil increase with the grade level and inputs per pupil can vary substantially between tracks in school. If school resources are not perfectly correlated over time, the results obtained from regressing current level of achievement on current measures of school resources may be less likely to show a statistically significant relationship between school inputs and learning.

A more realistic model of educational production would take the form:

$$EA_{it} = f(EA_{it-1}, HE_{it}, SE_{it}),$$

or, aggregating over time:

$$EA_{it} = f(EA_{i0}, HE_i', SE_i'),$$

where:

HE_i' = a vector of home environment variables cumulative from time 0 to time t

SE_i' = a vector of school environment variables cumulative from time 0 to time t

EA_{i0} = level of educational achievement upon entering school.

While avoiding a serious defect of cross-sectional research, studies employing a "longitudinal" model of achievement are nonetheless potentially subject to many of the same problems encountered in cross-sectional research (such as regressing individual achievement on average school resources). The only difference between the two models—and the difference is an important one—is that longitudinal research takes explicit account of the possible cumulative effects of school resources.

Adopting a model similar to the above, Hanushek[8] regressed third-grade verbal achievement on first-grade achievement and measures of school inputs received in grades two and three. His statistically significant results were a positive coefficient on verbal score of second- and third-grade teachers, a negative coefficient on percent of time spent on discipline by the third-grade teacher, and a negative coefficient on the number of years since the most recent educational experience for the second-grade teacher.

Another longitudinal study was undertaken by Winkler.[9] While longitudinal data on the school environment was available in that study, the same was not true of the home environment. The resulting model took the form:

$$EA_{it} = f(EA_{i0}, HE_{it}, SE_i').$$

If the home environment remains relatively constant over time, omission of longitudinal information should not seriously affect the results.

The measures of achievement used in the study are the percentile test scores in the eighth-grade Stanford Reading Achievement Test (EA_8) and the California Mental Maturity Test (EA_0) for grade one. Measures of the home environment include the number of cultural items (CLT) in the home (an index which takes on values from 0 to 7), number of siblings (SIB) at home, and a variable (which takes on the value 0 or 1) indicating whether or not the family owns its home (HOM). Measures of school inputs include aggregate expenditures per child on administrators and guidance counselors between grades one and eight (ADM), aggregate monthly expenditures on teacher salary between grades one and eight (SAL), aggregate student-teacher ratio between grades one and eight (S/T), and the proportion of a student's set of teachers from prestigious undergraduate colleges (BA). This last variable is thought to be a proxy for teacher verbal ability.

Also, two measures of school peer-group composition are included in the model. The proportion of school peers of low socioeconomic status in grades one through eight (SES) may influence student achievement through effects on the pattern of peer rewards and the amount of teacher time spent in nonlearning activities. The change in racial composition between elementary and junior high school (ΔB) may affect achievement by exposing students to different academic standards or by putting the student in a situation where he may feel socially threatened. Change in racial composition is equal to proportion of peers who are black in junior high school minus the proportion of peers who are black in elementary school. The equation estimated is then:

$$EA_8 = B_0 + B_1 EA_0 + B_2 CLT + B_3 SIB + B_4 HOM + B_5 ADM + B_6 SAL + B_7 S/T + B_8 BA + B_9 SES + B_{10} \Delta B$$

where the coefficients, B_0, B_1, ..., B_{10}, represent the change in the dependent variable resulting from a one-unit change in the corresponding independent variable on the right-hand side of the equation. In the language of economics these coefficients are called marginal products. The observations used to estimate the equation consist of 388 blacks and 385 whites who were in the secondary schools of a large, urban school district in 1964-65.

One objective of the study was to determine the extent to which the schools were responsible for the increase over time in the achievement gap between blacks and whites. Whereas, at grade one the average percentile test score was 52.71 for blacks and 59.61 for whites, by grade eight the corresponding figures were 30.08 for blacks and 60.57 for whites. The schools are responsible in some sense if blacks and whites were exposed to unequal school environments or if the productivity of school resources in producing student achievement differed between races.

Because blacks and whites attended schools which, especially in the primary grades, were racially segregated, there is no a priori reason to expect that they received identical amounts of school resources. Indeed, blacks and whites did not appear to receive equal school inputs; nor were they exposed to similar home environments. In the school, blacks receive more than whites in terms of cumulative expenditures on school administration ($316.49, compared with $272.72), and blacks had somewhat smaller class sizes. The aggregate student-teacher ratio was 253.63 for blacks and 262.86 for whites; dividing by eight, the number of years the sample was in school, the average class sizes were 31.70 and 32.86, respectively. On the other hand, blacks had lower-salaried teachers, a lower proportion of high-quality teachers, a higher proportion of low *SES* peers, and a larger absolute change in racial composition of the peer group than did whites. The cumulative monthly salary for teachers of blacks was $4,809.28 compared with $5,264.94 for teachers of whites; this corresponds to average (over eight years) monthly salaries of $601.16 and $658.12. The proportion of high-quality teachers was .44 for blacks compared with .63 for whites. Lastly, whereas the proportion of low *SES* peers for blacks was .43, the figure for whites was .20, and the average change in racial composition for blacks was −.20 and for whites was +.08.

The school environments were clearly not equal for blacks and whites, a fact that might not be important if factors in the school environment are not significantly related to achievement. Are small increases in school resources equally effective in terms of increasing black and white achievements? Answering this question requires separate estimations of the model of educational production for blacks and whites. The results with respect to the school environment are summarized in Table 3-1.

TABLE 3-1

Estimated Parameters of Educational Production Functions
for Blacks and Whites[a]

School inputs	Blacks	Whites
ADM	$-.019$	$.046^{b}$
	$(.033)$	$(.027)$
SAL	$.0046^{b}$	$.0099^{b}$
	$(.0027)$	$(.0039)$
S/T	$-.047$	$.074$
	$(.056)$	$(.076)$
BA	32.37^{b}	26.66^{b}
	(7.99)	(5.40)
SES	-5.21	-33.38^{b}
	(18.68)	(10.73)
Δ_{B}	21.68^{b}	-3.49
	(6.31)	(6.33)

[a]Standard errors reported in parentheses below parameter.
[b]Statistically significant at the .10 level or better.

For the black sample, the relationship between expenditures on administration and counseling, student-teacher ratio, and the proportion of low SES peers and student achievement are statistically insignificant. Increasing the determinants of teacher salary so that aggregate monthly teacher salaries were $1,000 higher ($125 per year) would, however, increase EA_{8} by .0046 × $1,000, or 4.60 percentile points. Also, increasing the proportion of high-quality teachers by ten percentage points would increase achievement by 32.37 X .10, or 3.24 percentile points. Finally, the change in racial composition at the junior high school level has an adverse effect on black achievement. Reducing the absolute change in racial composition by ten percentage points would increase achievement by 21.67 X .10, or 2.17 points. The policy implications of this finding are not clear, but one possible implication is that racial integration should be carried out as early in the school life of the student as possible. It should also be noted that other results for this sample indicated that having higher proportions of low *SES* peers is reflected in lower student achievement.

The major differences between the parameter estimates for blacks and those for whites are the statistically significant coefficients for expenditures on administration and counseling and for the socioeconomic composition of the school peer group. While school inputs are not equally effective for blacks and whites, there can be no clearcut conclusion that improving the school environment is more effective in terms of one group's achievement than of another's.

The relative importance of the school can be determined by calculating the proportion of the gap in eighth-grade achievement between blacks and whites, which can be accounted for by differences in the school environments to which blacks and whites were exposed. The estimated contribution of the school is determined not only by differences in the school environments but also by differences in the estimated production functions for blacks and whites. We can compute the gain in black achievement that would result if blacks received the same resources as whites. The gain is calculated by multiplying resource differences by the estimated productivities (for blacks) of the resources in question and adding the resulting numbers. If the coefficient representing resource productivity is statistically insignificant, however, we assign it the value zero.

Following this procedure, we compute that if blacks were exposed to the same school environment, including peer-group composition, as whites, they could be expected to have achievement scores 12.58 points higher. The estimated change in achievement is equal to 41 percent of the achievement gap, which is 30.49. The components of the school environment, purchased inputs and peer-group composition, explain 27 percent and 14 percent of the achievement gap, respectively.

   This exercise clearly demonstrates that, at least for the school district being studied, the racial achievement gap could be greatly diminished through reallocation of resources. As an extreme example, reallocating school resources such that whites had the present school environment of blacks and blacks had the present school environment of whites would result in a black average achievement equal to $30.08 + 12.58 = 42.66$ and a white average achievement equal to $60.59 - 15.25 = 45.32$ points. Policymakers can act to reduce the racial achievement gap by improving the school environment of blacks.

   It would be a serious mistake to conclude, on the basis of cross-sectional research, that there is no relationship between school resources and achievement because failure to include a measure of the importance of school resources over time may produce statistical results that significantly underestimate how important schools really are. The few longitudinal studies thus far conducted indicate significant school effects.

POLICY IMPLICATIONS OF RESEARCH
IN EDUCATIONAL PRODUCTION

   The policy question often asked is: "Do dollars make a difference?" Although the results of cross-sectional and longitudinal studies suggest that dollars *can* make a difference, this question is not a very meaningful one. The relevant question is: "*How* should dollars be spent to make the biggest difference?" Educational production research does not provide a direct answer to this question. Economic theory does, however, provide an analytical framework within which this fundamental policy concern can be addressed.

   School administrators typically have a fixed budget, B, and face the problem of how to allocate that budget such that output is maximized. This is in the class of economic problems dealing with maximization of output subject to a budget constraint. Assume that there are only two inputs, X_1 and X_2, which schools can buy at prices P_1 and P_2. The budget constraint then takes the form:

$$P_1 X_1 + P_2 X_2 = B.$$

   The constraint is plotted in Figure 2-1. If the entire budget were spent on X_1, the maximum number of units which could be pur-

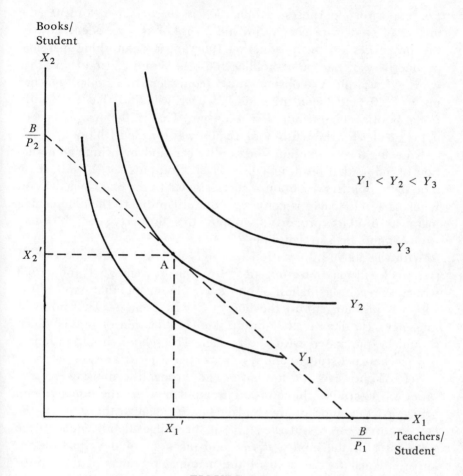

FIGURE 3-1
Diagram Illustrating Maximization of Output (Y),
Subject to a Budget Constraint

chased is B/P_1. Similarly, a maximum of B/P_2 units of X_2 could be purchased. The school can buy any combination of X_1 and X_2 which lies on or below the dotted line B/P_2, B/P_1.

Assume, also, that there exists an educational production function for the school, which states the maximum achievement, Y, attainable with any combination of inputs X_1 and X_2:

$$Y = f(X_1, X_2).$$

For expository purposes, assume X_1 is teachers per student (the inverse of student-teacher ratio) and X_2 is books per student. One of the properties of the production function is diminishing marginal productivity of one input holding the other input constant. In other words, if we hold X_1 constant at .05 (equivalent to a student-teacher ratio of 20) and begin increasing X_2, we will find that each additional book will contribute less to output. That is, the marginal product is smaller for the tenth book than it was for the fifth book.

Knowing the production function we can find an infinite combination of inputs that result in a given level of output, say, $Y = 50$. If we plot these points, we obtain a curve similar to the one labeled Y_1 in Figure 2-1. The curve is convex to the origin due to the diminishing marginal product property; without this property the Y_1 curve would simply be a straight line.

With the above information we can again ask: "What allocation of resources will maximize output?" In terms of Figure 3-1, the school wishes to reach the highest output curve obtainable; that curve is Y_2, which is just tangent to the budget line at point A. That point of tangency also dictates the appropriate combination of inputs which should be purchased with the budget. The school should purchase $X_1{}'$ teachers per student and $X_2{}'$ books per student.

Schools, however, do not have to go through the above exercise in order to determine the appropriate input mix. At the point of tangency, A, the slope of the budget line is equal to the slope of the equal output curve. But the slope of the budget line is equal to the price ratio of the inputs, P_1/P_2, and the slope of the equal output curve is equal to the ratio of the marginal products of the inputs, MP_1/MP_2. Hence, the necessary conditions for maximizing output subject to a budget constraint are:

$$\frac{P_1}{P_2} = \frac{MP_1}{MP_2} \ ,$$

which can be generally restated:

$$\frac{MP_1}{P_1} = \frac{MP_2}{P_2} = \ldots = \frac{MP_i}{P_i} \ .$$

In other words, the ratio of marginal product to input price should be equal for all inputs.

The important policy implications of research in educational production follow from the above conditions. Educational production functions provide estimates of the marginal products of inputs. For example, assume the functional form is linear, and we obtain the following estimated equation:

$$Y = 100.0X_1 + 2.3X_2 .$$

The coefficients of X_1 and X_2 are estimates of the marginal products of X_1 and X_2. The results say that increasing X_2 by one unit, or one book per student, should increase average student achievement in the school by 2.3 points. Thus, the production function parameters given in Table 2-1 are estimated marginal products.

Levin[10] provides a numerical example of the above exercise. Using data from the Coleman Report, he calculated marginal products and input prices as shown in Table 3-2. The computed ratios of marginal

TABLE 3-2

Prices and Marginal Products of Teacher Characteristics

Characteristics	Price/Unit	Marginal product	MP/P
Verbal score	23.98	.179	7.47×10^{-3}
Years of schooling	396.04	*	*
Years of experience	78.91	.060	$.76 \times 10^{-3}$

*Statistically insignificant from zero.

product to input price are not all equal and suggest that schools should hire teachers with those characteristics where the ratio is highest or change their salary schedules or do both. In the example shown in Table 3-2, schools should attempt to employ more teachers with high verbal score and fewer teachers with advanced degrees.

While research in educational production tells us that additional dollars of school expenditures can increase student achievement, the important policy question is how dollars should be spent to maximize achievement in the school. Educational production research provides us with estimates of the marginal productivities of school inputs, but no information is provided with respect to the costs or prices of those school inputs. In some cases that information is easily obtainable—for example, the cost of increasing average teacher experience by one year is given by the district salary schedule—but the costs or prices of other school variables may be very difficult to calculate. For example, what is the price of increasing teacher verbal score by one unit, or reducing racial segregation?

NEW DIRECTIONS IN RESEARCH

Future research promises to provide more meaningful policy implications than does the existing body of research in educational production. One new research area is microstudies of learning. The objective here is to obtain more precise measures of resources received by individual students, including teacher attitudes, style, and time. One example is the current research by Wiley[11] on the relationship between the amount of teacher time a student receives and subsequent achievement. Another example is the recent psychological research on mastery-learning, where the findings suggest new, more productive teaching strategies. Microstudies may reveal information on the process by which school inputs affect learning.

Another new direction in research is the attempt to find the educational production frontier. The economic production function assumes that administrators obtain maximum output from a given combination of inputs. In the real world, however, even in controlling for the influence of the home, schools may differ in terms of the gains in achievement obtainable from a given combination of inputs. The reason for this is that educational technology may differ between schools, or some input that varies between schools may have been ignored in the analysis. By locating those schools that appear to combine inputs most efficiently, we may discover which technology is superior or which inputs have been previously ignored. Carlson[12] has attempted to find a frontier production function for higher education, and Levin[13] has attempted the same for elementary and secondary education.

A third new direction in research is continued investigation of the longitudinal process of learning. In reviewing the evidence, Bloom[14] concluded that the level of achievement in the preschool and early school years largely determines the level of achievement in later years. This conclusion has provided part of the rationale for early childhood intervention programs, and it implies that school resources should be focused on those early years. Yet we observe that, in the

United States, per pupil expenditures typically increase with the grade level. And in a recent evaluation of early childhood intervention programs, Bronfenbrenner[15] concludes their long-run effects on achievement are negligible. The important policy question, which this research may help answer, is: "What is the optimal path of resource allocation over time in order to maximize some final measure of student achievement?" If a school has a limited budget per pupil to spend over a twelve-year period, how should those funds be allocated over time in order to maximize twelfth-grade achievement? Should resources be focused in the early years or the later years? Although Hanushek and Winkler[16] have done some exploratory research, the question remains unanswered. The output measure commonly used, scores on standardized examinations, presents a problem in longitudinal studies. The construction and content of standardized examinations can vary greatly over time, thereby making it difficult to precisely measure gain in a specific type of learning.

CONCLUSIONS AND A CAVEAT

Cross-sectional and longitudinal research undertaken to date has demonstrated a positive and significant relationship between some school inputs and student achievement, thereby showing that dollars can make a difference. Some surprising results are consistent across studies. For example, teacher verbal score appears to be an important factor in determining student achievement. Also, there is no demonstrated strong relationship between class size and achievement.

While some of the results are impressive, a caveat is in order. Research done to date should be properly considered to be in the realm of basic research. This does not imply that past research has no policy implications whatsoever, but there are enough deficiencies to warrant a healthy skepticism toward many results. The list of reasons for being cautious in drawing policy implications from the estimated models includes the following:

1. The results may be biased owing to omitted variables that properly belong in the models.
2. Results obtained for one group of students do not necessarily generalize to other groups of students.

3. In many cases we are not sure what a variable is measuring, and policy implications may vary greatly with alternative interpretations of the variables. For example, does teacher verbal score measure communication skills, intelligence, or some other characteristic?

4. Schools produce an entire vector of outputs, not just verbal achievement. A specific input may affect one output differently than another. For example, reducing class size may not improve achievement, but it may help reduce the student dropout rate.[17]

Furthermore, while existing research results indicate that changes in expenditures can affect student achievement, no one is yet able to tell a school district how much money should be spent per pupil or how much should be spent at different grade levels.

Future researchers and users of research findings should be aware of possible deficiencies in studies of educational production. The most promising new directions for future research appear to be better identification and measurement of schooling inputs and outputs as well as the schooling process itself. Microstudies of the classroom, for example, are likely to provide more detailed information on the process by which teacher characteristics affect student achievement. In addition, in order to answer the important question as to the optimal allocation of resources over the school life of a child, longitudinal research is required and should be given a high priority in terms of new research efforts.

NOTES

1. James S. Coleman *et al.*, *Equality of Educational Opportunity*, Office of Education, National Center for Educational Statistics, OE 38001 (Washington, D.C.: Government Printing Office, 1966), 25. Hereafter cited as the Coleman Report.

2. See Samuel Bowles and Henry M. Levin, "The Determinants of Scholastic Achievement—An Appraisal of Some Recent Evidence," *Journal of Human Resources* 3(Winter 1968), 3-24, for a detailed critique of the Coleman Report.

3. Student attitudes are endogenous if, as well as being determinants of achievement, they are in part determined by past and current achievement. Assuming attitudes are endogenous, it is erroneous to assume they are exogenous and to include them as right-hand variables in equations that are estimated using ordinary least squares. For an elaboration on this point, see Samuel Bowles, "Towards an Educational Production Function," in W. Lee Hansen (ed.), *Education, Income, and Human Capital* (New York: National Bureau of Economic Research, 1970), 18-19.

4. For example, using data from the Coleman Report, Bowles, *op. cit.*, and Eric A. Hanushek, *Education and Race* (Lexington, Mass.: Lexington Books, 1972), found positive, statistically significant relationships between teacher verbal ability and student verbal achievement.

5. For example, Jesse Burkhead, *Input and Output in Large-City High Schools* (Syracuse, N.Y.: Syracuse University Press, 1967), found the marginal product teacher experience to be .26 while Hanushek, *op. cit.*, found a marginal product of .14 for blacks and .07 for whites. Lewis J. Perl, however, in his "The Role of Educational Investment and Family Background in the Production and Distribution of Educational Services," unpublished dissertation, Department of Economics, University of California, Berkeley, 1970, found the estimated marginal product to be statistically insignificant.

6. See the results of Burkhead, *op. cit.*; Richard Raymond, "Determinants of the Quality of Primary and Secondary Education in West Virginia," *Journal of Human Resources* 3(Fall 1968), 450-70; and Perl, *op. cit.*

7. Martin T. Katzman, "Distribution and Production in a Big City Elementary School System," *Yale Economic Essays* 8(Spring 1968), 201-56; Raymond, *op. cit.*; and Burkhead, *op. cit.*, all confirm this finding, but Perl, *op. cit.*, did find a negative, statistically significant relationship between average class size in nonscience courses and a principal component measuring general ability.

8. Hanushek, *op. cit.*

9. Donald R. Winkler, "School Inputs, Educational Production, and the Achievement Gap between Blacks and Whites," paper presented at the Winter Meetings of the Econometric Society, Toronto, December 1972.

10. Henry M. Levin, "A Cost-Effectiveness Analysis of Teacher Selection," *Journal of Human Resources* 5(Winter 1970), 24-33.

11. David E. Wiley, "Another Hour, Another Day," Working Paper No. 3, University of Chicago, July 1973.

12. Daryl E. Carlson, "The Production and Cost Behavior of Higher Education Institutions," unpublished dissertation, University of California, Berkeley, 1972.

13. Henry M. Levin, "Measuring Efficiency in Educational Production," *Public Finance Quarterly* 2(January 1974), 3-23.

14. Benjamin S. Bloom, *Stability and Change in Human Characteristics* (New York: John Wiley and Sons, 1964).

15. Urie Bronfenbrenner, *A Report of Longitudinal Evaluations of Preschool Programs: Volume II, Is Early Intervention Effective?* (Washington, D.C.: Government Printing Office for the U.S. Department of Health, Education, and Welfare, 1974.)

16. Hanushek, *op. cit.*; Donald R. Winkler, "The Production of Human Capital: A Study of Minority Achievement," unpublished dissertation, Department of Economics, University of California, Berkeley, 1972.

17. Katzman, *op. cit.*, in fact, found the results did differ, depending on the measure of output used.

4. Social Science Evidence and the Objectives of School Desegregation

AUDREY JAMES SCHWARTZ

Few areas of social science research have stimulated as much interest and passion, in addition to methodological discussion, as research on the effects of segregated and desegregated schooling. These studies strike at the heart of the formal socialization process in American society and their findings bear significantly on the formulation of educational policy. Parents, politicians, educators, and laymen all want to know what research findings show about racial, ethnic, and socioeconomic integration of schools and especially its consequences on the academic achievement, values, and attitudes of pupils. They also ask if equality of educational opportunity can be attained by transporting pupils from segregated residential areas to desegregated educational environments and if it is realistic to expect schools to take the lead in integrating other major social institutions.

Widespread interest in such educational policy matters is well placed, for research shows that pupils are affected by other people in their schools. And because children will replace the present generation of adults, what they learn now will shape not only their own futures but the kind of society they will later create. A central function of formal education everywhere is to transmit to the young what a society believes ought to endure. Curricula are formulated to contain the essence of a society's culture, cadres of educators are trained to transmit it, and physical facilities are constructed so that pupils, educators, and curricula come together in the most fitting arrangement for deliberate socialization to occur. Social scientists are increasingly asked in what ways school desegregation will affect this process.

The objectives of desegregated education are directed toward both the individual and the society. For the individual, desegregated schools are expected to provide education that facilitates personal mobility, permits access to the "good life," and allows for increased options in the selection of adult roles. From the standpoint of society, desegregated schools are expected to foster a desegregated adult community—at least with respect to its secondary social structures— so that citizens will interact without regard to social origins and subpopulation membership. Also from the standpoint of society, desegregated schools are expected to allow for greater development of human resources, since loss of talent among low-income and minority groups due to poor education will presumably no longer obtain. The extent to which social science findings show that school desegregation is achieving these three objectives is the theme of this chapter.

ROLE OF INTEGRATED SCHOOLS IN FOSTERING INDIVIDUAL SOCIAL MOBILITY

Several social scientists have made the claim that the relationship between education—whether segregated or desegregated— and ultimate social status is trivial. So trivial, in fact, they contend that resources presently allocated to public schools would have greater mobility benefits if allocated directly to individual pupils or their parents to be used in a manner of their own choosing.

For example, a 1973 proposal by a panel of the President's Science Advisory Committee chaired by James S. Coleman recommended that the government give vouchers equivalent in value to the average cost of education through four years of college directly to youth at age sixteen instead of giving the usual subsidies to schools and colleges. Recipients could use these vouchers for formal education or for other forms of skill development at their own discretion and unused portions would be added to their social security annuities. This proposal is designed so that all youth will have an equal share of public educational expenditures, even if they do not take advantage of schooling opportunities.[1]

The notion of grants to parents for the education of elementary school pupils had been explored in a 1970 report to the U.S. Office of Economic Opportunity by the Center for the Study of Public Policy under the direction of Christopher Jencks. The report proposed that the value of each voucher be equal to the per pupil expenditure of the public schools in that geographic area and that children from families with below-average income receive additional payments to be spent on their education. Parents could enroll their children in any "approved" public or private voucher school in which there were vacancies. The report recommended the establishment of an agency to assure that schools (1) do not discriminate among applicants, (2) maintain educational standards, and (3) spend a substantial portion of each reimbursement directly on the pupil's education.[2] An experimental voucher system, which includes only public schools, is currently in operation in Alum Rock, California.

Jencks and several associates later expanded the idea of education vouchers from grants to parents of elementary school pupils to grants directly to adolescents. They recommended that those youth who receive relatively few benefits from schooling be permitted to use money normally spent on schools to subsidize other forms of job training, housing, or whatever each individual believed would be most useful. Grants could possibly take the form of lower taxes for those who do not go to school.[3]

Inequality Controversy—Do Schools Equalize Individual Opportunities?

The case against direct support of schools and against compulsory schooling is presented in the book *Inequality: A Reassessment of the Effects of Family and Schooling in America.* The argument is supported by intricate statistical analyses of several major data sets, including Project Talent longitudinal surveys of 5,000 high school pupils conducted in 1960 and 1963,[4] Equality of Educational Opportunity survey of some 650,000 elementary and secondary school pupils conducted in 1965 by Coleman and others,[5] and Occupational Changes in a Generation survey by Blau and Duncan under the auspices of the U.S. Bureau of the Census in 1962.[6]

The chief conclusion of the Jencks book and the one on which recommendations about formal schooling rest is that schools do very little to equalize opportunities of individuals. Regardless of the quantity and quality of resources allocated to educational programs, pupils perform at different levels on tests of cognitive ability and they stay in school for different lengths of time. Further, adults who have had the same quantity of formal schooling tend to occupy different positions in the occupational hierarchy and, more importantly to the argument, earn different amounts of money. Jencks and his associates conclude from these findings that schools are not instruments for social mobility.

Inequality quickly became controversial for it attacks the deeply held belief that education is necessary, if not sufficient, for individual social mobility and the attainment of some viable occupation. For example, Henry Levin suggested in a review that it resurrected the erroneous Horatio Alger myth in the guise of social science. Levin stated that the Jencks model attributes a large portion of unexplained income differences to luck when, in fact, the inclusion of other variables and different statistical treatment of the data would have substantially reduced these differences.[7] On the other hand, Beverly Duncan agreed that chance events do play a major role in our lives: missing a bus, feeling below par on the day of a test, and marrying someone whose brother becomes a successful politician should not be minimized. In her view the fact that the Jencks group was able to estimate about one-fourth of the income differences by family background, cognitive skills, educational attainment, and occupational status reflects well on sociological inquiry.[8]

One finding often overlooked in the spirited controversy surrounding *Inequality* is that the analysis showed that quantity of schooling definitely increases a person's chance to enter some high status occupation. "Schooling seems to be important in and of itself, not as a proxy for cognitive skills or family background."[9] This finding was not emphasized in the book because of the authors' major concern with success as measured by income. However, it should be noted that the relationship between education and occupational attainment had already been persuasively demonstrated by Blau and Duncan in what is often considered the most complete intergenerational study ever conducted. In their analysis of much of the same data used in *Inequality*, these researchers show that the influence of the amount of schooling on ultimate occupational status is considerable and, in fact, far greater than the influence of family social background.[10] For example, from an examination of these data by national origins, Duncan and Duncan concluded that schooling greatly reduces the impact of nationality on occupational achievement. Except for the overachievement of Russian-Americans (Jews) and the underachievement of Latin-Americans, "the notion of equal opportunity irrespective of national origins is a near reality."[11]

Differences in interpretation of the effects of schooling on adult opportunity made by the Jencks group and by Blau and Duncan lie largely in their measures of success. Unlike Blau and Duncan's analysis, which used occupational status as the prime dependent variable, the Jencks analysis used income. Further, it did not include income from sources other than salary, such as investments and expense accounts, nor did it include accumulated wealth. Thus, the finding often cited from *Inequality* that "there is nearly as much economic inequality among brothers raised in the same homes as in the general population"[12] does not consider the fact that one brother might be salaried with measurable income and the other a financier with no income for the purposes of the study. Also, the proportion of income variation that is explained would have been greater if such factors as geographic region, cost of living, age of individuals, etc. were considered.[13]

In a paper prepared for a *Harvard Educational Review* symposium on *Inequality*, James S. Coleman presents a statistical analysis that casts doubt on the Jencks claim that "fairly substantial reductions in the range of educational attainments do not materially reduce economic inequality among adults."[14] By dividing the coefficients of variation for the distributions of both the income and the educational attainment of young adults from 1929 to 1970 by the coefficient of variation for the year 1929, Coleman created an index showing inequalities in educational attainment and in income for each time period relative to 1929. The coefficients of variation (the standard deviations divided by the mean for each distribution) developed for *Inequality* are presented in Table 4-1. The similarity in the decline of inequality between education and occupation for each time period as shown by the Coleman index is presented in Table 4-2. Though other explanations could be offered, Coleman believes that this index "suggests that increasing equality of education does have a strong effect on increasing equality of income."[15]

TABLE 4-1
Coefficients of Variation Developed for *Inequality*

Year	1929	1935-36	1946	1960	1968	1970
Coefficient of variation for income:	1.23	1.09	0.87	0.83	0.72	0.75
Coefficient of variation for education:	0.42	0.37	0.30	0.28	0.25	0.23
Of people aged: in given year	25-34	22-31	22-31	26-35	29-33	26-30

Source: James S. Coleman, "Equality of Opportunity and Equality of Results," *Harvard Educational Review* 43(February 1973), 96. Copyright 1973 by President and Fellows of Harvard College.

TABLE 4-2
Coleman's Indices of Inequality for Selected Years

Year	1929	1935-36	1946	1960	1968	1970
Income:	1.0	0.89	0.71	0.67	0.59	0.61
Education:	1.0	0.88	0.71	0.67	0.60	0.55

Source: James S. Coleman, "Equality of Opportunity and Equality of Results," *Harvard Educational Review* 43(February 1973), 97. Copyright 1973 by President and Fellows of Harvard College.

Inequality focuses primarily on mobility opportunities for individuals, not for groups. It does, however, reach several significant conclusions about the relationships between race and other factors, including schooling, occupational placement, and income. With respect to race and schooling, the authors conclude that black pupils not only aspire to more education than do comparable white pupils, but they get more education as well. Young blacks have nearly caught up with whites in terms of educational credentials. "The overall differences between black and white educational attainment is much smaller than the difference between black and white test scores, occupational status, income, or almost anything else we can think of."[16]

The Jencks group also concludes that the relationship between educational attainment and income for blacks has been increasing since the mid-1960's. "While educational attainment and cognitive skills did not explain an appreciable fraction of the income difference between whites and blacks in the early 1960's, we may be moving towards a situation where they will be considerably more important."[17] With respect to desegregation, the social composition of elementary schools has a "modest effect on students' cognitive development" and the racial composition of schools "has a modest effect on black students' later occupational status."[18]

That education is irrelevant to life chances, an inference that is sometimes drawn from the Jencks study, must emphatically be rejected. In the American society, as in all post-industrial societies, education is necessary for occupational placement. The more skills a job entails, the more employment depends on achievement criteria that are supplied and certified by school.[19] In addition to giving most people a minimum level of competence, schools have the responsibility for selecting people to receive advanced formal education and for attesting to their capabilities. Although valid arguments have been made about whether required credentials are directly related to the ability to perform specific jobs and whether credentials create an artificial barrier between individuals and the jobs they are competent to perform,[20] the United States has developed a credentialed society in which many occupations are opened only to those who are formally certified by schools. As long as this situation obtains, decreasing support for formal education, as has been suggested by some voucher proposals, could do this generation of low-income and minority children irreparable harm. Whether they realize it or not, most of these children have few options other than schools with which to carve out viable occupational roles.

Desegregated Schools and Occupational Placement

Given the general association between educational level and occupational placement, one must ask if desegregated more than segregated schools provide mobility opportunities for low-income and racial-ethnic minority children. Most social science research findings suggest that they do. This was first brought to light in a study of black and white adult males conducted in 1966 for the U.S. Commission on Civil Rights under the direction of Thomas Pettigrew. Data were collected by the National Opinion Research Center from a sample of 1,624 men living in northern cities and comparisons were made between northern-born black males who had attended desegregated elementary schools for at least five years and those who had not. (Desegregated schools were defined as schools in which more than half of the student body is white and from which whites have not moved away in substantial numbers.) Pettigrew found that significantly more men from desegregated than segregated elementary schools held higher status jobs and earned above the median income of the sample.[21]

In a subsequent analysis of these data, Robert L. Crain also concluded that more black men who attended desegregated than segregated schools receive higher annual incomes and hold more prestigious occupational positions—many not traditionally available to blacks.[22] Crain attributed these employment opportunities to interracial contacts as adults made possible through desegregated schooling. He found that over one-half of the men who attended desegregated secondary schools, contrasted with less than one-third who attended segregated secondary schools, reported frequent interracial contact in social, occupational, church, and neighborhood settings.[23] Crain suggested that these contacts with whites provide blacks with a source of information about jobs that is not normally available to them:

It is common observation that one of the most significant forms of unfair employment practice is the hiring of new employees from referrals made by the present staff; if the staff is all white, the persons who apply will be friends, relatives, and neighbors who are also white. In a segregated community, Negroes must depend upon other Negroes for information about job opportunities. If Negroes are segregated into low-paying employment, they will, of course have limited knowledge of better paying opportunities.[24]

Effects of Interracial Schooling on Educational Attainment

Since quantity of schooling is related to occupational placement, the contribution of interracial schooling to ultimate social position can also be inferred from its direct effect on educational attainment. Crain concluded that the black alumni of northern desegregated schools, more than segregated schools, are likely to complete elementary and secondary education and to attend college.[25] Data supporting these conclusions are presented in Table 4-3, which shows the relationship between the racial composition of elementary and secondary schools attended and number of school years completed.

TABLE 4-3
Educational Attainment by Integration of Elementary and High School, Birthplace and Age Moved North, and Sex (percentages)

	Born in North			Birthplace and Age Moved North				
				Elementary and High School Integration				
				Born South, Moved North Before Age 10			Born South, Moved North After Age 10**	
Educational Attainment	Both Integ.	Mixed	Both Seg.	Both Integ.	Mixed	Both Seg.	Mixed	Both Seg.
Men:								
less than 9 years	8	*	12	12	*	20	*	37
9-11 years	28	23	36	33	29	57	48	32
12 years	32	45	28	24	51	20	24	19
some college	27	22	20	18	17	0	24	8
college grad.	5	10	4	12	3	3	3	4
TOTAL	100	100	100	99	100	100	99	100
(N)	(273)	(158)	(159)	(66)	(70)	(60)	(58)	(852)
Women:								
less than 9 years	6	*	16	11	*	30	*	25
9-11 years	37	48	35	50	39	36	44	34
12 years	32	31	25	25	41	22	47	26
some college	13	11	20	10	21	9	8	8
college grad.	12	10	5	3	0	3	. .	5
TOTAL	100	100	101	99	101	100	99	99
(N)	(310)	(157)	(153)	(107)	(96)	(69)	(106)	(1097)

Net effect of integration, $p < .05$ (one tailed).

Note: In this table, weighted N's are given in parentheses. The true N can be estimated by dividing the weighted N by 2.5.

*Since "mixed" category requires that the respondent attend high school, these cells all must be 0.

**Since Southern respondents could not have attended integrated elementary schools, there is no "both integrated" category here.

Source: Robert L. Crain, "School Integration and Academic Achievement of Negroes," Sociology of Education 44(Winter 1971), 6.

Crain analyzed these data further to determine if apparent advantages of desegregated over segregated education to black adults were spurious, that is, whether they were related to other factors that are also correlated with school racial composition. He definitely ruled out differences in family background as an explanation for the higher occupational status of adults from desegregated schools. "Surprisingly, Negro students in integrated schools do not come from higher status families than those in segregated schools . . . it is hard to imagine a 'selectivity factor.' "[26]

Crain believes that the quality of in-school factors other than the composition of the student body may account for some of the effects attributed to racial desegregation, but certainly not all. "Students in integrated schools are more studious and college-bound, which sets a 'school climate' more favorable to achievement. It is also true that the facilities and curriculum of the ghetto school are inferior, and this may make a difference at the high school level. But the quality index does not explain the difference between the integrated and segregated schools."[27]

In an attempt to discern long-term effects of school desegregation that may lead to eventual socioeconomic parity between blacks and whites, David J. Armor presented strong evidence for the "channeling" effect into college by middle-class suburban schools. He concluded from two separate studies that schools have a positive influence on rates of college going and on the quality of the colleges attended by black students.

One study was of Boston's METCO plan, a voluntary desegregation program begun in 1966 in which black students from Boston were enrolled in middle-class schools in 28 suburban communities. Two-thirds of the METCO students from the 1970 graduating class and the same proportion from a control group of siblings who remained in Boston schools were contacted in the spring of 1972 to learn about their post-secondary education. Eighty-four percent of the 32 suburban school graduates and 56 percent of the control group of 16 Boston school graduates had started some form of higher education. More importantly, METCO graduates were enrolled in what are generally considered higher quality institutions; for example, 56 percent of them compared to 38 percent of Boston graduates were enrolled in four-year colleges.[28]

Similar findings come from an unpublished report of the effects of "A Better Chance" program (ABC) on the graduation class of 1971. Forty high-ability black students in this very selective program were matched with 40 similar black students on background and achievement factors. All of the graduates of the ABC program, as contrasted with half of the comparison group, were enrolled in college. And two-thirds of the ABC graduates attended colleges of higher quality than those attended by the control group. Armor speculates that the impact of suburban schools on college attendance is probably due to better counseling and better contacts with college recruiting officers. He concludes that, for whatever reason, "black students attending such schools may have doors opened for them that are closed to students attending predominantly black schools."[29] However, he also points out that the college drop-out rate of METCO graduates is significantly higher than that of the control group so that similar proportions of each ultimately graduate from college. Nevertheless, the baccalaureate obtained by transported pupils are from higher prestige institutions, which gives them considerably more leverage in the occupational market.

Why do desegregated schools seem to increase rates of college-going and influence the quality of colleges attended by low-income and minority students? The answer often lies in the differences in educational climate provided by low-income and middle-income schools. It seems clear that the socioeconomic background of a student body is strongly related to the resources that become available for its education, including the quality and behavior of the school staff and the formal curricula. In combination with the values, norms, and academic behavior of the students, these resources create an educational climate that, in a very real sense, is a latent curriculum rivaling the formal curriculum in its socialization impact. Pupils who attend predominantly middle-class schools usually have teachers with greater skills[30] and classmates who demonstrate high levels of achievement when they enter school and show large gains at every grade level.[31] And since the physical well-being and normative socialization of middle-class pupils are assumed to be provided elsewhere, the staff and curricula of middle-class schools typically stress high levels of cognitive achievement. Middle-class secondary schools are viewed more as preparatory to college than as supplying terminal education.

However, the most significant socialization resource that schools offer pupils is not the teaching staff but the other pupils in the school. This is due partly to the influence of the student body on the recruitment and behavior of teachers and, more importantly, to the influence of pupils on one another. The academic expectations, the cognitive and social skills, the values and norms, and the behavior of individual pupils form a peer subculture that affects most students. The academic behavior of individuals is determined by the social pressures of classmates, along with their own home environment, scholastic ability, and academic values. In schools where academic performance, intellectualism, and subject-matter competence are emphasized and rewarded, pupils tend to conform to the scholastic norms of the majority and achieve at high levels.[32]

In addition to peer pressure toward achievement, middle-class schools have many college-oriented pupils, teachers, and counselors, as well as courses, to provide practical information about college admission. College going is stressed in both the formal and the latent curricula. Lower-status schools by contrast are oriented toward immediate employment upon school graduation. Teachers in these schools often have low expectations of pupils, and pupils have low expectations of themselves and of one another. Information pertaining to college is commonly lacking and courses required by colleges may be absent. Further, the occasional pupil who applies to college may be disadvantaged because of the stigma college admission officers sometimes attach to lower-status schools.[33]

INTEGRATED SCHOOLS AND AN
INTEGRATED SOCIETY

Another expected outcome of school desegregation is the creation of an integrated adult society in which prejudice toward culturally and racially different groups is at a minimum and individual alienation is all but absent. From their analyses of data supplied by northern-born black males, both Pettigrew and Crain present evidence that shows a negative relationship between desegregated education and racial prejudice. Pettigrew reported that more black men who attended desegregated than segregated schools: (a) prefer to live in desegregated neighborhoods, (b) live in mostly white neighborhoods, (c) have children in desegregated schools, and (d) have close friends who are white. His analysis of sample data from white adults indicates that those white males who attended desegregated schools continue to have more favorable attitudes toward integration.[34]

Crain's analysis indicates that northern black men who attended desegregated schools differed from those who attended segregated schools in the following ways:

(a) More of them disagree that "it is a hardship for a child to attend an integrated school."

(b) More of them express personal efficacy as measured by the "Perceived Control of the Environment Scale."[35]

(c) Fewer express prejudice against whites as measured by the "Anti-White Feeling Scale."[36]

He also shows that this favorable definition is related to adult interracial contacts. More than half of the black men who attended desegregated high schools, compared with less than one-third who did not, reported frequent interracial contacts in social, occupational, church, and neighborhood settings.[37]

The conclusions drawn by Pettigrew and Crain from the NORC data are supported in a study by Bonnie Bullough of black adults living in Los Angeles that shows a positive relationship between attendance at a desegregated school and personal values fostering interracial contacts in adult years. Bullough conducted interviews of 320 black middle-class men and women living in three different types of residential areas: the predominantly segregated white suburb of San Fernando Valley, the affluent integrated area of Baldwin Hills, and a predominantly segregated black neighborhood. She found that the proportion of the sample from each area that attended black segregated schools as children was highly correlated with the proportion of black adults living in each residential area.

The focus of Bullough's study was "to find those factors which prompt Negroes to seek effective integration, which in the North primarily means housing integration." She links opportunities that had been provided black schoolchildren for equal-status contact along racial lines to feelings of personal efficacy as adults, and ultimately to their choice of integrated living patterns. Personal efficacy was defined as both the extent to which people feel that they can control the outcomes of their own behaviors, as measured by the "powerless" scale,[38] and the perception people have of their own integration into the on-going society, as measured by the "anomia" scale.[39] Significantly more residents in desegregated than segregated areas indicated high personal efficacy on these measures.

Bullough concluded that the most salient factors for the racial integration of black adults are values and attitudes formed as children. "The participants in such an exchange do not necessarily learn brotherly love, but they do learn to communicate and negotiate with each other, and in the process, Negroes, at least, manage to establish a self identity for themselves in the white world."[40]

Table 4-4 shows the mean scores on these measures for the samples from each of the Los Angeles residential areas by experience with segregated and desegregated schooling. These data suggest that current differences in values and attitudes are related to past schooling; those who attended only segregated schools have the highest levels of powerlessness and "anomia." Bullough reports a slight, though not statistically significant, relationship between these scale scores and parental socioeconomic status, but contends that the relationship is not as strong as the racial composition of the school attended.

Strengthening the Racial-Ethnic Reference Group

The importance of a realistic definition of the social situation for the subsequent adjustment to adult society by low-income and racial-ethnic minority children is sometimes overlooked by evaluators of school desegregation programs. For example, in interpreting his research findings of black inner-city children transported to suburban schools, David Armor viewed as negative the evidence that desegregation "heightens racial identity and consciousness, enhances ideologies and reduces opportunities for actual contact between races."[41] He noted that after two years, black pupils in suburban schools of the Boston METCO project were more likely than the control pupils in segregated city schools to support the idea of black power. Many reported that, compared to their first year in suburban schools, they received less friendliness from whites, spent more free time with blacks, and observed more incidents of prejudice and less frequent interracial dating.[42] While Armor cautions that overt racial incidents are infrequent, he suggests that increased "ideological solidarity" by black METCO pupils is a negative consequence of school desegregation.

TABLE 4-4
Sense of Personal Efficacy and School Racial Composition

Schools attended		Valley	Baldwin Hills	Ghetto
Anomia				
Integrated	Mean	10.10	11.40	12.10
	S.D.	2.89	3.42	3.26
	N	(31)	(35)	(29)
Integrated at some levels	Mean	10.58	10.82	11.89
	S.D.	3.20	3.18	4.32
	N	(48)	(55)	(28)
Segregated	Mean	10.81	12.33	13.89*
	S.D.	4.03	3.42	4.59
	N	(22)	(30)	(46)
Powerlessness				
Integrated	Mean	2.06	2.06	2.79
	S.D.	1.46	1.59	2.01
	N	(31)	(35)	(29)
Integrated at some levels	Mean	2.48	2.15	2.92
	S.D.	1.52	1.57	1.78
	N	(48)	(55)	(28)
Segregated	Mean	3.09	2.97**	3.26
	S.D.	1.93	1.59	4.14
	N	(22)	(30)	(46)

*p < .05; F=3.93 within area between "segregation experience" groups
**p < .05; F=3.37

Source: Bonnie Bullough, "Alienation and School Desegregation," *Integrated Education* (March-April 1972), 33.

Because Armor's article, which appeared in the influential journal *Public Interest*, attracted a great deal of attention, Thomas Pettigrew and three Harvard colleagues who interpreted these data differently from Armor published a critical reply. They attacked Armor's work on a number of grounds: (a) the criteria he employed for "successful" school desegregation were unrealistically high, (b) the studies he used to draw conclusions about desegregation were negatively biased, and (c) the study of the METCO program from which most of his conclusions were drawn suffered from serious methodological weaknesses.[43] With respect to Armor's interpretation of "militancy," black consciousness, and solidarity, these critics suggested that, if such attitudes did develop in desegregated schools, they should be regarded as evidence of the success, not the failure, of desegregation.[44] This behavior represents a healthy adaptation to a realistic appraisal of the social situation.[45]

There are two points that should be made about the effect of school desegregation on the development of self-conscious attitudes by minority students. The first point is that exposure to an alien culture usually heightens the awareness of the uniqueness of one's own culture; as others react to it in patterned ways, it takes on added meaning. When low-income minority pupils interact with pupils from predominantly middle-class families, they observe cultural patterns that are different from their own and are forced to adjust their behavior to take account of these differences.

The second point is that the social and psychological stresses created by the coming together of young people with different cultural backgrounds usually require the gyroscopic function of one's own reference group. Glaring status differentials in terms of social class background and preparation for academic work, plus the reflections in school affairs of a prejudiced larger society, demand strong positive identification with one's own family culture. It would seem, then, that both of these factors indicate that group pride and solidarity are natural responses to a pluralistic student body.

Conflict Among Students

Critics of school desegregation sometimes allude to the extent to which conflict arises among pupils from different backgrounds. They view this conflict as evidence that desegregated schools cannot foster intergroup cooperation among adults. However, conflict is not confined to pupils from different racial-ethnic groups; it is observed, for example, among pupils of different regions and social classes, as well as between sexes. But news media tend to exaggerate disruptive racial incidents, thereby giving impetus to further incidents, and school administrators sometimes overreact, which has the effect of further upsetting pupils and alarming the adult community.[46]

A more important fact in interpreting evidence of conflict is that it is not necessarily bad nor is it necessarily disruptive. Contemporary sociologists have tended to minimize the extent to which conflict is an inherent part of the development of social groups. As Coser has pointed out, "a certain degree of conflict is an essential element in group formation and the persistence of group life."[47] When it is managed effectively, conflict can be used to identify and clarify inconsistencies in the basic assumptions of conflicting parties and can serve as a mechanism for mutual socialization, adjustment, and change. However, when conflict is stifled, it often changes into hostility, which reappears in the form of uncontrollable violence.[48]

SCHOOL INTEGRATION AND DEVELOPMENT OF HUMAN RESOURCES

The third objective of school integration—the fuller development of human resources—has been the major focus of most school desegregation studies. Taking the lead from the national Equality of Educational Opportunity study (referred to as the Coleman Report), most evaluators use standardized scores from tests of language and computational skills as indicators of school effectiveness, even though academic achievement is only part of what is required of well-functioning adults. Participation in an advanced technological society entails knowledge and skills in occupational and other public roles and a world view consistent with the social organization of formal adult life. These include: (a) *personal qualities* such as self-confidence, motivation, flexibility, and creativity, (b) *social qualities* such as knowledge of the *gesellschaft* norms of secondary social structures, interpersonal skills, facility in moving from one social role to another, and the ability to compete, and (c) *vocational skills* such as the capacity to perform at a minimum level in some useful occupation. These outcomes of schooling have been largely ignored in discussions of the effects of desegregated schools.

Nevertheless, the lack of evaluation studies should not obscure the consistent finding that there have been and continue to be striking differences in achievement levels (as measured by standardized tests) between low-income and racial-ethnic minority pupils on the one hand, and middle-class pupils on the other. The achievement gap among subpopulations was fully publicized in 1966 by the Equality of Educational Opportunity data of the Coleman Report. That survey showed that with the notable exception of Oriental-Americans and some native-Americans, minority pupils on the average score

TABLE 4-5
Nationwide Median Test Scores for First- and Twelfth-Grade Pupils, Fall 1965

Test	Racial or Ethnic Group					
	Puerto Ricans	Indian Americans	Mexican Americans	Oriental Americans	Negro	Majority
1st grade:						
Nonverbal	45.8	53.0	50.1	56.6	43.4	54.1
Verbal	44.9	47.8	46.5	51.6	45.4	53.2
12th grade:						
Nonverbal	43.3	47.1	45.0	51.6	40.9	52.0
Verbal	43.1	43.7	43.8	49.6	40.9	52.1
Reading	42.6	44.3	44.2	48.8	42.2	51.9
Mathematics	43.7	45.9	45.5	51.3	41.8	51.8
General information	41.7	44.7	43.3	49.0	40.6	52.2
Average of the 5 tests	43.1	45.1	44.4	50.1	41.1	52.0

Source: Coleman Report, 20

significantly below majority pupils on all tests of academic achievement in their first year of school and that this discrepancy continues at each subsequent grade.

The Coleman Report was based on a massive survey that supplied data on some 400 variables from a five-percent sample of the nation's schools. Information pertaining to home background, attitudes, and achievement was obtained from more than 650,000 pupils in grades 1, 3, 6, 9, and 12. Information about the education, experience, and attitudes of the professional personnel in these schools was obtained from some 60,000 teachers and 4,000 principals. The teacher questionnaire also included a 30-item vocabulary test to measure teacher verbal ability; the principal questionnaire requested information about school facilities, staff, programs, and curricula.

Data from the survey were made available to other investigators who performed rigorous analyses that, along with the initial report, were topics of extensive debate.[49] Regardless of the investigator and the statistical techniques employed, all analyses of the Coleman survey data point dramatically to the strong effects of family social background on pupil achievement.[50] This effect is so powerful that it overwhelms the effects of in-school factors on pupil performance, thereby limiting the extent schools by themselves can provide equality of educational opportunity.

Schools bring little influence to bear on a child's achievement that is independent of his background and general social context; and this very lack of an independent effect means that the inequalities imposed on children by their home, neighborhood, and peer environment are carried along to become the inequalities with which they confront adult life at the end of school.[51]

The comparatively small unique influence of schools on pupil achievement makes it extremely difficult to determine with precision which in-school factors make the most difference. But it is generally agreed that the other people in the school are the most important factor. The family background of the other students is the most influential and the quality of the teaching staff is second. Tangible resources, though significant, do not approximate the saliency of social interaction. In general, the Coleman data show that when family background is controlled for statistically, low-income and minority pupils enrolled in desegregated as opposed to segregated schools score significantly higher on tests of achievement. "The apparent beneficial effect of a student body with a high proportion of white students comes not from racial composition per se, but from the better educational background and higher educational aspirations that are, on the average, found among white students."[52]

There are very difficult methodological problems in unraveling the relative influences of school socioeconomic status and school racial-ethnic composition on pupil achievement. These influences have received much attention without arriving at definitive conclusions. Yet racial-ethnic minority families are poor in larger proportion than white families and most predominantly minority schools have large numbers of low-income pupils. As a result, the question of the relative influence of race and class need not be answered in order to address the effects of racial-ethnic school desegregation. Socioeconomic integration automatically brings about racial-ethnic integration because thus far there is an insufficient number of middle-class minority pupils.[53]

McPartland and York analyzed the Coleman data and, unlike the original analysis, concluded that racial composition alone affects the academic performance and attitudes of black pupils after differences in social class levels of schools are taken into account.[54] They attribute the inconsistencies between their own and the Coleman team's analysis to the fact that they focused on the characteristics of students within classrooms rather than within the entire school. "It is in the classroom within the school where the characteristics of the fellow students have their effects. . . . Negro students in segregated classrooms apparently do not derive benefits from attending majority white schools."[55]

McPartland further studied the Coleman data concentrating on ninth-grade blacks from the metropolitan northeast because this sample was the most complete. He observed that within many desegregated schools the formal programs tracked a large portion of black pupils into segregated classes where they received no particular benefits in terms of achievement growth.[56] The sources of influence on achievement, according to McPartland, are largely from social-psychological factors: absence of the stigma of inferiority, social integration among students, and the student environment. The racial composition of the desegregated class is related to a sense of personal efficacy; social integration is effective in creating changes in racial attitudes; and student environment, that is, the standards developed by the student body, is an important factor in academic growth.[57]

Cohen, Pettigrew, and Riley reanalyzed the Coleman data for ninth- and twelfth-grade black pupils to determine if the apparent effect of classroom racial composition actually resulted from the selection of the more academically-able black pupils into desegregated classrooms. They concluded that although there was some selectivity in curricular assignment, it does not totally account for the effect of class racial composition on the achievement of black pupils in desegregated classes.[58]

A group of social scientists at the U.S. Office of Education under the direction of George W. Mayeske analyzed the national sample of sixth-grade pupils in the Coleman Report in an attempt to explain observed racial-ethnic group differences in achievement test scores. Several new methodological techniques were employed to overcome important limitations in the original analysis. These new techniques include the use of criterion scaling in the treatment of missing data and in assigning values to independent variables, and the use of the "commonalities" technique for unraveling the unique effects of highly interrelated factors such as racial-ethnic group membership and family socioeconomic status.[59] This group performed two complementary analyses that yielded mutually consistent results supporting and expanding the earlier Coleman Report findings.

In the first analysis they were able to explain almost all the variation in achievement scores between racial-ethnic groups by factors that are "primarily social in nature and origin."[60] These factors included home background variables (family SES and family structure), family process variables (educational expectations and aspirations that parents have for children and the activities they engage in to support them), area of residence (national region and degree of urbanization), and the achievement and motivational levels of the other students in the school. Differences between racial-ethnic groups in achievement were statistically maximized through criterion scaling,[61] then each of the above variables was introduced, one at a time, in an attempt to minimize these differences. All of the variables, alone and together, reduced variation in achievement scores among racial groups.[62]

The Mayeske group employed the "commonalities" technique in a second analysis to determine the magnitude of each variable's contribution, including the racial-ethnic group variable, to achievement. Although the variables were highly intercorrelated, the researchers were able to conclude that "motivational and structural aspects of the family and the achievement and motivational level of the students one goes to school with" are the most salient in explaining differences in student achievement both before and after racial-ethnic group membership is taken into account. Educationally related child-rearing activities play a greater role in achievement than the racial-ethnic group, socioeconomic status of parents, or the type of school attended. The Mayeske group, like the Coleman group, concluded that social background of the other students is the most important in-school factor affecting the educational process and the quality of teaching personnel is second. These conclusions imply that schools do play an independent part in preparing children for the adult world.[63]

Selected Studies on School Desegregation and Pupil Achievement

Studies in desegregation seldom meet the criteria of well-controlled experimental design, for this would require pupils to be subjected to situations that are not always in their best educational interest. The classic experimental design entails the selection of two or more groups of pupils through random techniques. One group, the "experimental" group, undergoes the "experimental" treatment, in this case desegregated schooling. The other group, the "control" group, receives no special treatment. Both groups are evaluated on the outcomes of interest to the research before the experiment and again after its completion. The changes in outcomes in each group are assessed and the extent to which they differ is attributed to the experimental treatment. When these changes are sufficiently large that they cannot be attributed to chance factors, the effects of the treatment are said to be "statistically significant."

Evaluations of on-going desegregation programs present a number of methodological difficulties including noncomparable experimental and control groups or no control group at all, lack of pre-experimental evaluation data, changes in evaluation instruments during the experimental period, attenuation of the sample through pupil movement out of the school or refusal to cooperate, and restrictions over the control of relevant stimuli. Many strategies have been developed that approximate but do not entirely conform with the ideal model of experimental design. Thus quasi-experimental or natural research designs form the bulk of desegregation research.

Alan Wilson's work that appeared in the U.S. Commission on Civil Rights report, *Racial Isolation in the Public Schools*, has been uniformly praised for its methodological design. Wilson overcame some of the major criticisms leveled at the Coleman Report and other cross-sectional surveys in which all variables were measured at only one time. His access to longitudinal data permitted him to look at achievement gains of the same pupils at several points in their school career. In addition, he was able to control for the primary-grade I.Q. score of each member of his sample. In this way Wilson separated the effects of school experience from the effects of preschool learning and intellectual ability on academic achievement.

Wilson compared secondary school pupils whose primary-grade I.Q. scores were identical but had attended elementary and secondary schools with differing proportions of minority and low-socio-economic-status pupils. He concluded that the social class composition of schools—measured by the proportion of pupils whose parents were unskilled laborers, unemployed, or welfare recipients—has a significant impact on the academic development of white pupils and an even greater effect on the development of black pupils. This finding obtained regardless of the racial composition of the school. Unlike McPartland who concluded that the racial composition of the classroom was important in school achievement, Wilson contended that racial composition was relatively unimportant.[64] However, he did not analyze his data at the classroom level.

Evidence for the salutary effects of school desegregation on academic achievement of low-income and racial-ethnic minority pupils is contained in a host of independent studies. Although each has obvious methodological problems, many ingenious strategies have been employed to deal with them and each has its own strengths and makes its own compromises. Taken together, the pattern of findings lends support to the proposition that low-income and minority children benefit from the racial, ethnic, and socioeconomic desegregation of schools. This is not the place to review these many studies; instead, a few that show that fuller educational opportunities can be provided through school desegregation are discussed.

The evaluation of Sacramento's "Project Aspiration" in which the achievement gains of black pupils who were transported from ghetto to middle-class schools were compared with black pupils who remained in the ghetto indicates that, although every effort had been made to supply equal educational opportunity through traditional school inputs to both groups, the pupils in the racially-mixed schools had significant educational advantages brought about by the social composition of the student body.[65]

A similar study of Rochester's "Fifteen Point" Program shows that the desegregation of pupils at early grade levels is more effective than desegregation at higher grade levels. It also shows that arithmetic achievement in comparison with reading achievement is more responsive to changes brought about by school desegregation.[66]

Hartford's "Project Concern" also indicates that desegregation in early grades is most effective.[67] And studies of desegregated schools that occur naturally in Pittsburgh and in Boston again indicate that arithmetic achievement more than reading achievement is sensitive to the social context of the school.[68]

From the evaluation of the desegregation of the Berkeley school district comes the finding that, except for an occasional setback during the first year of total desegregation, reading achievement of both black and white students showed consistently positive change. Other studies have shown that achievement of white pupils is not negatively affected by changes in the racial composition of their schools.[69] However, a few studies suggest that achievement of white pupils may be depressed when there are large percentages of low-income and minority pupils.[70] A recent reanalysis of the Coleman Report's data by Jencks and Brown[71] indicates that for both black and white elementary school pupils there is greatest cognitive gain in schools with between 57 and 75 percent enrollment of white pupils.

Data from the desegregation of Riverside, California, schools have been analyzed in ways that point out some of the subtle processes of school desegregation. For example, minority pupils of high academic ability are more advantaged by school desegregation than minority pupils of moderate and low ability. Also, the achievement of minority pupils in desegregated schools is positively related to the level of ability of the other pupils in school.[72]

The kind of educational programs presented is found to be an extremely important factor in the achievement of minority pupils. Those that stress mastery of specific skills and attempt to communicate educational objectives to parents bring greater learning gains than do traditional programs.[73] This is illustrated by the dramatic effects of the Riverside compensatory educational program "Learning Achievement through Saturated Educational Resources" (henceforth LASER) in the primary grades of the 52-percent minority Longfellow school. The program was individualized for each student and was "competency based," which means that each pupil received instruction in specific skills until the skills were mastered and then moved on to other educational objectives. Great efforts were made to explain the program to parents and to involve them with their children's education and with the school.

After the first two years of operation (1970 and 1971), pupils who participated in the LASER program showed achievement increases in mean grade equivalent over previous pupils in the same grade. In spring 1971, second-grade pupils were performing at the 66th percentile in mathematics and third-grade pupils had a mean grade equivalent of 4 school years and 3 months in arithmetic. The evaluation data for second- and third-grade pupils in the LASER program are presented in Table 4-6.

TABLE 4-6
Median Grade Equivalent Scores for Longfellow School
on Stanford Achievement Tests

	1968	1969	1970	1971
Grade 2 (2.8)				
Total reading	2.5	2.8	2.9	3.2[a]
Arithmetic computation	2.8	3.1	3.6	
Arithmetic concepts	2.4	2.8	3.3	
Mathematics				66%[b]
Grade 3 (3.8)				
Total reading	2.9	3.3	3.7	4.0
Arithmetic computation	2.9	3.7	4.0	4.3
Arithmetic concepts	2.7	3.4	3.3	4.3

[a]Cooperative Primary Reading Test.
[b]Cooperative Primary Mathematics Test. (Computation and concepts are combined in a single test. No grade equivalents are given by the publisher. Scores are reported in percentiles.)

Source: Riverside Unified School District, *LASER Individualized Education* (Riverside, Cal.: Department of Research and Evaluation, 1971).

Influence of Teacher Attitudes on Pupil Achievement

The findings of another substudy of the Riverside evaluation project by Eugene Johnson show the influence of teacher attitudes and expectations about individual pupils on the achievement of those pupils. Dr. Johnson examined the relationship between the academic growth of elementary school pupils during the first year of Riverside desegregation and the perception of their teachers about their academic ability and motivation. He developed a teacher racial discrimination index that predicted the academic growth of minority pupils.

The racial discrimination index was formed by first determining the teacher's evaluation of the ability of all the minority pupils in the class relative to the ability of all the white pupils. This ratio was then divided by the ratio of predesegregation achievement test scores of minority pupils to comparable scores of white pupils. Teachers who accurately perceived the ability of their pupils had an index score of 1; those who underestimated the ability of minority pupils or over-

estimated the ability of white pupils had a score greater than 1, and
so on. Those enrolled in classes of teachers who scored low on this
index made greater academic progress than those of teachers who
scored high. The procedure for creating this index is as follows:

$$\text{Discrimination Index} = \frac{\overline{X}_{WB}/\overline{X}_{MB}}{\overline{X}_{WA}/\overline{X}_{MA}}$$

where

$\overline{X}_{WB}$ = average judgment of the brightness of whites in a classroom

$\overline{X}_{MB}$ = average judgment of the brightness of minority children in a classroom

$\overline{X}_{WA}$ = mean predesegregation standardized achievement of
white children a teacher is judging

$\overline{X}_{MA}$ = mean predesegregation standardized achievement of
minority children a teacher is judging.

Johnson divided his sample of 145 classrooms into high- and low-
discrimination classes defined by whether the teacher's discrimination score was above or below the median:

Analysis of variance shows that children in high and low discrimination classrooms do *not* differ significantly with respect to predesegregation achievement.
Children do differ, though, with respect to changes in achievement. In low discrimination classrooms all ethnic groups show little change from predesegregation achievement levels. But in high discrimination classrooms both minority
groups (especially blacks) show significant decreases in achievement while whites
show slight increases. . . . Those minority children doing *most well* predesegregation are *most* adversely affected by a classroom high in discrimination post
desegregation.[74]

Johnson's analysis underscores the sensitive relationship between a
child's performance and teacher expectations for that performance.
Special hardships are often created for minority pupils during early
stages of desegregation because of negative stereotypes. The situation
for minority pupils is further exacerbated by the fact that they seem
to be more sensitive than white pupils to the interpersonal behavior
of their teachers.[75]

INTEGRATING THE DESEGREGATED SCHOOL

These analyses illuminate the important distinction between integrated and segregated education in desegregated schools and show that school desegregation is but a first step in achieving the objectives of integrated education. It must be followed by other steps if an even more vicious form of racial isolation—the resegregated school—is to be avoided. Reports of minority pupils enrolled in schools that are merely desegregated indicate that they may suffer greater educational deprivation and social-psychological harm than minority pupils in traditionally segregated schools. In this situation they are not protected from the stigma of social inferiority that goes hand-in-hand with discriminatory attitudes. From research thus far it seems clear that minority pupils who perceive the social climate of their schools as prejudicial toward them and hostile toward racial interaction are not able to take full advantage of the other educational opportunities that desegregated schools can provide.

In spring 1972, a group of researchers under the direction of Jane Mercer at the University of California, Riverside, studied 55 desegregated elementary schools in four southern California school districts to determine the extent to which these schools were becoming educationally integrated. Integrated education was defined in their research as "the social process by which pupils, parents, and educators from a variety of ethnic backgrounds work together to develop a school organization which involves members of each ethnic group in equal-status relationships and which reflects the culture of each group in its program."[76]

This definition of integrated education, which includes both cultural and structural integration, is unusual on several counts. First, cultural integration does not exist unless the heritage and life experience of all the pupils are represented in the school program. The objective of the school program is to develop children who are bicultural—"children who have not only acquired the skills and knowledge needed to succeed in modern industrial America but have also become literate in their native tongue and have learned to understand and value their own cultural heritage." The definition is also unusual because structural integration does not exist unless "children, parents, and teachers of all ethnic groups acquire statuses and play roles in the school that are of equivalent power and prestige."[77]

Given these standards for school integration, it is not surprising that the Mercer team found no school with an ideal educational climate. They concluded that desegregated schools continue to favor Anglo children and their parents. From the sample of all the third-and/or sixth-grade pupils in each of the 55 schools, they found the achievement of Anglo pupils significantly higher than the achievement of either Mexican-American or black pupils. The teachers in each school held significantly higher educational and occupational expectations for Anglo children and perceived them as significantly more competent and sociable. Also, teachers perceived the parents of Anglo pupils as having more power in the community and being more able to influence school policy than the parents of either black or Mexican-American pupils.

With respect to the racial-ethnic composition of the teaching staff in the desegregated schools, ten schools had no minority teachers at all and only ten had 20 percent or more black teachers. Mexican-American teachers were employed in only 15 schools and there were never more than two on a teaching staff. Nor was there much evidence that school programs supported cultural pluralism. There was low usage of multi-ethnic reading materials and relatively little recognition of ethnic holidays. The Mercer team concluded that the desegregated schools in their study were far from developing integrated learning environments.[78] According to this and other studies, effective school integration requires meticulous planning so that the stresses that normally accompany new patterns of social interaction will be minimized.

Empirical evidence to support the proposition that school racial climates can be deliberately altered comes from several sources. In one study, a 1973 evaluation of the effects of the Federal School Assistance Program in desegregated southern high schools, Crain and York[79] show significant relationships among the academic performance of black males, their motivations and school morale, and the racial climate of their schools. They also show the racial climate of schools to be significantly affected by teacher behavior, which, in turn, seems to be influenced by formal school policies.

Crain and York compared 200 desegregated secondary schools that received federal funds to aid school desegregation with a matched sample of schools that did not. They found that after one academic year the achievement of black males was considerably higher in funded schools, though there was little difference in the achievement of black females or of whites of either sex. They also found that more black pupils in the funded schools were "happy" in school and more of them perceived the school staff as supporting desegregation. (Teachers in funded schools did in fact discuss racial issues in class more often and thought of their schools as racially tense less often.) The authors concluded that funded schools apparently had a more "egalitarian racial atmosphere than their matched controls and are more likely to be places where black students like school and feel a sense of belonging."

Crain and York also report important differences in the official policies between funded and unfunded schools. More funded schools provided human relations programs for teachers, revised their curricula during the school year, and increased their extracurricular activities geared to minority pupils. Whether these activities were directly responsible for the observed healthier racial climate, the greater sense of belonging by black pupils, and the higher academic achievement of black males cannot be determined from the design of this particular study. However, the authors suggest that the symbolic gesture of federal funding may have been more responsible for these consequences than actual in-school programs. Pressures from the federal government in the form of financial aid to make desegregation work could well have been interpreted by the school staff as an "instruction" to improve race relations within the school and as a "legitimation" of school desegregation policy.

Further evidence that school social climate can be manipulated through official school policy and in-service training for teachers is presented by Preston and Robinson[80] in their report on the results of desegregation workshops for in-service teachers in Houston that significantly reduced negative attitudes of white teachers toward black people in general. A biracial faculty of 20 educators and consultants met with 150 teachers for 12 successive eight-hour Saturday sessions in which films, lectures, and discussions were presented on racial problems. In addition, participants spent three hours each week in biracial sensitivity sessions designed to provide intimate equal-status contact between whites and blacks.

Comparisons between the interracial attitudes of white teachers before and after the program indicate that they became significantly more positive. However, changes in the attitudes of black teachers were minimal and none was significant in a statistical sense. In inter-preting this finding, Preston and Robinson note that materials pro-vided by the workshop were structured toward the modification of white misconceptions about blacks and virtually ignored black mis-conceptions about whites. From this they conclude that reduction in prejudice requires more than equal-status interracial contact; it also requires deliberate activities designed to reinforce it. Interracial workshops must include materials directed at the reduction of preju-dice toward all races, including white, if they are to be totally effec-tive.

A 16-month follow-up study, which compared the 350 institute participants with a random sample of 198 teachers from the same schools, indicates that the reduction in prejudice of white teachers is long-lasting. On every comparison between white institute teachers and the random sample regarding stereotyping, integrated inter-personal relations, and desegregation, institute participants were sig-nificantly less prejudiced.[81] Although differences between the atti-tudes of black teachers who did and did not attend the institute were not statistically significant, black institute teachers were consistently more favorable toward whites. This research supports the view that interracial contact can decrease prejudice under certain circum-stances, including equal status and common goals among participants and a social structure that supports the reduction of prejudice.

Further evidence of the effectiveness of positive intervention in desegregated situations is presented by Cohen and Roper. It is their position that in the American society the "belief systems concerning race and other status characteristics are so powerful that they will infect the interaction setting and will likely reinforce rather than change stereotypical beliefs."[82] These belief systems create wide-spread "interracial interaction disability," so that all participants in interracial groups—both black and white—will usually ascribe high status and general ability to white members, regardless of real com-petence. Expectations based on such stereotypes lead to self-fulfilling prophecies in interracial groups in which white participants usually become more dominant and more productive than black participants. "The low status member, expecting to be less competent than the high status member, initiates less at the outset, overevaluating the contribution of the more talkative high status members and under-evaluating his own contribution."[83]

Cohen and Roper report that they have been able to reduce "interracial interaction disability" by modifying the expectancies held by both white and black pupils about the competencies of the black pupils in advance of interracial group interaction. The procedure consists of (1) developing superior competence among black pupils in some task (for example, the ability to build a transistor radio), (2) demonstrating this competence by having black pupils instruct white pupils in this task, and (3) making certain that the superior competence of the black pupils is visible to all by repeating their teaching performance through videotape. Cohen and Roper report that the expectation for black performance is significantly increased in the black and white pupils who were exposed to the program. Black pupils in groups where all members received this treatment initiate many more activities than those who have not, which is assumed to be the most sensitive and reliable index of power and prestige order within the group.[84] This finding obtains only when both black and white group members are treated in advance. Apparently since "interracial interaction disability stems from expectations held by both races, it is necessary to treat expectations of both."[85]

SCHOOL DISTRICT DESEGREGATION AND "WHITE FLIGHT"

Needless to say, the imputed advantages of desegregated schools are not present in districts where pupils are mostly of one race or ethnic group. For this reason it is important to know if the implementation of desegregation affects a district's proportion of white pupil enrollments. It is sometimes suggested that, upon failure, white parents who actively resist school desegregation will seek alternative education for their children, either in private schools within the same district or in public schools in another area.

Coleman, Kelly, and Moore[86] analyzed school racial composition from school district reports submitted to the U.S. Office of Civil Rights for the years 1968 through 1972. They observed that although segregation between schools within most school districts declined during those years, segregation between school districts increased, especially between urban and suburban districts. By comparing scores on an Index of Segregation, based on the proportion of white children in the average black child's school (or school district) standardized by the proportion of whites in the district (or region), they concluded that segregation rates were lower and varied less from school to school within the same district than from district to district within geographical regions. For example, the Index of Segregation within districts for Southeastern U.S. decreased from .75 to .19 between 1968 and 1972, at the same time the Index of Segregation among districts in that region increased from .18 to .22.[87] The within-district data reflect results of official school desegregation policy, whereas the between-district data reflect the phenomenon of white suburbanization where larger proportions of white than black families move from cities to suburbs.

The Coleman group did not conclude that school desegregation *caused* white families to leave their neighborhoods, but they strongly suggest that desegregation hastened suburbanization in several large Southern school districts, most notably Atlanta and Memphis. However, they also concluded that in areas where there are high proportions of black families in cities and predominantly white suburbs, movement from cities "proceeds at a relatively rapid rate with or without desegregation."[88]

The findings of the Coleman group were somewhat garbled in the national news media and many accounts, contrary to fact, attributed to it empirical support for the position that "white flight" was created by school desegregation. Some of the confusion may have arisen because neither Coleman nor reporters took sufficient care to differentiate clearly between Coleman's personal opinions and the results of the research he and his colleagues carried out at the Urban Institute.

The same school district reports were subsequently analyzed by Pettigrew and Green[89] who concluded that school desegregation does even less to hasten "white flight" than attributed to it by Coleman. They published a lengthy article in the *Harvard Educational Review* showing their analysis. In addition, they take Coleman to task publicly for not making clearer distinctions in his public statements between his own value structure and the results of his research.

CONCLUSIONS

This chapter gives a general account of social science findings relating to the consequences of school desegregation for individuals and for the larger American society. It assumes that public policy to segregate schools has at its core three interdependent objectives: the fostering of individual mobility, the creation of a desegregated adult society, and the fuller development of the resource potential of the school-age American population. Data bearing on each of these objectives are sparse, beset with methodological difficulties, and often lead to conflicting conclusions.

One of the most intractable problems in the conduct of desegregation research is that objectives of school desegregation, like most educational objectives, are concerned with the kinds of adults schools produce. An evaluation of such long-range objectives requires an historical perspective, yet only a few studies cover both childhood and adult periods of sampled populations. Further, most of these studies have been unable to develop adequate controls over factors that might bear on the relationships of most interest.

Rather than use long-range objectives, most evaluations of school desegregation employ short-term outcomes such as cognitive achievement and attitudes about schooling. Aside from the question of the appropriateness of these measures, many of these studies contain methodological problems and they seldom meet the ideal of experimental design. Although many strategies have been developed to cope with this shortcoming, new techniques present new limitations. These studies do not always have adequate control over home background factors and frequently have no controls for the allocation of resources within schools, composition and social climate of classrooms, and teacher attitudes.

A third and related problem in school desegregation lies in the interpretation of findings. Disagreement among social scientists often takes the form of debate over methodology, although ideological differences are usually at the core. The spirited exchanges over the Coleman survey data pertaining to the use of statistical tools are an example. Debates such as these arise because some techniques will show weaker statistical relationships among a set of variables than other techniques; multiple regression analysis compared to analysis of variance is a case in point. Researchers tend to select the methods most likely to support their underlying hypotheses, while their critics demand to know why the data were not treated in a different manner.

Another source of contention among social scientists is the extent to which findings are of theoretical and practical importance. The Jencks group concluded that home background and quantity of education have little impact on adult occupational status because they accounted for only a portion of the total variation in income among adults. But other researchers view home background and education as theoretically and practically significant because they account for so large a portion of the variation that social scientists have been able to explain.

Lay people have even greater difficulty in understanding the meaning of research findings. Both pro- and anti-desegregation camps grasp at partial findings to support their own ideological positions. For example, studies showing no relationship between school desegregation and its presumed objectives are interpreted by some as negative evidence about school desegregation. But as Averch[90] pointed out, the absence of an observed relationship between school desegregation and scholastic achievement means that these studies did not uncover a positive relationship, not that a positive relationship does not exist. Social science, unlike its physical science model, is still very young and needs much more theoretical and methodological development in order to increase its explanatory power. Until that time, findings must be used with caution.

A fourth problem lies in generalizing from negative research findings about a specific program to general public policy. Policymakers sometimes conclude that desegregation can never achieve its objectives on the basis of past research without looking at the way a particular program was implemented. However, unfavorable evaluations come more often from poorly conceived and executed desegregation programs than from limitations in underlying theory about desegregation. A long tradition of sociological and psychological literature suggests that desegregated schools when properly managed can attain hoped-for objectives. It should not be assumed that because some desegregated schools fail to raise achievement test scores of low-income and minority pupils that theories about the socialization impact of school climate and the psychological effect of discrimination are in error. The few attempts to deal with attitudinal dimensions of school desegregation discussed above strongly suggest that it is possible to manage the climate of desegregated schools and classrooms and that this will contribute importantly toward desired objectives.

In sum, the drive toward integration ought not to be discarded on the basis of social science evidence. Aside from the limitations of the studies themselves, researchers and educators are just beginning to develop the experience and sophistication necessary to build integrated schools. A review of some of the more discrete and carefully controlled studies, such as those from Riverside, California, which examine different aspects of the educational process and their relationships to school outcomes, foster optimism that school desegregation can live up to its promises under certain circumstances. There must, however, be careful, long-range educational and social planning to include the relationship between pupils' in-school and nonschool experiences, the education and utilization of teachers, and the affective and cognitive climates of schools and classrooms.

NOTES

1. Panel on Youth of the President's Science Advisory Committee, *Youth: Transition to Adulthood* (Washington, D.C.: Government Printing Office, 1973), 169-70. Two dissenting members of the ten-person panel pointed out that youth and their families do not always have the capability to select appropriate opportunities for their own skill development and, also, that there are pronounced possibilities for exploitation by the recipients of vouchers. (Panel on Youth, 179).

2. Center for the Study of Public Policy, *Education Vouchers: A Report on Financing Education By Grants to Parents* (Cambridge, Mass.: The Center, 1970), 13-17.

3. Christopher Jencks *et al.*, *Inequality: A Reassessment of the Effects of Family and Schooling in America* (New York: Basic Books, 1972), 23.

4. Marion F. Shaycroft, *The High School Years: Growth in Cognitive Skills* (Pittsburgh, Pa.: Project Talent, University of Pittsburgh, 1967).

5. James S. Coleman *et al.*, *Equality of Educational Opportunity*, Office of Education, National Center for Educational Statistics, OE 38001 (Washington, D.C.: Government Printing Office, 1966). Hereafter cited as the Coleman Report.

6. Peter M. Blau and Otis Dudley Duncan, *The American Occupational Structure* (New York: John Wiley & Sons, 1967).

7. Henry M. Levin, "Schooling and Inequality: The Social Science Objectivity Gap," *Saturday Review* (11 November 1972), 49.

8. Beverly Duncan, "Comments on 'Inequality,'" *Harvard Educational Review* 43(February 1973), 124.

9. Jencks *et al., op. cit.*, 181.

10. Blau and Duncan, *op. cit.*, 201-2.

11. Beverly Duncan and Otis Dudley Duncan, "Minorities and the Process of Stratification," *American Sociological Review* 33(No. 3, June 1968), 363-64.

12. Jencks *et al., op. cit.*, 7-8.

13. Levin, *op. cit.*, 49.

14. Jencks *et al., op. cit.*, 255.

15. James S. Coleman, "Equality of Opportunity and Equality of Results," *Harvard Educational Review* 43(February 1973), 132.

16. Jencks *et al., op. cit.*, 142-43.

17. *Ibid.*, 219.

18. *Ibid.*, 30. There is a growing body of literature that examines the relationship between tangible resources allocated to schools and student outcomes, which leads to inconclusive results. A major review of input-output studies by the RAND corporation concludes that background factors tend to dominate the results to such a degree that there is little evidence that school resources have a powerful impact on student outcomes. Further, this body of research has not identified what particular resources should be provided to students. (See Harvey Averch *et al., How Effective Is Schooling? A Critical Review and Synthesis of Research Findings* [Santa Monica, Cal.: RAND, 1972], 48.) The RAND scholars reach similar conclusions about peer groups: "There is no evidence that a student body affects the performance of individual members of that student body." However, they point out that there is also no evidence to the contrary; "no researcher has shown that student-body effects do *not* exist" (*Ibid.*, 43). The conclusions of the RAND researchers are, in general, at odds with those of this chapter.

19. Burton R. Clark, *Educating the Expert Society* (San Francisco: Chandler, 1962).

20. For example, see Randall Collins, "Functional and Conflict Theories of Educational Stratification," *American Sociological Review* 36(No. 6, December 1971), 1002-19.

21. Thomas F. Pettigrew, "Adult Consequences of Racial Isolation and Desegregation in the Schools" in U.S. Commission of Civil Rights, *Racial Isolation in the Public Schools*. Vol. 1 (Washington, D.C.: Government Printing Office, 1967), 215-20.

22. Robert L. Crain, "School Integration and Occupational Achievement of Negroes," *American Journal of Sociology* 75(January 1970), 595.

23. Robert L. Crain, "School Integration and the Academic Achievement of Negroes," *Sociology of Education* 44(Winter 1971), 19.

24. Crain, "School Integration and Occupational Achievement of Negroes," 599.

25. Crain, "School Integration and Academic Achievement of Negroes," 7.

26. *Ibid.*, 11-12.

27. *Ibid.*, 17.

28. David J. Armor, "The Evidence on Busing," *The Public Interest* 28(Summer 1972), 105-6.

29. *Ibid.*, 106.

30. This assumes that teacher verbal ability is a measure of teacher quality. It has in fact been shown to be positively related to pupil achievement. (See David J. Armor, "School and Family Effects on Black and White Achievement: A

Reexamination of the USOE Data" in F. Mosteller and D. Moynihan (eds.), *On Equality of Educational Opportunity* [New York: Vintage, 1972], 192, 213.)

31. Coleman Report, 132 and 273-75; George W. Mayeske, "Teacher Attributes and School Achievement" in *Do Teachers Make A Difference?* U.S. Department of Health, Education, and Welfare (Washington, D.C.: Government Printing Office, 1970), 108.

32. Edward L. McDill, Edmund D. Meyers, Jr., and Leo C. Rigsby, "Institutional Effects on the Academic Behavior of High School Students," *Sociology of Education* 40(Summer 1967), 199.

33. The discussion of school social climate draws heavily from Audrey James Schwartz, *The Schools and Socialization* (New York: Harper and Row, 1975), chap. 7.

34. Pettigrew, "Adult Consequences of Racial Isolation and Desegregation in the Schools," *op. cit.*, 224.

35. *Perceived Control of the Environment Scale.* Crain, "School Integration and Academic Achievement of Negroes," 18-20.

    1. Good luck is just as important as hard work for success.

    2. Very often when I try to get ahead, something or somebody stops me.

    3. People like me don't have a very good chance to be really successful in life.

    4. Being a success is mainly a matter of hard work, and luck has little or nothing to do with it, or, Getting a good job depends mainly upon being in the right place at the right time. (Choose one.)

    5. When I make plans, I am almost certain that I can make them work, or, It is not always wise to plan too far ahead because many things turn out to be a matter of good or bad fortune anyway. (Choose one.)

36. *Anti-White Feeling Scale.* Crain, "School Integration and Academic Achievement of Negroes," 18-20.

    1. Sometimes when I am around a white person I'm afraid I might tell him what I really think about white people.

    2. I'm afraid I might lose my temper at something he says.

    3. The trouble with most white people is they think they're better than other people.

    4. If a Negro is wise, he will think twice before he trusts a white man as he would another Negro.

    5. Sometimes I would like to get even with white people for all they have done to the Negro.

    6. There are very few, if any white men who are really unprejudiced.

37. Crain, "School Integration and Academic Achievement of Negroes," 19.

38. Julian B. Rotter *et al.*, "Generalized Expectancies for Internal vs. External Control of Reinforcements," Psychological Monograph 80, 1966.

39. Leo Srole, "Social Integration and Certain Corollaries: An Exploratory Study," *American Sociological Review* 21(December 1956), 709-16.

40. Bonnie Bullough, "Alienation and School Desegregation," *Journal of Integrated Education* (March-April 1972), 29-35.

41. Armor, "The Evidence on Busing," 102.

42. *Ibid.*, 102-3.

43. Thomas F. Pettigrew *et al.*, "Busing: A Review of 'the Evidence,' " *The Public Interest* 30(Winter 1973), 88-91; Armor's response appears in "The Double Standard: A Reply," *The Public Interest* 30(Winter 1973), 119-31.

44. Pettigrew *et al.*, *op. cit.*, 90.

45. Armor makes the assumption that the Supreme Court's decision in *Brown v. Board of Education* (1954) was based in part on social science evidence which claims that social contact between different groups decreases intergroup hostility and prejudice. He points out that research to support this claim was carried out only in "naturally" desegregated settings and that "induced" desegregation might produce different results. For this reason, attitudes and social relations between the transported and host pupils were of special interest in his research. That these factors were not more positive after desegregation, coupled with the fact that achievement scores of transported pupils were not significantly raised, led Armor to conclude that public policy fostering school desegregation must be justified on grounds other than existing social science evidence (Armor, "The Evidence on Busing," 114).

46. U.S. Commission on Civil Rights, *Racial Isolation in the Public Schools* (Washington, D.C.: Government Printing Office, 1973), 9-10.

47. Lewis A. Coser, *The Functions of Social Conflict* (New York: Free Press, 1956), 3.

48. *Ibid.*, 152.

49. For example, see Frederick Mosteller and Daniel P. Moynihan (eds.), *On Equality of Educational Opportunity* (New York: Vintage, 1972).

50. Many of the criticisms of the initial Coleman Report are methodologically significant but substantively trivial. Analyses performed to meet methodological objectives leave the original qualitative findings relatively unchanged. Among the most important reanalyses are those by a Harvard faculty seminar in 1966-1967 (Mosteller and Moynihan (eds.), *op. cit.*). Under the co-chairmanship of Pettigrew and Moynihan these scholars conducted four different analyses of the Coleman data using a variety of statistical techniques. Their work was extremely technical and at times statistical virtuosity seemed to overshadow the theoretical and practical significance of the findings. Nevertheless, their conclusions were similar to those of the original Coleman team. Perhaps the most important contribution was Marshall S. Smith's discovery of an error in the original procedure for estimating school-to-school differences explained by individual home background. This error led to an overestimate of the unique effects that schools might have on their pupils. (Marshall S. Smith, "Equality of Educational Opportunity: The Basic Findings Reconsidered" in Mosteller and Moynihan [eds.], *op. cit.*, 231.)

51. Coleman Report, 325.

52. *Ibid.*, 307.

53. Eric Hanushek, "The Education of Negroes and Whites," unpublished Ph.D. dissertation, MIT, Cambridge, Mass., 1968; Nancy H. St. John and Ralph Lewis, "The Influence of School Racial Context on Achievement," *Social Problems* 19(Summer 1971), 68-79. There are some middle-class predominantly minority schools. One is the Windsor Hill elementary school in Los Angeles

where 90 percent of the pupils come from middle- and high-income black families. In 1969 the mean I.Q. of its sixth grade was 115 points, which is considerably above the national mean, and the mean reading achievement score was the same as the national norm (*Los Angeles Times*, 30 September 1969). See also Thomas Sowell, "Black Excellence—The Case of Dunbar High School," *The Public Interest* 35(Spring 1974), 3-21 for an article on the academically-excellent all-black Dunbar High School in Washington, D.C.

54. James McPartland and Robert L. York, "Further Analysis of Equality of Educational Opportunity Survey" in U.S. Commission on Civil Rights, *Racial Isolation in the Public Schools*. Vol. 2, *op. cit.*, 37.

55. *Ibid.*, 42.

56. James McPartland, "The Segregated Student in the Desegregated Schools: Sources of Influence on Negro Secondary Students," Report No. 21 (Baltimore, Md.: Johns Hopkins, 1968), 334.

57. *Ibid.*, 335-36.

58. David K. Cohen, Thomas F. Pettigrew, and Robert T. Riley, "Race and the Outcomes of Schooling" in Mosteller and Moynihan (eds.), *On Equality of Educational Opportunity*, *op. cit.*, 358-59.

59. For a description of these techniques, see Albert E. Beaton, Jr., "Some Mathematical and Empirical Properties of Criterion Scaled Variables" in George W. Mayeske *et al.*, *A Study of Our Nation's Schools: A Working Paper* (Washington, D.C.: U.S. Office of Education, 1969), 339-43.

60. This work along with that of Alan Wilson should shift the balance in the controversy reawakened by Arthur Jensen in "How Much Can We Boost IQ and Scholastic Achievement?" *Harvard Educational Review* 39(No. 1, Winter 1969), 1-123, over the origins of intelligence toward the environmentalist position. Wilson examined factors that were most related to the I.Q. scores of seventh- and tenth-grade pupils and found that race *per se* was not even statistically significant. Most important to the I.Q. of seventh-grade pupils were the academic quality of elementary schools, teachers' expectations, pupils' commitment to parents' goals, and pupils' feelings of personal efficacy. Most important for tenth-grade pupils were fathers' expectations, teachers' expectations, and pupils' educational aspirations. (Alan B. Wilson, "Sociological Perspective on the Development of Academic Competence in Urban Areas" in A. Passow (ed.), *Urban Education in the 1970's: Reflections and A Look Ahead* [New York: Teachers College Press, Columbia University, 1971], 135-37).

61. George W. Mayeske, "On the Explanation of Racial-Ethnic Group Differences in Achievement Test Scores." Mimeograph, 6.

62. *Ibid.*, 13.

63. *Ibid.*, 18-21.

64. Alan B. Wilson, "Educational Consequences of Segregation in a California Community" in U.S. Commission on Civil Rights, *Racial Isolation in the Public Schools*. Vol. 2, *op. cit.*, 202.

65. Sacramento City Unified School District, "An Evaluation Report on a Program of Compensatory Education E.S.E.A., Title I: Focus on Reading and Mathematics 1970-71" (Sacramento, Cal.: The District, 1971).

66. Rochester City School District, "Final Report: A Three Year Longitu-

dinal Study to Assess a Fifteen Point Plan to Reduce Racial Isolation and Provide Quality Integrated Education for Elementary Level Pupils" (Rochester, N.Y.: Division of Planning and Research, 1970).

67. Thomas W. Mahan, "Project Concern: 1966-1968, Hartford, Connecticut. Report to Hartford Public Schools" (Hartford, Conn.: The Project, 1968); Aline M. Mahan and Thomas W. Mahan, "Changes in Cognitive Style: An Analysis of the Impact of White Suburban Schools on Inner City Children," *Integrated Education: Race and Schools* 8(January-February 1970), 58-61.

68. Nancy H. St. John and Marshall S. Smith, "School Racial Composition, Achievement, and Aspirations," mimeograph, n.d.; Nancy H. St. John and Ralph Lewis, "The Influence of School Racial Context on Achievement," *Social Problems* 19(Summer 1971), 68-79.

69. Rochester City School District, *op. cit.*; Jayjia Hsia, *Integration in Evanston, 1967-71: A Longitudinal Evaluation* (Evanston, Ill.: Educational Testing Service, 1971); Mabel C. Purl, *The Achievement of Pupils in Desegregated Schools* (Riverside, Cal.: Riverside Unified School District, 1971).

70. Hanushek, *op. cit.*; St. John and Lewis, *op. cit.*

71. Christopher Jencks and Marsha Brown, "Research Note: The Effects of Desegregation on Student Achievement," *Sociology of Education* 48(No. 1, Winter 1975), 131.

72. Purl, *op. cit.*

73. Riverside Unified School District, *LASER Individualized Education* (Riverside, Cal.: Department of Research and Evaluation, 1971).

74. Eugene Johnson (private communication, December 20, 1971).

75. Nancy H. St. John, "Thirty-Six Teachers: Their Characteristics and Outcomes for Black and White Pupils," *American Educational Research Journal* 6(November 1971), 646.

76. Jane R. Mercer, Marietta Coleman, and Jack Harloe, "Racial/Ethnic Segregation and Desegregation in American Public Education" in C. Wayne Gordon (ed.), *Uses of the Sociology of Education* (Chicago: University of Chicago Press, 1974), 308.

77. *Ibid.*, 309.

78. *Ibid.*, 313-16.

79. Robert L. Crain and Robert L. York, *Southern Schools: An Evaluation of the Effects of the Emerging School Assistance Program and of School Desegregation* (Chicago: National Opinion Research Center, 1973).

80. James D. Preston and Jerry W. Robinson, Jr., "On Modification of Interracial Interaction," *American Sociological Review* 39(No. 2, April 1974), 283-85.

81. Jerry W. Robinson and James S. Preston, "Interracial Contact and Racial Prejudice," unpublished manuscript, n.d., 13.

82. Elizabeth G. Cohen and Susan S. Roper, "Modification of Interracial Interaction Disability: An Application of Status Characteristic Theory," *American Sociological Review* 37(No. 6, December 1972), 657.

83. *Ibid.*, 644.

84. *Ibid.*, 649.

85. Elizabeth G. Cohen, "Modifying the Effects of Social Structure," *American Behavioral Scientist* (July-August 1973).

86. James S. Coleman, Sara D. Kelly, and John A. Moore, *Trends in School Segregation 1968-73* (Washington, D.C.: The Urban Institute, 1975); James S. Coleman, "School Desegregation and Loss of Whites from Large Central-City School Districts," unpublished paper presented to the U.S. Commission on Civil Rights, Washington, D.C., December 1975.

87. *Ibid.*, 2-5.

88. *Ibid.*, 32.

89. Thomas F. Pettigrew and Robert L. Green, "School Desegregation in Large Cities: A Critique of the Coleman 'White Flight' Thesis," *Harvard Educational Review* 46(No. 1, February 1976), 1-53.

90. Harvey A. Averch *et al.*, *op. cit.*

PART TWO

The Public Policy Implications of Educational Research

5. Education, Life Chances, and the Courts: The Role of Social Science Evidence

HENRY M. LEVIN

INTRODUCTION

Public policy attempts to improve the "life chances" of youngsters from low-income and minority backgrounds have focused primarily on the schools. "Life chances" is defined as a child's future ability as an adult to participate fully in the social, economic, and political life of society. More narrowly, "life chances" may be considered in terms of such outcomes as ultimate earnings, occupational status, and political efficacy. The crucial role of the school in preparing students for these eventualities has been tacitly assumed. It is no surprise, therefore, that in their quest for greater equality among persons of different races and social class origins, both policymakers and the courts have devoted extensive efforts in an attempt to alter the organization and financing of education.[1]

There are three principal areas of reform to which policymakers and the courts have directed themselves in the last two decades:

Reprinted by permission from Henry M. Levin, "Education, Life Chances, and The Courts: The Role of Social Science Evidence," *Law and Contemporary Problems* 39(No. 2, Spring 1975), 217-40.

school desegregation, the provision of additional resources for the education of children from low-income families, and reform of state educational finance systems by reducing the reliance upon local property wealth as the determinant of local school expenditures.[2] Each of these reform measures comports with notions of basic fairness and, indeed, could be defended on these grounds alone. But this view of reforms—that they are essential in a "just" society—has been overshadowed by the claim that social science research has shown that the particular educational strategies offered to the courts enhance the life chances of children. Educational reform litigation increasingly relies on social science evidence, as seen in the challenges to school segregation, to the present methods of financing education, and to student classification policies.[3]

This article explores the appropriateness of using social science evidence as a basis for formulating public policy and for deciding law suits in these particular areas. In the course of this exploration, four questions have to be addressed: (1) To what degree can social science methodology determine the impact of schooling on such life chance outcomes as income and occupational attainment, separating out other factors influencing life chances such as family background and IQ? (2) To the extent that social science research presents conflicting theories of these relationships, why do some theories receive considerable attention in the policy arena while others do not? (3) What impact does social science evidence have on the evolution of law and public policy with respect to education? (4) Finally, what contribution can the social sciences make to the issues raised in litigation?

EFFECTS OF EDUCATION ON LIFE CHANCES

How might the social scientist attempt to trace the effects of a particular educational strategy on the life chances of an individual or group of persons? The difficulties inherent in this task can be illustrated by considering the fundamental characteristics of the problem. At the outset, there is a complex multitude of psychological, social, genetic, political, economic, and educational influences that can determine occupational attainments and earnings. The actual effect of education and of a particular educational environment is particularly difficult to trace because the outcomes that we wish to review are very much removed in both time and context from the schooling process. Typically, research in this area is intended to relate the income and occupation of an individual or a group of persons to the schooling which they received many years before and under circumstances very different from their present situations. Also, the educational experiences of an individual are so closely tied to his social class origin and family experiences that it is virtually impossible to isolate the distinct influences of each on life chances.

In addressing this issue, social scientists have two basic approaches at their disposal.[4] The first is the purely experimental approach. In theory, an experiment would select persons who were similar in every respect and assign them to a different quantity and quality of education, and then monitor them over their lifetimes in order to determine how the differences in educational experiences are translated into differences in lifetime experience. Such an experiment would probably require a minimum of thirty years and would have to ensure that the individuals in both the experimental and control groups were treated identically in their pre-adult years, with the exception of schooling. In other words, such factors as genetic background, family environment, community factors, medical care, nutrition, friendships, and so on, would have to be identical in order to draw an accurate inference about the effects of differences in schooling.

For obvious reasons, however, such an exercise is impossible. Not only do we lack the luxury of several decades or a lifetime to carry out research for impending policy decisions, but the conditions that we would have to place on the human subjects in order to conduct the experiment could very well raise questions about a violation of their constitutional rights.[5] Even were such an experiment feasible, we would not be able to generalize beyond the actual educational strategies that were utilized and the specific persons or groups of persons that were involved in the experiment. Since there are infinite combinations of both, even a relatively large scale experiment would reveal information about only a limited range of alternatives and population groups. Moreover, in a society such as ours, the relationship of education to one's life chances is likely to change from generation to generation, meaning that the results obtained from a particular experiment might not be applicable to conditions some forty years later when the experiment was finally completed.

Thus, the most powerful investigative tool that science has to offer for an understanding of the relationship between education and life chances is politically and practically infeasible. At best, experimentation can be used to test minor hypotheses that may be related to some later outcome.[6] For example, it may be possible to set up an experiment to determine the effect of teachers' attitudes on student achievement or educational aspirations, assigning students randomly to two different types of teachers, and holding other factors constant for the period of the experiment. Outcomes would be measured by standardized test scores and such elements of educational aspiration as incentive for further schooling. Even with this more limited type of experiment, it is a formidable endeavor to fulfill the *ceteris paribus* conditions. And even more problematical is the relationship of the experimental outcomes to life success. One would have to make the assumption that student test scores and attitudes are related initially to educational attainment, and ultimately to income and occupational attainment. While the logic of such a relationship may be compelling, any conclusion in this respect is beyond what could be substantiated by results from the experiment just outlined.

An alternative social science strategy that is used when direct experimental research is not feasible is the quasi-experimental approach.[7] This latter strategy represents an attempt to parallel the experimental conditions by using statistical procedures to "correct" for those factors that cannot be controlled experimentally. Sometimes the quasi-experimental approach is termed a "natural" experiment because data are collected from an actual life situation rather than an experimental one. For instance, a researcher who is interested in the effects of schools on life chances might collect historical data for a sample of adult males or females. These data would include the present earnings and occupation of the individuals, information on their parents' class origins, characteristics of the schools that they attended, information on their friends, their work experience, and so on. A statistical model would then be constructed in an attempt to determine the relationship between the educational variables and the occupational and income attainments of the sample being studied.

Quasi-experimental studies attempt statistically to relate all relevant factors that might explain a particular phenomenon. The success of such an approach is dependent upon the ability to identify and measure these factors and to relate them in the statistical analysis in a manner reflecting the true phenomenon. As mentioned previously, however, there are an unlimited number of potential influences on adult outcomes and there are a variety of plausible ways that each can be measured and related to other variables in the analysis. In an area where choices must be made among the myriad of possible variables, measures, and relationships, the complexity and arduous nature of this type of statistical analysis necessarily limits the researcher to a narrow set of alternative formulations. The actual choice of factors to be included in a study, the measures of those that are ultimately selected, and the structure used to relate them is in part determined by the personal predilections of the researcher.[8]

In summary, there are enormous difficulties in determining how a host of genetic, psychological, social, cultural, political, economic, educational, and chance factors determine a person's ultimate life attainments. These difficulties and the complex nature of the problem suggest the inability of social science research to derive answers that can be utilized with any reasonable degree of reliability. Indeed, it is little wonder that opinions on the subject differ as much among social scientists as they do among laymen. Because of the inherent inadequacy of our present tools, there is no social science consensus on the appropriate educational strategies for improving the life chances of children from low-income and minority backgrounds.[9]

HYPOTHESES ABOUT SCHOOLING AND ADULT ATTAINMENTS

The fact that social science has not provided a definitive or even a tentatively acceptable analysis of the relation between schooling and adult attainments does not mean that there exist no hypotheses on the subject. To the contrary, there are at least four such theories relating schooling to eventual adult occupation and income. Each of them presumes a relatively different educational approach toward improving the life chances of disadvantaged students.

Skills or Cognitive Achievement

Much of the literature on schooling and adult income is dominated by the notion that education produces verbal and mathematical skills as well as other knowledge that translate into higher productivity in the market place and consequently higher earnings. Under this hypothesis, the more cognitive knowledge that children acquire in school, the greater will be their life attainments. Accordingly, the effect of schooling on income is determined by the effect that schooling has on skills and knowledge. Those schools that contributed toward greater gains on achievement tests ostensibly would have the greatest impact on improving the future adult attainments of their pupils. Hence, the appropriate educational strategies would be those that are consistent with increasing the test scores of children from low-income backgrounds. The most notable of these approaches is the provision of additional educational resources as exemplified by programs of compensatory education in the elementary and secondary schools[10] and such pre-school programs as Project Head Start.[11] It has also been argued that greater social class and racial integration of schools will have this effect.[12]

Noncognitive Characteristics for Work Relations

In contrast to the cognitive achievement hypothesis outlined above, the second thesis views the school as inculcating students with the appropriate behaviors for occupying particular positions in the occupational or organizational hierarchy. Such characteristics as respect for rules, dependability, and internalization of the norms of the workplace have been found to be strong predictors of employee ratings by supervisors and of income levels.[13] The workplace is seen as a hierarchically differentiated organization in which different positions require varying worker characteristics:[14]

those at the base of the hierarchy requiring a heavy emphasis on obedience and rules and those at the top, where the discretionary scope is considerable, requiring a greater ability to make decisions on the basis of well-internalized norms. This pattern is closely replicated in the social relations of schooling. Note the wide range of choice over curriculum, life style, and allocation of time afforded to college students, compared with the obedience and respect for authority expected in high school.

According to the second hypothesis, while minimal skills are necessary for productivity, most of the discrepancy in occupational attainment and earnings is attributable to noncognitive work traits. Four of these work prerequisites—proper level of subordination, discipline, supremacy of cognitive over affective modes of response, and motivation according to external reward structures—have been identified.[15] Also identified are the ways in which the schools are structured to foster these traits. For example, subordination and proper orientation to authority along hierarchical lines are necessary in virtually all modern work enterprises. Thus, "[a]s the worker relinquishes control over his activities on the job, so the student is at first forced to accept, and later comes personally to terms with, his loss of autonomy and initiative to a teacher who acts as a superior authority, dispensing rewards and penalties."[16] Similarly, it is argued that other school practices are related to the requirements of the workplace; students from lower social class origins are being prepared to occupy lower status occupations and those from higher class backgrounds are being socialized to undertake professional and managerial roles.

This hypothesis suggests that the contribution of schooling should be evaluated in terms of its impact on creating productive worker characteristics. Unfortunately, the work hierarchy is so unequal in terms of job requirements, satisfaction, income, and prestige that providing everyone with the "most productive" traits is not likely to increase life chances for everyone. Rather, it would simply redistribute opportunities among the population with some individuals improving their standing and others losing ground in terms of productive adult roles. In contrast with the thesis that everyone's productivity is enhanced by the attainment of greater cognitive skills, it is difficult to argue that productivity for all individuals would rise with the inculcation of higher echelon occupational traits, so long as the number of such positions is rationed by the occupational pyramid. In short, the view that the schools affect the life chances of students by preparing them for particular levels of the work hierarchy suggests that schools perform their function when they differentiate and produce the highly unequal outcomes that correspond to adult roles.[17] The most that could be accomplished by the schools in such a world is that students from disadvantaged backgrounds would have the same chance to be prepared for particular roles as those from advantaged backgrounds, in contrast with the present system which relegates racial minorities and the children of the lower class to corresponding lower class adult roles.

Screening and Certification

The third major hypothesis of how education affects earnings and occupational status views the school as an organization whose principal function is to sort and select students. According to this interpretation, the schools carry out a sophisticated process of assessing the cognitive and personal attributes of a student and then assigning him to a particular educational fate. Through testing, ability grouping and tracking, curriculum assignment, grading systems, and stratification by social class among neighborhoods, the schools act as an enormous filter.[18] Students who have the low-level skills and personality characteristics suitable for the lower end of the work hierarchy are placed in slow ability tracks or in inner-city schools that provide them with little incentive for further schooling. In contrast, students with high test scores and with personality attributes that correspond with the upper level of the job hierarchy are encouraged to pursue further education and will be rewarded with the high grades which represent the admission requirement for obtaining superior educational credentials.

The screening and certification hypothesis assumes that the occupational and income attainment process for an individual is determined largely by the amount of schooling he has received, his field of study, and the prestige of the institutions that he attended.[19] Thus, the sorting and selection of each student according to his initial and developing characteristics are identified in the job market by an educational credential which is used to establish his place in the occupational structure. Since such credentials are awarded on the basis of "productive" characteristics, employers need only to find out which "certificate" an individual possesses in order to judge his suitability for a particular position.[20] The hypothesis thus suggests that schools do not serve to educate students but instead to select them for their future fates according to characteristics derived from their genetic heritage and non-school environments. It has been further argued that the traits used for selection have little to do with real productivity differences and that persons with higher educational credentials are simply placed in jobs that are ostensibly more productive because of such factors as, for example, greater capital investment per worker.[21]

Presumably, then, the reason that children from lower income and minority backgrounds do more poorly in both schools and later careers is that they are filtered out rather early on the basis of low initial test scores and personality traits deemed inappropriate for further educational selection. Their low educational credentials mean that they will occupy low productivity jobs with little hope of access to the more productive and remunerative ones.[22] The educational policy implications of this hypothesis are not unlike those of the second hypothesis discussed earlier, which is concerned with the non-cognitive characteristics or behavior appropriate at various levels. In both instances, the schools tend to reinforce the initial attributes of students; according to the third hypothesis, through selection and certification procedures, and according to the second hypothesis, through selection, differentiated preparation by category of student (especially social class), and certification. The major distinction between the two views of the educational process is that the sorting hypothesis assumes that the school has no educational effect on the student and that the observed differences merely reflect variation in natural endowments and out-of-school influences. The noncognitive socialization theory, on the other hand, assumes that schools do have an effect—that of further reinforcing these initial differences.

Only by eliminating all sorting and selection based on character-istics that coincide solely with race and social class will educational credentials be distributed in a more nearly random manner. Yet, since grades and examination scores are based substantially upon behavior and language styles which in turn are heavily determined by racial and social class backgrounds, drastically different criteria would have to be developed for determining a student's educational success.

Reduction of Social Class and Racial Frictions

The final hypothesis considers the attitudes of all students towards racial and social class differences. The premise is that the better all racial and social class groups understand each other, and the greater the number of intergroup contacts, friendships and inter-actions, the less racial and class conflicts there will be in adult life.[23] The role of the school in this regard is crucial, for racial, cultural, and social class diversity in the educational environment is considered to be a prerequisite to greater justice in the distribution of jobs and earnings among the population. It is assumed that such a policy would have a marked impact on reducing labor market discrimina-tion against racial minorities and members of the lower classes.

The obvious educational strategies that are consistent with this hypothesis are those which lie at the heart of the school desegregation movement. These include greater social class and racial heterogeneity among students and the introduction of a more multiculturally oriented curriculum. The former action would be accomplished through massive desegregation of schools, thereby increasing the diversity of student populations and of the resultant educational and social interactions. The latter approach, which emphasizes a greater balance among the cultural contributions of different social and racial groups, would be implemented through changes in instructional materials, teacher training, and teacher selection.

EMPIRICAL SUPPORT FOR THE HYPOTHESES

According to the conventional image of science, mere application of research methodology to competing hypotheses will reveal which one best describes the world. Thus, through the use of sophisticated empirical research techniques we should be able to distinguish among those approaches worthy of elevation to the level of explanatory theory and those which should be banished as falsehood. But, as noted previously, the tools of social science are inadequate for this task. The social science evidence that does exist is incomplete, fragmented, and applicable to narrow populations only. It cannot, therefore, be conclusive.[24]

Although each hypothesis can be shown as consistent with some observable facts, the same facts often lend support to more than one of the hypotheses. Table 5-1 represents a summary of the evidence in support of the four hypotheses linking education with the life chances of poor and minority students. The educational strategies and the measures of educational outcome that are consistent with each hypothesis are shown in this table. But beyond this, the important concern is whether certain specified educational outcomes have been produced successfully by the corresponding educational strategy. The extent to which the desired educational outcome is linked to such adult attainments as income and occupational status is of substantial concern as well. These aspects are essential to determining the degree to which we can expect a particular educational strategy to produce enhanced income and occupational positions. Accordingly, the summary of the evidence linking the educational strategy to a specified educational output, and the educational output to measures of life attainment is also provided in Table 5-1. It is impor-

TABLE 5-1
Summary of Evidence in Support of Four Hypotheses Linking Education to Life Chances of Low Income and Racial Minority Students

	Hypotheses			
	Cognitive Skills	Noncognitive Work Characteristics	Sorting and Selection	Reduction of Racial and Class Frictions
Educational strategy	Compensatory education and integration	Compensatory education and integration	Changes in selection mechanisms	Integration and multi-cultural environment
Measure of educational outcome	Test scores	Values, attitudes, behavior	Values, attitudes, behavior and test scores	Attitudes towards self and other groups
Evidence of strategy's success for enhancing educational outcome for poor and racial minorities	Weak	Weak	Weak	Inconclusive
Evidence linking educational outcome to income and occupational attainment	Consistent statistical tie, but only nominal effect	Strong inferential evidence, but little direct support	Not separable from cognitive and noncognitive results	Very little direct evidence

tant to observe that a lack of evidence for the impact of any particular strategy does not mean that the approach is without merit. It simply means that existing research—which may be quite minimal on the subject—has not provided sufficient empirical support for such a strategy.

Measures of Educational Outcome

The cognitive skills hypothesis has as its measure of educational outcome standardized test scores. Despite the fact that there are many and diverse measures of the broad range of cognitive skills, the evidence, as indicated below, is remarkably consistent whether IQ tests, achievement tests, reading tests, mathematics tests, or others are used. In order to raise the level of cognitive performance of low-income and minority youngsters, the educational strategies usually invoked are the provision of greater resources for compensatory education and racial and socioeconomic integration. The evidence is weak that either of these policies has significant impact on test scores. For example, neither the Coleman Report[25] nor subsequent studies, some of which used the data collected for the Coleman Report, found that differences in the level of educational resources have any major impact on test scores.[26] An analysis based on the statistical results of a number of these studies has shown that even major increases of those educational resources most related to test scores would not come close to eliminating the performance gap between white and black students.[27] Evaluations of compensatory education programs carried out under Title I of the Elementary and Secondary Education Act of 1965[28] similarly have been unable to demonstrate any significant relationship between increased resources and improved test scores.[29]

While some studies have suggested that both socioeconomic and racial integration improve the test scores of minority and low-income students,[30] these conclusions have been contested in other evaluations.[31] Thus, neither compensatory education strategies nor those related to desegregation show anything other than a weak relationship to cognitive gains. Even when statistical differences in favor of these strategies are reported, the improvement in cognitive skills is generally marginal.

Assuming that strategies other than compensatory education and racial and class integration could be found which did improve cognitive scores substantially, what would be the impact of such an improvement on income and occupational attainments of poor and minority youngsters? Numerous studies demonstrate a consistent statistical relationship between test scores and these measures of life success.[32] The explanatory significance of this relationship is nonetheless quite weak.[33] At most only about 10 percent of the differences in income can be explained by test scores, leaving 90 percent or more to be explained by other factors. Furthermore, relatively large increases in test scores are associated with only modest increases in income. While the apparent effect of test scores on occupational status is somewhat higher, it still only explains—at the most—about 25 percent of the variance.[34] Differences in test scores, therefore, are not a major factor in explaining why occupational attainments and incomes differ among various cross sections of the population. In summation, the hypothesis that improving the cognitive test scores will raise the adult attainments of children from low-income and minority families shows little promise of success because (1) available educational strategies have not demonstrated much success in improving test scores of these students and (2) increases in test scores show only modest effects on adult income and occupations.

Evidence on Noncognitive Work Characteristics

In contrast with the numerous studies exploring the relationship between test scores and increased resources or integration, there are few research studies devoted to the other hypotheses. Nonetheless, there have been some attempts to explore the noncognitive worker characteristics thesis. As indicated previously, the measure of educational outcome relating such traits to income and occupation are those values, attitudes, and behaviors which are required for work positions in a hierarchical setting. These include such characteristics as dependability, subordination to authority, respect for rules, and internalization of work norms.[35] Measures of noncognitive work traits have been demonstrated to be related to grades awarded by teachers, more so than are test scores.[36] However, there is apparently no study which has attempted to determine the *degree* to which the worker characteristics of poor and minority students can be altered by compensatory education or integration. Contrariwise, there is a strong presumption that the present approach will resist change because it is functional to the reproduction of the capitalist work hierarchy.[37] Accordingly, the relationship between the educational strategy and the desired educational outcomes must be considered as weak.

There is, however, evidence linking noncognitive outcomes to income and occupational attainments. The amount of schooling a person receives is a more powerful determinant of income and occupation than are test scores. For example, three studies using longitudinal data—permitting prior schooling experiences and test scores to be linked to earnings—have found either a nonexistent or a relatively negligible correlation between test scores and earnings. This is in contrast to the rather pronounced impact that the amount of schooling has on ultimate income.[38] Thus it appears that the amount of schooling a person receives has a considerable effect on adult success, independent of the cognitive skills attained from the educational process.

But there is additional evidence supporting the noncognitive work characteristics hypothesis: teachers tend to award higher grades to students who exhibit personality characteristics functional in the work hierarchy.[39] One study of a sample of workers from three different enterprises found that these personality traits or characteristics are related both to supervisors' ratings and to earnings, even after differences in cognitive skills among employees is accounted for.[40] Obviously, much more research is needed in this area, but the view that noncognitive educational outcomes have more important influences on life attainments than cognitive ones has considerable support. Nevertheless, the lack of evidence indicating that educational strategies can alter the distribution of these traits suggests that the policy implications of this hypothesis are minimal.

Evidence on Sorting and Selection

The difficulty in evaluating the sorting and selection hypothesis is that there is virtually no reliable way to distinguish its effects from those generated by the cognitive and noncognitive socialization hypotheses. Essentially, the difference between the sorting and selection hypothesis and the other two is that the former assumes that schools do not produce the cognitive and noncognitive traits that are reflected in educational attainments and credentials. Rather, schools simply identify and select students according to those traits which they already possessed or acquired outside of the school setting, and bestow upon them differing educational rewards.

Whether schools sort according to already-existing characteristics or actually inculcate these characteristics in students cannot be determined without very intensive studies. Possibly both aspects are prevalent but there is no apparent evidence that permits differentiation between the two.[41] Thus, any evidence tending to support the cognitive and noncognitive socialization hypotheses would certainly be consistent with a sorting and selection hypothesis as well.

Evidence on Reduction of Frictions Between Races and Classes

Finally, the hypothesis on reducing racial and social class frictions measures educational outcome by the attitudes of representatives of each group towards themselves (self-image and sense of efficacy), as well as by attitudes that connote an understanding and acceptance of members of other groups. Whether the educational strategies of desegregation and multi-cultural emphasis[42] have long-run effects on attitudes and behavior is questionable. That the evidence in these areas is both controversial and contradictory is reflected in recent debates on the subject.[43] In some instances desegregation of the schools appears to have improved the self-images of racial minorities and racial attitudes of both majority and minority students;[44] in other cases there seem to have been no effects, or even negative ones.[45] One of the basic problems that pervades this research is the questionable reliability and stability of any measure of human attitudes. Given the variable quality of desegregation efforts and multi-cultural educational programs, it is not surprising to find such a divergence of results.

There is at least some empirical evidence supporting the view that socioeconomic integration improves the life chances of low-status children. An analysis of data collected for a sample of youngsters then in the ninth grade, supplemented by follow-up information on their subsequent schooling, occupational attainments, and income nine years later, indicates that students who had similar test scores and social class backgrounds as well as educational attainments had higher incomes if they had attended secondary schools with other students from high socioeconomic backgrounds.[46] A particularly interesting aspect of this study was that low-status individuals appeared to "gain" more than twice as much income from this effect as did the high-status individuals. However, even this finding applies only to the young adults in this particular sample. Furthermore, it is not clear why socioeconomic composition per se should lead to higher incomes.

SOCIAL SCIENCE AND THE CHOICE OF A STRATEGY

The difficulty of using social science research to determine how different educational strategies can be used to affect the future life chances of low-income and minority students is clear. While virtually all of the four hypotheses discussed above have some support, the results are ambiguous and inconclusive. Advocacy of any particular approach, therefore, is not based so much upon its general acceptance in the scientific community as it is upon the predilections of researchers and policymakers. The fact that they as well as the courts have not been neutral among competing ideas suggests that it is useful to explore the reasons that particular strategies are selected.

At the outset, one may very well ask how social science researchers can commit themselves to a particular hypothesis or approach on the basis of ambiguous, fragmented, and often contradictory findings. The answer, seemingly, is that researchers often have commitments based upon deeply ingrained social experiences that affect their understanding of how society functions. The natural consequence of these experiences encourages the social scientist to accept the evidence which reinforces his own experience and to be skeptical of that which does not.[47] As Polanyi has noted:[48]

I start by rejecting the ideal of scientific detachment. In the exact sciences, this false ideal is perhaps harmless, for it is in fact disregarded there by scientists. But we shall see that it exercises a destructive influence in biology, psychology and sociology and has falsified our whole outlook far beyond the domain of science.

To a substantial degree the social scientist is himself a product of the very forces he wishes to study. Long before he has received his professional training he is exposed to such phenomena as class, race, family structure, money, prices, religion, industry, politics, work, the messages of the media on all of these subjects, and more. His perspective of the world is largely a cumulative result of his role as a child, student, sibling, husband, consumer, professor, rich man, black, woman, mother, and so on. All of these roles have defined the boundaries of experience which in turn mold his social reality.[49] In a more specific sense, the social scientist who studies the effects of schooling on achievement has been socialized to a large degree by his own particular experiences during his education. His knowledge about the determinants of poverty is influenced by his own class origins and experiences. His image of political reality is conditioned by his own interactions with the political system and other institutions that inculcate political attitudes. Interacting with these influences is his professional training which emphasizes particular metaphysical and epistemological frameworks for viewing the world.

Moreover, since researchers are not randomly assigned to studies, the effects of the researcher's commitment and ideology on the interpretation of research findings is not a chance event. To the contrary, there is a self-selection of problems by researchers according to their predilections, as well as the selection by government and other decisionmakers, based upon the "outlook" of the researcher and the sponsoring agency. Social science investigators choose those problems that interest them and to which they feel they can contribute something of value. Of course, research support is also a prerequisite, but most social science analysts—particularly in the academic setting —have a choice of problems on which to focus. Public policy-oriented research has a substantive or topical component that may or may not be of interest to potential investigators. Such motives as a sincere wish of the individual to improve government decisionmaking are often strong factors in the choice of problems, but they also coincide with a deep personal involvement in the outcome of the study. That is, the researcher is likely to have relatively strong viewpoints about what proper policy should be in advance of his research.

The agencies that support research are just as likely to select a researcher on the basis of his values as on his "scientific" competence. As Paul Samuelson has remarked:[50]

The leaders of this world may seem to be led around through the nose by their economic advisers. But who is pulling and who is pushing? And note this: he who picks his doctor from an array of competing doctors is in a real sense his own doctor. The Prince often gets to hear what he wants to hear.

It would be inconceivable to think of the United States Commission on Civil Rights hiring a researcher for his neutrality on the desegregation issue. Indeed, we expect that government decisionmakers seek out those investigators who are sympathetic to the agency's own orientation.

Obviously, these phenomena dovetail very closely with the use of social science evidence in the courts. Legal proceedings are endeavors in advocacy, each side seeking that "evidence" which will support its own position. There is always some social science evidence on virtually any phenomenon, so one must ask what types of evidence are likely to be drawn into the courts. I assert that the social science evidence which courts are likely to receive has the following attributes: (1) It tends to be based upon complex, statistical methodologies that are generally beyond the experience and the competence of the court to question. (2) It directly supports or refutes the matter under consideration. (3) It is based upon a theory which is credible and understandable to the court. (4) And, finally, it implies a remedy that is readily within the court's power and is politically feasible.

The first requirement evolves from the image that the layman has of science. "Good" social science is characterized by large data sets, complicated statistical methodologies, and an aura of technical competence. While the researcher has made many personal judgments with respect to his formulation of the problem—selection of a framework for the analysis, definition and measurement of variables, technique of data analysis and interpretation of results—all will tend to be obscured by what appears to be a strictly technical analysis. The greater the methodological sophistication, the more difficult it is to demystify the analysis and the more tempting it becomes to see "the emperor's new clothes." The bias in favor of sophisticated empirical studies also rules out the consideration of hypotheses that are not conducive to empirical evaluation.

The second requirement suggests that ambiguity in research findings will be shunned. Alternative interpretations of the results can obviously be dangerous to the advocate who uses the evidence to support his client's case. Thus, the social science research that is utilized must unequivocally support the particular objectives of the advocate. This tends to eliminate any opportunity for a thoughtful analysis of all of the competing hypotheses.

The third requirement, that the social science evidence presented to the court be based upon a credible hypothesis, is illustrated by the fact that while social science research in the Marxian tradition may be both extremely sophisticated and unambiguous, the theory upon which it is based may not be acceptable to those heavily indoctrinated with the capitalist viewpoint.

Another example: no evidence has been presented in either the desegregation or the school finance cases that argues in favor of the noncognitive worker characteristics hypothesis as an explanation of the effects of schools on the life attainments of children from low-income and racial minority backgrounds.[51] To the educated layman the cognitive skills theory is much more credible than the noncognitive one.

Finally, the requirement that the social science evidence presented to the court implies a remedy that is both within the court's remedial powers and is politically feasible, is illustrated, for example, by the fact that given the present institutional framework, it is not possible for the court to interfere with family child-rearing for educational purposes. Yet studies have shown that such interventions will improve the life chances of students from low-income families.[52]

In light of these principles it is understandable that the courts and other policymakers have focused primarily on the cognitive skills approach. Firstly, the research in this area, beginning with the Coleman Report[53] and the "Racial Isolation" report of the U.S. Commission on Civil Rights the following year,[54] has the aura of being methodologically sophisticated and empirical. Enormous data sets (about 650,000 students and 70,000 teachers comprise the Coleman Report data), sophisticated methodologies such as multiple regression analysis, and quantification of educational outcomes as reflected in test scores, create a strong image of valid scientific endeavor. Secondly, these studies purport to show unambiguously that socioeconomic and racial integration as well as certain school resources improve the test scores of low-income and minority students. Thirdly, educated men tend to believe that cognitive test scores are important determinants of life chances because they are likely to attribute their own educational and occupational success to their relatively high levels of knowledge and skills rather than to "less rational" factors such as those related to family socioeconomic origins. Cognitive skills are an attractive basis for constructing the meritocracy.[55] Finally, implementation of the desegregation and compensatory education strategies implied by the cognitive hypothesis are within the powers of the courts and educational decisionmakers.

EFFECTS OF SOCIAL SCIENCE EVIDENCE

Thus far, it has been argued that the social sciences cannot produce conclusive results that would support a particular educational strategy for improving the life attainments of students from low-income and minority families. Also, it has been asserted that the evidence that does enter the courts or policy arena is considered and utilized on the basis of factors other than its scientific "validity." What are the implications of these assertions for the evolution of public policy and the law?

There are three possible cases. The first is the happy one where the evidence presented is somehow the "best" that is available. In other words, the evidence is based upon the clearest attainable picture of the world and is unequivocally better than that which supports alternative hypotheses on the subject. It is not clear how this would happen but to the degree that it does occur, it can be viewed as advancing the wisdom of the legal system. The second case is a less benevolent one in which the social science evidence, while representing just one among competing views on the subject, nonetheless carries the day. To the degree that the results of the research are erroneous, the use of social science may be harmful.

But in many ways it is the third case that is most interesting. Here social science evidence is used to support both sides of a legal dispute.[56] In educational finance litigation, the constitutionality of state school finance systems was challenged on the ground that they provided lower quality education for children in low property wealth districts than for those in more affluent districts. The defense relied upon social science research which, they asserted, indicated no relationship between the level of expenditures and the quality of an education program. The defense arguments were buttressed by the Coleman Report[57] and other research,[58] tending to show that there was little or no causative effect between educational expenditures and other measures of school quality and student achievement. The plaintiffs countered with witnesses and research that disputed the methodologies and data employed in the studies cited by the defense, and which indicated a correlation between increases in educational resources and improved pupil achievement.[59] In some cases the plaintiffs won the argument;[60] in others, the courts were unpersuaded.[61]

Even where both sides draw upon social science evidence and the court decides between the two competing presentations, there is a possibility that use of such evidence will tend to redefine the issue itself. Presentation of evidence on the relationship between educational expenditures and cognitive achievement implicitly narrows the context within which the effects of unequal expenditure patterns will be considered. While the two sides to this debate disagree on the effect of school resources, both have accepted the view that standardized achievement scores are the appropriate focus for exploring educational outcomes. Since courts and policymakers generally find it easier to understand a point of agreement than of contention, such points of accord have more influence on the assimilation of the policy implications of research than the conclusions of the research itself. Thus, much of the legal debate surrounding the challenge to present methods of financing education does not address the basic unfairness reflected by state arrangements to spend more on the education of children in rich districts than in poor ones. Rather, the prima facie inequities are ignored as the courts are tortured with the convoluted arguments provided by social scientists about whether money makes a difference for "poor kids."[62] It is unfortunate that the issue has now become framed in terms of whether additional expenditures for children in poor school districts will raise their test scores.[63]

A second example of the tendency of a tacit consensus among litigants having a greater influence on policy formation than the actual research results, is the controversy over the effects of school desegregation. Until the mid-1960's, the case for racial desegregation was one that was based largely upon the type of society one envisioned.[64] For those who equated a fair society with the absence of racial separation, segregation of schools was contradictory. For those who defined a fair society in other ways, racial isolation in the educational system was of little consequence. The argument was primarily a moral one, dealing with normative visions of the world.[65]

With the advent of the Coleman Report and the 1967 Report of the U.S. Commission on Civil Rights, *Racial Isolation in the Public Schools*, a new dimension was added. These studies attempted to demonstrate that segregated school environments retarded the test scores of black children and other students from lower socioeconomic backgrounds. By 1972, serious questions were being raised about the validity of the earlier findings. Reanalysis of the Coleman data did not support the hypothesis that the test scores of black students were a function of the racial composition of the schools.[66] A subsequent analysis of several longitudinal studies of the effects of busing argued that the data do not support the conclusion that racial integration of schools in itself will improve the achievement levels of racial minorities and that there is at least some evidence that harmful changes in attitudes take place.[67]

The results of this study were shocking[68] due to the fact that heretofore there seemingly had been one point of agreement in the social science studies on desegregation—that "[i]ntegrated education will enhance the academic achievement of minority groups, and thereby close (or at least substantially reduce) the achievement gap."[69] Despite the very contradictory literature on school desegregation, the case for desegregation was seen as hinging *primarily* on whether it improves the achievement test scores of minority students. Rather than considering what kind of educational policy regarding school racial patterns is consistent with our democratic ideals, the issue seems to be whether or not blacks and other minorities gain a few more points on a vocabulary or reading test. This standard is far removed from the declaration of the Supreme Court of 1954 that the separation of black children "because of their race generates a feeling of inferiority as to their status in the community that may affect their hearts and minds in a way unlikely ever to be undone."[70] At this stage, the issue has thus been cast in terms of the achievement scores of blacks rather than in terms of the larger moral and human dilemmas raised by segregated public institutions. There is little doubt that the research agenda has framed the issue.

CONCLUSION

What is the proper role of social science in charting educational policy for improving the life chances of low-income and minority students? The answer to that question is not clear. The question of the relationship between educational influences and actual adult status addresses a very complicated area of social and individual behavior. In particular, little is known about the effects of different school environments on human behavior, about underlying theories of human productivity and its determinants in a particular social setting, about the myriad of other influences that can intervene between the educational strategy and the adult outcomes many years hence, and about the appropriate measurements of even those factors that do seem relevant. Further, the fact that experimentation as an empirical investigating tool is politically and practically infeasible limits severely our ability to uncover the true relationships.

Some observers may react to these conclusions by suggesting the social science evidence in these complicated areas is likely to be so misleading and value-laden that we ought to ignore it.[71] In contrast, some technocrats will argue that the case *against* the ability of social science to validate the relationships between education and life chances has been overstated and that rapid scientific advances in research methodology will even nullify those anomalies which have arisen. Both of these views assume that the social sciences must play a deterministic role in contributing to policy or that they can play no role at all. Yet, it may be the heuristic aspects of social science research which are most useful.

Alice Rivlin has suggested that we acknowledge the development of a "forensic social science," rather than pretending "to be part of the tradition of balanced, objective social science in which the scholar hides (or claims to hide) his personal biases, and attempts to present all the evidence on both sides of a set of questions so that the reader may judge for himself."[72] Using the notion of a forensic social science for addressing policy issues,[73]

scholars or teams of scholars take on the task of writing briefs for or against particular policy positions. They state what the position is and bring together all the evidence that supports their side of the argument, leaving to the brief writers of the other side the job of picking apart the case that has been presented and detailing the counter evidence.

The problem with such an approach is that it assumes that all of the sides will be fairly represented. But adversary proceedings normally are based upon only two conflicting points of view.[74] Moreover, the fact that the epistemology of the social sciences itself limits the analysis to a specific set of hypotheses (particularly ones that have readily identifiable empirical consequences) suggests that the issue might be framed in an erroneous manner. Of course, this type of bias can be avoided by permitting non-social scientists to enter the forum to present their views and argue their evidence. It is not clear what criteria would be used to select such witnesses nor is it obvious how one could determine how many points of view should be permitted. It is also not clear that the courts would attach great weight to "non-scientific" presentations. Finally, the court lacks expertise in selecting among alternative presentations that are grounded in complex statistical procedures and highly technical language.[75] Of course, the court could hire its own experts for examining and interpreting the evidence, but what guarantees the objectivity of the "wise men" who advise the court?[76]

Social science research can best be used to frame the issues and their consequences rather than to obtain conclusive evidence on what is right and what is to be done. This approach requires a recognition that while many aspects of the world cannot be quantified or analyzed in a social science setting, such factors should be considered along with the results of social science research.[77] It is not clear that utilization of social science research in this manner is consistent with an adversary framework. Further, if social science findings increasingly are used to create what appear to be technical issues out of essentially moral dilemmas, this presents a potential social danger. The apparently increasing reliance of the courts on social science evidence suggests that intensive debate on these issues should be given high priority.

NOTES

1. David L. Kirp and Mark G. Yudof, *Educational Policy and the Law* (Berkeley, Calif.: McCutchan Publishing Corp., 1974), chs. 4, 6, 7.

2. A recent summary of these strategies is contained in Report of the Senate Select Committee on Equal Educational Opportunity (92nd Cong., 2d Sess.), *Toward Equal Educational Opportunity* (Washington, D.C.: Government Printing Office, 1972). See also J. E. Coons, W. H. Clune III, and S. D. Sugarman, *Private Wealth and Public Education* (Cambridge, Mass.: Belknap Press, 1970); John D. Owen, *School Inequality and the Welfare State* (Baltimore, Md.: Johns Hopkins, 1974); Arthur Wise, "School Desegregation: The Court, the Congress, and the President," *School Review* 82(1974), 159.

3. Kirp and Yudof, *op. cit.*

4. For the best discussion of the experimental and quasi-experimental approaches in a related context, see Donald T. Campbell and J. C. Stanley, *Experimental and Quasi-Experimental Design for Research* (Chicago: Rand McNally, 1966). For a more skeptical statement on the ability of social science research to provide "proof" for a theory, see Donald T. Campbell, "Qualitative Knowing in Action Research," Kurt Lewin Award Address, Society for the Psychological Study of Social Issues, Meeting with the American Psychological Association, New Orleans, September 1, 1974 (to be published in *Journal of Social Issues*). See also Jay Katz, *Experimentation with Human Beings: The Authority of Investigator, Subject, Professions and State in the Human Experimentation Process* (New York: Russell Sage Foundation, 1972).

5. It is very difficult to explain the experimentation in such precise terms that a layman will understand the full implications of the testing and thus be able to provide an effective waiver. Compare the requisite standards for full

consent in the area of medical experimentation and research. See *Kaimowitz v. Department of Mental Health,* Civil No. 73-19 434-AW (Mich. Cir. Ct., July 10, 1973) for a judicial response to the legal and medical issues posed by experimental psychosurgery. In that case, the court determined that the consent must be competent, voluntary, and knowledgeable. (*Ibid.,* 31-32.) See also Herch and Flower, "Medical and Psychological Experimentation on California Prisoners," *University of California Davis Law Review* 7(1974), 351.

6. A creative attempt at using experimental methodology to ascertain the effects of intervention on racial interactions is found in Elizabeth Cohen and Susan S. Roper, "Modification of Interracial Interactions Disability: An Application of Status Characteristic Theory," *American Sociological Review* 37(December 1972), 643-57.

7. See Campbell and Stanley, *op. cit.*

8. See generally Henry M. Levin, "Schooling and Inequality: The Social Science Objectivity Gap," *Saturday Review* 55(November 1972), 49.

9. See Address by David Campbell, *op. cit.*

10. In addition to programs under Title I of the Elementary and Secondary Education Act, 20 U.S.C. § 241 (1970), several states provide funds for compensatory programs. See, *e.g.,* Cal. Education Code § § 6499.230-6499.238 (West 1975); Wisconsin Stat. Ann. § § 115.90-115.94 (Supp 1974).

11. Project Head Start, instituted under authority of Title II of the Economic Opportunity Act of 1964, 78 Stat. 516 (1964), as amended 42 U.S.C. § 2781 (1970), offers a variety of health, social and educational services to enable pre-school children from deprived families to enter kindergarten or first grade.

12. See James S. Coleman, "Towards Open Schools," *Public Interest* 9(Fall 1967), 20-27.

13. Richard C. Edwards, "Alienation and Inequality: Capitalist Relations of Production in a Bureaucratic Enterprise," unpublished dissertation, Department of Economics, Harvard University, July 1972.

14. Samuel Bowles, "Understanding Unequal Economic Opportunity," *American Economic Review* 63(May 1973), 346, 353.

15. Herbert Gintis, "Education, Technology and the Characteristics of Worker Productivity," *American Economic Review* 61(May 1971), 266.

16. *Ibid.,* 274.

17. See Henry M. Levin, "A Conceptual Framework for Accountability in Education," *School Review* 82(May 1974), 363-91.

18. See Ivar Berg, *Education and Jobs: The Great Training Robbery* (New York: Praeger, 1970); Hall, "On the Road to Educational Failure: A Lawyer's Guide to Tracking," *Inequality in Education* 12(1970), 1; David L. Kirp, "Schools as Sorters: The Constitutional and Policy Implications of Student Classification," *University of Pennsylvania Law Review* 121(1973), 705; Sorgen, "Testing and Tracking in Public Schools," *Hastings Law Journal* 24(1973), 1129. Use of the term "filter" is adopted from Kenneth Arrow, "Higher Education as a Filter," *Journal of Public Economics* 2(1973), 193.

19. See generally Samuel Bowles, "Unequal Education and the Reproduction

142 CHAPTER 5

of the Social Division of Labor," in Martin Carnoy (ed.), *Schooling in a Corporate Society* (New York: David McKay and Co., 1972), 36-66; K. Karabel, "Community Colleges and Social Stratification," *Harvard Educational Review* 42(November 1972), 521-62.

20. See Arrow, *op. cit.*; Michael Spence, "Job Market Signaling," *Quarterly Journal of Economics* 87(August 1973), 355.

21. See Lester C. Thurow, "Education and Economic Equality," *Public Interest* 28(Summer 1972), 66; Ivar Berg, *op. cit.*

22. See David M. Gordon, *Theories of Poverty and Underemployment* (Lexington, Mass.: Lexington Books, 1972). See also Bennett Harrison, "Education and Underemployment in the Urban Ghetto," *American Economic Review* 62(No. 5, 1972), 796.

23. "Contacts that bring knowledge and acquaintance are likely to engender sounder beliefs about minority groups. . . . Prejudice . . . may be removed by equal status contact between majority and minority groups in the pursuit of common goals. The effect is greatly enhanced if this contact is sanctioned by institutional supports (i.e., by law, custom, or local atmosphere), and if it is of a sort that leads to the perception of common interests and common humanity between members of the two groups." Gordon W. Allport, *The Nature of Prejudice* (Reading, Mass.: Addison-Wesley Publ. Co., 1954), 268, 281; see Morton Deutsch and Mary E. Collins, *Interracial Housing: A Psychological Evaluation of a Social Experiment* (New York: Russell & Russell, 1951); John Dollard, *Caste and Class in a Southern Town* (Garden City, N.Y.: Doubleday, 1957); Gunnar Myrdal, *American Dilemma* (New York: Harper & Row, 1962). But see David J. Armor, "The Evidence on Busing," *Public Interest* 28(Summer 1972), 90, 102-5; David J. Armor, "The Double Double Standard: A Reply," *Public Interest* 30(Winter 1973), 119, 127-29.

24. See Address of David Campbell, *op. cit.*

25. James S. Coleman *et al.*, *Equality of Educational Opportunity*, Office of Education, National Center for Educational Statistics, OE 38001 (Washington, D.C.: Government Printing Office, 1966). Hereafter cited as Coleman Report.

26. See, *e.g.*, Christopher Jencks *et al.*, *Inequality: A Reassessment of the Effects of Family and Schooling in America* (New York: Basic Books, 1972), 93-95, 255.

27. Martin Carnoy, "Is Compensatory Education Possible?" in M. Carnoy (ed.), *Schooling in a Corporate Society, op. cit.*, 175.

28. 20 U.S.C. § 241 (1970).

29. See, *e.g.*, Michael J. Wargo, G. Kasten Tallmadge, Debbra D. Michaels, Dewey Lipe, and Sarah J. Morris, *ESEA Title I: A Reanalysis and Synthesis of Evaluation Data from Fiscal Year 1965 through 1970* (unpublished document on file at American Institute for Research, Palo Alto, Calif., March 1972); Henry M. Levin, "Effects of Expenditure Increases on Educational Resource Allocation and Effectiveness" in John Pincus (ed.), *School Finance in Transition: The Courts and Educational Reform* (Cambridge, Mass.: Ballinger Publishing Co., 1974), 177. A study prepared by the RAND Corporation acknowledges that "[v]irtually without exception, all of the large surveys of the large national compensatory education programs have shown no beneficial results on average."

Harvey Averch *et al., How Effective Is Schooling? A Critical Review and Synthesis of Research Findings* (Santa Monica, Calif.: RAND, 1972), 124-25. The study, however, is quick to note that "the evaluation reports on which the surveys are based are often poor and research designs suspect." (*Ibid.*, 125.) The caveat points to such factors as non-random assignment of children, bias in project selection, "continuation" of the questionable evaluation procedures. (*Ibid.*, 106-7.) Consequently, "no . . . assurance is possible . . . that the survey evaluations used in arriving at such a verdict were themselves an accurate description of the real world. . . ." (*Ibid.*, 105.)

  30. See Coleman Report; U.S. Commission on Civil Rights, *Racial Isolation in the Public Schools.* 2 vols (Washington, D.C.: Government Printing Office, 1967); Thomas F. Pettigrew, Elizabeth L. Useem, Clarence Normand, and Marshall S. Smith, "Busing: A Review of 'The Evidence,' " *Public Interest* 30(Winter 1973), 88-131.

  31. See David J. Armor, "The Evidence on Busing," *Public Interest* 28(Summer 1972), 90-126; Samuel Bowles and Henry M. Levin, "The Determinants of Scholastic Achievement—A Critical Appraisal of Some Recent Evidence," *Journal of Human Resources* 3(Winter 1968), 3-24; David K. Cohen, Thomas F. Pettigrew, and Robert T. Riley, "Race and the Outcomes of Schooling," in F. Mosteller and Daniel Moynihan (eds.), *On Equality of Educational Opportunity* (New York: Random House, 1972), 343-70; Eric Hanushek and John F. Kain, "On the Value of Equality of Educational Opportunity as a Guide to Public Policy," in F. Mosteller and D. Moynihan (eds.), *On Equality of Educational Opportunity* (New York: Random House, 1972), 116-45; Nancy St. John, "Desegregation and Minority Group Performance," *Review of Educational Research* 40 (February 1970), 111-33; Marshall Smith, "Equality of Educational Opportunity: The Basic Findings Reconsidered," in Frederick Mosteller and Daniel P. Moynihan (eds.), *On Equality of Educational Opportunity* (New York: Random House, 1972), 230-342.

  32. See O. D. Duncan, D. L. Featherman, and B. Duncan, *Socioeconomic Background and Achievement* (New York: Academic Press, 1972); Jencks *et al., op. cit.*; Thomas Ribich and James Murphy, "The Economic Returns to Increased Educational Spending," 1974 (mimeo; to appear in *Journal of Human Resources*); P. Wachtel, "The Effect of School Quality on Achievement, Attainment Levels and Lifetime Earnings," unpublished paper, New York University Graduate School of Business Administration, May 1974; Z. Griliches and W. Mason, "Education, Income, and Ability," *Journal of Political Economy* 80 (May-June 1972 Supplement), S74-103; William H. Sewell and Robert M. Hauser, "Causes and Consequences of Higher Education: Models of the Status Attainment Process," *American Journal of Agricultural Economics* 54(December 1972), 851-61; Paul J. Taubman and Terence J. Wales, "Higher Education, Mental Ability, and Screening," *Journal of Political Economy* 81(January-February 1973), 28-55.

  33. Samuel Bowles and Valerie Nelson, "The Inheritance of IQ and the Intergenerational Reproduction of Economic Inequality," *Review of Economics and Statistics* 56(February 1974), 39-51.

  34. See generally, O. D. Duncan, D. Featherman, and B. Duncan, *op. cit.*;

Jencks *et al., op. cit.*; Bowles and Nelson, *op. cit.*; Griliches and Mason, *op. cit.*; Sewell and Hauser, *op. cit.*

35. See, *e.g.*, Richard C. Edwards, *op. cit.*; Bowles, "Understanding Unequal Economic Opportunity," *op. cit.*; Samuel Bowles and Herbert Gintis, "IQ in the U.S. Class Structure," *Social Policy* 3(November-December 1972, January-February 1973), 65; Gintis, *op. cit.*

36. See Gintis, *op. cit.*

37. Bowles, "Understanding Unequal Economic Opportunity," and "Unequal Education and the Reproduction of the Social Division of Labor," *op. cit.*

38. See Ribich and Murphy, *op. cit.*; Wachtel, *op. cit.*; Sewell and Hauser, *op. cit.* Even when test scores are included in the analysis, the effect of schooling alone on earnings is not significantly reduced. See Bowles, "Understanding Unequal Economic Opportunity"; Gintis, *op. cit.*; Griliches and Mason, *op. cit.*

39. See Gintis, *op. cit.*

40. See Edwards, *op. cit.*

41. A related question is the degree to which educational credentials reflect differences in productivity as opposed to their role in screening employees for particular occupational positions without regard for productivity. Compare Taubman and Wales, *op. cit.*, with Richard Layard and George Psacharopoulos, "The Screening Hypothesis and the Returns to Education," *Journal of Political Economy* 82(September-October 1974), 985.

42. See pp. 126-29.

43. See Armor, "The Evidence on Busing," and "The Double Double Standard: A Reply," *op. cit.*; Pettigrew, Useem, Normand, and Smith, *op. cit.*

44. See Allport, *op. cit.*; Deutsch and Collins, *op. cit.*; Dollard, *op. cit.*; Myrdal, *op. cit.* See also W. Epps, "The Impact of School Desegregation on Aspirations, Self-Concepts and Other Aspects of Personality," *Law & Contemporary Problems* 39 (No. 2, 1975) at 300 for a review of the research on the impact of desegregation on self-esteem, and Elizabeth Cohen, "The Effects of Desegregation on Race Relations," *Law & Contemporary Problems* 39(No. 2, 1975) at 271 for a review of the research on the impact of desegregation on interracial relations.

45. See Armor, "The Evidence on Busing," and "The Double Double Standard: A Reply," *op. cit.*

46. See Ribich and Murphy, *op. cit.*

47. See generally Peter L. Berger and Thomas Luckman, *The Social Construction of Reality* (New York: Doubleday and Co., Inc., 1966); T. S. Kuhn, *The Structure of Scientific Revolutions* (Chicago: University of Chicago Press, 1962); Karl Mannheim, *Ideology and Utopia* (New York: Harcourt, Brace, and Co., 1936); Robert K. Merton, *Social Theory and Social Structure* (Glencoe, Ill.: The Free Press, 1949), and *The Sociology of Science*, ed. Norman W. Storer (Chicago: University of Chicago Press, 1973); Michael Polanyi, *Personal Knowledge* (Chicago: University of Chicago Press, 1958); Karl R. Popper, *Objective Knowledge: An Evolutionary Approach* (Oxford, Eng.: Clarendon Press, 1972); Yehuda Elkana, *Rationality and Scientific Change*, unpublished manuscript, Department of History and Philosophy of Science, Hebrew University, Jerusalem,

1972, and *The Theory and Practice of Cross-Cultural Contacts* (Jerusalem: Hebrew University, 1972, mimeo).

48. Polanyi, *op. cit.*, p. vii.

49. Berger and Luckman, *op. cit.*

50. Paul A. Samuelson, "Economists and the History of Ideas," *American Economic Review* 52(March 1962), 1, 17.

51. But cf. *Serrano v. Priest* Civil No. 938,254 (Cal Super. Ct., April 10, 1974). In that case, conflicting evidence was introduced on the proper test to be applied in determining the quality of education existing within a school district, defendants urging the "pupil-achievement standard" while the plaintiffs urged a "school-district-offering standard." (*Ibid.*, 52.) The controlling dispute did not focus on the relationship between noncognitive theories of education and life attainment, and much of the opinion *was* cast in terms of the skills and cognitive achievement hypothesis. See, *e.g., ibid.* at 89. By holding for the plaintiffs, however, the court accepted the testimony that "Standardized achievement tests . . . are not appropriate for measuring the degree of attainment of many of the educational goals of the State. . . ." They "do not measure for progress in the affective domain—a pupil's personality characteristics, interests and attitudes, interpersonal skills and socialization skills." (*Ibid.*, 91.) In concluding that standardized tests are not determinative of the quality of an educational program, the court also adverted to the parties' stipulation to the following: "That a child's self-concept can be improved by the educational process; that the educational process can reinforce a child's negative self-concept; that schools can, do, and should, play a role in providing a child with acceptable social values and behavior norms; that schools can, do, and should, play a role in equipping children with what it takes to get along in a technological society; that schools can, do, and should, play a role in making children better future citizens; that many components of a good education are not measured by pupil performance on achievement tests; that many aspects of a student's capabilities and progress are not measured by performance on achievement tests; and that the scope of skills measured by achievement tests is limited."

52. See, *e.g.,* Bowles, "Unequal Education," and "Understanding Unequal Economic Opportunity"; R. D. Hess, V. Shipman, and D. Jackson, "Early Experience and the Socialization of Cognitive Modes in Children," *Child Development* 36(1965), 869-86; E. G. Olim, R. D. Hess, and V. Shipman, "Role or Mothers' Language Styles in Mediating Their Pre-School Childrens' Cognitive Development," *School Review* 75(Winter 1967), 414-24.

53. See Coleman Report.

54. See U.S. Commission on Civil Rights, *op. cit.*

55. See Richard Herrnstein, *IQ in the Meritocracy* (Boston: Atlantic Monthly Press, 1973); Michael Young, *The Rise of the Meritocracy* (London: Thames and Hudson, 1958); Bowles and Gintis, *op. cit.*

56. In *Hobson v. Hansen,* 327 F. Supp. 844 (D.D.C. 1971), Judge J. Skelly Wright commented on the utilization of expert social science in an adversary proceeding: "Plaintiffs' motion for an amended decree and for further enforcement has now been argued and reargued via a series of motions and written

memoranda for one full year. During this time the unfortunate if inevitable tendency has been to lose sight of the disadvantaged young students on whose behalf this suit was first brought in an overgrown garden of numbers and charts and jargon like "standard deviation of the variable," statistical "significance," and "Pearson product moment correlations." The reports by the experts—one noted economist plus assistants for each side—are less helpful than they might have been for the simple reason that they do not begin from a common data base, disagree over crucial statistical assumptions, and reach different conclusions. Having hired their respective experts, the lawyers in this case had a basic responsibility, which they have not completely met, to put the hard core statistical demonstrations into language which serious and concerned laymen could, with effort, understand. Moreover, the studies by both experts are tainted by a vice well known in the statistical trade—data shopping and scanning to reach a preconceived result; and the court has had to reject parts of both reports as unreliable because biased. Lest like a latter day version of Jarndyce v. Jarndyce this litigation itself should consume the capital of the children in whose behalf it was brought, the court has been forced back to its own common sense approach to a problem which, though admittedly complex, has certainly been made more obscure than was necessary. The conclusion I reach is based upon burden of proof, and upon straightforward moral and constitutional arithmetic." (*Ibid.*, 859.)

57. See Coleman Report.

58. See generally, Jencks *et al.*; Mosteller and Moynihan (eds.), *On Equality of Educational Opportunity, op. cit.*

59. See, *e.g.*, James Guthrie *et al., Schools and Inequality* (Cambridge, Mass.: MIT Press, 1971); Eric Hanushek, *Education and Race* (Lexington, Mass.: Lexington Books, 1972); Bowles and Levin, *op. cit.*; Hanushek and Kain, *op. cit.*

60. See, *e.g., Serrano v. Priest*, Civil No. 938,254 (Cal. Super. Ct., April 10, 1974); *Robinson v. Cahill*, 62 N.J. 473, 303 A.2d 273 (1973).

61. See, *e.g., Jensen v. State Bd. of Tax Comm'rs*, Civil No. 24,474 (Ind. Cir. Ct., January 15, 1973).

62. It seems inconceivable that prior to the Coleman Report a state would defend its arrangements to spend more money for the education of children in wealthy districts than in poor ones by arguing that dollars do not affect educational outcomes. I believe that this assertion would seem incredulous to a court. Common sense suggests that if higher expenditures make a difference for children in wealthy districts, they also make a difference for pupils in poorer districts. At the least, a court should question why a state sanctions such high expenditures in wealthy districts if such resources are "wasted." Cf. *Hobson v. Hansen*, 327 F. Supp. 844 (1971), where the court stated that the defendants "cannot be allowed in one breath to justify budget requests to the Congress and to the District of Columbia City Council by stressing the connection between longevity and quality teaching, and then in the next breath to disavow any such connection before the court." (*Ibid.*, 855.)

63. See Paul D. Carrington, "Financing the American Dream: Equality and School Taxes," *Columbia Law Review* 73 (October 1973), 1227.

64. See generally Kenneth Clark, "Social Policy, Power, and Social Science Research," in *Perspectives on Inequality*, Reprint Series No. 8 (Cambridge, Mass.: Harvard Educational Review, 1973), 77.

65. Compare Cahn, "Jurisprudence," *New York University Law Review* 30(1955), 150 with Clark, "The Desegregation Cases: Criticism of the Social Scientists' Role," *Villanova Law Review* 5(1960), 224.

66. See Cohen, Pettigrew, and Riley, *op. cit.*, 439-50, 356.

67. Armor, "The Evidence on Busing," *op. cit.*

68. The critics moved in quickly to question the criteria, statistical procedures, choice of studies reviewed, and other aspects of the Armor analysis. See Pettigrew, Useem, Normand, and Smith, *op. cit.* The reply to this criticism also quickly followed. See Armor, "The Double Double Standard: A Reply," *op. cit.*

69. Armor, "The Evidence on Busing," and "The Double Double Standard: A Reply," *op. cit.*

70. *Brown v. Board of Education*, 347 U.S. 483, 494 (1954).

71. In *Rodriguez* Justice Powell noted that in view of the division of opinion among "scholars and educational experts . . . [on] the extent to which there is a demonstrable correlation between educational expenditures and the quality of education," the judiciary should refrain from deciding the issue. 411 U.S. at 42-43. See also *ibid.*, n.86.

72. Alice Rivlin, "Forensic Social Science," *Harvard Educational Review* 43(1973), 43.

73. *Ibid.*

74. While in most school litigation expert testimony is offered by both parties to the dispute, see, *e.g.*, *Serrano v. Priest*, Civil No. 938,254 (Cal. Super. Ct., April 10, 1974); in *Robinson v. Cahill*, 118 N.J. Super. 223, 287 A.2d 187 (1972), only the plaintiffs introduced expert witnesses on the relationship between expenditures and achievement.

75. See note 56.

76. And even if the court's own expert is "objective," by what criteria, for example, is he to choose between two competing economic theories?

77. See Address by David Campbell, *op. cit.*

6. Public Policy, Desegregation, and the Limits of Social Science Research

THEODORE M. HESBURGH, C.S.C.

> While you and i have lips and voices which
> are for kissing and to sing with
> who cares if some oneeyed son of a bitch
> invents an instrument to measure Spring with?
>
> e.e. cummings, "voices to voices, lip to lip"
> *Poems, 1923-54* (New York: Harcourt Brace
> Jovanovich, Inc., 1954)

Since the days of Thomas Jefferson, we as a nation have assumed that education is a means of achieving equality in our society. Recently this assumption has been challenged by a number of social scientists, most notably James Coleman, Daniel Patrick Moynihan, Christopher Jencks, and David Armor.

This chapter examines some of the social science analyses that bear on educational achievement and integration and suggests that there are philosophical, political, and moral reasons for not regarding social science research as a foolproof guide to enlightened public

The author would like to acknowledge the generous scholarly assistance of Howard A. Glickstein and John T. Bannon of the Notre Dame Center for Civil Rights in the preparation of this chapter.

policymaking. The chapter is divided into four parts. The first examines various arguments concerning the Coleman Report, Jencks's *Inequality*, and Armor's research on busing. Each of these social science studies, directly or indirectly, deals with the relationship between educational achievement and integration and is indicative of the nature and complexity of the issues involved in attempting to use social science research as a guide to public policy. The second part of the chapter deals with the two broad intellectual traditions of social science and their relationship to the methodological positions taken by contemporary social scientists. The basic philosophical assumptions inherent in social science research are seldom made explicit, and yet these philosophical assumptions must be taken into account if we are to evaluate realistically the role social science should play in the making of public policy. The third part of the chapter explores the relationship between public policy and the social science expert, which, of course, involves the political uses of social science knowledge. The last part of the chapter suggests the possibility that morality and history may be firmer guides to enlightened public policy than contemporary social science research.

THE DEBATE OVER SOCIAL SCIENCE STUDIES OF SCHOOLS

Throughout our nation's history, society has recognized the essential role of public education in the life of its citizenry.[1] Government officials, educators, and others have assumed that a child's cognitive skills, that is, the ability to communicate in verbal and quantitative terms, are in large measure determined by the child's experience in school. This prevailing conception of public education has been challenged rather suddenly by various social science studies, and the challenge has come at a time when black Americans are in a position to make their influence felt in the nation's largest school systems. Instead of focusing on what needs to be done to improve the school systems, we find ourselves debating whether it is schooling or socioeconomic background that determines educational achievement.

The Coleman Report

Since the publication of *Equality of Educational Opportunity*,[2] popularly known as the Coleman Report, in 1966, there has been a growing and widespread debate among social scientists about the relative influence of school and socioeconomic status on a child's performance in the classroom. Is it family background and socioeconomic status that make the difference, or is it the child's experience in the school that is the determining factor? The Coleman Report concluded that academic achievement depends more on family background than on what happens in the classroom. According to the Report, the schools fail to narrow the gap between students who are advantaged and students who are disadvantaged, and disadvantaged students are likely to leave school in an academically weaker position, relative to their peers, than when they entered. Coleman and his followers[3] contend that schools receive students who already differ in knowledge, skills, and attitudes, thus beginning their formal education at different starting points. Formal education does little to close the gaps between students.

Since the release of the Coleman Report, educational sociologists, statisticians, and other groups of social scientists have analyzed and reanalyzed both the Report's methodology and its conclusions, and a number of reports have reaffirmed the Report's findings. Some social scientists, however, differed with the conclusions of the Coleman group. Their studies showed that there was a clear and independent relationship between what schools did and the results they produced. Critics of the methodology used in the Coleman Report cited research studies showing that children from disadvantaged homes generally attended schools having fewer and lower-quality educational services, as well as less experienced teachers and administrators. These same critics concluded that the facilities and the quality of education in a school had a direct bearing on how well children performed.[4] A 1969 Urban Coalition study, for example, found a direct positive relationship between the quality of school services provided for students and their academic achievement. Higher-quality school services were associated with higher levels of academic achievement. The Urban Coalition study concluded that schools have an effect that is independent of the child's socioeconomic environment; schools definitely make a difference.

Who is correct? Are the conclusions of the Coleman Report essentially accurate, or are the critics of the Report on firmer ground? How does a public policymaker determine who is correct?

Jencks's *Inequality*

Any public policymaker in the area of educational achievement and integration confronts a dilemma when he attempts to determine how much weight he should give a social science study. Christopher Jencks, in the controversial study, *Inequality*,[5] went beyond the findings of the Coleman Report and argued not only that schools do not overcome the effects of educational disadvantage, but also that schools are basically unable to improve substantially the academic performance of disadvantaged children. According to Jencks, it is one's family background that is the most important determinant of educational attainment. After family background, the most important determinant of educational attainment is cognitive skills. Just how closely cognitive skills relate to educational achievement is extremely difficult to determine because such skills can only be measured by tests, and test scores quite probably reflect noncognitive differences like those that exist between home environments. Jencks contends that qualitative differences among schools explains only a very small percentage of the variations in student educational achievement. His study challenges the egalitarian assumption that schools are an instrument in equalizing status and income and suggests that income redistribution would be a more effective way of equalizing earning power.

Criticisms of Jencks's *Inequality* has been both forceful and widespread. Aside from the ever-present methodological arguments, *Inequality* has been criticized on other grounds.[6] First, its limited perspective on the function of schools has been challenged.[7] *Inequality* is preoccupied with the measurable effects of various school inputs upon student performance in later life. What the study ignores is the school's obligation to help students get the most out of their experiences, the school's obligation to help students translate their experiences into a meaningful process of development.

Inequality has also been criticized by those who feel it is an example of a new tradition of "forensic social science."[8] Forensic social scientists marshal social science arguments for or against particular policy positions and often assume the task of writing social science "briefs" for or against a particular policy. Social scientists, taking a counterposition, then destroy the opposition's argument with their amassed counterevidence. There is doubt among some social scientists as to whether this is a legitimate function for social scientists to perform, and professional organizations of social scientists will eventually have to deal with this problem.[9]

Another criticism of *Inequality* is that it has done a disservice to children from minority backgrounds and those who come from low-income families by enabling school officials to shift their responsibility to society-at-large.[10] Many social critics voice the truism that overall social change, as well as equality of educational opportunity, is needed to right the wrongs American society has perpetrated on its minorities. *Inequality* seems to suggest, however, that there is no need to be concerned with education because only with social, political, and economic change will there be educational gains. Critics of Jencks's position suggest that the failure of the educational system is to be found in the schools rather than in the students and that what is actually needed is "help" for the schools. Critics also question Jencks's inference that schools are doing the best they can to improve student performance. The burden of performance, say the critics, should be moved from the students to the schools; student performance can be improved when educational decisionmakers have the desire and the long-term commitment to make schools accountable for their behavior.

The public policymaker quickly learns that social scientists are not in agreement over the role schools play in the quest for equality of educational opportunity. This lack of agreement among social scientists has been emphasized by briefly examining the basic findings of both the Coleman Report and Jencks's *Inequality*, along with the criticisms of those studies. This same lack of consensus among social scientists can be seen in the narrower, more focused debate between David Armor and Thomas Pettigrew over busing, integration, and educational achievement.[11]

The Armor-Pettigrew Debate

David Armor, a former Harvard sociologist, wrote a highly publicized article concerned with the effects of busing on black students in the Boston METCO program. In his study he also reviewed a number of other programs. The METCO program buses black students of all age levels from Boston to predominantly white, middle-class schools in the suburbs. Armor challenged the assumptions of social scientists and policymakers who postulated that school integration had positive effects for black students. He claimed that many social scientists and policymakers uncritically assumed that school integration would promote black achievement, give blacks higher aspirations, raise their self-esteem, give them more opportunities for higher education, and improve race relations. Armor studied each of these factors. He examined and compared tests of reading and arithmetic skills between a group of students who were bused and a control group of black students who were not bused, and he found that the students in the bused group showed no significant gains in either reading or arithmetic skills. Educational aspirations, Armor concluded, did not increase for the bused students; in fact, he found that there was a significant decline. Armor also found that integration did not reduce racial stereotypes or increase racial tolerance, a finding that contradicted one of the basic tenets of social science theory. According to Armor, his data showed that integration heightened racial identity and consciousness, enhanced ideologies that promoted racial separation, and reduced opportunities for actual contact between the races. On the question of opportunities for higher education, however, Armor found substantial evidence that black students attending middle-class suburban schools were more likely to be admitted to higher-quality institutions of higher education than students attending predominantly black schools.

Armor concluded, then, that four of the five premises underlying the METCO program and similar busing programs were not supported by the data. He also concluded that integration programs are open to serious question.

Thomas Pettigrew, a Harvard social psychologist, strongly challenged Armor's research and conclusions. Pettigrew disagreed with Armor on four major grounds. First, Pettigrew argued that Armor established unrealistically high standards by which to judge the success of school desegregation. Armor evaluated just one academic year and concluded that school desegregation had not succeeded because it had not led to increased achievement, to higher aspirations, to greater self-esteem, to further interracial tolerance, and to better life opportunities for black children in that short period of time. Armor, moreover, did not distinguish between various types of interracial schools. On the one hand there are "desegregated" schools, where children of different races merely come together in the same building and classrooms, and, on the other hand, there are "integrated" schools where there is effective interaction among the pupils.

Pettigrew next criticizes the Armor article because it presents selected findings from selected studies. According to Pettigrew, seven relevant, well-known investigations of busing programs that reported achievement gains for black students were not even mentioned, and those busing investigations that were reviewed in the article were cursorily reviewed. Negative findings, consistent with the article's analysis of school integration, were emphasized, while a number of positive findings from the same busing studies were either obscured or ignored. The positive findings were ignored because Armor utilized overly rigorous standards. One example of this is Armor's comparison of the achievement gains of black students in desegregated schools with the achievement of whites. A more obvious comparison would have been the comparison of black achievement gains in desegregated schools with black achievement gains in black schools.

Pettigrew's third major disagreement with Armor's article is that its conclusions rest primarily on findings from one short-term study conducted by Armor himself. This study examined the voluntary busing programs in metropolitan Boston called METCO, which was mentioned earlier. Pettigrew found that the METCO study had serious methodological shortcomings. The primary deficiency concerned the lack of an adequate control group. To test the effects of busing and school desegregation, the appropriate control group should consist exclusively of children who are not bused and who do not attend desegregated schools. Armor, however, compared a group of children who were bused to desegregated schools with another group of children, many of whom were also bused to desegregated schools. Without an adequate control group, the METCO study was scientifically worthless as a study of busing and school desegregation. Since this study was the basis for Armor's evidence concerning the efficacy of busing, his conclusions are open to serious question.

Pettigrew raised yet another objection to Armor's article, and it concerned Armor's basic assumption about racial change. Armor viewed public school desegregation as basically a technical matter, rather than a moral or legal one, a matter for social scientists rather than moralists, legislators, or judges. Armor's article ignored the moral and constitutional rights of black children to equal educational opportunity; it ignored the immoral and illegal segregation of black children in our school systems. And, finally, the article ignored the capacity of law to affect racial change, the capacity of law to help end racial discrimination and prejudice.

We have now examined three well-known controversies that have implications in the area of educational achievement and integration. In each of these controversies, both sides relied extensively on the use of social science evidence. That social science evidence can be used by both sides in a particular controversy is considered extremely disheartening by some; yet there are both philosophical and political reasons to explain why this is so.

THE INTELLECTUAL TRADITIONS OF SOCIAL SCIENCE

The philosophical reasons why social science evidence can be used by both sides in a controversy revolve around two major conflicting intellectual traditions within the social sciences.[12] Man's achievements in manipulating the physical environment have been impressive, and success has encouraged utilization of scientific procedures to gain command of the social environment. The extension of scientific procedures into the social sphere has been accompanied by considerable criticism from those scholars who question the adequacy of scientific procedures as they are applied either to individuals or to social groups. A considerable number of scholars have yet to be convinced that social researchers can become scientists. On another occasion I commented upon the relationship between the physical and social sciences:

The social sciences are mainly parvenus among the sciences. They came upon a field already largely occupied by the physical and natural sciences. It is human and understandable that, in an effort to be comfortable in already occupied territory, the newcomers took on the protective coloration of the place and times, adopting the reigning regime's proudest title of science—as if this were the only source of respectability and pride—and adopting the title of science in an altogether too univocal sense.

There followed many other understandable developments: the amassing of data for the sake of data, the attempt to quantify the unquantifiable, the cult of mathematical verification in an effort to establish theories ultimately beyond mathematics, the worship of objectivity to an extent that often sterilized what might have been very fruitful research, the confusion between counting heads and establishing what are essentially philosophical norms, the blurring of what is average and what is truly significant, the development of so-called scientific terminology and occult nomenclature that allowed an esoteric statement of obvious fact to masquerade as scientific wisdom when it was in fact not only not worth stating, but was stated in murky and turgid rhetoric. Regarding this latter point, may I say that the inability to communicate signals the end of usefulness for any element in a culture, be it religion, art, or science.[13]

Two major intellectual traditions have competed for support among social scientists. These two traditions, the neo-idealist and the positivist, differ, both with respect to how they view the subject matter of social science and with respect to their research methodology. The neo-idealist tradition emerged from Kantian and Hegelian idealism, which was the basis for the works of a brilliant, creative group of German social theorists influential during the latter half of the nineteenth century. Perhaps the most prominent member of this distinguished group was Max Weber. Weber reasoned that natural science and social science were distinctive bodies of knowledge, distinctive because of the nature of the subject matter with which each dealt. And, from this basic assumption, Weber further reasoned that natural scientists and social scientists must utilize different methodologies and research strategies. Unlike the natural scientist, the social scientist had to consider both the historical aspect of human action and the subjective aspect of human experience. Weber concluded that social scientists had to gain an understanding of human social reality and its symbols, attitudes, and values. In other words, the social scientist had to "get inside" his subject matter.

The positivist tradition in social science is in direct opposition to the neo-idealist school of thought. Positivism does not accept the proposition that the natural and social sciences are distinct branches of knowledge, and social scientists in this school assume that they can obtain objective knowledge in the social sphere just as the natural scientist does in the natural world. The positivist believes that natural science and social science share a basic methodology. Even though the subject matter of these two branches of knowledge may differ, both employ the same logic of inquiry and similar research procedures.

This brief examination of the philosophical debate between two groups of social scientists is intended to suggest that this still unsolved, and perhaps unsolvable, debate holds a lesson for those who perceive social science as a unified body of knowledge and who expect consistency in both methodology and results from social scientists. The debate, sometimes heated, poignantly illustrates the foolhardiness of relying on social science alone to provide answers to pressing social problems. Different social scientists proceed from different philosophical positions, and, because of this, they employ different research strategies and methodologies. In light of this, is it not presumptuous to expect that they reach the same conclusions? I suggest that it is.

PUBLIC POLICY AND THE SOCIAL SCIENCE EXPERTS

Earlier I mentioned that there were both philosophical and political reasons for the use of social science evidence by both sides in any given controversy. The philosophical reasons having been briefly surveyed, I now turn to the political aspects of the problem. Where a policymaker is deluged with a mass of social science information, should his political judgment be heavily influenced by his social science advisers? The problem of the relationship between public policy and social science expertise is a political one because the policymaker must decide just how much weight social science expertise will be given in any particular situation.

A pervasive fear of modern man is that of being governed by a scientific elite, and there is, among some people, a deepening fear that democracy may be obsolete because so many important political decisions turn on seemingly abstruse technical questions about which political decisionmakers lack sufficient information or understanding to sustain informed opinions. While these fears are understandable, they are not well founded. There are forces at work that help keep the social science expert in his place. In almost any controversial issue there are sure to exist a wealth of social science data and arguments that can be utilized by both sides. This being so, social science evidence on a controversial issue is seldom conclusive. While some political decisionmakers make an honest attempt to weigh available social science data before they take a stand on a political issue, other political decisionmakers who have already taken a position on an issue, whether because of their constituency or because of a deeply held belief, look for expert opinions to strengthen their positions and to provide politically viable rationalizations for them. I sometimes suspect that much of the deference accorded social scientists by some legislators and administrators is simply a useful way to obtain more or less sophisticated rationalizations with which to defend previously taken positions. Many political decisionmakers are quite skilled in getting from experts the kinds of information and conclusions for which they are looking. This political use of social science knowledge is one of the forces that control the social science adviser.

It is vitally important, here, that we understand that political decisionmaking often involves fundamental, ethical judgments which, more likely than not, cannot be resolved by social science. Conceptions of justice, the location of power, and the distribution of resources become more difficult when men have different interests and different values, and ethical judgments concerning these matters depend upon the relative power of various factions and the ethical and moral sensitivity of the society in which they occur.[14] Attempts to reduce such questions of value to objectively neutral, scientific consideration give rise to the myth that there is a value-free social science that overrides individual moral sensitivity. Without values there can be no discernment, no judgment, and no relevance to the important and pressing problems of our time.

Few public issues can be resolved by appeals to social science. Does anyone really believe that social science experts can prescribe with any degree of finality what would be fair and equitable for minorities with respect to equal educational opportunity? We must constantly be on guard against the arrogance and pretentiousness of many who claim social science knowledge. It is important to note that facts seldom speak for themselves. Experts, of necessity, render judgments, not facts, and, in matters of judgment, the influence of what one wants the answer to be simply cannot be excluded from consideration. As one perceptive science instructor at Harvard University wrote, in a slightly different context:

[t]he answer must be social and political and the sooner we realize how much of science is so influenced, the sooner we will demythologize it as an inexorable "truth-making machine."[15]

When evaluating social science controversies, it is sometimes less important to investigate the details of a particular argument than the ideological determinants that influence participants. This is not what many of us learned in school, and many of us wish it were not so. We were taught to challenge the argument, not the person who espoused it. A powerful trend in modern thought, however, is the claim that much of man's important thinking is prompted by anxieties and

goals rather than by rules of abstract logic.[16] And, on this point intellectual movements as diverse as existentialism, pragmatism, and the
sociology of knowledge agree. This argument could, of course, be
carried too far if all policy arguments degenerated into attacks upon
the motives and values of those who advocate different policies.
Some attempt must be made to settle social science arguments on
social science grounds, but we must not be misled by the vision of a
neutral, objective, value-free social science. Kenneth Clark addresses
this problem in his latest book and stresses the importance of using
moral guidelines in the responsible exercise of one's intelligence.[17]
One of Clark's concerns is that excessive emphasis on social science
objectivity would preclude the making of moral judgments and result
in a rejection of one's responsibility to remedy the unfair treatment
of minorities in American society. Along with Clark, I see no reason
why the social scientist cannot also be a philosopher or a theologian,
or both, if this would enrich his primary intellectual endeavor in
social science, particularly as regards its most central and complex
focus: the human person. Too much emphasis on social science
objectivity can lead to callous moral irresponsibility, a problem not
peculiar to social science. One commentator, speaking on the natural
sciences, has noted that, throughout our history,

> statements that seem to have the sanction of science have been continually in-
> volved in attempts to equate egalitarianism with sentimental hope and emotional
> blindness. People who are unaware of the historical pattern tend to accept each
> recurrence at face value: that is, they assume each such statement arises from the
> "data" actually presented rather than from the social conditions that truly in-
> spire it.[18]

Today, too many social scientists reject their obligation to challenge and probe the status quo, thus refusing to play their role as
social critics. Other social scientists, while they do not abandon their
role as social critics, suggest solutions so unworkable as to be of little
use to a concerned policymaker. And, all too often, social scientists
fail to consider the use that partisans will make of their studies.
While this should obviously not deter the social scientist from publishing his findings, it should make him a bit more responsible in
those areas where research findings are, at best, tentative and inconclusive. Modern social science, overconcerned with "objectivity"
where objectivity may not even be possible, poses special dangers for

those who perceive the role of social scientist to be that of social critic. Under the guise of objectivity, the social scientist can easily become an apologist for the status quo. While it would be misleading to believe that most or even a majority of social scientists have chosen for themselves the role of social apologist, social scientists do seem to be moving away from the more socially relevant models devised by colleagues like Gordon Allport and Gunnar Myrdal. Social science seems to be used increasingly, by some social scientists and some policymakers, to rationalize moral and ethical indifference to the plight of racial minorities and the poor. Social science concepts, methodology, and language should not be allowed to disguise this troublesome trend. If social science is to be relevant in this age of social change, it must become more concerned with what social change is all about; in short, social science must become increasingly critical of the status quo and increasingly aware of the world's monumental problems.

History, Morality, and the Public Policymaker

Social science research is but one element of the highly complex problem of attempting to achieve some semblance of social justice in a racially biased society. A public policymaker today should understand that there are deficiencies in even the most carefully carried out social science research. He must become aware of philosophical and political problems associated with the use of such research and learn to evaluate it within the context of history and morality. In the sensitive area of race relations, in general, and school desegregation, in particular, both history and morality provide insights that help the policymaker view social science research in perspective.

Let us assume that social science research shows that school desegregation provides limited benefits to black children. It would be well to look to history before we reject desegregation too readily. History reveals the enormous burdens that all-black institutions have carried in our society. As a result of slavery—labeled our "peculiar institution" by historians—things black are stigmatized. The black man and his institutions have been stamped with a badge of inferiority from which black Americans have yet to recover. I recognize, of course, that in recent years black leaders have made great strides in encouraging black pride. I also recognize that black political power is growing and is capable of exerting significant influence toward strengthening predominantly black institutions. These factors must be taken into account when considering alternatives to school desegregation, but I still think we have a long way to go before our society recognizes black institutions as being the equal of white institutions and treats them accordingly.

The stigma attached to all-black schools and the characteristics of education in such schools were studied intensively by the Commission on Civil Rights and reported on in *Racial Isolation in the Public Schools*. The Commission found that:

Predominantly Negro schools generally are regarded by the community as inferior institutions. Negro students in such schools are sensitive to such views and often come to share them. Teachers and administrative staff frequently recognize or share the community's view and communicate it to the students. This stigma affects the achievement and attitudes of Negro students.[19]

The Commission heard many witnesses who described the dimensions of this problem. Calvin Brooks, a black high school student who testified at a Commission hearing in Cleveland, described the environment at his school and its effects on the students:

. . . it had an effect because they were there and all they saw were Negroes and they were raised in an environment of poverty and the building was old and it had an effect I don't know of—of hopelessness. They didn't think that they could do anything because their fathers had common labor jobs and they didn't think they could ever get any higher and they didn't work, some of them.[20]

Charles Pinderhughes, a psychiatrist who testified at the Commission hearing in Boston, traced the stigma involved in attending a predominantly Negro school back to the institution of slavery. The Commission's general counsel asked Dr. Pinderhughes: "[I]t is generally believed that most ethnic and religious groups have not been disadvantaged by being segregated in schools? Is it different for Negroes?" Dr. Pinderhughes replied that there was "a vast difference." The system of slavery in this country, he testified, assigned to Negroes certain functions designed to rob them of power, to exploit them, and to keep them in a position inferior to that of whites.[21]

According to Dr. Pinderhughes, since Negroes have been much more limited in their mobility than other groups because of racial discrimination, "there has been little opportunity for diffusion of the basic elements in their old roles. The lack of diffusion in these roles has maintained certain characteristics that might be thought of as remnants of a slave culture caste, which still prevail."[22]

In the view of Dr. Pinderhughes, the racially isolated school, instead of serving as an agent through which blacks can move freely in American society, is partly responsible for transmitting this slave psychology:

[T]he school is one of the major participants in the transfer of culture to young people. Where we have primarily a single ethnic group in a school, the school serves as a vehicle for conveying the characteristics of that group. So a school in an Irish community will perpetuate and help to produce Irish youngsters; and in a Jewish community, Jewish youngsters; and in a Negro community, the same unfavorable stamp which I have described, will be pressed, or the school will participate, at least, in the transmission of it.[23]

History not only reveals the heavy psychological burdens that have been placed on all-black institutions, but it also offers proof that all-black institutions almost invariably suffer in tangible ways. It is well established that, during the period of "separate but equal" schools, the separation was rigidly enforced and the equality, flagrantly violated. Courts repeatedly found inequalities between black and white schools in terms of buildings and other physical facilities, course offerings, length of school terms, transportation facilities, extra-curricular activities, cafeteria facilities, and geographical convenience.[24] Mary E. Mabane (Liza), a teacher at South Carolina State College, described what it was like to go to a separate but unequal school:

It's when you're in the second grade and your eye reads the name "Bragtown High School" and you also see in the front of the book "discard" and even though you're only 7 years old you know, as you turn the pages that have tears patched with a thick yellow tape, that you're using a book that a white girl used last year and tore up, and your mother is paying book rent just like her mother paid book rent. You get the second-hand books. And it gives you a thing about second-hand books that does not go away until you are teaching yourself and are able to buy all the new ones you want.[25]

Nor did *Brown v. Board of Education* put an end to such inequalities. In 1968 a hearing by the Commission on Civil Rights in Alabama focused on sixteen counties with significant black populations. The Commission found that 80 percent of all substandard schools in the area were black. White schools proportionately had four times the space of black ones. In Clarke County, only one white school had an insurance valuation of less than $110,000, and that was valued at $52,000. No black school was valued at more than $20,000, and two were valued at $750. White school libraries averaged 13.8 books per pupil; black schools, 5.7.[26] Black Americans are not the only minority group shortchanged. The Edgewood School District in San Antonio is predominantly Mexican-American. It adjoins the Alamo Heights District, which is almost exclusively Anglo. Edgewood, which taxed itself at a higher rate than did Alamo, spent $356 per pupil for the 1967-68 school year, while Alamo spent $594.[27] Facts like these may not convince social scientists, but they carry great weight with practical parents. A black mother in North Carolina, for example, explained her support of busing:

Within one month, the parents of the white children who were bused managed to get the black school painted, repairs made, new electric typewriters and sewing machines, and the shelves filled with books. . . .
I contend that busing for one year will upgrade our schools quicker than anything the President or Congress can do.[28]

In Boston today there are black parents who are willing to endure the turmoil that school desegregation has created in that city because they are convinced that "green follows white."[29] They feel that money and good teaching only come into schools where there are whites. To demonstrate this, blacks in Boston point to a dilapidated black school that was given new equipment before white students arrived.[30]

It is evident, therefore, that history, both past and contemporary, has a lot to teach us about school desegregation controversies, and social science studies must be viewed against this history by those in policymaking positions. There are also moral considerations that affect public policy. The principle of equality before the law, which is deeply rooted in our system of justice, dictates that a remedy not be withheld from an individual or group because the objectives of that individual or group lack approval or because granting relief would prove inconvenient or burdensome. It is this principle that is at stake in most big-city school desegregation controversies.

In Boston, for example, District Judge W. Arthur Garrity did not examine social science studies to convince himself that widespread school desegregation was required; he was not engaged in "social engineering." Judge Garrity issued his orders because he was committed to the principle of equality before the law. The proof in the case before him demonstrated conclusively that segregated schools existed in Boston because of deliberate and illegal acts of public officials. It was not happenstance; nor did many individuals simply act according to their own preferences. School segregation was officially created and sanctioned in Boston. Judge Garrity, after recounting the history of deliberate actions to keep Boston's schools segregated, concluded: ". . . the defendants have knowingly carried out a systematic program of segregation affecting all of the city's students, teachers and school facilities and have intentionally brought about and maintained a dual school system."[31] This type of official lawlessness also resulted in far-ranging court orders in Charlotte-Mecklenburg, Richmond, and Detroit. To have condoned such lawlessness would not only have subverted the law; it would have been highly immoral as well. Even if social science data had cast doubt on the efficaciousness of school desegregation, this still would not have made segregation acceptable. Such data have no relevance when a court is faced with a school system that has been officially segregated, for the court is legally and morally bound to enforce the principle of equality and to undo the illegal conduct.

I do not believe social science techniques have been refined to the point where we can rely on the results of that research alone to suggest policies that history has demonstrated will not work. Nor do I believe, with due regard to my own calling, that we should ordain social scientists as the priests of our public policymakers. Those entrusted with making public policy must look to the ethical and moral principles that underlie our Judeo-Christian heritage for guidance. Perhaps many of the difficulties we find ourselves in today would be less severe if we were more often guided by those principles rather than by revelations culled from regression tables. I confess that my formula may be old fashioned, but I have found no better.

NOTES

1. U.S. Commission on Civil Rights, *Racial Isolation in the Public Schools* (Washington, D.C.: Government Printing Office, 1967), 1-2.

2. James S. Coleman et al., Equality of Educational Opportunity, U.S. Office of Education, National Center for Educational Statistics, OE 38001 (Washington, D.C.: Government Printing Office, 1966). Hereafter cited as Coleman Report.

3. Obviously there are differences among Coleman, Christopher Jencks, and David Armor with respect to methodology and conclusions. Coleman, for example, may have doubts about the ability of schools to close the achievement gap, but he does believe in school integration and the benefits that flow from it. Armor, on the other hand, challenges the whole notion of school integration. Jencks contends that schools are incapable of closing the achievement gap and reaches the conclusion that what is needed is not school reform but broad social changes. The conclusions of all three writers, however, stress the limitations of the public schools in performing their traditional functions.

4. Report of the Senate Select Committee on Equal Educational Opportunity, Toward Equal Educational Opportunity (Washington, D.C.: Government Printing Office, 1972), 167-69.

5. Christopher Jencks et al., Inequality (New York: Basic Books, 1972).

6. See Harvard Educational Review 43(February 1973), where a number of researchers in the field of education present their views on inequality; also available as Perspectives on Inequality, Reprint Series No. 8 (Cambridge, Mass.: Harvard Educational Review, 1973).

7. See Kenneth Clark, "Critical Issues in Minority Education," in When the Marching Stopped (New York: National Urban League, 1973), 121-28.

8. Ibid.

9. Gideon Sjoberg and Roger Nett, A Methodology for Social Research (New York: Harper and Row, 1968), 76-80.

10. See Clark, op. cit.

11. See David J. Armor, "The Evidence on Busing," Public Interest 28(Summer 1972); Thomas F. Pettigrew et al., "A Review of the Evidence," Public Interest 30(Winter 1973).

12. Sjoberg and Nett, op. cit., 1-13.

13. See the address given by the Reverend Theodore M. Hesburgh, C.S.C., at the dedication of the Institute for Social Research, University of Michigan, Ann Arbor (March 30, 1966), 5-6.

14. For the classic American statement on the nature, causes, and effects of factions, see James Madison, Federalist, No. 10.

15. Stephen J. Gould, "Racist Arguments and I.Q.," Natural History 29(May 1974).

16. See Karl Mannheim's classic work, Ideology and Utopia: An Introduction to the Sociology of Knowledge (New York: Harcourt Brace Jovanovich, 1955).

17. Kenneth Clark, The Pathos of Power (New York: Harper and Row, 1974).

18. Gould, op. cit.

19. U.S. Commission on Civil Rights, op. cit., 204.

20. Ibid., 194.

21. See U.S. Commission on Civil Rights, *A Time to Listen ... A Time to Act* (Washington, D.C.: Government Printing Office, 1967), 47.

22. *Ibid.*, 48.

23. *Ibid.*

24. Cases are collected in Howard A. Glickstein and William L. Want, "Inequality in School Financing," *Stanford Law Review* 25(1973), 342-43.

25. *New York Times,* March 15, 1972, p. 47, cols. 1-3.

26. U.S. Commission on Civil Rights, *Cycle to Nowhere* (Washington, D.C.: Government Printing Office, 1968), 13.

27. *San Antonio Independent School District v. Rodriguez,* 411 U.S. 1, 12-13 (1973).

28. Cited in U.S. Commission on Civil Rights, *Your Child and Busing* (Washington, D.C.: Government Printing Office, 1972), 15.

29. *New York Times,* October 6, 1974, p. 46, col. 4.

30. *Ibid.*

31. *Morgan v. Hennigan,* Civil Action No. 72-911-G (E. D. Mass., June 21, 1974).

7. The Cost-Quality Debate in School Finance Litigation

JOHN E. McDERMOTT

INTRODUCTION

Since the appearance in 1966 of the *Equality of Educational Opportunity Report* (the Coleman Report),[1] social science researchers have been attacking one of America's most cherished beliefs: that education may be used as an instrument to reduce social inequality.[2] Social scientists of national reputation, including the Coleman team, members of the faculty seminar at Harvard that reanalyzed the Coleman Report findings,[3] Christopher Jencks,[4] and others, claim that beyond some minimum per pupil expenditure level, there is little or no statistical relationship between dollars spent per pupil and student performance on standardized achievement tests. Put another way, higher expenditures do not produce higher student achievement. Home background and other socioeconomic

Adapted, with permission, from John E. McDermott and Stephen P. Klein, "The Cost-Quality Debate in School Finance Litigation: Do Dollars Make A Difference?" which appeared in a symposium on Future Directions for School Finance Reform in *Law and Contemporary Problems* 38(No. 3, Winter-Spring 1974), published by Duke University School of Law, Durham, North Carolina. Copyright, 1974, by Duke University.

factors account for variations in pupil achievement, not inequalities in school expenditures. Armed with a seemingly irrefutable array of statistics and data, and having employed the most sophisticated social science research techniques, the conclusion is thus reached that inequalities in schools have little effect on student outcomes, as measured by pupil performance on standardized achievement tests.

Yet the research findings have not been relegated to some dusty corner of academia.[5] As the cost of public education has soared and the demand for accountability by state legislatures has gathered momentum, the Coleman Report and similar research have been cited increasingly by policymakers who question whether increasing school expenditures will improve the quality of education. The issue has also emerged in courtrooms across the country in lawsuits attempting to remedy intrastate and intradistrict disparities in per pupil expenditures. If money does not matter, so the argument goes, then fiscal disparities from district to district or school to school do not result in unequal educational opportunities afforded school children.

The traditional concept that the efficacy of schools is linked substantially to expenditures is, however, not without its defenders. Those defenders concede that American society has been naive in its faith that education can cure every social ill, but urge that a reprieve be granted before discarding the traditional importance attached to schooling. The reprieve should be granted because of evidence that suggests that social science research findings, given the present state of the art, are inadequate as a tool for making public policy decisions about educational opportunities.

The focus of this chapter is on the appropriateness of using the judicial process as a forum for resolving the cost-quality debate in educational finance. The relationship between social science and public policy has always been less than amicable, which is perhaps as it should be. But the courtroom is a narrower and more rigidly circumscribed context in which to resolve the tension between science and policy than the legislative and administrative arenas. Principled adjudication adorns itself with avoidance techniques to preserve the separation of powers and to avoid infringing on legislative prerogatives. Where, as here, satisfactory definitions of equal educational opportunity are elusive and where the impenetrable jargon of science threatens the proper functioning of the adversary process, courts justifiably should be loath to intervene in matters relating to the financing of public education. The challenge to the school finance reform lawyer, and the purpose of this chapter, is to discover some intermediate ground, some judicially manageable standard that permits the judicial machinery to operate, but avoids settling the scientific dispute.

JUDICIAL STANDARDS OF EQUALITY OF EDUCATIONAL OPPORTUNITY

What norm or standard exists for defining equality of educational opportunity? Educators have not satisfactorily defined the concept, perhaps because the concept's historical content is not static, but evolutionary. Professor Coleman has noted the change in expectations of schooling: the school is no longer viewed as a passive instrument, rather our society has come increasingly to rely on schools to solve complex social problems such as poverty, crime, and racial discrimination.[6] Yet schools are ill-equipped to fulfill such a mission. Their function is education, not social reform. To place on schools the responsibility for solving problems over which they have little or no control is to doom the public school system to certain failure. In any event, defining equality of educational opportunity is a hazardous undertaking when no social consensus exists as to the proper role of schools.

Judicial response under such circumstances is predictably poor. Courts in school finance litigation, in the absence of Coleman Report-type evidence on school outputs, often assume a cost-quality relationship;[7] other courts accept Coleman Report-type evidence at face value in rejecting plaintiffs' claims.[8] Seldom does the adversary process work effectively. Nevertheless, past judicial attempts to construct standards of equality of educational opportunity offer an introduction to the available options. Eight different standards have been considered: (1) equal dollars per pupil, (2) needs, (3) no judicially manageable standards, (4) maximum variable ratio, (5) negative definition, (6) inputs, (7) outputs, and (8) minimum adequacy.[9]

McInnis v. Shapiro

The first three standards are amply illustrated in *McInnis v. Shapiro*,[10] where plaintiffs attacked the interdistrict expenditure inequalities of the Illinois school financing system. Plaintiffs claimed that the fourteenth amendment commanded that expenditures be distributed *only* on the basis of the educational needs of pupils. The court first rejected any rigid dollar equality standard of educational opportunity, noting that expenditures are not "the exclusive yard-stick of a child's educational needs."[11] Perhaps the only point of agreement on the part of educators, courts, and laymen is that a "one-dollar one-scholar" measure of equality is inappropriate. Absolute dollar equality would ignore variations in costs and educational needs from district to district. Fear was also expressed in *McInnis* that leveling high-expenditure districts downward would produce uniform mediocrity and stifle local experimentation.[12] No court has ever adopted such a standard; even courts that find a relationship between cost and quality, and regard dollar expenditures as one relevant criterion for measuring equal educational opportunity, disavow that an equal-dollars-per-pupil result is in any way legally required.[13] Moreover, because the reasons for appropriate expenditure disparities are several, a "needs only" standard of expenditure distribution was also unacceptable in *McInnis*. A standard was needed that was flexible enough to accommodate competing financial claims, a standard in other words, that was consistent with some acceptable concept of proportional equality, or, as it were, the principle of justified inequality.

Yet the articulation of such a standard was thought in *McInnis* to be "a basic policy decision more appropriately handled by a legislature than a court."[14] Complaining that educational need was a "nebulous concept" beyond judicial competence to define, the court refused to decide the case on its merits, and declared that "there are no 'discoverable or manageable standards' by which a court can determine when the Constitution is satisfied and when it is violated."[15] A similar result was reached in *Burrus v. Wilkerson*,[16] where the court, in upholding Virginia's system of school financing declared, "Courts have neither the knowledge nor the means nor the power to allocate the public monies to fit the varying needs of these students throughout the state."[17] Thus, to be successful, school finance litigants must construct a standard for measuring equality of educational opportunity that permits appropriate expenditure variation but is also judicially manageable.

Maximum Variable Ratio

One solution is a maximum variable ratio standard for measuring equality. Such a standard, while essentially arbitrary, would permit expenditure variations within a specified range, thereby providing school districts with some financial flexibility in responding to local problems. One court suggested, but did not order, that variations in operating expenditures due to local initiative might be permissible "to the extent of 10 percent or 15 percent of the level of income guaranteed for the district by the state in any year."[18] The variable ratio approach can be combined with existing categorical aid programs so as to apply only to ordinary operating expenditures. Hence, in *Hobson v. Hansen*,[19] a case involving disparities in per pupil expenditures among schools within a single school district, Judge J. Skelly Wright, angered by the fact that the Washington, D.C., school system had not reduced expenditure disparities as ordered in an earlier opinion, ordered that disparities in per pupil expenditures for teachers' salaries not exceed a five-percent variation except for "adequate justification," which was defined to include compensatory and special education programs. Yet an approach using a maximum variable ratio standard is fraught with problems. The standard assumes the adequacy of the state-guaranteed minimum above which expenditures may vary; if the assumption is false and the ratio is set too low, then the policy demand would become intense. The standard is probably unworkable unless special categorical programs and capital outlays are excluded. There is also the problem of deciding on an appropriate ratio. If the ratio is set too high, serious inequalities will result; if set too low, the system will be unresponsive. Because of the lack of criteria with which to make these judgments, a judicial solution of this nature, involving as it must the imposition of a particular method of school finance on the legislature, raises serious separation of powers issues.

Negative Standards

A fifth standard of measuring equality of educational opportunity in school finance litigation is a negative definition, that is, to define what equality of educational opportunity is *not*, to limit one's examination to what a state may not do in the distribution of educational revenues, rather than ordering what a state must do. The

"fiscal neutrality" principle of Professors Coons, Clune, and Sugarman is the outstanding example of the negative standard approach.[20]
Fiscal neutrality requires that each school district receive the same
revenue for the same tax rate, that only those expenditure disparities
resulting from differences in local district taxable wealth are unlaw-
ful, or, put in the terminology of its proponents, "the quality of education must not be a function of wealth other than the wealth of the
state as a whole."[21] A negative fiscal neutrality standard satisfies the
requirement of flexibility because it does not require exact dollar
equality. Although the standard implicitly assumes a cost-quality
relationship with respect to the dollar variance among districts
caused by wealth differences, expenditures may fluctuate among districts for any reason other than district wealth. The larger question
of what differences other than wealth are legitimate is left unanswered, a real advantage to a court that desires to avoid deciding
that larger question. Fiscal neutrality, in other words, satisfies the
requirement of a judicially manageable standard, for a court need not
itself define what equal educational opportunity is in all its dimension. Judicial concern is concentrated solely on wealth-produced
expenditure disparities. Fiscal neutrality provides dollar flexibility, a
manageable standard, and by eliminating the contaminant of wealth,
significantly reduces current interdistrict expenditure disparities.

Yet the fiscal neutrality standard, although achieving some success
in state and lower federal courts,[22] was rejected by the United States
Supreme Court in *Rodriguez v. San Antonio Independent School
District*[23] and has been the subject of sharp criticism from commen-
tators, partly for not going far enough,[24] partly for going too far,[25]
and partly because the solution tendered by the Coons team—"district power equalizing"—was unacceptable.[26] A common criticism is
that under a power-equalized school finance system, expenditures
will still vary, not according to wealth, but according to tax rate.
Whereas Professor Coons would justify what he admits would be
qualitative differences in a power-equalized system on the basis of
local control, others have found that claim inconsistent with the
asserted fundamentality of education, for it would allow a child's
education to be poorer where the community was feckless. The criticism, in short, was that the negative definition did not go far enough,
did not reach to other equally impermissible variances in spending.
District power equalizing may itself be unconstitutional because

spending will vary with the chosen tax rate, an influence which may also be impermissible. Perhaps a more satisfactory approach would be to expand the negative standard to include other inequities. In any event, so long as there is consensus on what does *not* justify expenditure disparities, the negative definition of equality of educational opportunity should be regarded as a viable judicial approach to measuring equality.

Inputs

A sixth measure of equal educational opportunity is "inputs"—equality in the level of educational resources (which may vary in price between districts) brought to bear on a child's education. Such an approach is consistent with the historical origin of the equal protection clause, which is concerned with treating persons equally, not with making them equal. Justice Marshall, dissenting in *Rodriguez,* suggested such a standard: ". . . the question of discrimination in educational quality must be deemed to be an objective one that looks to what the State provides its children, not to what the children are able to do with what they receive."[27] Marshall, noting the disparities in teacher training, teacher-student ratio, and other resource inputs, argued that "[d]iscrimination in the opportunity to learn that is afforded a child must be our standard."[28]

Marshall's focus on objective educational inputs is firmly rooted in separate-but-equal cases such as *Sweatt v. Painter* where inputs, both tangible and intangible, were the standard of equality in comparing the University of Texas School of Law with the separate black law school:

[W] e cannot find substantial equality in the educational opportunities offered white and Negro law students by the State. In terms of number of the faculty, variety of courses and opportunity for specialization, size of the student body, scope of the library, availability of law review and similar activities, the University of Texas Law School is superior. What is more important, the University of Texas Law School possesses to a far greater degree those qualities which are incapable of objective measurement but which make for greatness in a law school. Such qualities, to name a few, include reputation of the faculty, experience of the administration, position and influence of the alumni, standing in the community, traditions and prestige. It is difficult to believe that one who had a free choice between these schools would consider the question close.[29]

More recently, Judge Wright in *Hobsen v. Hansen* declared that "if whites and blacks, or rich and poor, are to be consigned to separate schools pursuant to whatever policy, the minimum that the Constitution will require and guarantee is that for their objectively measurable aspects these schools be run on the basis of real equality."[30]

Although an objective approach is certainly desirable, an inputs standard, without more, not only fails to respond to countervailing scientific research as to the educational consequences of input disparities, but is subject to the same objections as an equal dollar standard. Equality of inputs is either a rigid standard that does not permit variations to meet special needs or costs, or, if variations are to be permitted, leaves the judiciary without adequate standards to determine when equality has been achieved.

Outputs

A seventh definition of equality of educational opportunity is "outputs"; that is, the effects of different educational investments are gauged in terms of pupil performance on standardized achievement tests. On the basis of social science research which finds an insignificant relationship between variation in expenditures and variation in test scores, the argument is made that disparities in expenditures do not result in unequal educational opportunities. Those courts that have been confronted with social science evidence of this sort have demonstrated an inability to deal with it adequately, largely because such evidence often goes unrebutted.[31] Seldom has the adversary process worked effectively so as to permit serious and thoughtful judicial examination of the cost-quality issue. The evidence presented is often only the tip of the social science iceberg, and often not analyzed carefully or expertly by lawyers on either side or by judges. Judicial opinions treat the social science evidence curtly and shallowly, and demonstrate a crucial lack of appreciation for the myriad of issues inherent in that evidence. The alien and imposing terminology of science has often found lawyers woefully unsuited to perform their adversary role and led judges to take repose in the seeming certainty of numbers. The intersection of law and social science is one of tension, nowhere more so than in educational inequality litigation. Before an outcome definition of equality is deemed acceptable, a more careful examination is due that intersection.

In Part One of this volume, several eminent social scientists have critically reviewed social science research evidence on school effectiveness. Each concludes that the state of the art of educational evaluation is too primitive to be relied on in making public policy decisions about education. Any effort to measure equality of educational opportunity in terms of student achievement must inevitably run the risk of masking actual school effects and of attributing to schools a failure to change those dimensions of achievement patterns not within their control. Because of the effect of other factors over which the school has no control, such as home background, schools cannot and should not be held accountable for the achievement patterns of students, for schools account for only part of the variation in achievement. In order accurately to assess the independent effect of school variables on achievement, controlled studies under experimental conditions are necessary before arriving at any causal conclusions about school effects.[32] In sum, considering the substantial problems arising from the use of standardized achievement test scores as measures of educational opportunity among school districts, and the substantial methodological difficulties in attempting to correlate school inputs with school outcomes, it seems unwise, at least at the present time, to use an output measure of equality of educational opportunity.

For purposes of educational inequality litigation, social science output research arguably can even be deemed legally irrelevant. Under the equal protection clause, the concern is with whether government treats people equally, not with making people equal or with equality of results emanating from a distributed benefit or with what extent people take advantage of the benefit, for the latter are beyond the capacity and power of governments and schools to control. Equal protection decisions have never required proof of the *effects* of unequal governmental treatment. As Professor Yudof has observed:

In *Sweatt v. Painter*, should the Court have decided not only that resources and facilities and intangible factors were unequal between the black and white law schools, but also that Mr. Sweatt would have been a more successful student and lawyer if he was permitted to attend the white institution? Must the reapportionment decisions fall if proof is not forthcoming that reapportioned legislatures act more responsibly and pass qualitatively superior legislation? Were the voting rights cases wrongly decided in the absence of proof that they would result in the election of different candidates?[33]

Indeed, without research, without testing by the state defendants (many states have no state-mandated testing program), there would be no way for school finance plaintiffs to prove injury. Where equality and equal protection analysis are concerned, the focus is on the rationality and fairness of how government distributes benefits, not with what people happen to do with those benefits. Input-output research would seem to be irrelevant to that inquiry. The words of Professor Edmond Cahn are singularly applicable here:

I would not have the constitutional rights of Negroes—or of other Americans—rest on any such flimsy foundation as some of the scientific demonstrations in these records [in *Brown v. Board of Education*, 347 U.S. 483 (1954)] ... [S]ince the behavioral sciences are so very young, imprecise, and changeful, their findings have an uncertain expectancy of life. Today's sanguine asseveration may be cancelled by tomorrow's new revelation—or new technical fad. It is one thing to use the current scientific findings, however ephemeral they may be, in order to ascertain whether the Legislature has acted reasonably in adopting some scheme of social or economic regulation; deference here is shown not so much to the findings as to the Legislature. It would be quite another thing to have our fundamental rights rise, fall, or change along with the latest fashions of psychological literature.[34]

Before deciding that education is at a deadend, which is the logical result of saying educational inequalities do not make a difference, important avenues of improvement must genuinely be exhausted. Until this is done, this society should not mortgage away tomorrow's human capital—and certainly not on the basis of exploratory research findings more defective than informative.

Minimum Adequacy

A final standard of equal educational opportunity is minimum adequacy, employed by the majority in *Rodriguez*.[35] In most states, a foundation program financing scheme is utilized, which is based on the premise that the state should guarantee every pupil a "minimum acceptable level of school support."[36] Above that level, districts are free to spend as they wish, but the revenue must be raised locally. A minimum adequacy definition predicates the foundation program as the limit of the state's responsibility for providing equality in its educational offering. So long as the state provides every child with a minimally adequate education, differences in spending beyond that specified minimum are not judicially significant. The adequacy standard is judicially manageable; it does not forbid expenditure differences, and it allows Courts neatly to avoid the necessity of resolving the cost-quality debate. No research challenges the importance of a basic minimum level of expenditure; the controversy relates to the educational consequences of spending inequalities above that basic level.[37] Justice Powell, influenced by the existence of this controversy and the lack of judicial tools for resolving it,[38] found an adequacy standard the solution to a vexing problem.

Yet the minimal adequacy perception of equality is not without serious difficulties. The extension of that test to any fundamental interest or to any other suspect classification other than wealth rests upon dubious legal precedent. In fact, Powell offers no authority to support such a claim. A cursory examination of voting and race cases will reveal the inaccuracy of the claim. In the reapportionment cases, the issue was not whether citizens were denied the right to vote; they were not. The issue was the relative importance of each vote. With respect to racial segregation, an era of "separate but equal" (not "separate but adequate") litigation weighs heavily against the adoption of a minimally adequate definition of equality. The issue in *Plessy v. Ferguson*[39] was not whether black citizens were denied boat transportation; they were not. The issue in *Sweatt v. Painter*[40] was not whether Sweatt was denied a legal education; he was not. The issue in desegregation cases after the *Plessy* rationale was discredited was not whether black children were denied an education; they were not. In each case, the inequality was relative. Adequacy and equality are not the same thing, and were never considered so prior to *Rodriguez*.

Nor does the adequacy standard enable courts to avoid the qualitative issue. As Justice Marshall's dissent correctly notes, the majority opinion does not specify applicable standards for determining what level of expenditure is constitutionally adequate.[41] Further, what may be adequate for one type of pupil may not be for another. Disadvantaged or handicapped students may require expenditures in addition to the foundation program guaranteed minimum expenditure level in order to receive an adequate education. Determining what those varying levels of adequacy are will require articulation of manageable standards. To rely on an equal dollar definition of adequacy (and the foundation program level of support is an equal dollar result) is no more defensible than to rely on an equal dollar definition of quality. Both standards are rigid and fail to permit justifiable variations. Marshall's criticism of Powell's double standard treatment is telling: "One would think that the majority would heed its own fervent affirmation of judicial self-restraint before undertaking the complex task of determining at large what level of education is constitutionally sufficient."[42]

There is an even more fundamental difficulty with the adequacy definition. The Texas system of financing public education was upheld because that system served a rational state purpose, that is, local fiscal control. Yet there is an inconsistency in using an adequacy standard to avoid resolving the social science debate while at the same time employing a justification for permitting relative spending disparities that itself presumes the existence of a cost-quality relationship. Justice Powell described the importance of local control in the following terms:

In part, local control means . . . the freedom to devote more money to the education of one's children. Equally important, however, is the opportunity it offers for participation in the decision-making process that determines how those local tax dollars will be spent. Each locality is free to tailor local programs to local needs. Pluralism also affords some opportunity for experimentation, innovation, and a healthy competition for educational excellence.[43]

Yet local control over financing and, thus, over program planning, occurs only above the state-guaranteed foundation program minimum level of expenditure. If local control means all that Justice Powell says it does, then a relationship between cost and quality must exist, for how else does a school district tailor local programs to local needs, experiment, innovate, or compete for academic excellence? Local control implies control over something that has meaningful content. If there is no relationship between cost and quality, then local control has no meaning and expenditure inequalities that use local control for their justification can have no rational basis.[44] For the system to be "rational" (at least if local control is the rational basis offered), the Court must go beyond an adequacy definition of equality. Justice Powell, in short, has employed a double standard, refusing to decide the cost-quality issue and then presuming the existence of the challenged relationship in order to justify the system's inequalities.

Because *Rodriguez* is law for the federal courts, there remains the question of what measure of inequality resulting from a state's school finance system will successfully support a federal claim for relief. One can speculate that in a state where the average per pupil expenditure substantially exceeds the foundation program minimum, where evidence supports the qualitative inadequacy of the minimum expenditure level, where there are demonstrated inadequacies in the educational programs of low-wealth districts, and where there exists little local option—factors that can currently be demonstrated in many states—a federal suit might succeed and still be consistent with *Rodriguez*. Focusing on a specific group of districts in which the programs and opportunities afforded are inadequate and in which the access to the financial wherewithal to remedy those inadequacies is effectively foreclosed will bring an important particularity to inter-district school finance litigation lacking in earlier fiscal neutrality litigation. The educational process will become paramount and fiscal issues secondary. The group of districts and the number of children will be smaller in number than that conceived in previous fiscal neutrality litigation, but more compelling because their plight is undeniable. State forums, however, are more likely to offer enhanced opportunities for successful school finance litigation. Whatever the forum, a more satisfactory approach to the problem of defining and measuring inequality of educational opportunity needs development.

LITIGATION STRATEGIES FOR RESOLVING
THE COST-QUALITY DEBATE

A Negative Inputs Standard

The preceding analysis of the social science research evidence may simply confirm the wisdom of regarding the qualitative issue, and the cases in which it is raised, as non-justiciable because of a lack of judicially manageable standards. Yet it would be unfortunate if this scientific debate removed disputes from the judicial process. Although courts are expected to reach correct and just decisions, a far more essential function of courts is to settle disputes as best they can. That function becomes more, not less, compelling when the dispute is difficult to resolve. To allow science to inhibit the functioning of the legal process is a foreboding precedent in a world becoming increasingly technocratic. It is particularly impor- tant that arbitrary inequalities in the way government treats individ- uals not be removed from judicial inquiry simply because there exists an unresolved and perhaps unresolvable scientific dispute over the effects of that differential treatment.

Given the standards of educational opportunity delineated in the first part of this chapter, what judicial approach is most likely to achieve equity in light of the social science debate over the efficacy of education? Straightforward definitions of equal educational opportunity must give way to hybrid solutions and a multiplicity of approaches developed to meet varying contexts.

Basically, we believe that a negative inputs or expenditures stan- dard of equal educational opportunity should be adopted. An inputs standard defines and evaluates educational opportunities in terms of the programs, services, and facilities made available to children, and thus is a "school concept" of educational opportunities. Inputs are chosen because the focus is on what the state provides to the child, not on what the child does with what the state provides him, as that is beyond the power of the school to control. The word "quality" should perhaps be avoided, for that connotes an attribute that goes beyond opportunity, beyond what the school itself provides.

An inputs standard alone would require an equal dollar revenue distribution and hence the negative standard applies. The focus is on what the state must not do, not what it must do or how it must distribute expenditures and resources. The concern is only with ex- penditure or input inequalities that lack rational justification, such as wealth-created disparities. The state is left free to vary expenditures and inputs in order to reflect variations in costs and needs.

We are not so disingenuous as to suggest that eliminating unjusti- fied financial disparities will achieve equal educational opportunity in all of its dimensions, only that a negative inputs standard preserves the dispute-settling function of the judiciary while at the same time is mindful of judicial limitations. While schools cannot be held re- sponsible for the test performance of children, they can be held accountable for the quality of the school services provided, the "inputs" to the educational process. Schools cannot make children equal, but what they provide to children can be made equal, with appropriate adjustments for special problems such as the need for compensatory, vocational or special education. Money, of course, is not the whole answer, but it is the instrument by which a district can purchase the needed inputs to attain educational excellence. Opinions vary on how districts can most wisely and efficiently invest their financial resources to achieve the highest possible quality of educational opportunity. But there is no disagreement that the level of financial resources available to a district is an ever present factor that constrains a district's effort to perform its mission. At the very least, equality of financial resources is a threshold condition for achieving equality of educational opportunity.

Application of the Standard

Proof of the input-opportunity relationship in the affirmative case should be limited to demonstrating existing inequalities in inputs and to presenting testimony of school personnel on the educational consequences of input disparities. Research evidence should be avoided during the affirmative case and held for rebuttal, a strategy consistent with the notion that output research is not relevant to equal protection analysis. Input evidence alone should establish a prima facie case of inequality of educational opportunity. Plaintiffs should prevail where no social science evidence is offered to rebut the input-opportunity relationship or where such evidence is deemed legally irrelevant.

The cost-quality relationship may also be regarded as admitted because of the conduct of the state in encouraging spending above the foundation plan, and the testimony of state and local defendants that expenditures beyond the foundation program can be important educationally if spent wisely. Assertions by the defendants regarding the value of local control also represent an admission on the cost-quality issue, for the very concept of local control predicates a relationship between cost and quality.

Where social science research evidence is offered in school finance litigation to rebut the input-opportunity relationship and that evidence is accepted by the trial court in resolving the cost-quality issue, the burden of proof can be shifted to defendants who are challenging the legislative declaration of fact underlying the entire financing structure, *i.e.,* that money matters. In effect, in school finance litigation plaintiffs are contending that state financing statutes declare the cost-quality relationship, and defendants are contending that there are no rational bases for those explicit and implicit statutory declara-

tions. This is a unique reversal of positions in constitutional litigation. If the state is to be permitted to question what should be
viewed as legislative factual determinations, then the burden of proof
in such an inquiry should properly rest with the party challenging the
validity of such statutes.[45]

Defendants' research evidence should be rejected for still another
reason. Wealth-created expenditure disparities have been defended on
the ground that the school finance system advances the state interest
in encouraging local fiscal control, an argument that was accepted by
the United States Supreme Court in *Rodriguez*. Yet there is a fatal
inconsistency between defending the system on the basis of local
control and contending that cost and quality are not related. As already argued, if expenditure disparities above some base level
expenditure have no educational consequence, then local control has
no meaning and there would be no state interest that would validate
the financing system. If the state purports to defend the system's
irregularities on the basis that expenditures above some minimum
level are, in effect, wasted, then the local control justification ought
not to be available to it or, alternatively, the state should bear the
burden of proof in demonstrating the rationality of the local control
justification. Indeed, by proving that money is unimportant past a
minimum level, the state has offered proof against itself and high-
spending districts of such a serious nature as to warrant a taxpayers'
suit against the state and/or high-spending school districts for an illegal expenditure of public funds.

CONCLUSION

The strategies offered here for measuring equality and for
resolving the cost-quality issue are specific, practical, and operational. They are designed solely for the narrow context of the judicial process. No specific school finance system is proposed as a
remedy; that is the function of the legislature. Our suggestions are
intended simply to preserve the dispute-settling function of the legal
process against a threatened erosion by the intimidating aura of
scientific certainty. Science is responsible for a quantum increase in
the complexities surrounding the mission and importance of schooling, yet institutional decisionmaking must adapt to that complexity,
must preserve its integrity and independence. Nowhere is the very

effectiveness of our institutions to adapt to scientific complexity being more tested than in the cost-quality debate in school finance litigation.

NOTES

1. James S. Coleman *et al., Equality of Educational Opportunity,* Office of Education, National Center for Educational Statistics, OE 38001 (Washington, D.C.: Government Printing Office, 1966). Hereafter cited as Coleman Report.

2. G. Hodgson, "Do Schools Make a Difference?" *Atlantic Monthly* (March 1973), 35-46.

3. *See generally* F. Mosteller and D. Moynihan (eds.), *On Equality of Educational Opportunity* (New York: Random House, 1972).

4. Christopher Jencks *et al., Inequality: A Reassessment of the Effects of Family and Schooling in America* (New York: Basic Books, 1972).

5. That an attempt was made to do so is suggested in D. Moynihan, "Sources of Resistance to the Coleman Report," *Harvard Educational Review* 38(1968), 23.

6. James S. Coleman, "The Concept of Equality of Educational Opportunity," *Harvard Educational Review* 38(1968), 7.

7. "Presumably students receiving a $1000 education are better educated than [sic] those acquiring a $600 schooling." *McInnis v. Shapiro,* 293 F. Supp. 327, 331 (N.D. Ill. 1968), *affd mem. sub nom. McInnis v. Ogilvie,* 394 U.S. 322 (1969).

8. *See Jensen v. State Bd. of Tax Comm'rs.* No. 24,474 (Ind. Cir Ct., Jan. 15, 1973).

9. In 1968, Arthur Wise suggested nine definitions of equality of educational opportunity: (1) negative, (2) full-opportunity, (3) foundation, (4) minimum-attainment, (5) leveling, (6) competition, (7) equal-dollars-per-pupil, (8) maximum variance ratio, and (9) classification. A. Wise, *Rich Schools, Poor Schools* (Chicago: University of Chicago Press, 1969), 143-59. Wise's standards have been criticized as being too vague for judicial use (David Kirp, Book Review, *Yale Law Journal* 78(1969), 908, 915), yet courts again and again have unknowingly utilized these standards, or variations thereof.

10. *McInnis v. Shapiro,* 293 F. Supp. 327 (N.D. Ill. 1968), *affd mem. sub nom. McInnis v. Ogilvie,* 394 U.S. 322 (1969).

11. 293 F. Supp. at 335.

12. *Ibid.,* 331, n11.

13. In holding the state's system of financing schools unconstitutional, a lower court in Idaho said that the state is not "obligated to insure that all districts have the same dollar input per pupil. The state may recognize differences in educational costs so long as the differences are based on relevant economic and educational factors." *Thompson v. Engelking,* Civil No. 47,055 (Idaho Dist. Ct., Nov. 16, 1973).

14. 293 F. Supp. at 332.

15. *Ibid.*, 335.

16. 310 F. Supp. 572 (W.D. Va. 1969), *affd mem.* 397 U.S. 44 (1970).

17. *Ibid.*, 574.

18. *Sweetwater County Planning Comm. v. Hinkle*, 491 P.2d 1234, 1238 (Wyo. 1971), *juris. reling.*, 493 P.2d 1050 (Wyo. 1972).

19. 327 F. Supp. 844, 863-64 (D.D.C. 1971).

20. J. Coons, W. Clune, and S. Sugarman, *Private Wealth and Public Education* (Cambridge, Mass.: Harvard University Press, 1970).

21. *Ibid.*, 2.

22. *Rodriguez v. San Antonio Independent School Dist.*, 337 F. Supp. 280 (W.D. Tex. 1971); *Van Dusartz v. Hatfield*, 334 F. Supp. 870 (D. Minn. 1971); *Serrano v. Priest*, 5 Cal. 3d 584, 487 P.2d 1241, 96 Cal. Rptr. 601 (1971); *Caldwell v. Kansas*, Civil No. 50,616 (Kan. Cir. Ct., Aug. 30, 1972).

23. 411 U.S. 1 (1973).

24. Berke and Callahan, "*Serrano v. Priest*: Milestone or Millstone," *Journal of Public Law* 21(1972), 23.

25. Paul D. Carrington, "Financing the American Dream: Equality and School Taxes," *Columbia Law Review* 73(1973), 1227; Stephen R. Goldstein, "Interdistrict Irregularities in School Financing: A Critical Analysis of *Serrano v. Priest* and Its Progeny," *University of Pennsylvania Law Review* 120(1972), 504.

26. S. Michelson, "What is a 'Just' System for Financing Schools? An Evaluation of Alternative Reforms," *Law and Contemporary Problems* 38(1974).

27. 411 U.S. at 84.

28. *Ibid.*

29. 339 U.S. 629, 633-34 (1950).

30. 269 F. Supp. at 496.

31. *Hollins v. Shofstall*, No. C-253652 (Ariz. Super. Ct., June 1, 1972), *rev'd*, 110 Ariz. 88, 515 P.2d 590 (1973); *Jensen v. State Bd. of Tax Comm'rs*, No. 24,474 (Ind. Cir. Ct., Jan. 15, 1973); *Robinson v. Cahill*, 62 N.J. 473, 303 A.2d 273 (1973).

32. See Gilbert and Mosteller, "The Urgent Need for Experimentation" in F. Mosteller and D. Moynihan (eds.), *On Equality of Educational Opportunity, op. cit.*, 371.

33. Mark Yudof, "Equal Educational Opportunity and the Courts," *Texas Law Review* 51(1973), 411, 504.

34. E. Cahn, "Jurisprudence," *New York University Law Review* 30(1955), 150, 157-58, 167.

35. 411 U.S. at 25, 37, 45.

36. California Education Code § 17300 (West 1969).

37. "[I]t must be stressed again that we are not assessing the *absolute* effect of schools on achievement but rather the effect of schools on variation in achievement levels. We have no doubt that schools have an overall baseline effect. This baseline effect is probably fairly uniform for all schools, because school factors may be relatively equalized with respect to minimum standards. But, given variation in verbal achievement, especially that between black and white students, we are searching for factors which might reduce the difference.

School factors may be important for a certain basic level of achievement, but this does not necessarily mean that *improving* those factors will help bring black achievement closer to white achievement. If one wants to reduce this differential, Coleman's and our analyses point to family-background factors as the more promising area for improvement." David Armor, "School and Family Effects on Black and White Achievement: A Re-examination of the USOE Data," in F. Mosteller and D. Moynihan (eds.), *On Equality of Educational Opportunity, op. cit.,* 225.

38. Justice Powell declared that the judiciary would be "well advised to refrain from interposing on the states inflexible constitutional restraints that could circumscribe or handicap the continued research and experimentation so vital to finding even partial solutions to educational problems and to keeping abreast of ever-changing conditions." 411 U.S. at 43.

39. 163 U.S. 537 (1896).

40. 339 U.S. 637 (1950).

41. *Ibid.,* 89.

42. *Ibid.*

43. *Ibid.,* 49-50.

44. "While the correlation between expenditure per pupil and the quality of education may be open to argument, the Court must assume here that it is high. To do otherwise would be to hold that in those wealthy districts where the per pupil expenditure is higher than some real or imaginary norm, the school boards are merely wasting the taxpayers' money. The Court is not willing to so hold, absent some strong evidence. Even those who staunchly advocate that the disparities here complained of are the result of local control and that such control and taxation with the resulting inequality should be maintained would not be willing to concede that such local autonomy results in waste or inefficiency." *Van Dusartz v. Hatfield,* 334 F. Supp. 870, 874 (D. Minn. 1971).

45. Such an approach was used in *Hobsen v. Hansen,* 327 F. Supp. 844, 860-61 (D.D.C. 1971), *Natonabah v. Board of Education,* 355 F. Supp. 716, 724 (D.N.M. 1973), and *Larry P. v. Riles,* 343 F. Supp. 1306, 1309 (N.D. Cal. 1972).

8. Equal Educational Opportunity and the Distribution of Educational Expenditures

HENRY M. LEVIN

Public educational investment represents the principal method by which our society attempts to equalize opportunity among children born into different circumstances. Given the crucial conceptual role of the educational system, the allocation of public funds for the attainment of equal educational opportunity has become a focal social concern in recent years. In 1971, the California Supreme Court, in the landmark case of Serrano v. Priest,[1] declared that the California system of financing education "with its substantial dependence on local property taxes and resultant wide disparities in school revenue, violates the equal protection clause of the Fourteenth Amendment . . . because it makes the quality of a child's education a function of the wealth of his parents and neighbors." Although a similar challenge to the Texas scheme of financing education was rejected by the United States Supreme Court in San

This paper was prepared for a special issue of Education and Urban Society, published in February 1973, and addressed to educational financing in light of Serrano v. Priest. The author has drawn heavily upon his reports to the New York State Commission on the Quality, Cost and Financing of Elementary and Secondary Education. Reprinted, with minor revisions, from Education and Urban Society 5(February 1973), 149-72, by permission of the publisher, Sage Publications, Inc.

Antonio Independent School District v. Rodriguez,[2] recent victories in state courts in New Jersey, Idaho, and California suggest a thorough overhaul of the traditional mechanisms for financing education.

In response, state legislatures and the federal government have initiated a frenzied search for alternatives for supporting the schools.[3] In some states, there are recommendations for a shift to income and sales taxes, while in others the legislatures are considering statewide, uniform property taxes. There are indications that the federal government may also get into the act with the President's announcement in early 1972 that a federal value-added tax is being studied as a substitute for the school-related property tax levy.[4]

The emphasis in both the legal cases and the recent federal activity has been on the improvement of equity with regard to the support of the educational function. That is, the palliatives to the traditional approach have stressed primarily the criterion of fairness in the underlying system of taxation. Much less research and discussion have been generated on the optimal distribution of educational investment among children of social groups. This is especially surprising given the substantial discussion in recent years on the difficulty of achieving equal educational opportunity among youngsters born into disadvantaged circumstances.[5]

The purpose of this paper is to address the distribution and composition of educational investment among social classes. Though a more equitable educational system might improve relative opportunities among children from modest circumstances, there is abundant evidence that suggests we cannot and should not rely upon the educational system alone for this task. Even with the same nominal amounts of schooling, it appears that nonwhites earn considerably less than whites and that persons from lower socioeconomic origins show lower occupational, income and educational attainments than persons from higher origins.[6] Whether this is due to discrimination or to a class structure that reproduces itself is beyond the scope of this study.[7] Yet it is important to assert at the outset that educational reform is not a substitute for social reform, although the former can certainly be an integral part of the latter.[8]

EQUALITY OF EDUCATIONAL OPPORTUNITY

Any attempt to equalize educational opportunity must begin with the rationale for doing so. Definitions of equal educational opportunity such as "equal access to education," or "enabling each child to maximize his potential" abound in the educational literature, but they offer little insight into educational policy. Both of these suffer from ambiguity since they are subject to a wide variety of interpretations. Moreover, what applications are attempted tend to define education as only *formal schooling*, despite the plethora of educational experiences and influences that take place outside the schools.

If we return to the origins of the American public schools, we see that the discussion and ferment that led to universal public schooling was heavily dominated by the conception that education was the best path to "equal opportunity." Indeed the rise of the "common school" is associated with the often-quoted statement by Horace Mann: "Education, then, beyond all other devices of human origin, is the great equalizer of the conditions of men—the balance-wheel of the social machinery."[9]

This movement did not represent a quest for a classless society as much as it reflected a search for fairness in the race for life's rewards. As Tyack suggests:

For the most part the workingman did not seek to pull down the rich; rather, they sought equality of opportunity for their children, an equal chance at the main chance. Indeed, in their arguments they appealed, as did the conservatives, to the past: they were only trying to realize "those cardinal principles of republican liberty which were declared in '76, and which can only be sustained by the adoption of an ample system of public instruction, calculated to impart equality as well as mental culture. . . ." When Robert Owen and his followers in New York suggested that all children be taken from their parents and educated in boarding schools where they should have the same food, clothes, and instruction, the workingmen rebelled. They did not want a classless society, nor did they wish to disrupt the basic social institution, the family. Disadvantaged they might be, but they were proud and hoped to better their lot within society as it was.[10]

That is, equality of opportunity in this sense would not lead to equality of outcomes; for it was tacitly recognized that a functioning society required manual laborers, farmers, clerks, and mechanics, as well as lawyers, physicians, managers, and professors. By equality of opportunity was meant "an equal start for all children in the race for life, but their assumption was that some would go farther than others."[11] Differences in ability, effort, luck, and preferences would create differences in outcomes among individuals, but the common school would assure that representative individuals born into any social class would have the same opportunity to achieve status as persons born into other social classes. That is, the opportunities for achieving life success for a son would not be determined by his father's achievements, but only by his own. This major accomplishment would be attained through the common school such that " 'all men are born free and equal'; which equality is preserved until destroyed by the varying degrees of personal merit."[12]

Of note was the fact that equal educational opportunity was considered to be the antecedent for equal opportunity per se. That is, the goal of the common school was equal opportunity and equal educational opportunity represented the means of achieving the goal. Implicit in this policy was the view that, in a just society, the average child from any social origin would begin his adult life with equal chances of success relative to that of a child from another stratum.

It is now clear, in retrospect, that the schools have not achieved this goal. Occupational success, scholastic achievement, and educational attainment of children are still positively correlated with those of parents, although the correlations might have been even higher in the absence of universal schooling.[13] The children of the poor will experience lower incomes, poorer housing, lower occupational status, substandard medical care, and other deficiencies relative to children born into higher socioeconomic strata. The failure of the common school to achieve the social mobility dream must surely raise questions about the role of schooling in achieving equality. Is the job too great for the schools to achieve or is the failure due to a lack of a social structure and commitment that would enable us to truly equalize life's chances for the children of our society?[14]

Human Capital Embodiment

One way of answering that question is to analyze the nature of the task with regard to its implications for educational policy. A useful method of doing this is to view the problem in the context of human capital formation. The concept of human capital has enabled the economist to study how investments in health, education, and training of people lead to increasing productivity and welfare. In essence, the productivity of a population can be related to its human capital embodiment, which is in turn determined by investments in housing, health, nutrition, education, training, and so on.[15]

When translated into monetary terms such as increased labor productivity, it appears that the return on investment in human capital often exceeds the return on physical capital (buildings, equipment, etc.).[16]

Let us assume a world in which the opportunities of a particular group of persons are determined solely by the amount of human capital which they possess. That is, we presume that there exists no discrimination in either labor or consumer markets, so that opportunities are determined only by capabilities reflected in human capital embodiment. In such a world, those populations with less human capital would always achieve less lifetime success than those with larger endowments. Indeed, that is the plight faced by children born into disadvantaged families, for by reason of birth alone their families will be able to invest less in them than will their counterparts in more advantaged circumstances.

Families from low socioeconomic origins have a much lesser ability to invest in their offspring in a large variety of areas that affect child development. Before birth, the lower-social-class child is more likely to face prenatal malnutrition.[17] It appears that such nutritional deficiencies may stunt the development of the brain and learning ability.[18] He is less likely to receive adequate medical and dental care as well, so he is more prone to suffer from a large variety of undetected, undiagnosed, and untreated health problems.

The meager income levels associated with lower socioeconomic families translate into less-adequate housing services as they affect child development. Substandard housing exacerbates health problems through inadequate plumbing, increased probability of fires, and other accidents, deficient protection from the elements, and a higher probability of rodents and vermin. As expected, substandard housing tends to be concentrated heavily among the poor and nonwhite.[19] Moreover, children need space and privacy to grow and develop skills that require thought and concentration. The Census Bureau assumes that more than one person per room represents an overcrowded condition, and in 1960 there were about 4 million households living in *standard* units that were overcrowded. For the population as a whole, "three out of ten nonwhite households were crowded in 1960, and one out of ten white households."[20] Research suggests that housing characteristics bear a direct relationship to both the health and productivity of their occupants.[21]

Special Role of the Family

In addition to deficiencies in nutrition, medical services, and shelter, families from lower socioeconomic backgrounds are less able to provide other material inputs which increase human capital. For example, limited family income inhibits or precludes travel and exposure to the large variety of worldly experiences that increase the knowledge and sophistication of the more advantaged child. Perhaps even more important, both the quality and the quantity of parental services as they affect human capital embodiment and future productivity tend to be lower for the disadvantaged child.

Such children are more likely to receive limited parental attention because they are frequently situated in families with many children and where one or both parents are missing.[22] Moreover, in nonwhite families, the mother is more likely to have a job in order to augment the inadequate family income.[23] Further, the lower educational levels of the parents themselves limit the amount of knowledge that they can transmit to their children.[24] While this is a particular drawback in the area of verbal skill development, it is also an inhibiting factor in the embodiment of the more general psychosocial behavior which is required for participation in existing social institutions.[25] The result is that parents with greater educational attainment themselves inculcate in their children much higher skill levels than do parents with less education. Indeed, the association of parental education and socioeconomic status with children's scholastic performance is probably the most consistent finding in studies of academic achievement.[26]

Implications for Financing Equal Educational Opportunity

In summary, if we use the human capital paradigm for diagnosing the problem of moving toward equal opportunity, we can draw the following inferences:

1. To put children born into different social classes on the same starting line for life's rewards will require equal capital embodiment among such groups of persons at the time that they have attained adulthood. This criterion assumes the absence of discrimination against persons from disadvantaged backgrounds. To overcome the obstacles of discrimination may require greater capital embodiment in the children drawn from lower social strata and racial minorities.

2. Differences in capital embodiment among populations stem from many sources, including housing, health services, nutrition, and family investment in educational services and experiences.

3. There is every indication that the differences in capital embodiment when valued in monetary terms are massive, and equalization will require both a heavy social commitment and prodigious public expenditures.

If equal opportunity depends upon equal capital embodiment, then the very circumstances into which the disadvantaged child is born will mean a lower level of investment, capital embodiment, and opportunity for him than for his more advantaged counterpart. Only government intervention is capable of reducing this inequality, since the family and other private sources of investment will always tend to reinforce the disproportionately higher capital embodiment in middle- and upper-class children.

The common school reformers believed that universal public schooling alone could equalize opportunity, partly because they tacitly underestimated the extent of capital embodiment disparities and partly because they had an enormous amount of faith in the efficacy of formal schooling.[27] Indeed, in the mid-nineteenth century, it was probably quite reasonable to believe that equal schooling would give everyone the same chances. First, it was obvious in those days that persons with the highest educations shared the most enviable positions in government and enterprise, so education appeared to be the great path to mobility. Second, the concept of the common school, where children of the rich and poor would sit side by side receiving the same indoctrination conjured images of unprecedented equality. This was particularly poignant in contrast with the elitist educational institutions and social structures of Europe. Taken together, the expectation was that the then revolutionary concept of universal common schooling in a unique society like America could equalize opportunity for all of its citizens.[28]

But, given the assumptions of the capital embodiment model, even equal schooling between children drawn from different social classes will not equalize proficiencies and opportunities. Rather, adding the same educational investment to each group will merely sustain the absolute differences in human capital. Clearly, to equalize capital embodiment will require far greater public investments in the disadvantaged than in the advantaged child if the "opportunity gap" is to be closed. Not only does the child from a disadvantaged background begin school with lower capital embodiment, but he receives less in terms of nonschooling investments even while attending schools. If educational investment is going to narrow the gap, it follows that more must be spent on the education of the disadvantaged child than the advantaged one. How much more depends upon the effectiveness of educational investment in increasing the productive capital of the disadvantaged as well as the urgency with which equality is desired.

The construction of a plan for financing equal educational opportunity is faced with a myriad of difficulties. Although the previous section outlined a criterion for assessing equality, it is not an easily measurable one. Moreover, the traditional concepts of schooling might not yield easily to necessary changes given that they protect many powerful vested interests. Yet, it is possible to set out certain principles that can be operationalized in such a way as to improve the probability of equal outcome (even if not fully attaining it). Bowles takes a more pessimistic view.[29]

Commitment to Equality

Before proceeding, it is important to note one other obstacle to creating a fairer system of educational finance. It is not clear that there exists a powerful commitment to equality in the manner that we have outlined in the previous section.[30] To achieve equal educational opportunity in this sense will require a transfer of wealth (taxes) from the richer and more powerful to the poorer and weaker segments of the population. Any legislator who votes in favor of such a plan is voting in favor of reducing the lead in the race for life's rewards for children from the upper classes. To add insult to injury, the middle-class parent would be expected to pay to decrease his own child's life chances while enhancing those of the child from lower origins. Yet consider that the political support for most legislators comes from lobbyists who represent interests of middle- and upper-class America as well as voters whose financial contributions, political participation, and ballots are heavily weighted in favor of richer constituents.

If the first rule of politics is self-survival, then few legislators will show the altruism to increase taxes for the middle and upper classes to effect a salutary improvement in the life conditions of the lower classes. This is not to say that minimal social welfare programs will not be supported, for this society has developed a clear commitment to ensuring a bureaucratic-type subsistence for the poor. But such subsistence programs represent insurance against civil disruption much more than serious attempts at equalizing opportunities. Public welfare programs allow life to proceed for the poor in a dreary, underhoused, underfed, undignified, publicly spied upon, and routinized way, but they do not promote social mobility or self-reliance.[31]

Unfortunately, even among the many legislators who espouse egalitarian goals, a personal commitment to this philosophy is not tantamount to a political commitment. The realities of political life force many public representatives to compromise their consciences at the roll call. Nevertheless, one can still ask what criteria might be used to finance equal educational opportunity if that millennium were to arrive. Accordingly, the remainder of this paper will outline those guidelines by discussing the necessary composition of compensatory education programs, the size of the compensatory investment, the definition of "disadvantaged," and a heuristic application.

Composition of Compensatory Educational Investment

Capital embodiment in a population is defined as the sum of investments from a variety of origins that determine that group's productive capabilities. Sources of such investment include parental interactions, nutrition, health, shelter, and formal education among others. That the disadvantaged share less of these inputs over their lives than the advantaged is a prime cause of inequality of opportunity. Thus, the goal of society would appear to be to equalize average capital embodiment in some sense between the advantaged and the disadvantaged.

If increased educational investment in the disadvantaged is the policy instrument by which this is to be achieved, there exists a basic contradiction in defining the nature of that educational investment. Assume a capital embodiment function,

$$K_{it} = f[M_{i(t)}, D_{i(t)}, N_{i(t)}, S_{i(t)}, F_{i(t)}, I_{i(t)}] \qquad [1]$$

Let K_{it} represent the total capital embodied in the ith population at time t; $M_{i(t)}$ represents the cumulative investment up to time t for medical services; $D_{i(t)}$ signifies the cumulative investment to time t for dental services; $N_{i(t)}$ denotes a comparable measure for nutritional inputs; $S_{i(t)}$ represents the inputs from shelter; $F_{i(t)}$ signifies the cumulative inputs to time t from family interactions and experiences; and $I_{i(t)}$ represents the cumulative effect of the formal instructional services of the school.

In order to understand the nature of educational investment, it is necessary to delineate the relations among these variables in obtaining capital embodiment. Since capital embodiment is defined as the total investment in a population that enables that group to pursue productive opportunities (jobs, income, political power, and so on), it is important to note that not all investment is productive in this sense. For example, beyond certain nutritional requirements, additional dietary inputs do not contribute to the productivity of the individual. Rather, they are eliminated from the body or stored in the fatty tissues, and an excess of alimentary inputs over actual needs for growth and maintenance will be wasted (or even injurious). This is likely to be true of all of the sources of input into capital embodiment function. That is, it is probable that the law of diminishing marginal returns is applicable to the investment function such that concentration on any single source of investment will be wasteful or at least less optimal than dividing investment over all of the requisite inputs.

A second assumed property of [1] is that the effect of any additional input through one source of investment will probably depend upon the levels of investment from other sources. For example, a child with inadequate nutrition or medical care (e.g., untreated vision problems) will likely have a much greater difficulty in learning for any level of instructional inputs than a child who has received higher levels of investment in N and M.

Both these properties suggest that, if equality must be brought about through educational policy alone, then educational services must include far more than instructional services.[32] To a certain degree, the various investment sources might represent substitutes for each other in producing capital embodiment. For example, good instructional services may be able to compensate for many of the educational inputs that the family would normally provide. Yet, as we noted in a previous example, instructional services are probably not substitutable for a protein or vitamin B deficiency, a need for eyeglasses, or a debilitating systemic infection. Accordingly, the compensatory educational budget must be allocated among a variety of investment inputs to obtain a substantial increase in productive capital embodiment of the disadvantaged.

Certainly, the schools have made nominal efforts in these directions with their provision of minimal dental services, free or low-cost milk programs, school lunches, and so on. Both Title I of the Elementary and Secondary Education Act of 1965 and Head Start emphasized that the provision of such "life support" services were legitimate educational inputs.[33] Yet their importance has been understated in the actual world of expenditures, where the lion's share of so-called compensatory monies is allocated to reduced class sizes and for remedial reading and other instructional specialties.

In the view of this researcher, a much greater portion of investment for equalizing the opportunity for the disadvantaged must take the noninstructional route. More specifically, the following areas of investment are suggestive.

1. A full range of medical and dental services must be considered for children from families who have been excluded from the privileged world of regular and competent diagnosis and treatment. Emphasis should be not only on remedial aspects of health, but also on preventive ones.

2. The role of the schools in providing adequate nutrition should be explored. School breakfasts, as well as free dietary supplements, might represent ways in which the educational system could aid nutrition.

3. Alternatives to private provision of shelter are difficult to suggest. Clearly, study space and room for other activities might be provided for students from substandard and overcrowded housing. Personal development often requires privacy, conditions that may be physically impossible to attain in the existing housing of students from disadvantaged backgrounds.

4. Family inputs can be enhanced through greater school-community involvement. Some methods of doing this include the use of the school for community activities and as a community center as well as the initiation of programs that require parental input, such as tutoring. A greater policymaking role for the community is also a possible approach to increasing family inputs.[34]

5. Instructional inputs have been the traditional area in which school strategies have been implemented. Unfortunately, the specific approaches that have been adopted have often been unimaginative, with heaviest emphasis on increasing personnel within existing programs rather than altering the very programs that have most often been characterized by failure.[35]

More attention must be devoted to alternative instructional approaches if the efficacy of instructional expenditures is to rise.

Thus, equalizing investment for the disadvantaged requires a broad array of programs, not just instructional ones. Unless instructional inputs are completely substitutable for nutritional, health, and other inputs in contributing to the physical, cognitive, and emotional development of youngsters, it will not be possible to achieve equality of opportunity through instructional programs alone. Moreover, even if it were technically possible to substitute heavy doses of instruction for health and other deficiencies, it is likely to represent a very costly strategy relative to a more balanced approach. This can be illustrated by [2] and [3]. The former represents a budget for achieving equality of opportunity.

$$B_{it} = P_1 M_t + P_2 D_t + P_3 N_t + P_4 S_t + P_5 F_t + P_6 I_t \qquad [2]$$

B_{it} represents the budget during the period t for increasing the capital embodiment of the ith population, and $(P_1, P_2, \ldots, P_6)$ represent the unit costs for each additional input of medical services, dental services, nutritional services, shelter, family services, and instructional services, respectively.

Assume that we wish to minimize the budget required to obtain a particular level of capital embodiment during the next period $K_{i(t+1)}$ for the disadvantaged population. Given a choice of the various types of investments in the capital embodiment function 1 and their relative costs $(P_1, \ldots, P_6)$, we wish to determine the minimum budget (total cost) necessary to reach $K_{i(t+1)}$. The standard cost-minimization model would lead to the investment guideline represented by [3], where total investment would be allocated among all inputs until their ratios of marginal products of capital embodiment relative to cost per unit of input were equal for all inputs. Now, if all

$$\frac{\partial K_i/\partial M}{P_i} = \frac{\partial K_i/\partial D}{P_2} = \ldots = \frac{\partial K_i/\partial I}{P_6} \qquad [3]$$

investment were limited to instructional inputs, [3] would be violated, as in [4].

$$\frac{\partial K_i/\partial M}{P_i} = \frac{\partial K_i/\partial D}{P_2} = \ldots > \frac{\partial K_i/\partial I}{P_6} \qquad [4]$$

In the case of [4], the overinvestment in instruction has yielded a smaller contribution to capital embodiment than other alternative investments. Thus, a larger total budget is required than if resources were allocated among all inputs according to their additional productivities. This is the case where an expenditure on eyeglasses or nutritious breakfasts represents a less costly way of increasing student proficiencies than reductions in class size or than alternative instructional approaches. Even if such narrow indicators of capital embodiment as reading scores are used, there is *no* evidence to suggest that instructional investments are more effective relative to their costs than other strategies.[36]

The Magnitude of Differential Investment

The logic of greater educational expenditures on the disadvantaged is straightforward, but the magnitude of the differential must depend on a number of factors. These factors include the relative efficacy of educational investment for achieving equality, the priority for achieving equality, and institutional constraints on expenditure policy.

One way of determining the relative efficacy of educational investment for achieving equality is to think of minimum and maximum values between which there is a range of equalizing effects. That is, let us assume that average educational expenditures on nondisadvantaged children can be represented by E, and we wish to spend more than E for disadvantaged ones. Since the differential in expenditures between the two groups can be characterized by its relationship to E, we can conceive of the ratio d, which denotes the additional multiple of E that is applied to educational spending on disadvantaged students. Thus, per pupil expenditures on each group can be characterized by E for advantaged students and $(E + dE)$ for disadvantaged ones. If $d = 1$, then spending on the disadvantaged would be twice that on the advantaged; a value of $d = .5$ denotes a 50 percent differential, and so on.[37]

What should be the minimum and maximum values for d? The minimum value should be set at the threshold level, where differential expenditures bring about differential effects. Since the advantaged student continues to receive higher levels of capital investment from his family and other sources during the school period, a minimum differential is needed simply to compensate for ongoing differences in out-of-school influences.[38] Thus, a minimum effort might be needed in order to obtain any effect. The maximum possible value would depend on that point at which additional expenditures yielded no additional increment to human capital. That is, at some point a saturation level is reached, so that additional spending during that period will have no effect on increasing human capital among the disadvantaged relative to that of the advantaged.

Figure 8-1 shows the illustrative minima and maxima for differential educational expenditures in favor of the disadvantaged under three sets of investment decisions. The schedule represented by $f_1(I)$

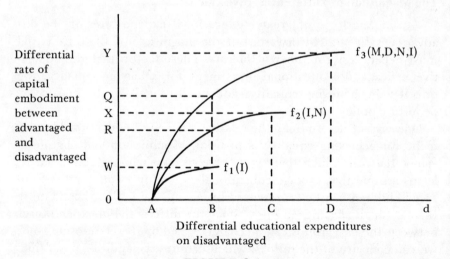

FIGURE 8-1
Illustrative Minima and Maxima for Differential Educational
Expenditures on the Disadvantaged

assumes that investment can be channeled to the disadvantaged only through instructional approaches; $f_2(I, N)$ signifies the hypothetical investment relationship when nutritional and instructional approaches are used; and $f_3(M, D, N, I)$ denotes the differential investment effect when medical, dental, nutritional, and instructional services are combined in compensatory programs.

In this illustration, a minimum differential of A is required in order to obtain a threshold difference in the rate of capital embodiment between the advantaged and disadvantaged. That is, A represents the minimum value for d at which educational investment differences in favor of the disadvantaged will increase human capital at a faster rate for the disadvantaged than for the advantaged.

While the minimum differential is shown as being invariant in this illustration, the maximum is dependent on the nature of the investment. The saturation point where additional investment fails to contribute to differential capital embodiment is at B for instructional approaches alone, at C for instruction and nutrition combined, and at D for medical, dental, nutritional, and instructional services combined. That is, the maximum differential is an increasing function of the range of services included in the compensatory investment. When the instructional route alone is selected, the saturation point is reached quickly, while, when investment is distributed across a wider range of services, the potential maximum differential for addressing the equalization of capital embodiment between the two populations is much higher.

A second characteristic of Figure 8-1 is that the rate of equalization per amount of differential investment is an increasing function of the range of services offered. At the saturation point for instructional services alone, B, the rate of equalization is W; but if the same differential $(d=B)$ were applied to instruction and nutritional services, a rate of equalization R would be attained; and if the wider range of services reflected by f_3 were utilized, the rate of equalization of capital embodiment would be higher yet at Q. This phenomenon is reflected by [3] and [4], suggesting that the larger the range of compensatory services offered, the greater the impact of differential expenditures.

Yet, minimum and maximum differentials yield only the technically feasible values that might be applied to compensatory spending. The actual level selected depends not only on this information, but also on the relative priority that the society places on equal opportunity. In the past, the value of d has been negative, a fact which does little to support the view that a large value for d would be feasible politically. That is, traditionally the states have spent greater amounts on the schooling of advantaged students than disadvantaged ones.[39] The larger the value of d—up to the technically feasible maximum—the faster the rate of progress toward equal capital embodiment among populations. Given the large divergencies in capital embodiment that exist at present, even maximum values may mean a time-path to equality that must be measured in centuries. Neither the available technology nor the apparent priorities suggests any rapid movement toward equal capital embodiment.

Defining the Population of Disadvantaged

One of the difficulties in assigning expenditure levels for the education of different groups is that the population does not divide neatly into population groupings of advantaged and disadvantaged. That is, the spectrum of human capital embodiment operates along a hierarchy just as the associated distribution of family wealth and income. Since wealth and income are distributed among the population along a continuous path from abject poverty to fabulous wealth, with the majority of the population between these two poles, it is not an easy task to set out who is disadvantaged by simply drawing a poverty line. When such a device is used to delineate a population, one is confronted with the absurdity that a very small difference in income (or wealth) can transfer a family from poverty status to a nonpoverty one and vice versa. For example, if all families with less than $3,000 are declared to be in poverty, then a family with $2,999 in income is considered to be destitute while one earning $3,001 is not. Yet, for practical purposes, both families are equally poor.

In an excellent analysis of education and poverty, Ribich[40] has outlined a conceptual method for handling this difficulty. Children from families in the lowest income stratum can be considered fully disadvantaged and deserving of a full measure of compensatory expenditure. Students drawn from the lower-middle-income stratum are considered partially disadvantaged with a need for a smaller amount of compensatory spending. Finally, pupils from families at the middle of the income distribution or above are not considered disadvantaged. Thus, they would receive no compensatory monies.

Figure 8-2 illustrates the simplest way of weighing the differential. The horizontal axis shows family income, and the vertical one shows

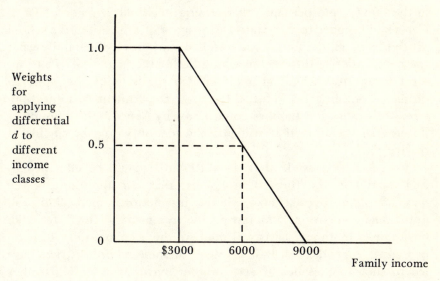

FIGURE 8-2
Weights for the Compensatory Spending Differential

the weight that we will apply to each income class when computing the compensatory differential per student. If we assume that students from families below $3,000 in annual income are fully disadvantaged and those drawn from families with over $9,000 in annual income are not disadvantaged at all, the respective weights for these two extremes are 1.0 and 0. That is, students from the lower-income category would receive a compensatory expenditure equal to (1.0) d and those in the higher bracket would receive none (0) d. Students from families between the $3,000-$9,000 limits would benefit by some ratio of d depending upon where they were on the spectrum. In this illustration, students from families with about $4,500 in annual income would benefit by $(.75)$ d; pupils from families with $6,000 would receive $(.5)$ in compensatory spending and so on.

Accordingly, the amount of differential expenditure for equalizing capital embodiment could be calculated simply by knowing the number of students drawn from each income class and the appropriate weights. In this way, it would even be possible to coordinate compensatory spending with the state income tax. All households would be required to file a tax return, even if they received no income during the year. Based upon the family income, number of children in the family, and perhaps other criteria, the State Division of Taxation would report to the State Department of Education, the school district in which the family was enrolled, and the eligible family what the compensatory differential would be for the next year. Thus, no local means test would be required. On the basis of the April 15 deadline for filing tax returns, the State Department of Education, school districts, and families could know by May 15 the amount of differential spending that students and schools would be eligible to receive.[41]

Indeed, it is possible that the differential could be allocated to each family in the form of a voucher that was applicable to the purchase of approved services, whether instructional, medical, dental, nutritional, and so on.[42] Moreover, the treatment of the differential on a family-by-family basis will improve the accountability of compensatory expenditures. Past practices of some school districts have led to such monies being used for the education of students other than those who were eligible under the law.[43]

A Heuristic Approach to Financing Education

One way of suggesting how to implement some of the concepts that were described in the foregoing analysis is to suggest a general approach for allocating the state educational budget. The total expenditure for the ith school district might be represented by [5].

$$T_i = EN_i + aN_i + C_i + D_i + dE \sum_{j=1}^{n} W_i N_{ji} \qquad [5]$$

T_i is the total expenditure for the ith district, E denotes the basic per pupil expenditure that applies to the student membership of the district N_i; a represents a cost differential that is applicable only to those districts where labor, land, and other costs are higher than normal; C_i denotes a flat sum allocable to the district by the state for mandated transportation; D_i is a flat sum allotted to the district according to the state formula for educating exceptional children and similar tasks; d is the differential ratio of E for equalizing opportunity; W_j is the weight for the jth income class; and N_{ji} represents the number of pupils drawn from the jth income class.

If the state were to assume all the costs of education, it might allocate all monies in [5] directly to school districts except for the last element, the compensatory education portion. This amount might be allotted directly to parents in the form of a voucher as described previously. Families might be given the choice of a large variety of compensatory services both within and outside the school. Moreover, even if part of the voucher were applied to narrow instructional services such as reading, the student and his family might be able to select alternatives to the public schools for this function. That is, private firms and other groups would be certified to compete for student vouchers.

In such a case, accountability would be established by requiring that all approved firms or groups must record the progress of each child and supply such information to the child's parents, the school, and the state accrediting agency; moreover, differential success of firms would also be published at stated intervals, perhaps annually or biannually. Under this arrangement, the public schools would also be eligible to receive vouchers, providing that they fulfilled the accountability requirements of the state. Children could be released from part of the standard curriculum to receive such specialized services.

The logic underlying this plan is based upon the fact that the schools have shown their greatest failures in adapting to the individualized needs of their students. Even the approaches made toward compensatory education have emphasized a curriculum or a technique for all of the so-called disadvantaged students in the school or even in the school system. It would seem that the market approach would work best for specialized educational needs in the sense that the firms could concentrate on fairly narrow objectives, while allowing the schools to concentrate on the broader aspects of education, especially those that require a close tie to the general needs of the community.

NOTES

1. *Serrano v. Priest*, 5 Cal. 3d 584 at 589 (1971).
2. *San Antonio Independent School District v. Rodriguez*, 411 U.S. 1 (1973).
3. See, for example, Citizens Commission of Maryland Government, "A Responsible Plan for the Financing, Governance, and Evaluation of Maryland's Public Schools" (Baltimore, 1971); New York State Commission on the Quality,

Cost and Financing of Elementary and Secondary Education, *Report* (New York, 1972).

4. F. V. Fowlkes, "Economics Report—Administration Leans to Value-added Tax to Help Solve National Fiscal Crises," *National Journal* (February 5, 1972), 210-19.

5. *Harvard Educational Review* 38(Winter 1968).

6. Lester C. Thurow, *Poverty and Discrimination* (Washington, D.C.: Brookings Institution, 1969); G. Hanoch, "An Economic Analysis of Earnings and Schooling," *Journal of Human Resources* 2(Summer 1967), 310-29; Samuel Bowles, "Schooling and Inequality from Generation to Generation," *Journal of Political Economy* 80(May-June 1972), S219-51; Z. Griliches and W. M. Mason, "Education, Income, and Ability," *Journal of Political Economy* 80(May-June 1972), S74-103.

7. Samuel Bowles, "Unequal Education and the Reproduction of the Social Division of Labor," in Martin Carnoy (ed.), *Schooling in a Corporate Society* (New York: David McKay, 1972), 36-66.

8. That is, even in an "unfair" society, an improvement in one part of the system is still preferable to no improvement at all.

9. Horace Mann, *The Republic and the School* (New York: Columbia University Teachers College, 1957).

10. David B. Tyack, *Turning Points in American Educational History* (Waltham, Mass.: Blaisdell, 1967).

11. Arthur Mann, "A Historical Overview: The *Lumpenproletariat*, Education, and Compensatory Action," in Charles U. Daly (ed.), *The Quality of Inequality: Urban and Suburban Public Schools* (Chicago: University of Chicago Press, 1968), 9-26.

12. Mann, *op. cit.*; E. Abbott and S. P. Breckenridge, *Truancy and Nonattendance in the Chicago Schools* (Chicago: Arno, 1971).

13. For research on these relationships, see Griliches and Mason, *op. cit.*; Bowles, "Schooling and Inequality from Generation to Generation"; O. D. Duncan, *Socioeconomic Background and Occupational Achievement Extensions of a Basic Model* (Washington, D.C.: U.S. Department of Health, Education, and Welfare, 1968).

14. This question is raised in H. M. Levin, "Social Utility, Equal Educational Opportunity, and Educational Investment Policy," Report to the New York State Commission on the Quality, Cost and Financing of Elementary and Secondary Education, Part 2 (July 1971).

15. T. W. Schultz, "The Human Capital Approach to Education," in R. L. Johns *et al.*, *Economic Factors Affecting the Financing of Education* (Gainesville, Fla.: National Educational Finance Project, 1970), ch. 2; G. S. Becker, *Human Capital* (New York: Columbia University Press, 1964).

16. T. W. Schultz, "The Rate of Return in Allocating Investment Resources to Education," *Journal of Human Resources* 2(Summer 1967), 293-309.

17. U.S. Department of Health, Education, and Welfare, *Perspectives on Human Deprivation: Biological, Psychological and Sociological* (Washington, D.C.: Public Health Service, 1968); A. D. Berg, "Nutrition as a National Priority:

Lessons from the India Experiment," *American Journal of Clinical Nutrition* 23(November 1970), 1396-1408.

18. N. S. Scrimshaw and J. E. Gordon (eds.), *Malnutrition, Learning and Behavior* (Cambridge, Mass.: MIT Press, 1968).

19. President's Committee on Urban Housing, *A Decent Home* (Washington, D.C.: U.S. Government Printing Office, 1968).

20. *Ibid.*

21. R. G. Healy, "Effects of Improved Housing on Worker Performance," *Journal of Human Resources* 2(Summer 1971), 297-309.

22. U.S. Department of Labor, *The Negro Family: The Case for National Action* (Washington, D.C.: Government Printing Office, 1965); for trend data, see R. Farley, "Family Types and Family Headship: A Comparison of Trends among Blacks and Whites," *Journal of Human Resources* 6(Summer 1971), 297-309.

23. According to the Department of Labor survey taken in March 1966, 47.17 percent of nonwhite mothers with children under the age of eighteen were in the labor force, while the comparable figure for whites was 34.3 percent. U.S. Department of Labor, *Wage and Labor Standards, Negro Women in the Population and in the Labor Force* (Washington, D.C.: Government Printing Office, 1967).

24. Ellis G. Olim, Robert D. Hess, and Virginia Shipman, "The Role of Mothers' Language Styles in Mediating Their Preschool Children's Cognitive Development," *School Review* 75(Winter 1967), 414; Robert D. Hess, Virginia Shipman, and D. Jackson, "Early Experience and the Socialization of Cognitive Modes in Children," *Child Development* 36(December 1965), 869-86.

25. For an excellent review, see U.S. Department of Health, Education, and Welfare, *Perspectives on Human Deprivation: Biological, Psychological and Sociological*, chs. 1, 2.

26. See, e.g., J. S. Coleman *et al.*, *Equality of Educational Opportunity* (Washington, D.C.: Government Printing Office, 1966).

27. L. A. Cremin, *The American Common School: An Historic Conception* (New York: Bureau of Publications, Teachers College, Columbia University, 1951), chs. 1, 2.

28. For a general social and political comparison of the United States and Europe in the 1830's, see A. de Tocqueville, *Democracy in America* (New York: Alfred A. Knopf, 1946).

29. For a more pessimistic view, see Bowles, "Schooling and Inequality from Generation to Generation."

30. H. M. Levin, *op. cit.*

31. F. F. Piven and R. A. Cloward, *Regulating the Poor: The Function of Public Welfare* (New York: Pantheon, 1971); I. Kristol, "Welfare: The Best of Intentions, the Worst of Results," *Atlantic* 228(August 1971), 45-47.

32. The assertion that noninstructional services are provided at adequate levels by other agencies is not supported by fact. See, for example, the reports issued by the Select Committee on Nutrition and Human Needs of the U.S. Senate in August and September of 1969 and in January of 1971.

33. For example, of almost $700 million of Title I allocations spent during the regular school year of 1967-68, about $26 million was allotted to food services and $19 million to health services. See U.S. Department of Health, Education, and Welfare, *Statistical Report Fiscal Year 1968: A Report on the Third Year of Title I ESEA, OE-37021-68* (Washington, D.C.: U.S. Office of Education, 1970).

34. H. M. Levin (ed.), *Community Control of Schools* (Washington, D.C.: Brookings Institution, 1970).

35. For a panoramic view, see A. Stein, "Strategies for Failure," *Harvard Educational Review* 41(May 1971), 158-204.

36. In fact, one of the reasons that instructional remedies have shown such poor results may stem from the interdependence between other types of student well-being and academic performance.

37. In the context of the model outlined in H. M. Levin, "Social Utility, Equal Educational Opportunity, and Educational Investment Policy," it is obvious that $d = P_2/P_1 - 1$.

38. For example, Dugan estimated that the market value of the flow of mother's educational services to the child between grades 1 and 12 was only $3,000 for a student whose mother was a grade school graduate, but over $8,000 for a student whose mother graduated from college. D. Dugan, "The Impact of Parental and Educational Investment upon Student Achievement," paper presented at the annual meeting of the American Statistical Association, New York City, August 21, 1969.

39. J. E. Coons, W. H. Clune, III, and S. D. Sugarman, *Private Wealth and Public Education* (Cambridge, Mass.: Belknap Press, 1970); J. W. Guthrie, G. B. Kleindorfer, H. M. Levin, and R. T. Stout, *Schools and Inequality* (Cambridge, Mass.: MIT Press, 1971).

40. T. I. Ribich, *Education and Poverty* (Washington, D.C.: Brookings Institution, 1968), ch. 2.

41. Income averaging for a three- to five-year period might be used as the basis for computing eligibility. In this way, temporary fluctuations in family income would not create spurious fluctuations from year to year in student expenditure. Family size and other relevant characteristics might be used to calculate the amount of the educational differential.

42. For readings on vouchers, see Milton Friedman, *Capitalism and Freedom* (Chicago: University of Chicago Press, 1962), ch. 6; Center for the Study of Public Policy, *Education Vouchers: A Report on Financing Elementary Education by Grants to Parents* (Cambridge, Mass.: Center for the Study of Public Policy, 1970); H. M. Levin, "The Failure of Schools and the Free Market Remedy," *Urban Review* 2(June 1968), 32-37.

43. R. Martin and P. McClure, *Title I of ESEA: Is It Helping Poor Children?* (Washington, D.C.: Washington Research Project and NAACP Legal Defense and Educational Fund, 1969).

9. Equality in Education

GREGORY S. KAVKA

Judges, lawyers, educators, legislators, administration officials, and concerned citizens are currently wrestling with numerous
political and legal issues concerning the operation, structure, and
financing of various elements of the American educational system. A
commonly stated and agreed upon aim of those debating these issues
is the attainment of the American ideal of equality within our educational system. There is a great deal of uncertainty, however, about
how this aim is to be achieved. Such uncertainty stems not only from
limited empirical knowledge, but also from a lack of sufficient understanding of the central concepts of equality, equal treatment, and
equal opportunity as they apply in educational contexts. I shall
attempt to clarify some of the important conceptual and theoretical
issues involved in the debate over equality in education. I hope thereby to establish that the ideal of equality must be supplemented by a
theory about the proper aims of our educational system if we are to
reach substantive conclusions about educational policy. Clarifying
the concept of equality in education requires some preliminary investigation into the general notions of equality and equal opportunity and the moral basis for advancing them as appropriate social
goals.

EQUALITY

The ideal of equality involves two distinct but related claims: first, the descriptive claim or the assertion that all human beings are, in some sense, equal to one another; second, the prescriptive claim or the recommendation that all human beings ought to be treated equally.

To understand descriptive equality, we must discover what is involved in the claim that two (or more) entities are equal to one another. What are we asserting when we state that "X and Y are equal" or "X is equal to Y"? In some limited contexts such statements function as identity statements which assert that entities X and Y are really the same entity. Thus, for example, the statement "$2 + 2 = 4$" asserts that the number obtained by adding two and two just is the number four. Usually, however, statements of equality do not assert the identity of the objects involved; they merely assert sameness or likeness in particular respects.[1] For example, if we say that two youngsters got equal pieces of pie, we are not claiming that they received the *same* piece of pie, but, rather, that the pieces they received were of the same size. Insofar as the youngsters were interested only in the amount of pie they got, they could have traded pieces, and neither would have gained or lost by the transaction. In general, then, it appears that statements of equality assert sameness or interchangeability in a particular respect or particular respects. Or, to put the same point somewhat differently, such statements assert the common possession, by the objects in question, of some set of attributes, or possession of those attributes in like degrees.

Any attempt to apply this analysis of equality statements to the claim that all human beings are equal immediately causes problems. For, according to the above analysis, what is being asserted is that all human beings are alike in certain respects, that there are certain features which all human beings possess or which they possess in like degree. If we actually look at the features of persons which we normally regard as most significant, however, we immediately discover that people vary immensely with respect to those features. People are not all equal in terms of size, physical strength, appearance, intelligence, moral virtue, creativity, sensitivity, amount of factual knowledge, or other similar attributes. It is no easy matter, therefore, to identify significant ways in which all human beings are alike. Such an undertaking seems exceedingly important, however, since defenders of equal treatment generally base their case on claims of descriptive equality, holding that it is in virtue of their *being* equal that men ought to be treated equally.[2] Unless a way can be found to interpret the claim that all men are equal so that it is at least approximately true and involves significant similarities, the usual ground of the demand for equal treatment will disappear.

The authors of the Declaration of Independence and the United Nations Declaration on Human Rights, as well as others who have regarded all men as equal, were certainly aware that people are not equal in terms of strength, virtue, intelligence, or similar features. Insofar as they made genuine assertions of descriptive equality, they must have been referring to men's common possession of certain very general characteristics. It seems to me that they were referring to features so general and so obvious that they are often overlooked when one is seeking the basis for claims of human equality.[3] These general features fall roughly into three categories: vulnerability, capacity for happiness, and moral capacity.

Vulnerability. Human life is finite and fragile. Human beings may die from old age, disease, starvation, or physical damage caused by natural objects or other men. Because they are vulnerable to death, all human beings share certain basic needs—food, clothing, shelter, protection from violent attack, and medical care. Men are vulnerable not only to death, but also to pain. Hunger, injury, and disease cause physical pain. Disappointment, shame, loneliness, and lack of affection from others cause emotional pain. Though human beings differ in degree of vulnerability owing to differences in their circumstances or psychological characteristics, they do share the basic capacity to be hurt—to suffer pain or death.

Capacity for happiness. Just as human beings share a capacity for suffering, they also share the opposite capacity for enjoyment and satisfaction. Like other animals, human beings are capable of experiencing (and often do experience) physical pleasure. Yet, unlike the other animals, human beings are capable of certain activities involving satisfactions and valuable experiences of a higher order. As rational forward-looking creatures, human beings are capable of planning for the future, adopting and realizing goals, plans, and aspirations. Because they are also self-conscious, human beings are capable of feeling pride in their accomplishments and of gaining self-respect based on a feeling of the worth of their plans, aspirations, and activities.[4] Human beings are also capable of entering into positive relationships with other persons—bestowing affection on others and receiving affection in return. They can feel a sense of togetherness with others that makes possible solidarity and identification with large groups and humane causes. Briefly stated, as rational, self-conscious social animals, we share the capacity for living a satisfying human existence, for being happy in a sense that goes beyond mere enjoyment of physical sensations.

Moral capacity. It is generally felt that, whatever their natural gifts or social position, human beings have a capacity for moral goodness. Men are capable of caring for others, of acting from nonselfish motives, of cooperating with others to advance the common good. Not all human beings actualize these capacities to any great extent, but it is generally held that even the most evil of men are capable of rehabilitation and reform.[5] Some philosophers, like Kant, have linked the capacity for moral reform with the idea that human beings are rational agents and are thus capable of free choice and commitment to moral rules.[6] The notion finds expression in the Christian religion through the doctrine of the possibility of redemption through faith and repentance. Our system of criminal punishment is also based on the assumption that prisoners are generally capable of reform, while the modern science of psychiatry attempts to deal with many moral defects as curable diseases of the human organism. Thus, the view that most all human beings possess the capacity for virtue, for the attainment of moral worth, is deeply embedded in our moral tradition.

I suggest that we interpret "all men are equal" as an assertion of the general facts that human beings are vulnerable, that they are capable of happiness, and that they are capable of moral virtue, in the senses I have just spelled out. Admittedly, the descriptions that I have provided are both vague and wide ranging. Yet I feel that they at least begin to capture the flavor of unarticulated values and processes of reasoning underlying the claim of descriptive equality. This way of interpreting the claim that all human beings are equal does, however, raise a serious question concerning the truth of the claim. Is it true that *all* human beings actually possess these general features? Are there not people so mentally disturbed that they are incapable of either happiness or moral virtue? Certainly there are people living in comas from which they will never emerge, who lack the capacity to feel pain as well as the capacity for happiness and moral behavior. Young children lack the understanding and conceptual apparatus necessary for moral behavior. Is it not, then, strictly speaking, false that all human beings are equal in the sense of sharing the general features I have specified?

There are, as I see it, two different approaches to dealing with this problem of human beings who lack the requisite features. Both approaches involve conceding that the claim "*all* human beings are equal" is not strictly true and must be replaced by the slightly weaker claim that *almost all* human beings are equal. The approaches differ, however, in how they treat the implications of this concession with regard to the claim to equal treatment of the "exceptional cases." According to the first approach, the claim to equal treatment based on human equality is valid not only for those who presently possess the features in question, but also for those beings who have had, or will in the normal course of events come to have, those features as well. Thus, those who are mentally ill or permanently comatose but who once had the capacity for happiness and moral behavior and young children who will, in the normal course of events, develop such capacities deserve equal treatment despite the present lack of these capacities. This approach, as I see it, seems to imply a claim to equal treatment for fetuses and perhaps even fertilized ova since they will, in the normal course of events, become persons with the capacity to be hurt, happy, and moral.[7] I prefer a different approach which holds that human beings who lack the requisite general features are not deserving of equal treatment on the same basis as those who do possess these features. Thus, young children can be subordinated to their parents,[8] and the mentally ill can, in certain cases, be treated without their consent, even if we require consent as a condition of treatment for other persons. This is not to say that human beings lacking the general features in question do not deserve *humane* treatment (for example, psychiatric care, medical sustenance, protection from harm), but only that they do not necessarily have a claim to equal treatment with other human beings based on the usual claims about human equality. In fact, it seems to me that we have a moral obligation to help those human beings who lack the capacities for happiness and moral behavior to develop those capacities if it is possible for them to do so, but such an obligation is not based on any claim to equal treatment which these human beings have.[9]

Even supposing a completely satisfactory solution to this problem of "exceptional cases," there is still the problem of showing how the claim that all (or almost all) human beings are vulnerable, capable of happiness, and capable of moral virtue supports the prescriptive judgment that all (or almost all) human beings ought to be treated equally. In other words, how does descriptive equality lead to prescriptive equality? I can offer only the bare outlines of an answer.[10]

It is assumed here that all human beings possess the characteristics of vulnerability, capacity for happiness, and moral capacity as spelled out above.[11] That each human is capable of continuing to live or of dying, of suffering or of being happy, implies that what happens to every single human being matters from the point of view of any moral system that values human life and happiness. Because human life is precarious and each of us has the capacity to live a happy life, the basic needs whose satisfaction is a prerequisite of our survival and happiness—the need for food, shelter, clothing, medical care, protection from violence, affection—are, morally speaking, worthy of consideration. This does not mean that the well-being of all creatures capable of experiencing satisfaction or enjoyment is worthy of the same consideration. Human beings differ from other animals in that humans possess the capacity for higher-order satisfactions. This, then, is a general reason for giving the basic needs of human beings priority over the needs of other animals and for promoting human survival in preference to the survival of other living things. Since all human beings possess the capacity for higher-order happiness, however, it would appear that, in the absence of specific compelling reasons to the contrary, the basic needs of all human beings are worthy of *equal* consideration. From the point of view of morality, there are no inherent differences in the significance and importance of the happiness of different human beings; there is no general class of persons whose needs should take precedence over the needs of other persons in the same way human needs take precedence over animal needs.

Our common vulnerability points the way to a different sort of equality as well—equality of status in our dealings with one another. Such vulnerability implies a common need for cooperation in two senses. Vulnerability to death and injury at the hands of our fellows implies the need for cooperation in the minimal sense of mutual restraint from attack.[12] Vulnerability to cold, hunger, disease, and other exigencies of the environment implies a common need for cooperation in the more positive sense of engaging in group activities designed to promote group safety and material prosperity. As human beings capable of feeling affection for others and a sense of togetherness with them, we are all capable of reaping both the psychological and the material benefits of cooperation. As rational moral beings we have the capacity to arrange and carry out complex activities for the mutual benefit of ourselves and others. The fact that all human beings share the need for cooperation, the capacity to cooperate, and the capacity to benefit from such cooperation implies that they are in basically similar situations with respect to one another insofar as cooperative action is concerned. This similarity of situations suggests initial equality of status as an appropriate basis for their dealings with one another. Since no human being is so powerful that he can afford not to cooperate, and no human being is so weak that his cooperation may not prove helpful, cooperation should rest on the single condition relatively acceptable to all—equality of status.

Equality of status as a basis of interaction is also implied by men's common possession of moral capacities. As free rational agents, people are capable of sincere disagreement about the correct course of group and individual action. Recognizing that each person possesses the capacity for moral goodness requires respecting sincere viewpoints, principles, judgments, and claims. No view may be dismissed out of hand just because of whose view it is. Each person's views must be considered on their own merits if we concede that each person is capable of discovering and following the path of moral truth and virtue. Treating each person's view on its merits in the course of decisionmaking amounts to according each person initially equal status in the cooperative process.

To summarize, the basic point of the argument is that, in circumstances of common vulnerability, capacity for happiness, need for cooperation, potential to gain by cooperation, and potential disagreement about how to cooperate, the most sensible basis for human interaction seems to be an assumption of equality, that is, equal status for all and equal consideration of each person's basic needs. The argument is essentially a negative one: lacking a rational basis for distinguishing persons as generally more or less worthy of good treatment, and aware of their common needs and general capacities for contributing to society, we seem to have no good reason for treating persons *un*equally. As John Locke put it, there is "nothing more evident than that creatures of the same species and rank, promiscuously born to all the same advantages of nature and the use of the same faculties, should also be equal one amongst another without subordination or subjection."[13]

It might be objected that, along with the common features most all men share, there are also certain conspicuous and significant differences among men that might justify or even require differences in the way they are treated. I take this to be true, but deny that it is inconsistent with the claim that all men ought to be treated equally. If we examine the notion of equal treatment more closely, we notice that treating people equally does not necessarily coincide with treating them the same way. Suppose one child wants to go to the zoo and another to the movies, and their mother takes them to the zoo. If the child who wanted to go to the movies complained, the mother could hardly reply, "Don't complain. I treated you both equally, I took you both to the same place." Sameness of treatment means equality of treatment only if the parties so treated do not differ in relevant respects. To take both children to the zoo was to treat them unequally in view of their different desires and preferences.

The observation that what counts as equal treatment depends upon the relevant features of the persons so treated and their circumstances leads to the formulation of a fundamental principle of equality that I call the *principle of formal equality*.[14] The principle may be stated as follows: any difference in treatment of different persons must be based on relevant differences between these persons or their situations. The principle really says no more than that any difference in treatment must be based on relevant reasons. As such, it seems to be a requirement of rational action, and anyone who knowingly violates the principle could be said to be acting irrationally in the sense that he ignores relevant considerations or bases his action on irrelevant ones.

The principle of formal equality demonstrates that the defender of equal treatment is not committed to the absurdity of disregarding significant differences between persons in the course of deciding how to treat them. This principle, because it is merely a formal principle, is of limited significance with respect to solving the problem of what it is to treat people equally. It tells us that differences in treatment should be based on relevant differences between persons, but it places no restrictions on what may count as relevant differences. As far as the principle itself is concerned, a judge could give one robber a life sentence and another one day in jail on the grounds that the latter and not the former had a red-haired grandmother, and he could still claim to have treated them equally. For the principle of formal equality to be effective, it must be supplemented by criteria of relevance that indicate what sorts of differences between people are relevant to what sorts of treatment they might receive.

It is impossible to state a general principle indicating what differences between people are relevant reasons for treating them differently because what counts as a relevant difference depends upon the kind of treatment in question and the specific context in which the question of treatment arises. A few general points about relevance can, however, be made. First, there are many instances in which it is clear that people are being treated differently for irrelevant reasons and, therefore, that they are being treated unequally. Thus, though we could not state precisely what differences might justify a judge's giving two persons who commit the same crime different sentences, we know that such features as the prisoner's hair color, skin color, and ethnic background are not among those that might be relevant. Second, it seems that the needs and desires of the parties involved, with respect to the treatment to be accorded them, are almost always relevant considerations in determining how they are to be treated according to equalitarian principles. If an individual has an extra orchestra ticket to give away, the fact that one of his friends wants to go to the orchestra performance while another friend does not constitutes a relevant difference between the two friends. The ticket can be given to the first friend without treating the two friends unequally. Similarly, that one man is starving and needs food to survive while another is well fed, constitutes a relevant reason for giving an extra loaf of bread to the former rather than the latter.

Third, it is generally felt that a person's deserts are relevant to the question of equal treatment. To give everyone what he deserves is to treat eveyone equally in an important sense.[15] The problem, as Aristotle notes, is that men disagree about the features men must have to deserve benefits. Aristotle lists "wealth," "excellence," and "being a free man" as candidates for characteristics that make one deserving of good treatment,[16] and we might add "moral virtue," "effort," "ability," "training," and "contribution to the common good" to this list. As in the case of equal treatment, there are no universal criteria to be appealed to here; there is no general answer to the question of what features make a person deserving. The relevant features vary according to the nature of the treatment that is said to be deserved.[17] The criminal deserves to be punished because he committed the crime; the runner deserves the trophy because he crossed the finish line first; the student deserves to be praised by her teacher because she worked so hard and wrote such a good paper. In the absence of a general criterion of desert, recognizing desert as a criterion of equal distribution does not take us very far toward a general formula of equal treatment.[18]

Finally, it may be pointed out that what count as relevant differences may depend upon the established rules or the aims of a given social practice.[19] For example, it is a standard practice at most American racetracks to provide a small weight allowance for horses ridden by apprentice riders. This practice establishes the apprentice-nonapprentice distinction as relevant with respect to the question of how much weight a horse ridden by a given rider should carry, and an apprentice rider could rightfully claim discrimination and unequal treatment if his horse were forced to carry equal weight with horses ridden by veteran riders. Taking an example related to the aims of a social practice, we might say that the primary aim of our system of criminal laws is to protect citizens from unjust harm. These considerations make the fact that person A committed a crime while person B did not clearly a relevant reason for punishing A but not B, for punishing lawbreakers can reasonably be expected to deter crime and thus protect citizens. Punishing an innocent person (B), however, harms someone unjustly. We return to this point about the aims of a practice when considering the application of the principle of equality in educational contexts.[20]

EQUAL OPPORTUNITY

One form of equal treatment often advocated in the political arena is income equality. Those who support equal incomes for all citizens, so-called egalitarians, usually base their position on two sorts of arguments. The first, a utilitarian argument, is based on the assumption that we should seek to maximize human happiness. Since income generally has declining marginal utility, that is, an extra dollar of income produces less extra happiness the more money the person receiving it already has, egalitarians suggest that the best way to maximize happiness is to equalize incomes.[21] The second argument results from applying the formal principle of equality. According to that principle, people should have equal incomes unless differences between them constitute relevant reasons for giving some people more income and others less. It is argued, however, that the usual reasons given to justify differential incomes—for example, different degrees of ability or different contributions to the common good— are not really relevant to the question of income distribution. Hence, we ought to do away with income inequalities based on such criteria.[22]

The mainstream of American political thought opposes income equality and tends to counter egalitarian arguments with two of its own. The first of these questions the claim that utilitarian considerations favor income equality. Although it is conceded that income equality would maximize happiness if total national income were a fixed quantity, it is argued that a national policy of income equality would significantly reduce total national income by removing the incentive for people to work hard, take profitable risks, and make innovations at all levels of the economic process. It is claimed, therefore, that the choice is not between two ways of dividing up a fixed national income pie, but between distributing a smaller pie equally or a significantly larger pie unequally. And it is pointed out that, even if there is a decreasing marginal utility of personal income, it is plausible to suppose that more utility is produced by distributing unequal shares of a significantly larger national income than would be produced by distributing equal shares of a much smaller national income.

The second of the counterarguments claims that the egalitarian is making a mistake in overlooking people's deserts in developing arguments for equal income. It is claimed that some people *deserve* more income than other people because they work harder, because they contribute more to the social product of the nation, because they are willing to take financial risks others are unwilling to take, because they sacrifice more time and effort in acquiring skills necessary to perform their jobs, or for some other reason.[23] The desert theorist holds that such considerations do constitute relevant reasons for treating individuals differently with respect to distribution of income.

These two arguments, although they are often mixed or elaborated in various ways, seem to form the basis for the standard conclusion in American political thought that income equality is not an appropriate national goal. Instead, the generally accepted goal is a highly competitive system in which some occupations carry with them high incomes, power, and status, and in which people have equal *opportunity* to enter and achieve success within these occupations. In other words, the ideal of income equality is rejected in favor of a competitive system governed by a different sort of equality—equality of opportunity.

What is equality of opportunity? Before seeking an answer to that question, we should note that there are different sorts of equal opportunity: equal educational opportunity, equal occupational opportunity, and equal political opportunity, among others. The American ideal of equal opportunity primarily involves equal occupational opportunity,[24] assuming that the same jobs generally carry with them the most income, the highest status, and the greatest amounts of power. If one accepts this premise, a system of equal occupational opportunity assures equal opportunity with respect to income, status, and power. For our purposes, we may accept this assumption and treat equality of occupational opportunity, income opportunity, and status opportunity interchangeably.

The first point to notice about equal occupational opportunity is that it does not imply that everyone has an equal probability of securing a high-level job and earning a large income. Equal opportunity does not require that unskilled and ineffective workers have as good a chance to serve in desirable jobs as skilled, trained, and effective workers. Nor does it require that persons with varying degrees of intelligence and other native abilities be equally likely to end up in the most desirable occupations. A system that assured such results would require random or arbitrary placement in jobs, which is totally at odds with the ideal of equal opportunity.

If equal occupational opportunity does not mean that everyone has equal probability of ending up in the top economic stratum, what does it mean? It means essentially that competition for desirable jobs is fair. Fair, first, in the sense that desirable jobs are bestowed on individuals because they possess the appropriate skills, merits, or abilities, not on the basis of factors that are irrelevant to the question of how well the individual would do the job if hired. In other words, equal opportunity requires that desirable jobs be assigned to those prospective employees best qualified to do those jobs well. If, for example, doing a certain job requires being able to lift fifty-pound boxes for hours at a time, it is consistent with equal opportunity to eliminate any candidates physically unable to do this, but it would violate the canons of equal opportunity to disqualify a candidate for the job solely on the basis of sex. Of course, there will be in any given case possible grounds for controversy as to whether this condition is being fulfilled since neither the exact nature of the job, the nature of the appropriate qualifications, nor the best way of measuring these qualifications in prospective applicants is likely to be precisely defined for most jobs. The general notion of hiring on the basis of relevant qualifications is clear, however, even if its application in particular cases may not be.

Satisfaction of this first requirement of fair competition is not enough, however, to ensure equality of opportunity. Even if the requirement were strictly satisfied, there could be inequalities owing to the fact that different members of society do not have equal opportunities to develop either the skills, abilities, or habits that would qualify them for desirable occupations, or the desire and self-confidence necessary to make them compete for these desirable positions.[25] Thus, for example, even if national tests and licensing practices ensured that only those best qualified to become doctors became doctors, we could not say that there was equal opportunity for all to become doctors unless all individuals had equal access to the training necessary to enable them to pass the tests and fulfill other licensing procedures. As a matter of fact, whole groups within our society—the poor, ethnic minorities, women—are such that members of those groups have generally not had an equal opportunity to acquire the knowledge or skills necessary to become doctors, lawyers, businessmen, government officials, and so forth. Barriers interfering with equal opportunity to acquire qualifications have been of various sorts: economic, cultural, psychological, and legal. As long as, and to the extent that, such barriers remain in existence, we cannot be said to have a system based on equal opportunity, even if desirable jobs are doled out solely on the basis of genuinely relevant qualifications.

There is a second requirement of fair competition that makes up the ideal of equal opportunity: persons from all social groups[26] and backgrounds must have an equal chance to develop their natural ability to acquire the qualifications needed to obtain desirable jobs, as well as an equal chance to develop the motivation to compete for such jobs. In other words, full equality of opportunity requires that all discriminatory barriers be removed so that persons from different groups, if equal in natural talent, have equal probability of being successful. Of course, this requirement can never be totally satisfied since we lack knowledge of how to help people turn their natural talents into economically valuable skills, and, even if we had such knowledge, ensuring an equal chance to develop individual talents would probably require almost complete control of a person's environment. Supporters of the ideal of equal opportunity must still try, if possible, to remove those social conditions or practices known to keep members of certain social groups from having an equal chance to acquire qualifications for economic success.

I have suggested that the concept of equal opportunity has two components: jobs distributed on the basis of qualifications, and equal chances for persons in various social groups to develop their natural abilities to obtain these qualifications. It might be said that this conception of equal opportunity does not go far enough because it favors people with more natural talents. Possession of natural talents is, after all, a matter of chance; no one earns or deserves his genetic makeup. Should we, therefore, seek to reduce or remove income differences based on natural differences between people by, for example, supplying the less intelligent with more education and training than the more intelligent?[27] I admit that I am not sure how to deal with the problem of natural inequalities in useful social skills, but I do not think that compensating for such inequalities is part of the traditional ideal of equality of opportunity. The traditional notion of equal opportunity is not seen as a means of making the naturally unequal equal. Equal opportunity is supposed to offer everyone a fair chance to compete, but this is not supposed to ensure everyone success in the competition or even equal probabilities of success. So, while there may be some political or moral reasons for compensating those who have natural deficiencies, such compensation is not part of the ideal of equal opportunity.[28]

A further point about the second requirement of fair competition is worth noting. That requirement makes explicit reference to social *groups* in stating that equally capable individuals from all groups should have equal chances to develop the qualifications necessary for occupational success. This raises the question as to whether equal opportunity is an ideal designed to promote the advantage of social groups per se, or only to give individuals within those groups a fair chance of success.[29] It seems clear to me that equal opportunity is something owed to individuals—the traditional supporting arguments about desert and incentives clearly imply this.[30] Social groups are mentioned in the specification of the second requirement of fair competition only in a negative sense. Membership in a group is not supposed to affect, directly or indirectly, an individual's chances for success within a system if the system offers genuine equality of opportunity. Of course, a social group that has been discriminated against would benefit greatly from the establishment of a system that provides true equal opportunity since this would require an end to discrimination and would doubtless work to the economic benefit of the members of the group. But the point of offering equal opportunity is to treat individuals fairly and justly as individuals, not to ensure that any particular group gets its share of the social pie.

This distinction between the individual group member and the group must also be kept in mind when we look at what constitutes evidence that persons have not been offered equal opportunity. If an individual does not succeed in occupational competition, there are four possible explanations: bad luck, lack of natural ability, poor performance or motivation for reasons apart from natural ability, or inequality of opportunity. Unless there is clear evidence that an individual has been discriminated against in some way, it seems nearly impossible to conclude that failure was due to lack of equal opportunity since it would be difficult to eliminate conclusively bad luck or personal deficiencies as possible explanations. When, however, we are dealing with large social groups in trying to determine whether the members of those groups are being offered equal opportunity, the situation is somewhat different. If a group has a high failure rate, bad luck is not a plausible explanation because of the statistical probabilities involved. Furthermore, poor performance or motivation not based on lack of natural ability would, if it were widespread among members of a social group, indicate that members of that group were being subjected to social-environmental disadvantage and thus were not receiving full equality of opportunity. Thus, for example, if most women do not have the desire to compete for good jobs and the confidence necessary to succeed in such competition, and this is not due to natural (that is, biological) differences between men and women, then women are not being offered an equal chance to acquire the qualifications for success and do not have full equality of opportunity.[31] There are only two alternative explanations of why members of a given social group have a high failure rate in a competitive society: either the members of that group are not being offered full equality of opportunity, or they are, on the average, less endowed with the natural abilities and capacities that lead to competitive success. This narrowing of explanatory possibilities explains, perhaps, the recently revived interest in the issue of black versus white intelligence.[32] It is an undisputed fact that the occupational "failure" rate within our society for blacks is disproportionately high, and this must be explained either in terms of the natural inferiority of blacks in some relevant respect (for example, intelligence), or it must be conceded that America still offers most of its black citizens much less than equality of opportunity.

To understand the ideal of equal opportunity, it is necessary to investigate not only what equal opportunity is, but also its philosophical basis, the ideology that underlies the pursuit of equal opportunity as a social goal. We have already discussed the main elements in the philosophical defense of equal opportunity, but they require reemphasis because the philosophical basis of equal opportunity is often misunderstood. In this regard I am particularly concerned to rebut the views about the ideology of equal opportunity put forth by Christopher Jencks and others in their influential book, *Inequality: A Reassessment of the Effect of Family and Schooling in America*. I feel that Jencks is fundamentally confused about the philosophical reasoning that underlies the quest for equal opportunity in American society.

The aim of *Inequality* was, according to Jencks, "to show that equalizing opportunity, especially educational opportunity, would not do much to reduce economic inequality . . . ."[33] The enemy to be confronted is "the liberal notion that equalizing educational opportunity will equalize people's incomes."[34] It is clear, from these remarks and the structure of the argument of *Inequality*, that Jencks regards the liberal argument for equal opportunity to run roughly as follows:[35]

1. Income equality is a desirable result.

2. Income equality can be attained by equality of occupational opportunity.

3. Equality of occupational opportunity can be attained through equality of educational opportunity.

Conclusion. We should seek equality of educational opportunity, which will bring about income equality.

Inequality's attack on this argument focuses largely on the third premise. Much of the book involves presenting and discussing empirical evidence that equal educational opportunity would not lead to equal occupational opportunity. Jencks accepts the first premise, regarding it as a common ground between himself and his liberal opponents.[36] The second premise is attacked by pointing out that, even in a system of equal opportunity, some people succeed and some fail, and there will, therefore, be differences between incomes.[37] The liberal supporter of equal opportunity is in effect accused of confusing equal opportunity with equal results.

It is important for the understanding of equal opportunity as a political ideal that we see that Jencks has fundamentally misconceived the liberal position. Far from adopting the first and second premises in his argument for equal opportunity, the liberal supporter of equal opportunity rejects both. While Jencks interprets the liberal as advocating equal opportunity as a means to equality, the liberal argument for equal opportunity takes as its starting point the desirability of a system of competitive inequality.[38] The real liberal argument, as opposed to the view Jencks seems to be attacking, goes something like this:

Income equality is an impractical, undesirable result. It is impractical because it would destroy incentives; it is undesirable in any case because it does not take account of people's deserts, the differences in their contributions to the common good. What is desirable is a system of fair competitive inequality, with some provision made to care for those with special needs and to satisfy the basic needs of those who fail in the fair competition. Such a system has the following advantages: there are sufficient incentives to ensure national income is near maximum; people receive the incomes which they deserve in terms of their contribution to society; the basic needs of all are provided for. It appears that the appropriate social goal for

America is a system of equal opportunity supplemented by an adequate welfare system.

Contrasting this argument with the one stated above, we see that, far from aiming at equality, equal opportunity presupposes *in*equality. The whole point of the ideal of equal opportunity is to achieve an effective compromise between various different moral values: equality, utility maximization, rewards proportioned to desert, and satisfaction of basic needs. Whether or not we agree with the liberal argument, it is a powerful one that is worth taking seriously. It would be a mistake to dismiss it on the grounds that it is based on a confusion between equal opportunity and equal results; it is not.

EQUALITY IN EDUCATION

Having investigated the concepts of equality and equal opportunity, the results can be applied to the sphere of education. A consideration of equality in education is followed by a discussion of equal opportunity in education.

What does treating people equally with respect to their education amount to? Clearly, it does not require ensuring that all children leave the educational system with the same level of cognitive skills. Not only might this be an impossible goal, but, even if it could be attained, it would require gross inequities in the treatment of those entering school with varying degrees of cognitive skills and ability.[39] Equal treatment might be defined in terms of equalization, between and within school districts, of such measures as expenditures per pupil, teaching hours per pupil, or years spent in school by the average pupil. While equalizing such measures would doubtless make our treatment of pupils more equal than it is now, it would not amount to equal educational treatment because education depends on the nature and quality of the student's interactions with his teachers and classmates and not just on the amount of time or monetary resources invested in his education.[40]

Discussions of educational quality immediately raise a new issue. Because different students are different in their educational needs, interests, and abilities, the exact nature of quality education varies from student to student. Offering quality education for all involves recognizing and dealing with individual differences, not treating everyone the same. Here we have a specific application of a general principle noted above:[41] equal treatment is different from sameness of treatment and involves differences of treatment based on relevant differences in the parties receiving such treatment. Our problem is that of identifying the relevant differences between persons that justify treating them differently in educational contexts.

Two relevant differences between students immediately come to mind: differences in desire and in the ability to learn. It might seem that to give similar amounts of education to persons wanting it and to persons not wanting it is to treat them unequally, and that equal treatment requires giving more education to those who want it. Similarly, to give like amounts of higher education to good students able to make use of it and to poor students less able to make use of it would seem to involve inequality in the sense of overlooking relevant differences. Does not equality require that the more able students be given readier access to the limited resources of institutions of higher education? The problem with these arguments, of course, is that, by accepting desire and ability as the criteria of educational opportunity, we would thereby increase the advantages of those entering the educational system with motivation and ability and the disadvantages of those entering the system from culturally or cognitively disadvantaged backgrounds. In other words, these arguments sound plausible only if we ignore another extremely important difference between students—difference in educational *needs.*

As we have seen, need often is a relevant criterion for determining what constitutes equal treatment. The fact that persons from certain social groups or backgrounds have greater educational needs is often used as the basis of a strong argument for programs of compensatory education for members of such groups—head start programs, special training in the English language in schools for nonnative speakers. Given the importance of education in our social-economic system, it seems we cannot ignore differences in persons' educational needs and still claim to offer equality of educational treatment to all. To understand equality in education, then, we must look more closely at the concept of need.

What is it to need something? Clearly it is different from merely wanting something, for we may want something (for example, a Cadillac) without needing it and may need something (for example, antibiotics for a strep throat) without wanting it.[42] An important clue about needs is the fact that statements of the form "Person P needs X" are generally incomplete or elliptical; to need something is to need it *for something*.[43] In general, I think we can say that statements of the form "P needs X" are abbreviations for statements of the form "P needs X for Y" where Y stands for some aim, purpose, or goal of P, or some benefit to P. Thus, for example, "John Smith needs \$75,000 right away" is elliptical for "John Smith needs \$75,000 right away to pay his lawyers."

To need something is to need it for something else. But what is the relationship that holds between two things when one is needed for the other? It appears that the first thing is a necessary means to the second thing. In other words, "P needs X for Y" means roughly the same thing as "X is a necessary condition of P attaining (obtaining, doing) Y" or "P cannot attain (obtain, do) Y without X." On this analysis, John Smith needing \$75,000 amounts to his being unable to attain the goal of paying his lawyers without receiving \$75,000. There is more to it than this, however. For suppose I say to you that I need to borrow your baseball bat, and it turns out that I intend to use it to brain a noisy neighbor. Upon discovering my intentions, you would be perfectly justified in replying that I do not *really need* the baseball bat, and that it was misleading to suggest that I did. Yet it remains true (we may suppose) that I cannot brain the neighbor without obtaining your bat. What this suggests to me is that a statement about needs implies that the thing needed is a necessary means for attaining a *valid* or *proper* aim or goal. In my neighbor's view, I do not really need the baseball bat, because he does not regard the aim which I cannot accomplish without that bat as being valid or proper. This observation about needs reveals that the concept of need is an essentially normative one. This is because one's view of whether something is really needed or not depends upon a normative judgment of whether or not the end for which it is needed is a valid or proper one.[44]

What this analysis of needs implies is that what is regarded as constituting an educational need, calling for special treatment in an educational context, will depend upon what are regarded as valid and proper ends of the educational system and of the persons affected by that system. It may be that children in a certain social group need compensatory programs in order to compete successfully with children from other social groups for jobs when they finish school, but that they need different sorts of educational programs if they are to preserve their cultural identity throughout their school years and during their later life. Which programs we adopt to fulfill their educational needs depend upon which objectives we regard as valid educational ones—improved competitive status in adult life or preservation of cultural traditions.[45] If, in turn, we define equal treatment in terms of equal consideration within the system of the educational needs of all, what constitutes equal treatment will turn out to depend upon what we regard as the valid objectives, goals, aims, and purposes of the educational system as it applies to the individual.

A similar conclusion can be arrived at by a less circuitous route. The principle of formal equality, stated earlier, requires that differences in treatment be based on relevant differences between the persons so treated. In discussing this principle, I pointed out that what constitutes a relevant difference in the context of a given social practice or institution often depends upon the aims, goals, and purposes of that practice or institution.[46] If we apply this principle to education, we conclude that what constitutes a relevant difference depends upon the aims and purposes of educational institutions. If a primary aim of those institutions is to ensure the production of a finely trained, intellectually elite class, it may be within the bounds of equal treatment to have special tracks in the educational system to supply superior education to those with special intellectual gifts. Or the aim may be to supply the culturally disadvantaged with tools to compete with other adults in the economic sector, to preserve the cultural identity of ethnic minorities, or to allow each individual to develop his own reasoning powers. Or it could be a variety of other things. In each case, a different aim may well lead to a different conception of what constitutes equal treatment. It follows also that the lack of a clear conception of the aims of education leaves a person largely unequipped to develop a clear view about what constitutes equality in education.

We might call this conclusion about the variation of criteria of equal treatment in education according to one's view of the aims of education the *indeterminacy of educational equality*. According to this conclusion, there is no determinant answer, independent of a specification of the aims and purposes of our educational institutions, to the question of what equality in education is. It might be thought we can escape this conclusion of indeterminacy by switching our focus from the notion of equal treatment in education to the notion of equal educational opportunity. After all, is it not educational opportunities which we wish to equalize rather than other features of the educational process? Let us look then at the concept of equal educational opportunity to understand what it is and to see if it can supply us with a focal point for public policy.

EQUAL EDUCATIONAL OPPORTUNITY

Discussion of the relationship between education and equal opportunity requires, first, noting the important distinction, frequently overlooked, between offering equal opportunity *within* the educational system and achieving equal opportunity *through the use of* the educational system. The former is defined as requiring that the two criteria of fair competition be satisfied with respect to access to scarce educational resources, especially at the higher levels. In other words, access to higher education is to be based solely on qualifications, and persons of equal natural ability from all social groups are to have an equal chance to develop such qualifications. Equal occupational opportunity through the use of the educational system, on the other hand, requires that the educational system operate as the primary social means of seeing that the second criterion of fair competition is satisfied with respect to occupational opportunities. In other words, the educational system is to be operated so as to ensure that equally talented individuals from different social groups have an equal chance to develop the qualifications necessary to obtain desirable jobs.

These two distinct concepts are often confused with one another because, based on the standard model of equal opportunity in America,[47] their operations are supposed to coincide. According to this model, equality of opportunity within the educational system is *the* way of guaranteeing that people from various ethnic, racial, religious, and sexual groups have equal opportunity to obtain qualifications for high-status, high-income jobs. By making primary and secondary education available to all and by basing admission to college and graduate and professional schools on demonstration of qualifications, we ensure that, regardless of their backgrounds, persons have a fair chance to compete for success in obtaining the educational credentials that amount to certificates of admission to the more desirable occupations. If this model were correct, offering equality of opportunity within education would be a necessary and sufficient condition for satisfying the second requirement of equal occupational opportunity.

Unfortunately, however, the model is incorrect and inadequate. If the educational system were the only aspect of a person's environment that affected his development of occupational qualifications, then perhaps the model would be satisfactory, but cognitive, social, and psychological influences of various kinds outside the school system affect a child's development in important ways. These influences may operate in such a way as to place most children from certain social groups at a serious competitive disadvantage throughout their school careers. Upon entering school, such children may lack the linguistic facility to profit from their schooling; the positive attitude toward learning that is a prerequisite for benefiting from school; or familiarity with concepts, subjects, and events discussed in school and known to most of their classmates. The upshot of all this is that equal opportunity within the schools may serve only to perpetuate or even increase the competitive advantages of certain social groups in comparison with others. Despite equal opportunity within the educational system, members of some groups will not have had overall environments that offered them an equal chance to develop the qualifications needed to enter into and succeed in desirable occupations.

Compensatory Inequality

This divergence between equal opportunity in education and equal occupational opportunity raises the possibility that it might be necessary to offer *un*equal opportunities in education as a means of promoting equal occupational opportunities. This idea is an attractive one because access to educational resources is one means of individual economic success that society has comparative control over, and thus it is a resource leading to individual success that society can attempt to dole out to correct imbalances in the distribution of other unfathomed and uncontrollable factors determining who shall succeed and who shall fail. Given that, in our society, schools serve as selection and certification agencies for prospective employees, one way to enable members of certain groups in society to be more successful occupationally is to increase their access to such certification by increasing their access to higher educational institutions. Given, however, the social disadvantages that members of certain groups have faced, it is necessary to relax formal selection requirements of certain institutions of higher learning (and certification) to ensure that representative numbers of members from these groups receive such certification.[48] Selection policies of this sort can be called programs of *compensatory inequality*. They involve inequality in the sense that they allow access to certain educational resources, that is, unequal as measured by the traditional criteria of qualification—grades, test scores, and so forth. Such inequality is compensatory because it is designed to make up for and to balance out other social disadvantages of those now being given preferred treatment.[49] In other words, compensatory inequality in education involves attempting to ensure certain persons an equal chance to develop job qualifications by compensating them for the social barriers they face in seeking to acquire such qualifications through special access to certain educational resources that help to develop these qualifications.

Programs of compensatory inequality, which involve different admission standards for members of different racial, sexual, or ethnic groups, have caused a great deal of controversy in this country recently. The moral issues involved are extremely complex, and I will not attempt to deal with them fully here. I will, however, make a few general comments on certain aspects of the matter that are closely related to equality of opportunity. As I see it, two essentially different sorts of arguments favor compensatory policies of this kind.[50]

The first sort of argument contends that it is not proper to use only traditional criteria—grades, test scores, and personal recommendations—to compare applicants for admission to certain institutions of higher education. It is claimed that, in the case of members of disadvantaged groups, test scores and past grades are not necessarily accurate indicators of ability and likely future performance in a favorable educational environment. That is, a less distinguished record in high school or college for a minority student may be stronger evidence of overall academic or professional promise than a somewhat better record achieved by a student who faced fewer social obstacles to educational achievement. Thus, some degree of relaxation of standards of admission for minority students may represent merely a correction of the normal standards as measures of likely future performance.

A slightly different argument of this sort focuses on criticism of the present criteria of success and competence within institutions of higher education and various high-income, high-status professions. It is claimed, for example, that, from the point of view of society as a whole, a physician's willingness to treat and ability to relate to poor people, and his personal dedication to alleviating suffering, are just as important as his technical knowledge and diagnostic skill and that, therefore, such traits are valid criteria for the selection of candidates for admission to medical school and for deciding who is to be licensed to practice medicine. If it is conceded that minority group members are more likely to possess these desirable traits, this would, according to the argument, constitute a valid reason for offering admission and certification to minority candidates, even if their grades and test scores were lower than those of other candidates and even if their grades and test scores were so much lower that we would expect them to perform less well than other candidates by present (inadequate) standards of academic and professional competence.

Essentially, then, the thrust of the first sort of argument is to attack the adequacy of traditional standards of admission, certification, and competence. Such arguments contend that traditional standards are wrong and that, therefore, admissions policies that involve inequality with respect to those standards need not involve inequality when judged by reference to proper standards that allow for special traits, special problems, and special potential for social contribution possessed by members of disadvantaged social groups. In other words, according to this argument the admissions policies that we have labeled policies of compensatory inequality are really, from the proper perspective, programs of *equal* treatment since they treat members of different groups differently only on the basis of relevant differences between the members of these groups. Such policies appear to involve inequality only because present criteria of admissions recognize some of the relevant differences between candidates while ignoring others that are equally important.

The second sort of argument for programs of compensatory inequality in admissions does not presuppose the inadequacy of traditional criteria of admission. Rather, it tries to justify the application of unequal standards to members of different groups on the grounds that such inequalities are perhaps necessary in the short run if we are to attain true equality of opportunity in the long run. Short-run inequalities are necessary, it is claimed, because placing representative numbers of members of disadvantaged groups in successful social positions is a prerequisite to ending negative social attitudes that encourage continued discrimination against members of such groups. In other words, competent[51] role models from disadvantaged groups are needed to help convince skeptical majority group members that members of disadvantaged groups can "do the job" if given the chance and to convince skeptical members of disadvantaged groups that it is possible for them to succeed if they are willing to work hard and compete.[52] Given the virtual impossibility of offering equality of hope to younger members of disadvantaged groups without these groups being significantly represented in society's upper stratas, reaching a state of true equal opportunity may well require unequal admissions standards for different groups as a temporary measure. It is a case of buying future equality by sacrificing a certain amount of equality in the present.

These seem to me to be the two strongest sorts of argument one could offer in favor of compensatory inequality in education. There are also powerful moral arguments against compensatory inequality. The main such argument revolves around the claim that practices of compensatory inequality involve injustices to those individuals denied access to educational resources despite having better qualifications than minority students who receive such access. It is claimed that the rules of access to educational institutions have been (in the ideal, if not in reality) based on merit, with those best qualified according to certain relevant criteria (grades, test scores, and so forth) being granted admission. In line with these long-established practices, students have developed legitimate expectations about the conditions of their competition with others and the rewards they are likely to receive if they work hard and get good grades during the earlier phases of their education. Changing the rules of competition to favor those having such apparently educationally irrelevant features as a certain skin color or sex would do an injustice to persons having such expectations.[53] Furthermore, it might be pointed out that compensatory admissions policies would increase the representation of certain social *groups* in college, graduate schools, and professional schools. But the focus on group membership means there is still no guarantee that equal opportunity for the individuals involved is advanced by such policies. Thus, policies favoring the admission of members of group X may benefit a member of group X who encountered few social obstacles to education, while, at the same time, they may hurt an individual who, while not a member of one of the designated disadvantaged groups, actually faced greater obstacles. In other words, the salient criteria employed in differential admissions policies (race, sex, or ethnic background) do not in individual cases exactly coincide with the social disadvantages that must be compensated for if each individual is to be afforded an equal chance to become a success. Inevitably, "compensation" will go to many relatively advantaged individuals, thus increasing their advantage, and many of those who need compensation will not receive it because they are not members of an appropriate group. The latter could reasonably claim to have suffered injustices under the system of compensatory inequality.

One way of summarizing these conflicting moral considerations about compensatory inequality would be to point out that compensatory inequality represents a kind of schizophrenic tension in the liberal concept of equal opportunity as spelled out above. One aspect of equal opportunity requires that hiring, promotions, and admissions be based on the possession of relevant qualifications. The other aspect of equal opportunity requires giving all persons (regardless of what group they come from) an equal chance to develop those qualifications. Because education is regarded as a part of this system of equal opportunity in two distinct ways, these aspects of equal opportunity may conflict. If, on the one hand, we apply the principle of relevant qualifications to the question of access to higher education itself, we may conclude that equal opportunity and compensatory inequality are incompatible. Regarding the educational system as only one part of the total social environment which determines an individual's opportunity to develop occupational qualifications, we may, on the other hand, view compensatory inequality in the educational system as a necessary means of assuring individuals from various disadvantaged social groups an equal chance to develop qualifications for employment. Thus, there is a tension between the two aspects of equal opportunity. It seems we can give everyone an equal chance to develop job qualifications only if we sacrifice the principle of assigning certain desirable positions (that is, admission to institutions of higher learning) solely on the basis of qualifications. Equal occupational opportunity through education can be reached only, if at all, by replacing equality of opportunity in education by programs of compensatory inequality.

Equal Opportunity in Education

If, as I have suggested, we cannot justify equal educational opportunity by appeal to the standard model of how equal opportunity should operate in America, the question arises as to whether equal educational opportunity is a desirable social goal at all. Jencks, who concludes from his data analyses that equal educational opportunity would not significantly reduce inequalities outside the educational sphere, concludes that "the case for distributing school resources and opportunities equally . . . is no different from the case for making the distribution of public parks, trash collection, or other public services equal."[54] I disagree, and I would like to explain why by looking at the concept of equality of educational opportunity more closely.

According to the standard American model, higher education is seen as a means to success and high income and, thus, as a prize which people should have an equal opportunity of capturing. With this view, both of the criteria of equal occupational opportunity can be transferred and directly applied to the realm of education. Equal educational opportunity requires that those best qualified attend higher educational institutions. It also requires that persons with equal natural abilities from different social groups and backgrounds have equal chances to obtain the necessary qualifications. It is felt that universal, free, compulsory primary and secondary education are necessary to satisfy the second condition, but that quota systems and differential admissions criteria for different racial or ethnic groups are inconsistent with the first requirement. This conception of equal educational opportunity seems to lose much of its force when its impotence as a means of attaining equal occupational opportunity is revealed.

There is, however, an alternative conception of equal educational opportunity where education itself, on all levels, is seen as a good. Equal opportunity is not equal opportunity to compete to get into law school or college; it is having an equal chance to learn, to develop one's intellectual abilities, one's personality and talents. According to this conception of education, equality of opportunity may involve different people being treated differently in the educational system because they have differing intellectual needs, abilities, and interests. Equal opportunity is not equality in competitive terms, but an equal chance to profit in one's own way from learning, and perhaps an equal claim on scarce educational resources which can be used to one's own intellectual benefit. Of course, such a notion of equality of educational opportunity is not completely separate from the competitive notion. The two are linked if it is felt that higher education is the best vehicle for personal intellectual development or that competition for success within the educational system contributes to personal development in its own right.

The point I wish to stress, however, is that we need not look at equality of educational opportunity as merely being a means to some social end of group equality or equality of opportunity. The developmental conception of equal educational opportunity rests on a different view of the significance of education. Education is primarily valuable, not as a means of material success, but as an end in itself or as a means of spiritual success.[55] That is, education contributes to the happiness and quality of life of persons in a way that is independent of its effects on their employment prospects. Education supplies people with knowledge and, what is more important, it may make them learn to think seriously, to examine their lives and their social environment critically. Thus, education provides direct links to two of the fundamental features shared by human beings—the capacity for happiness and the capacity for morality—for it contributes to their living at a higher level of awareness and self-consciousness, which is what makes education different from caring for public parks and collecting trash. Education of some sort is necessary for personal moral development and happiness. As human beings with the capacity for happiness and moral action, we all have, prima facie, an equal claim on the opportunity to learn and develop our intellectual powers, a claim independent of the relationship (or lack of one) between education and income.

Looking at these two very different concepts of equal educational opportunity, we see the reemergence of the principle of indeterminacy of educational equality. What constitutes equal opportunity in education cannot be specified without considering the aims and purposes of educational institutions any more than what constitutes equal treatment in education can be so specified. If you see the aim of educational institutions as that of certifying the most able persons and routing them into the most important jobs so that economic productivity will be maximized, then you see a competitive educational system that advances the best performers to the next level as constituting equal opportunity in the educational sphere. On the other hand, if you see the point of the educational system as being that of ensuring equality of occupational opportunity by preparing the socially disadvantaged to compete for the best jobs, programs of compensatory inequality look like educational equality of opportunity to you.[56] Finally, if you think the point of education is to develop the individual's intellectual capacities and powers of critical thought, equal educational opportunity may, as you see it, involve widely varying programs adapted to the abilities, interests, and needs of different students. Most of us, at some deep level undisturbed by careful, reflective thought, hold some combination of these views about the proper aims of education. We somehow hope that our educational system can accomplish all purposes at once—promote efficiency, ensure fair competition for jobs, contribute to the intellectual development of most all members of the society. But whether our aims for the educational system are single or multiple, the basic principle remains undisturbed. Determining what constitutes equality within an educational system requires some sort of theory about the point, or aims, or purposes of that educational system.

We might hope that moral philosophy would supply a ready solution to our indeterminacy problem by designating a particular aim or purpose as *the* morally proper aim or purpose of our educational system. I consider this to be a false hope. All of the aims mentioned—economic efficiency, fair job competition, and citizens' intellectual development—are morally admirable ones. A further aim of our educational system, the promotion of scientific research and the expansion of the frontiers of human knowledge, is also a worthwhile social aim. I am aware of no generally accepted philosophical basis for selecting one of these admirable aims over the others as being the proper aim of our educational institutions.[57] No doubt, depending upon the particular views they hold, moral philosophers and social theorists will disagree with one another about which of these aims ought to be promoted through the educational system (and which ought to be promoted only by other social institutions), about the relative importance of the different aims in question, and about the exact nature of the aims in question (for example, what constitutes fair job competition). Neither among citizens nor moral philosophers is there presently enough of a consensus about the aims of our educational system to allow us to give any precise account of what would constitute equality in the context of that system.

How, then, are we to deal with questions concerning equality that arise in educational contexts? It might be suggested that, lacking a consensus, a democratic society such as ours ought to decide such questions through the normal workings of the political process. I think this is inevitably what will happen, and it is probably what ought to happen. But I wish to make clear that, in saying this, I am not advocating that these issues be decided by the prejudices of the uneducated and the arbitrary passions of voters and politicians. The political process, as I conceive it, is fueled by ideas and arguments as well as by passions. The advocacy of a particular conception of equality in the political arena, and the development of social-educational theories to support that particular conception of equality, may occur together—each contributing to the other. The need for supporting arguments to be used in the political process gives impetus to the articulation and development of the underlying social-educational theory. Conversely, the nature of the developing theory may lead to changes in the political position offered or in some of the arguments adduced in its defense. It is hoped that, as this process of political competition backed by social theory development plays itself out in the future, a reasonable consensus about the aims of our educational system will develop, and well-supported substantive criteria of equality will come to be generally accepted as applicable to our educational institutions. If such a consensus fails to develop, at least we will have a clearer idea of what fundamental differences in social goals and educational theory separate the competing parties in disputes concerning equality in education.

Thus, I am not suggesting that the banner of equality should be laid down. I am only suggesting that bringing everyone under the banner of equality will not solve most major substantive disagreements about educational policy. What is required is a shift in emphasis toward developing conceptions of what our educational institutions are for, and what they should be like, in order to support particular substantive interpretations of educational equality and equal opportunity.

THE PROBLEM OF MEANS

Perhaps it is overly pessimistic to suggest, as I have above, that there is no consensus in American society about the primary aims of our educational system. One goal of that system has received considerable attention and public support during the last twenty years: the achievement of equal occupational opportunity in our society by offering equal educational opportunities to members of all social groups. While there may be some dissenters, I think it is fair to say that the vast majority of Americans have come to support this goal and that many of them regard it as one of the most important goals of our educational system.[58]

Let us suppose then, for purposes of discussion, that everyone now agrees on this particular aim—equal occupational opportunity through equal educational opportunity—as being the proper aim of our educational system. It seems to me that we would still be faced with significant problems in formulating general educational policies intended to realize the ideal of equality. One such problem is the problem of measurement. How are we to measure equality so as to determine whether or not we have achieved it or are approaching it? Though there may be immense practical difficulties, I do not regard this problem as insoluble. I have pointed out that, while it is difficult to determine whether an individual has received equal occupational opportunity, it may be possible to determine by statistical evidence whether members of a particular social group are being offered equal occupational opportunity.[59] The simplest test is to determine whether members of a particular racial, ethnic, or sexual group are as occupationally successful, on an average, as members of our society as a whole. If members of such a group are significantly less successful, this is strong indirect evidence that equal opportunity for members of that group has not been attained.[60]

Just as there are rough measures of whether members of certain groups are being offered equal occupational opportunity, we often can, in theory, determine whether changes in opportunity are attributable to changes in the educational system. Suppose, for example, that the average income of members of disadvantaged group X goes up 5 percent faster than the national average over a certain period of time. A breakdown of the statistics might reveal that the average income for members of group X having a given level of education has not increased at all, but the overall increase is attributable to an increase in the average level of education of members of the group. If this latter increase can be shown to be attributable to programs specifically intended to extend the educational opportunities available to members of group X (it occurs with appropriate time lag after colleges have started making special efforts to recruit applicants from group X), we could fairly conclude that society has moved closer to offering members of group X equal occupational opportunity by offering them more equal educational opportunities.

I would submit, then, that, for those seeking to promote equal occupational opportunity through the educational system, the central problem is not the problem of measurement. I think such persons would agree that we could tell we were approaching equal opportunity if the test scores of minority students were to go up significantly relative to the general population and if minority group representation in desirable occupations were to approach the point at which it would correspond to the percentage of the population made up of members of those groups. The central problem confronting us if we seek equal opportunity through education is *the problem of means.* The fact is that we do not know what to do within the educational system to significantly affect the above-mentioned indicators of equal opportunity.[61] Recent sociological evidence suggests that the commonsense solutions to the problem—racial and economic integration in the schools, equalizing expenditures per pupil—just do not work.[62] We do not know how to raise minority test scores significantly; nor do we know how to significantly increase representation of minority groups in professional schools and desirable occupations without employing some form of preferential hiring or admissions.

Actually, the apparent impossibility of solving the problem of social inequality by educational means alone should not come as a great surprise. Our educational system is only one part of a larger and more complex system of social institutions. It is this social system as a whole that operates to the disadvantage of women and minority-group members, and it apparently damages their life prospects in a way that cannot be cured solely by the medicines available within our educational system (or at least any such medicines presently available).

Surprising or not, these negative sociological findings have serious and unavoidable implications with respect to the goal of equal occupational opportunity through education. They suggest that offering equal opportunity within the educational system will not be enough to ensure minority-group members equal occupational opportunity. Achieving equal occupational opportunity may require programs of compensatory inequality within the educational system as well as changes in noneducational institutions of our society. In other words, if the sociologists are right, the educational goal supported by most Americans—equal occupational opportunity through equal educational opportunity—is not attainable. To attain equal occupational opportunity, other means are needed.

In view of the discouraging sociological data, how might those who have sought to help the disadvantaged by offering them educational equality (henceforth called reformers) sensibly proceed? Three steps seem reasonable at the moment. First, reformers should support further research on educational methods and programs that might significantly help the disadvantaged. For while spending money (or integrating schools) per se does not seem to help the education of the disadvantaged much, it may be that spending money (or integrating schools) in certain particular ways will have more significant beneficial effects. The fact that we do not yet know how to help the disadvantaged by education does not mean that we can never find out how to do so. Hence, recent negative findings should not discourage further research efforts. Reformers also should seriously consider the merits and demerits of various programs of compensatory inequality within the educational system.[63] It may be that some programs will be effective in improving the occupational prospects of members of certain disadvantaged groups and ought to be implemented for that reason. Finally, those seeking to improve the lot of the disadvantaged should face up to the fact that changes in the educational system alone cannot bring equal opportunity to our society. Changes in other institutions must be made as well. Discrimination in hiring and promotion must be attacked directly. Better housing and more jobs must be provided to the poor to improve the social environment in which poor children grow up. If such changes are not made, our society will not be offering its members equal opportunity even if it offers free quality education to all.

What of the more traditional approaches to dealing with problems of inequality, such measures as integrating the schools and equalizing per pupil expenditures across and within school districts? Should reformers continue to concern themselves with these matters? In spite of evidence that these measures have little impact by themselves, it seems important that efforts to implement them not be abandoned. While such measures apparently are not sufficient to produce the desired results, they may be necessary parts of the most effective cure. For example, while simply equalizing expenditures may not do much if money is used in traditional ways, we may in the future discover ways of helping disadvantaged children that are effective but expensive. Implementing beneficial programs may well require greater expenditures on the education of poor children than would be available under present programs of financing schools largely through local taxes. Equalizing expenditures might make the extra money available where the need is greatest.

A more basic and more important reason to continue reform efforts goes back to the idea of persons being of equal status because of their common vulnerability, their capacity for happiness, and their moral capacity.[64] As a society which accepts the equality of persons as a fundamental moral and political postulate, our society is committed to according essentially equal status to all of its members. It is in line with this notion of equal status that we regard all as equal persons before the law and refuse to grant titles to citizens. According persons equal status involves regarding them as equally important and equally worthy of receiving society's aid and protection. Therefore, insofar as society treats some individuals better than others without sufficient reason, it acts as if the former were more important than the latter, and fails to accord equal status to the latter. And insofar as a society *appears* to treat certain individuals or groups better than other individuals or groups without sufficient reason, it *appears* to accord a higher status to the former.

It is in this context that we must view questions of integration and expenditures within our educational system. For, in contemporary American society, education is generally regarded as an extremely important good. Education is thought to be directly beneficial to an individual's personal development and is thought to promote (and reflect) his competitive position in society. It follows that if society treats, *or appears to treat*, certain groups better than other groups so far as educational benefits are concerned, this appears to reflect a significant societal judgment about the relative importance or status of the groups in question. This is especially true if the groups so differentiated once had different legal statuses in society. Thus, for example, if blacks, who once had inferior legal status, go to separate and inferior schools from whites, this reinforces the lingering prejudice that blacks are inferior by suggesting that they are so regarded by society.

Now as far as equality of status goes, appearances are extremely important. If a person or group appears to be regarded as lowly or inferior by society, people who observe this (including the person or group so treated) will generally tend to accept the implied judgment and henceforth treat the person or group as lowly or inferior. We may therefore say about equality what is often said of justice: it is important not only to treat people equally, but also to appear to treat them equally. Hence, even if the current evidence indicates that integration and more equal expenditures per pupil will not improve the education of disadvantaged children very much, it may, nevertheless, be important that integration and a policy of equalizing expenditures be carried out. This is because of the danger that failure to implement such programs would, in the present climate, reinforce prejudicial attitudes and undermine belief in the equal status of all citizens.[65] The principle of equality, in other words, has enormous symbolic importance in any society which strives to be just, an importance which certainly warrants at least the attempt to move in what we believe is in the right direction, however much we may disagree over aims or the order of aims.

CONCLUSIONS

My general conclusions, then, are as follows. We cannot determine what constitutes equal treatment or equal opportunity in the context of our present educational system without clarification of the aims of that system. There is not, at present, sufficient agreement among Americans about the aims of our educational system to allow us to arrive at a consensus about what would constitute equality in education. We are, therefore, required to develop a morally acceptable conception of the role our educational system ought to play in our society before we can hope to develop an adequate and workable concept of equality in education. In the meantime, we can serve the ideal of equality only in a limited way: by removing obviously arbitrary inequities in the educational system, inequities that belie the equal status of all citizens in our society.

My position is best understood, I think, as a view about the proper relationship between morality and educational policy. While I agree with many supporters of educational equality that moral considerations must be the foundation of sound educational policy, I strongly disagree about the point at which these moral considerations must be brought to bear on educational policy. It will not do to simply attempt to apply the abstract moral ideal of equality to the current educational system. In most cases, this only leads to confusion and irreconcilable conflicts that stem from the multiple and possibly conflicting aims of our educational system. Rather, moral considerations must be brought to bear at the prior stage of developing a sound social-educational theory. Only when backed by such a theory will the concept of equality have definite and precise application in the context of our educational institutions.

NOTES

1. If we accept Leibniz' principle of the identity of indiscernibles, which says that if objects X and Y are the same in absolutely all respects then they are really the same object, we can view identity statements as the limiting case of general statements of equality which assert sameness in some respects. For a discussion of the principle of identity of indiscernibles, see Bertrand Russell, *The Philosophy of Leibniz* (London: Allen and Unwin, 1937), ch. 5.

2. Thus, for example, the authors of the Declaration of Independence wrote, "We hold these truths to be self-evident, that all men are created equal, that they are endowed by their Creator with certain inalienable rights, that among these are life, liberty, and the pursuit of happiness." This passage clearly links the idea of descriptive equality with the claim to be treated equally with respect to the basic rights to life, liberty, and the pursuit of happiness. Compare the statement, "All human beings are born free and equal in dignity and rights," from Article 1 of the Universal Declaration of Human Rights, General Assembly of the United Nations, December 10, 1948.

3. Here, as elsewhere, I am indebted to Bernard Williams' excellent essay, "The Idea of Equality," in P. Laslett and W. G. Runciman (eds.), *Philosophy, Politics, and Society* (London: Blackwell, 1962). I differ from Williams somewhat, however, in identifying what the general features that most all human beings possess are.

4. On the relationship between self-respect and one's plans and aspirations, see John Rawls, *A Theory of Justice* (Cambridge, Mass.: Harvard University Press, 1971), sec. 67.

5. This attitude of recognizing the potential morality of all men seems to lie behind Ghandi's refusal to regard his political opponents as enemies, and his belief that nonviolence can be used to save the oppressor as well as the oppressed. See Mohandas K. Ghandi, "Non-violence," in

Jeffrey G. Murphy (ed.), *Civil Disobedience and Violence* (Belmont, Calif.: Wadsworth, 1971), 95-96.

6. See Immanuel Kant, *Fundamental Principles of the Metaphysics of Morals,* tr. Thomas Abbott (Indianapolis, Ind.: Bobbs-Merrill, 1949).

7. It might be thought that this problem can be avoided by limiting the claim to equal treatment to those *persons* (rather than beings) who have had, or will in the normal course of events come to have, the general features in question. The difficulty arises in attempting to defend this limitation against a charge of arbitrariness. If what confers the claim to equal treatment is having once achieved the status associated with the possession of certain characteristics or having the potential to develop such characteristics, it seems inappropriate to afford the claim only to a certain class of beings who have that potential or have achieved that status.

8. Cf. sec. 55 of John Locke's *Second Treatise of Government,* ed. Peter Laslett (New York: New American Library, 1965), 346-47.

9. As I see it, this obligation is based on two different sorts of moral considerations: the utilitarian principle of benevolence toward all sentient creatures, and the perfectionist principle that rationality and human freedom should be promoted whenever possible.

10. The sketch of an argument I offer in some ways resembles Locke's argument in his *Second Treatise of Government,* and it has some affinities with Hobbes' *Leviathan* (New York: Collier, 1962), ch. 13.

11. For convenience in stating the argument, I ignore the problem of exceptional cases. The qualification that the argument refers only to those human beings who possess the three general features I have listed is to be understood throughout.

12. For Hobbes, the vulnerability to death at the hands of others is by itself enough to establish the basic equality of men. He writes: "They are equals, who can do equal things one against the other; but they who can do the greatest things, namely, kill, can do equal things." Thomas Hobbes, *De Cive,* ch. 1, sec. 3, in Bernard Gert (ed.), *Man and Citizen* (New York: Doubleday, 1972), 114.

13. Locke, *op. cit.,* sec. 4, 309.

14. I borrow this title from J. R. Lucas, "Against Equality," *Philosophy* 40 (October 1965), 296-307.

15. See Aristotle, *Nicomachean Ethics* (Indianapolis, Ind.: Bobbs-Merrill, 1962), ch. 5, sec. 3.

16. *Ibid.,* 118-19.

17. See Joel Feinberg, "Justice and Personal Desert" in his *Doing and Deserving* (Princeton, N.J.: Princeton University Press, 1970), 61.

18. One of the major virtues of laissez-faire economic theory, according to its proponents, is that it solves the problem of desert with respect to one important kind of treatment—the receipt of income. According to this view, what income a person deserves depends upon the demand for his goods and services in a free economy. This is because high demand for a product or service means people want the product or service a great deal, which indicates that supplying it constitutes a contribution to the general happiness. Thus, the supply and demand

system purportedly operates to ensure that people are rewarded with incomes roughly proportional to their economic contributions to the general happiness of society.

19. I would limit the application of this principle to cases in which the established practice and its aims are not substantially unjust. Thus, even if a policy of racial discrimination, for example, were firmly established as a social institution in a given society, this would not make racial differences relevant reasons for treating people differently in social and economic life.

20. See p. 36, below.

21. See, for example, Christopher Jencks et al., *Inequality* (New York: Basic, 1972). Hereafter cited as *Inequality*.

22. See, for example, the appendix to Feinberg, *op. cit.*

23. Cf. n. 19, above. See also Stanley I. Benn and Richard S. Peters, *Social Principles and the Democratic State* (London: Allen and Unwin, 1959), 138-40.

24. By equal occupational opportunity, I mean equal opportunity to enter desirable occupations *and* equal opportunity to advance and succeed within a given occupation.

25. Someone might object to the inclusion of the chance to develop the desire to succeed and self-confidence as part of equal opportunity, on the grounds that equal opportunity refers to being able to compete on fair terms *if you want to compete*, and has nothing to do with other factors determining whether or not you choose to compete. To convince ourselves that this objection is mistaken, we need only imagine a society in which a certain class of persons have formally open to them the channels of developing marketable skills. They have so systematically been taught by social mores to regard themselves as inferior or inadequate or to think of competition for high status and high income as an inappropriate goal for members of their class, for example, that they rarely take advantage of the opportunity to develop their skills and compete for high-income positions. It is clear that such a society does not offer the members of this class equal opportunity because it systematically operates in such a way as to ensure that they lack sufficient motivation to compete and succeed. I am grateful to Virginia Warren for bringing this aspect of equal opportunity to my attention.

26. The notion of a social group used here includes groups identified by racial, ethnic, cultural, sexual (e.g., female), political, or economic (e.g., lower-class) criteria. It does not include groups defined by characteristics which are directly relevant to one's ability to perform diverse socially useful tasks (e.g., intelligent). On this point, see pp. 24-25, below.

27. For a brief discussion of this proposal, see *Inequality*, pp. 74-75. The underlying idea that we ought to arrange social institutions so as to reduce the effects on income of natural differences between persons is presented in John Rawls, *op. cit.*, 15, 102.

28. For a statement of a similar conclusion with respect to the legal guarantee of equality under the equal protection clause of the United States Constitution, see "Developments in the Law—Equal Protection," *Harvard Law Review* 82 (No. 5, 1969), 1189.

29. The relevance of this distinction to Jencks's analysis and conclusions is discussed in Lester C. Thurow, "Proving the Absence of Positive Associations," *Harvard Educational Review* 43 (February 1973), 107-109; and in Beverly Duncan, "Comments on *Inequality*," *ibid.*, 125-26.

30. See pp. 18-19, above, for statement of these arguments. The desert argument clearly deals with the deserts of individuals rather than groups. The incentive argument most effectively supports the doctrine of equal opportunity for *individuals*, since incentives will operate most efficiently if persons expect to be rewarded economically if and only if they work hard, innovate, etc., rather than if their social group as a whole works hard, etc. It is clearly the courts' view that the constitutional guarantee of equal protection under the law applies to individuals rather than groups. See "Developments in the Law—Equal Protection," 1111.

31. *Cf.* n. 25, above.

32. See, for example, Arthur R. Jensen, "How Much Can We Boost IQ and Scholastic Achievement?" *Harvard Educational Review* 39(1969), 1-123.

33. Christopher Jencks, "*Inequality* in Retrospect," *Harvard Educational Review* 43(No. 1, 1973), 138.

34. *Ibid.*, 164.

35. See *Inequality*, especially ch. 1.

36. See *Inequality*, pp. 7, 11, and Jencks, "*Inequality* in Retrospect," 154.

37. See *Inequality*, 7, where Jencks writes, "Since a competitive system means that some people 'succeed' while others 'fail,' it also means that people will end up unequal."

38. Jencks's error is not, after all, as blatant as this sentence implies because, as Jencks notes, equality of income distribution is a matter of degree. Thus, one of the aims of many supporters of equal opportunity may be to reduce the *amount* of income inequality within a system of competitive inequality. My main point against Jencks remains unaffected, however: the central value underlying the ideology of equal opportunity is fairness of distribution, not equality of distribution.

39. The system might function by keeping people in school until they attained a certain score on a general standardized test and *no longer*, so that those able to pass the test upon entrance would not be allowed in school. On this plan, some children might never get into school; other persons might never leave it. Cf. *Inequality*, 74.

40. It may be that failure to use more specific measures of educational quality accounts, to some degree, for Jencks's negative conclusions concerning the relationship between education and cognitive skills. See Alice Rivlin, "Forensic Social Science," *Harvard Educational Review* 43(No. 1, 1973), 69.

41. See p. 13, above.

42. There is a somewhat different sense of "need," in which a need can roughly be equated with an urgent or strongly felt desire. Educational needs are not, however, needs in that sense, and I ignore that sense in what follows.

43. I owe this point to the late Arnold Kaufman.

44. Actually, it turns out that statements about needs are normative in another respect as well, and hence are doubly normative. For the notion of a

"necessary condition," used in the above analysis of needs, refers to a condition which is "necessary" in the sense of being the most reasonable or acceptable way of accomplishing the end in view. Thus, "I need to borrow a cup of sugar to make this cake" does not imply that there is no other way to make the cake, but only that all the available alternatives are undesirable or less acceptable for some good reason. What constitutes a good reason for regarding an alternative as unacceptable depends on the circumstances in the particular case. In general, the more reasons there are against using the "needed" thing, the stronger the reasons must be for eliminating the alternatives before we will agree that the thing in question is really needed. In other words, being needed involves being the least unacceptable means available for attaining the desired end. Speaking more formally, the analysis of need statements offered is: X needs Y if and only if there is a Z such that (1) Z is a valid or proper aim or purpose of X, (2) Y is a means of X attaining Z, and (3) there is no means of X attaining Z which is, all things considered, as acceptable as Y. The doubly normative nature of need statements is revealed by the appearance of normative terms ("proper," "valid," "acceptable") in two different clauses of this analysis.

45. I do not mean to imply that these particular ends must be mutually exclusive—they may or may not be depending upon whether competitive success in the society requires assimilation into the majority culture.

46. See p. 16, above.

47. This model seems to be one of the primary targets of Jencks's argument. See *Inequality*, especially ch. 1.

48. It may also be necessary to treat members of these groups differently once they enter these institutions to ensure that representative numbers of them receive certification. This may involve offering members of these groups special tutoring, counseling, reduced course loads, special financial aid, etc. Compensatory programs of this sort have tended to evoke less controversy than has the application of different admissions standards to members of different groups, but they raise some of the same moral problems since they seem to involve unequal distribution of educational resources.

49. The notion of compensatory inequality could be widened to include compensation for natural as well as environmental disadvantages. See *Inequality*, 74-75.

50. With certain modifications, the arguments for and against compensatory inequality which I give below could be applied to programs of compensatory inequality in employment as well as education. For more detailed discussion of compensatory inequality, see T. Nagel, "Equal Treatment and Compensatory Discrimination," *Philosophy and Public Affairs* 2(No. 4, 1973), 348-63, and J. Thompson, "Preferential Hiring," *ibid.*, 364-84.

51. The restriction to *competent* role models is crucial here since working with or serving under incompetent persons from disadvantaged groups would probably lead to increased prejudice on the part of majority group members. It is thus crucial that admissions and certification standards for members of disadvantaged groups not be lowered so far that many markedly unqualified persons become doctors, lawyers, teachers, government officials, etc.

52. Successful persons from disadvantaged groups may help reduce discrimi-

nation or its effects in other ways as well—by offering advice and counseling (from the point of view of someone who has overcome similar problems) to disadvantaged students and workers, by serving in their professional capacities as nondiscriminatory employment officers and admissions committee members, etc.

53. This difficulty is a specific instance of a rather general problem concerning justice. If the rules or operation of a social practice are somewhat unjust, but in the course of the operation of that practice people come to accept it and form their expectations based on it, it seems we are doing an injustice to some if we leave the practice as it is, and an injustice to others if we change the rules in the midst of the game thus disappointing what seem to be their reasonable expectations. The only solution seems to be a compromise in which we try to change the rules so as to eliminate the original injustices in such a way as to minimize the disappointment of legitimate expectations during the transitional period.

54. *Inequality*, 17.

55. Cf. Phillip Jackson, "After Apple-Picking," *Harvard Educational Review* 43(No. 1, 1973), 51-60.

56. Persons holding this view would probably reject the label "compensatory inequality" in favor of something like "compensatory equality." *Cf.* p. 43, above.

57. Someone might point out that, of the aims mentioned, only the intellectual development of citizens and the promotion of research can be said to be *educational* aims. This is true, but it only implies that educational institutions may have noneducational functions, not that the other functions are improper or less important than the educational functions of these institutions.

58. Jencks notes that this goal formed the basis of the war on poverty of the 1960's. See *Inequality*, 7.

59. See pp. 26-27, above.

60. This assumes that there is no valid scientific evidence that members of the group in question are, on the average, deficient in socially productive natural attributes (e.g., intelligence, creativity). If there is such evidence, we must accordingly reduce the success rate which is to serve as our criterion of whether members of the group in question are being offered equal opportunity. Of course, to avoid circularity, we must reject all attempts to treat a group's lowly economic position as evidence of its members' low average intelligence. On this last point, cf. N. J. Block and Gerald Dworkin, "IQ: Heritability and Inequality, Part 1," *Philosophy and Public Affairs* 3(No. 4, 1974), sec. V, 373-78.

61. This is the main conclusion of *Inequality*. Cf. H. M. Levin, "Education, Life Chances, and the Courts," (see Chapter 5).

62. See *Inequality*, especially chs. 2, 3.

63. Some of the moral issues raised by programs of compensatory inequality are discussed briefly on pp. 41-47, above.

64. See pp. 4-12, above.

65. A somewhat different sort of argument for equal expenditures could be developed along the lines suggested by the remarks on pp. 49-50, above. Such an argument would stress the intrinsic and personal benefits of education as opposed to the economic and social benefits that form the basis of the arguments presented in this section.

10. Social Science, Accountability, and the Political Economy of School Productivity

JAMES W. GUTHRIE

Since the 1950's there has been a growing increase in public demand for systematic assessment of school effectiveness. Accountability, however, is only as good or as bad as the standards with which it operates. Unfortunately, social science research has failed to provide satisfactory standards and criteria with which to evaluate the performance and effectiveness of schools. Accountability, it would seem, is a dubious enterprise without such criteria. The intent of this chapter is to (1) trace the political and economic roots of the renewed school evaluation movement; (2) analyze the characteristics of schooling that imbue it with an extraordinary resistance to scientific measurement techniques and the consequences of that resistance for school evaluation efforts; and (3) propose a plan for assessing overall school effectiveness that adjusts for the vast scientific vacuum regarding educational processes, embraces both state and local school district interests, and subjects school policy determination to lay control while simultaneously protecting the professional prerogatives of educators.

The author gratefully wishes to acknowledge the assistance of Diana Thomason, Research Associate, Childhood and Government Project, University of California, Berkeley, in the preparation of this chapter.

THE RISING DEMAND FOR EVALUATION

"Sharpening the Knife That Cuts the Public Pie"[1]

One source of the increased public concern for assessing school effectiveness stems from soaring national school costs. For example, in 1930, the national average per pupil expenditure for the United States was approximately $100. The equivalent figure in 1974 was in excess of $1,100.[2] Even when discounted for inflation, this represents a fivefold expansion in school costs over a thirty-year period. Total expenditures for U.S. elementary, secondary, and post-secondary schooling were approximately $90 billion in 1974, and, despite mid-1970's enrollment declines, this figure is projected substantially to exceed $100 billion by 1980.[3] This places educational expenses close to or ahead of national defense as a public sector undertaking.

For a number of years, annual school expenditures have been growing more rapidly than the economy as a whole, and today they equal approximately 8 percent of Gross National Product (GNP).[4] In absolute dollar terms, more is spent on schooling in the U.S. than in any other nation, and, as a share of GNP, it is exceeded only by developing nations where the absolute dollar base is small.

As a percentage of total elementary and secondary school expenditures, the federal government's contribution rose from approximately 4 percent in 1958 to a high point of 8 percent a decade later. Since that time, federal funds have stabilized and now consistently account for between 7 and 8 percent of the financial burden of lower education. Thus, the overwhelming proportion of spiraling school costs have been borne by state and local revenue sources. Nationally, almost 85 percent of locally generated school revenues are derived from taxes on real property,[5] a highly visible tax. In order to meet school costs, local authorities raise approximately $30 billion a year from this source. It is no wonder that local taxpayers and parents insist that boards of education increase the efficiency of schools by trying to find out what works and what does not.

However, the most persistent and well formed pleas for school evaluation have stemmed from state officials[6] because, at the state level, education is in direct competition with other public services for scarce resources. Local boards of education most assuredly are scrutinized when they raise taxes for schools. However, the overwhelming majority (85 percent) can do so exclusive of any concern for funding other public endeavors; they are "fiscally independent," meaning simply that they have their own taxing powers. State officials are in a different position because they must oversee the generation of revenues for a wide range of services, such as transportation, safety, health, welfare, as well as for schools. Since World War II, expenditures for all these services have risen as fast or faster than school costs. Education now finds itself in the unsettling position of having to compete vigorously with other public services for state resources. Therefore, state officials have been seeking more precise information about various public programs through performance budgeting, cost/benefit analyses, evaluation studies, and a seemingly never-ending stream of numbers to justify spending increases. Education is no exception to this phenomenon.[7]

Accountability

The movement that resulted from the escalating demands for assessment of school effectiveness is known by many names, the most widespread is "accountability." As with many fashionable labels, accountability is an imprecise term with different connotations depending on the audiences involved. It has served as a semantic umbrella over school administrators, state and local budget officials, legislators, taxpayer organizations, and a number of informed laymen, all of whom desire better information as to what they receive for school dollars spent.

Accountability strategies and tactics have mushroomed at state and local levels. Attempts to evaluate schooling tumble out of legislative hoppers *ad nauseum*. The bills are seldom thoughtful. The fact that they are enacted is a triumph of faith over experience because few of them have had a significant impact on any state's public school system. For example, in 1967 the California legislature mandated that every school district install a Program Planning and Performance Budgeting System. (This legislation was subsequently rescinded when it became evident that such measures were impractical, not to mention terribly unpopular politically with teacher organizations.[8]) The legislature, apparently learning little from its PPBS experience, subsequently produced the Stull Act which mandated local assessment of teaching performance. In addition, the Assembly and Senate established a Joint Education Committee on

Goals and Objectives to promulgate statewide local citizens' meetings to develop statements of school purposes. Presumably these were to provide a base against which school performance could be measured. Neither the Stull Act nor the Goals and Objectives Committee have had a significant impact.

The most widely used accountability tactic has been statewide testing programs. According to a joint publication of the Education Commission of the States and the Educational Testing Service, thirty states had a form of statewide testing program in 1972.[9] In some ways, the system established in Michigan in 1971 is the most famous, or infamous, example of statewide testing as an accountability procedure. The legislature approved, and the state Education Department administers, a statewide system of "criterion referenced" tests (this term will be explained later in the chapter). Districts characterized by high concentrations of low scoring children are accorded added state funds for compensatory education programs. However, unless the district displays achievement gains for such pupils in subsequent years, the added funding is supposed to be reduced or withdrawn. This plan, whatever its virtues, and there appear to be several, has created substantial controversy. Opponents allege that the idea is a fascist plot to permit the state to dictate learning objectives. Yet others complain that the withdrawal of funds from "non-performing" districts hurts most the very children the program was designed to help. Opponents also assert loudly that the program encourages cheating and misrepresentation of student performance and displaces important but difficult to measure school goals in areas such as literature and health.[10]

While states have been active in attempting to achieve accountability, local boards of education and schools of education have not shirked what they perceived to be their responsibilities. Organizations such as the Educational Testing Service have held national conferences drawing on the wisdom of experts from numerous disciplines to help master the complexities of school evaluation.[11] Academics have offered numerous plans for measuring how well schools perform. In so doing they usually have not felt handicapped by their relatively scant practical knowledge regarding schools.[12] Various national associations of school officials have met on accountability hundreds of times and have devoted substantial portions of their national publications to the topic.[13] The New York City Board of Education negotiated an agreement with its teachers to the effect that the Board and Union would work jointly to develop an accountability mechanism. The outcome was a well publicized conference at which there was a presentation of several controversial plans.[14] These schemes were given consideration, but none has yet to be implemented.

The private sector has not been neglected in attempts to install educational accountability plans. Many of the models proposed for assessing school performance and much of the accompanying technical jargon are adapted from industry and business, usually without attempting to modify them for public sector purposes. Indeed, accountability is a generic term usually associated with private enterprise. The technical-industrial model includes schemes such as "Management By Objectives" (MBO), Program Performance Budgeting Systems (PPBS), systems analysis, Program Evaluation and Review Technique (PERT), performance contracting, educational production function analysis, Competency Based Teacher Education (CBTE), and learner verification, all of which have their analogs in efforts to understand and maximize output in manufacturing organizations. Despite the best intentions of school boards, administrators, teachers, and the public, none of these technical-industrial schemes has succeeded significantly in providing policymakers and clients with information about what does and does not work in schools. Further, these techniques have steadfastly failed to relate dollar costs to school effectiveness. Policymakers at all levels of government are as ignorant today as they were a decade ago about what school programs will provide the most "educational bang for the taxpayers buck." Worse yet, in many ways these technical models of accountability have been counterproductive because they have fostered false hopes and thereafter provoked unnecessary cynicism and bitterness among educators and laymen alike.

The Technical-Industrial Accountability Model

The generalized model now widely proposed for increasing school productivity and achieving accountability contains components that assume the existence of: (1) one or more agreed upon pupil products or learning outcomes, (2) a scientific instrument for measuring student progress toward those outcomes, (3) a knowledge base, or technology that can specify the appropriate treatment of a particular child to enable him or her to accomplish the desired learning outcome, and (4) research techniques that make it possible to separate schooling effects from out-of-school influences (such as home environment and individual IQ) on student achievement.

These assumptions are expressed through a technical apparatus comprised of one or more of the following features: standardized tests to measure school output, specification of various school inputs (expenditures per pupil, teachers' salaries, pupil/teacher ratios, etc.), IQ tests to capture the learning potential of the students involved, proxy measures for family and neighborhood social environment, and statistical procedures, usually regression equations, to permit the separation of non-school factors from schooling effects.

This model for measuring efficiency or productivity is adapted from the private sector where analyses are frequently conducted to assess the optimum mix of manufacturing materials and techniques to minimize production costs and maximize profit. In the industrial field these are known as production function analyses. When applied to education, the scientific expression of these analytic components takes the form of the following generalized equation:[15]

$$A_{it} = g \, F_{i(t)}, \, S_{i(t)}, \, P_{i(t)}, \, O_{i(t)}, \, I_{it}$$

where:

A_{it} = a vector of educational outcomes for the ith student at time t.

$F_{i(t)}$ = a vector of individual and family background characteristics cumulative to time t.

$S_{i(t)}$ = a vector of school inputs relevant to the ith student cumulative to t.

$P_{i(t)}$ = a vector of peer or fellow student characteristics cumulative to t.

$O_{i(t)}$ = a vector of other external influences (the community, for example) relevant to the ith student cumulative to t.

I_{it} = a vector of initial or innate endowments of the ith student at t.

The major problem with the technical model is that its assumptions are invalid. Little or no agreement exists among the public on the expected outcomes of schooling; conventional instruments for measuring pupil progress toward learning objectives are highly inaccurate; very little is known scientifically about how children learn, or how teachers should teach; it is virtually impossible to obtain sufficient information to "control" for out-of-school factors such as home background and neighborhood environment; and existing means for measuring a student's innate or genetically endowed intellectual capacity appear badly flawed. In short, unlike many manufacturing processes, schooling presently is in a very low state of technological development and simply does not fit an industrial model for assessing productivity. After having viewed the technical accountability model from many perspectives and after having attempted to employ it for analytic purposes, the economist Henry Levin wrote:

the lack of similarities among the production techniques used by different schools may mean that neither average nor frontier findings can be applied to any particular school. Indeed, in the extreme case, each individual school is on its own production function (which varies according to the outputs being pursued), and evaluation results for any group of schools will not be applicable to individual schools in the sample.

While measurement of educational production may be a useful exercise in itself, it is not clear that such studies can help us to improve the efficiency of the educational sector. In particular, our focus on a single and measurable output, student achievement, not only limits the analysis considerably; but it may provide policy recommendations that would reduce the economic efficiency of the educational industry if they were adopted. Perhaps the only generalization that one can make from this pessimistic overview is that the analysis of production of public activities is fraught with difficulties that are unusually severe given the present analytical state of the art. The implications of estimates of public sector production functions for improving social efficiency should probably be stated with far greater modesty than they have been. They may be totally misleading.[16]

SOCIAL SCIENCE, THE LACK OF EVALUATION CRITERIA, AND THE CONSEQUENCES FOR ACCOUNTABILITY

The Principle of Analytic Territoriality

Education is an applied endeavor intended to accomplish a broad range of outcomes and utilizing a vast mix of services and personnel specializations. Consequently, it lends itself to many different social science analytic approaches. Because of the central importance of individual learning to schooling, the discipline of Psychology has the strongest ties to education. However, of late, Economics, Sociology, Political Science, and Anthropology have begun to renew their concern for schools as social institutions. Each of these disciplines is heavily devoted to its own analytic assumptions, professional biases, and core of conceptual interests. Thus, one of the immediate problems regarding social science and the assessment of school effectiveness is the relative absence of a common framework from which to view schooling and the instructional process.

It is not overly fanciful to assume that a group of social scientists visiting a school for a week would each focus on a separate set of activities. For example, an anthropologist or historian visiting an elementary classroom might explore the degree to which schools reflect and inculcate the norms and values of the larger community and society; a sociologist might focus on patterns of cooperation and strife between students of varying socioeconomic and racial origins; an economist might investigate the work incentive system or absence of specialization among school workers (teachers); the psychologist might concentrate on the amount of positive reinforcement teachers provide students during instruction; and a political scientist would attempt to define the power relationships between principal and teachers. In short, differences in frames of reference and the possessive nature of some social scientists regarding what is rightfully within their discipline's professional domain render the short run probability of a unified analytic approach to the study of school effectiveness very slim.

Lack of Social Science Knowledge

Even if social scientists could agree on what needs to be known about school effectiveness and cooperated in seeking a synthesis of disciplines, problems would not be solved soon. The complexity of a human endeavor such as learning defies simple cost-effectiveness analysis. Questions regarding the measurement of pupil learning potential and effective teaching techniques are vastly complicated. For example, to inquire if schools are effective assumes that (1) we have agreement on what it is schools should do, (2) we concur on how to measure these outcomes, (3) there exist means for diagnosing particular students' abilities to accomplish school objectives, and (4) we have knowledge of the instructional settings and techniques capable of moving a student, or groups of students, from what he or she now knows to where he or she should be or wants to be on the knowledge spectrum. *In fact, social science knowledge about schooling fails to meet any of these assumptions.*

Disagreement Over Goals of Schooling

Clearly, the goals of schooling have been a topic for philosophic consideration and practical conversation for literally thousands of years,[17] but the amount of time given to the problem has not resulted in a resolution. Only under the most autocratic national systems of education is there ever a clear pronunciation on the ends to which schooling should be directed. To be sure, even in a complicated and overlapping set of school jurisdictions such as we have in the United States, there can be a modicum of agreement on the purposes of schooling. However, such a consensus, at least when it is stated publicly, is generally so abstract as to be vapid.

For example, most citizens concur that schools should strive to teach basic reading, writing, and counting skills, good citizenship, tolerance of fellow citizens, good habits of health and safety, occupational training, patriotism, life adjustment, physical fitness, and on and on. The difficulty comes when efforts are made to arrive at priorities among these goals or when the objectives are made specific. How much effort should be given to teaching youngsters patriotism? Is this best done by teaching "critical thinking," which might very well result in students questioning national endeavors such as military action in Viet Nam? Or, should students, particularly at an early age, simply be taught "My country, right or wrong"? Perhaps students should be steeped more intensely in health and personal hygiene. After all, what could be more important than understanding how one's body functions, the requirements of basic nutrition, and the dangers of substances such as alcohol, tobacco, and addictive drugs? Yet again, it can be argued that America is not facing a crisis of patriotism and health anywhere near the degree to which it is experiencing a complete moral breakdown. Crime, divorce, child abuse, refusal to work, personal dishonesty, and government scandal all abound. This line of thought would have schools stress personal values, virtue, and strong discipline.

The argument over educational priorities and objectives takes place at every level of government.[18] Local and state statutes and federal government educational provisions are filled with confusing and conflicting rhetoric regarding the purposes of schooling. For example, it has been virtually impossible to determine if the Elementary and Secondary Education Act (ESEA) is a success or failure because nowhere is it clear what the act was supposed to accomplish. Is it intended to enrich the alleged cultural impoverishment of low-income children, teach them to read and count as well as their middle-class counterparts, or subsequently ameliorate their depressing rate of unemployment?

Disagreement over the purposes of schooling has been widespread from the first days of our republic and has increased as immigration patterns and geographic expansion began to forge a pluralist value system.[19] Moreover, our present period of life-style transition, religious relativism, and increased secularism are not likely to evoke cultural homogeneity and value harmony in the near future.

Today a growing number of radical social scientists and revisionist historians believe there has been, *de facto*, a hidden school agenda strongly held to by the majority, or at least the decisionmaking majority, of America's citizens. They contend that, as our economy has shifted from family farming and crafts to mass production, the nature of work has largely determined the expected student outcomes. Schools, in this view, have been expected to produce a docile work force and to reproduce the U.S. social-class structure from generation to generation. Sufficient exceptions to strict reproduction of social-class lines have been permitted to sustain the myth of individual equality and social mobility. On balance, however, lower-class children have been taught only enough to permit them to fit comfortably into low-status manual-labor and assembly-line jobs while children of the elite have been equipped with the knowledge, skills, and attitudes to enable them to rule over and profit from the labor of their lower-class counterparts. Under this persuasion, disagreement over the goals of schooling is but a camouflage concealing the fact that the hidden agenda of schooling was agreed upon and perpetuated with socially devastating effects on lower-class children.

This is an enticing interpretation because it parsimoniously accounts for many "facts" surrounding the failure of much of modern schooling. Nevertheless, we do not totally accept the argument because the evidence appears too complex to fit such a simple theory. Further, it is hard to believe that so many well-meaning people have for so long deluded themselves into believing that schooling was in fact a means to liberate rather than enslave children from low-income households.[20]

The point to emphasize is that the objectives held for schools are nowhere clear or simple. In the absence of consensus about school goals, typically a compromise of either of two sorts is struck by policymakers. One route is, in effect, to have no goals for schools or to have them stated so abstractly as to render them vapid, platitudinous, and, most importantly, immeasurable. The second route is to try and accommodate all tastes by having a multitude of objectives to be accomplished by the schools. The inevitable outcome is that many of them end up being antithetical or internally inconsistent. Whichever alternative is pursued, the end product is the same; in the absence of an agreed upon and consistent set of educational objectives, there is no baseline against which to measure the productive use of school resources.

Absence of a Measurement Technology

If by some miracle there is significant agreement on what schools are expected to accomplish, the overwhelming problems of assessing school effectiveness still remain. One reason for this is the primitive state of educational measurement. What is particularly disheartening in this regard is that testing probably has attracted more sustained research by better brains than any sphere of schooling. Scholars in this field are consistently among the brightest and best trained in all of educational research. However, in keeping with the problem of analytic territoriality referred to earlier, it is very difficult to attract psychologists away from their historic concerns for research about individuals and thereafter to induce them to cooperate with economists, sociologists, and politicians to resolve the thorny problems of finding an acceptable means for measuring school output. Space does not permit a detailed explanation of all such measurement problems, but several of the more significant ones are described below.

Normative Testing.[21] The emphasis in standardized testing has been on the development of predictive instruments, which make it possible to rate an individual taking the test in relation to others who have previously been examined on the same test. He scored "at the 90th percentile," "at the median," or "in the bottom quartile."

These are all normative statements that illustrate the dominant testing technology. These statements do not provide substantive information on what the test taker knows, how many questions he or she answered correctly, or whether or not the individual is qualified or competent on the substantive dimension being assessed. However, it does provide a ranking that frequently has powerful predictive validity. Literally millions of academic and employment decisions have been based on this kind of testing. Many colleges utilize the Scholastic Aptitude Test (SAT) in determining admission eligibility. Graduate schools of all kinds use a higher powered version, the Graduate Record Examination (GRE), for admission purposes. The military has long used the Armed Forces Qualification Test (AFQT). Government agencies and private firms administer tests to winnow the pool of job applicants, and school districts frequently use the National Teacher Examination (NTE) to assess the qualifications of potential employees.

Despite widespread popular acceptance and use, norm-referenced tests do not accurately assess school effectiveness because of the manner in which the tests are constructed. In assembling "good" test questions it becomes crucial to identify items that discriminate or separate examinees and distribute them over a range of correct answers. If all examinees made the same score, the test would be useless for predicting performance on some subsequent task; it would not permit discriminating judgments to be made. Thus, a norm-referenced test maker discards easy questions—those which are frequently answered correctly. Similarly, items to which no one can respond correctly are omitted.

Through repeated rounds of use, test items are continually purified in terms of their ability to discriminate among examinees. Even though norm-referenced tests are intended to measure a form of academic achievement, in time these examinations become much like IQ tests, filled with a number of abstractions. In this form, a standardized test published by a national testing company may contain very different items from what a classroom teacher has been attempting to convey to his or her pupils.

Interpreting the Metrics of Learning. A related social science weakness concerns measurement yardsticks or the scale or metric applied to measure how much gain or loss a student or group of students has experienced over a given period of time. This is an agonizing technical problem that probably is better understood by illustration. An ideal test instrument would be based on a set of evenly-spaced linear increments. For example, on a test composed of 100 questions, we would know that a student receiving a raw score of 75 was better informed regarding the subject matter at hand than a student who scored 25, and also that the former knew the subject matter three times better than the latter. However, such assumptions regarding linearity and systematic value of higher scores are implausible because of the construction of current norm-referenced tests. All that can be deduced from a norm-referenced test score is that the individual student in question scored higher, or lower, than most students.

The concept of grade equivalency scores is intended to impute greater meaning to norm-referenced testing. For example, a student scoring at the 4.5 grade level answered enough test items correctly to match the number typically answered correctly by youngsters in the fifth month (January) of the fourth grade. (The school year for grade equivalency reporting purposes is 10 months in length.) If the student is in fact in the second month of the third grade, then we know that he or she is testing higher than most third graders; in fact he or she is scoring as high as the average student in the middle of the fourth grade.

In another example, if a second-grade student scores 2.1 on a reading comprehension test in September and scores 4.5 in the spring of the same school year, we would know that he or she had learned substantially more than would normally be expected of a student in a school year. We could then say that the student, the teacher, the home, or all three, had performed well. Indeed, if all students or a major proportion of students in a class, school, or school district had made such gains, we would judge the situation very productive.

However grade equivalency statements are often deceptive. For example, frequently a gain of one month on a test score means that the student correctly answered only two or three more test items than the norm. In a reading comprehension test, this may mean correctly answering two or three vocabulary items. Who honestly believes that knowing a few more vocabulary words ranks a student a month ahead of his or her academic peers? At present, we can not be sure that our test instruments are of sufficient precision to permit such inferences. However, the grade equivalency mechanism provides the illusion of great specificity, and laymen and professional educators will undoubtedly continue to rely on the device because it provides a medium of understanding that otherwise is absent. However, consumers of school productivity studies should realize that such a metric is at best a slender reed upon which to base policy judgments.[22]

Criterion-Referenced Tests. An alternative is for educators to switch to criterion-referenced tests, which assume test questions can be devised to assess the degree to which a student has mastered a given body of knowledge. The criterion for including a test item is simply the degree to which it accurately reflects understanding of some facet of the subject matter to be mastered. For example, the written examinations most states use for testing driver's license applicants are criterion referenced. They are designed to test a candidate's comprehension of driving regulations and road related facts that one must know in order to drive safely. The tests are *not* designed to distinguish between those who know the facts best and those who know them only marginally; no effort is made to rank applicants. An applicant who responds to all questions correctly is not entitled to drive faster, longer, or according to a different set of rules than the applicant who passes the test by the margin of a single correct answer. Usually, there is a cutoff point and those who score below that point fail and must retake the test; those who score above the cutoff point are simply judged as passing.

Given the conceptual simplicity of criterion-referenced testing, why not design such tests and administer them statewide? Then we would know how many children had mastered mathematics, reading, civics, biology, French, and whatever else we wanted them to know. But the principal problem with criterion-referenced tests is who is to decide what is to be tested. A battery of test questions implies a set of learning objectives. Who determines these objectives? What constitutes the criterion of mastery? When can a student be said to know enough? These value problems have seriously emasculated most widespread criterion-referenced testing efforts.

For example, in the late 1960's two U.S. Office of Education commissioners, Francis Keppel, and his successor, Harold Howe II, mounted a nationwide testing program (National Assessment of Educational Progress—NAEP) utilizing criterion-referenced tests. The objective was simple—to determine how much American school-age youngsters knew. Were American schools succeeding or failing? At that time, there was no way of telling, and, for the most part, there still is not.

The politics of this endeavor are lengthy and Byzantine. Initially, the American Association of School Administrators (AASA) threatened to scuttle the effort and recommended that local school districts refuse to administer the tests. There were fears in other parts that the federal government would operate the testing program and it would be a precursor of a national system of education (read "Communism"). School practitioners appeared fearful of the possibility of comparisons, school to school, district to district, etc. The threat that the test results might be used for evaluation purposes was sufficient to mobilize almost every segment of America's professional educators in opposition. Only when the evaluation threat was defused, and much of the potential usefulness of the tests diluted, was the NAEP permitted to operate. The compromise finally struck was to have the program administered by the Education Commission of the States (ECS) in such a way as to preclude any useful comparisons between units of school management. Test results were not permitted to be compared between schools, districts, or states.[23] The Michigan accountability effort, relying on criterion-referenced tests, has had to overcome similar problems. In short, widescale use of criterion-referenced tests for purposes of assessing school effectiveness and studying productivity may be a technical possibility, but clearly it is not yet a political probability.

Problems With Process

In the absence of agreement on the product of schooling or how to measure it, concern for school efficiency and effectiveness has sometimes concentrated on process. The rationale is that there must exist a body of "best practices" that, if uncovered, would increase school effectiveness. Generally, the search for successful school practices focuses on the teacher. Regrettably, however, there has never been a definitive study of what constitutes an effective repertoire of instructional behaviors. Even the relatively unsophisticated scientific step of recording how good teachers act in the classroom has never taken place.

In the early days of scientific medical practice, physicians' descriptions of successful clinical procedures were published in medical journals. The authors never claimed to have performed thousands of such operations or to have treated a representative sample of patients by the new procedure. Rather, they simply recorded what they had done and why they thought it was effective. By implication, other physicians were invited to add their findings to the pool of practical knowledge. Indeed, this reporting procedure still takes place and is a useful contribution to improving modern health practices. It is not a replacement for, but a useful adjunct to, large-scale, scientific laboratory research. Similarly, if teachers had conducted "clinical" classroom research beginning a half century ago, today we might have a knowledge base of teacher behavior. Regrettably, such a base does not presently exist. Moreover, until teacher training institutions, school districts, and other related agencies begin to train teachers in the methods of clinical research and provide them with the setting and incentives to conduct studies, we will never be able to take advantage of the natural experiments and potential research studies in America's classrooms. Further, teachers will continue to miss an excellent opportunity to enhance their personal self-respect and image as professionals interested in improving their skills and adding to a scientific body of knowledge and practice.

Social scientists have fared little better than professional teachers in their efforts to determine effective teaching practices. Social science research, most of it conducted in the 1960's, almost totally excluded teacher behavior from consideration. For example, the renowned Coleman Report[24] contained no measures of teacher behavior. The Report employed what researchers label "status" variables rather than process measures. The Coleman team collected information regarding teachers' age, years of experience, and level of education. One can construct a hypothetical argument as to how such measures might be reflected in the behavior of teachers, and thus they may be important dimensions upon which to collect data. However, presumably, if a teacher has an effect on student learning, it is through the teacher's action. Thus, the important variable should be teacher behavior, measures of instructional processes, or teacher-student interaction.

Coleman Report findings are subject to debate on several grounds. However, the inability of this competent team to capture the essence of schooling—teacher behavior—dramatically illustrates the present impotence of social science in assessing school effectiveness. Moreover, until techniques for observing, recording, and analyzing teacher behavior improve, future prospects for gaining additional knowledge are dismal.

Inability To Control for the "Outside"

Evaluation schemes displaying even a modicum of sophistication attempt to take account of the fact that much of what a child is able to learn is beyond the ability of schools to control. For example, though no one is absolutely sure how important it is, it generally is conceded that human beings vary with regard to their genetically endowed learning capacity. Presumably, this innate intellectual capacity is established at the child's conception and is a learning factor beyond the ability of schools to manipulate. Similarly, there probably is no stronger social science finding than the relationship between school achievement and the student's family and neighborhood environment. Yet, with a few exceptions, educators cannot arrange for a home environment that motivates children to learn or provides them with the necessary experiences to benefit from schooling.

Researchers have devised several means to take such out-of-school influences on learning into account. However, these measures are woefully inadequate. Genetically endowed intelligence is almost impossible to measure accurately. Even psychologists readily admit that they do not know what IQ tests measure. These tests depend on a child manipulating physical materials or responding to pencil and paper tests. Yet, the ability to understand questions is affected not only by one's innate intelligence but also by one's environmental experiences. Frequently, the environment includes school. At present it is impossible to obtain a measure of intelligence untarnished by environment. Thus, IQ scores may be highly confounded. The outcome is that it is difficult to impossible to control for innate ability in a school effectiveness effort.

Controlling for a child's social environment outside of school is equally frustrating. The typical procedure here is to find measures that purport to capture the essence of a child's social circumstance, and then apply statistical controls for them. Even if one concedes the somewhat dubious proposition that a mathematical equation can hold human characteristics equal, the proxies for children's social background are almost always incomplete or flawed. The measures frequently used are parents' occupation, education, and income. Sometimes these are supplemented by an index of possessions in the home and a judgment as to the financial value of the home itself. In some instances these data are gathered directly from the student or parents. More frequently, they are pieces of information averaged for census tracts. Sometimes, student social background data are simply the best judgments of observers or a school principal. Even when such pieces of information are correctly gathered, they tend to be but fragmentary indicators of a child's social circumstances. If a well educated, financially comfortable home almost always provided emotional succor and intellectual stimulation, whereas economically and academically impoverished parents inevitably produced poor scholars, we might have more faith in superficial social measures. However, the exceptions to such simple scenarios are legion. Sufficient numbers of children deviate from the statistical norm with regard to these background proxies, that one almost inevitably concludes that, at best, they are of limited validity and, at worst, may be useless.[25] The situation is summed up succinctly by a RAND Corporation researcher who wrote:

> Evaluations that use imperfect information run into both analytical and political problems. Educational accountability systems based on achievement scores are an instance. Such systems frequently turn out to be *irrelevant* to policy decisions, *resisted* by educational groups that fear unflattering comparisons and the misuse of results, and *infeasible* given faulty data and limited time and money.
>
> Accountability systems in state governments are increasingly widespread, and state governments seem to be more and more important as educational policymakers. In the state I rename Fulano, accountability ran into political opposition and feasibility constraints which are instructive to examine. Policymakers consistently and mistakenly saw important statistical issues as merely 'technical' questions. Actually, these *statistical issues were at the heart of more relevance, less resistance, and greater feasibility.*[26]

Teacher Training Deficiencies

In the absence of an ability to specify school outcomes or appropriate teacher behavior, a last-gasp policy effort has been made in many states to prescribe the manner in which teachers should be trained. This appears to be a particularly hollow hope. Without sound information about good teacher practices gained from clinical studies and large-scale social science research, the prospect of outlining an exact teacher training program is an illusion at best. Nevertheless, the early 1970's were filled with the promises of evangelists regarding the merits of Competency Based Teacher Education (CBTE).[27] This fad, now apparently waning somewhat, was adopted in various forms by many states.[28] It is not clear, however, how many are in fact now enforcing the provisions.

Competency Based Teacher Education assumes a linkage can be built between particular sets of teacher behaviors and specified student outcomes. A teacher training and credentialing scheme would consist of a long list of prescribed teacher behaviors. For example, if students are learning how to find the lowest common denominator when doing sums, then the teacher should follow instructional procedures $l \ldots n$. In order to become licensed or credentialed, a teacher trainee would demonstrate proficiency on these and other instructional dimensions. In short, the trainee would have to show that he or she could competently perform the desired instructional behaviors to move students from learning point A to learning point B.

This approach appears reasonable and thus has attracted the allegiance of a number of laymen and even some professional educators. However, no body of scientific findings exists that links any one or set of teacher activities with any particular set of learner outcomes. A devastating blow to the CBTE concept is dealt by Heath and Nielson, who after having reviewed every conceivable item of related research, state:

Our analysis of this literature leads us to three conclusions: First, the research literature on the relation between teacher behavior and student achievement does not offer an empirical basis for the prescription of teacher-training objectives.

Second, this literature fails to provide such a basis, not because of minor flaws in the statistical analyses, but because of sterile operational definitions of both teaching and achievement, and because of fundamentally weak research designs.

Last, given the well-documented, strong association between student achievement and variables such as socioeconomic status and ethnic status, the effects of techniques of teaching on achievement (as these variables are defined in the PBTE research) are likely to be inherently trivial.[29]

Thus, the list of competencies that teachers should have are either so abstract as to be meaningless or, if precise, rooted in a quagmire of invalid research. Whatever the reason, the end result is the same—

CBTE provides no short-run hope for effectively increasing school productivity. In fact, if teacher trainees are coerced into adopting teaching behaviors that are counterproductive, school effectiveness will suffer.[30]

Professional Resistance to Productivity Measurement and Evaluation

Professional educators, teachers in particular, have been overwhelmingly critical of efforts to measure school productivity and to evaluate their performance. In part this reticence can be explained by fear of the consequences; if evaluated and found wanting, then the outcome may not be pleasant. However, given the inadequacies of the current state of the evaluation art, this reluctance is also substantially justified. Teachers fully understand that there is little consensus on the expected outcomes of schooling, and this puts them in a position of uncertainty. For example, they reasonably fear being subjected to a cross fire wherein some significant client segment holds them responsible for achieving one set of outcomes while another segment expects them to reach a different or, worse yet, antithetical set of objectives. The teacher then is in a zero-sum situation where to satisfy one client component is inevitably to displease the other.

Another educator concern is that the focus on measurable objectives will trigger a goal displacement process. Efforts to accomplish those goals that are measurable will shove aside those that do not lend themselves to quantification. For example, knowing that he or she is to be evaluated on students' reading, a teacher may consciously neglect social studies, health, or music components of instruction. Worse yet, quantification of objectives can establish a hidden incentive system. If a teacher is to be evaluated on the average increase in student reading achievement in a class, the teacher might wisely choose to focus on the brightest quartile of students. By concentrating instructional efforts in this manner, bright students' reading scores might escalate sufficiently to pull the entire class average up several points. Whereas, in fact, the less able students in the class remained stable or lost ground in terms of achievement. The professional concern of many teachers for the welfare of their students would probably inhibit them from subverting their efforts to such a degree. Nevertheless, a possibility exists that a reward system based exclusively on narrow measurement of quantifiable learning objectives might incite distorted teacher behavior.

Infringement on Professional Autonomy. Since teachers are professionals or quasi-professionals, and therefore concerned with their client's welfare, they may resist pressures to specify both objectives and treatment. Teachers desire the freedom and day-to-day autonomy to establish standards themselves, or, at the least, to participate with clients or public officials in the setting of school performance standards. A teacher might reasonably argue: "I am not worrying now about teaching Johnny to read. I won't neglect reading, but he has recently undergone a debilitating personal trauma, and the most important thing I can accomplish for him is to teach self-reliance, restore personal confidence, assist in building a positive self-image, etc. Only after his psyche is returned to a healthy state can he learn effectively. By requiring me to concentrate on reading (or any other substantive area), you are impairing my ability as a professional to facilitate the welfare of my client."

Concern for Subjective Judgment. Teacher tenure is frequently cited as the soft underbelly of school effectiveness. However, those who advocate abolition of tenure forget that once teachers owed their jobs to a system of political spoils. Failure to support the proper candidate or insistence on principles of academic freedom meant loss of one's job. Personal favoritism was widespread and teachers felt their dignity and professional independence seriously compromised as a result. Tenure provides protection against such abuses for teachers who successfully negotiate a probationary period (usually three years). Despite tenure protection, teachers frequently perceive themselves as vulnerable to administrative whim. Even if not subject to dismissal, a tenured teacher's prerogatives could be curtailed; one's teaching assignment within a school or district and other important matters relating to working conditions were subject to administrative discretion. Consequently, teachers sought protection from arbitrary administrative action through formalized rules and grievance procedures negotiated at the bargaining table. Despite such gains in job protection and standards of treatment, teachers continue to be reluctant to accord administrators wide discretion in evaluating their classroom performance. While acknowledging the need for evaluation, teachers want specific and objective standards so that there is little or no room for discriminatory treatment or personal favoritism.

To be acceptable to teachers, evaluation schemes must be deperson-alized and standardized. Because it is difficult to construct objective standards for measuring effective instruction, teachers have fre-quently resisted systematic evaluation schemes.

Sometimes this resistance takes the form of overt political action to defeat an evaluation plan at the state or local school district level. At other times, it takes the form of simple footdragging so as effec-tively to destroy an evaluation plan. This is well illustrated by edu-cators' general refusal to comply with California's PPBS mandate and Stull Act requiring specification of objectives for assessment of teacher and administrator performance. Professional educators, though usually willing to agree that an enterprise as costly and im-portant as schooling must be subjected to measurement and evalua-tion,[31] are generally reticent to approve any practical plan and, in particular, any scheme that provides financial reward or punishment.

The reluctance of professional educators to be subjected to sys-tematic scrutiny is illustrated in an Educational Research Service sur-vey of school districts of varying size. Small school districts (between 300 and 3000 students) were the most reticent to release standard-ized test scores to the public; only 9 percent of those sampled would make test score data available publicly. The most open school dis-tricts, somewhat surprisingly, were the largest sampled (enrollments of 25,000 or more). Almost half of the large districts reported test results to the press. However, of the districts that released test scores, less than half published them in a fashion that would permit achieve-ment comparisons from school to school.[32]

Dysfunctional Consequences of Technical Accountability Model

The crucial assumptions of the technical accountability model are supported neither by scientific findings nor by political realities. At best, there is only minimal societal consensus on the goals of schooling and pedagogues do not know well how to measure progress toward goals or what treatment to prescribe for any particu-lar child to achieve a particular goal. Despite the absence of such critical pieces of information, financially pressured public officials, well intentioned laymen, and misguided professional educators con-tinue to try to implement an accountability system premised on a nonexistent educational science.

Because the technical model is conceptually and practically unsound, it fails to correct the ills for which it is intended. It does not (1) offer a sound system of incentives for professional educators; (2) provide consumers with information they can use in choosing school services; (3) deliver useful feedback either to educators or to laymen as to how well schools are working; (4) provide a framework in which to conduct research and effectiveness studies to improve school services; (5) offer any basis to decide which teachers and administrators are effective and which are incompetent; and (6) provide clues as to where added financial resources should be spent. The list of failures extends on and on.

The inability of the technical accountability model to achieve the expectations held for it is provoking a number of counterproductive consequences. Professional educators, largely reacting to the inadequacies and inequities foisted on them by today's accountability efforts, are increasingly resisting any evaluation attempts. One typical argument is: "Standardized tests do not accurately measure what a child has learned in school. The child's home environment has been shown to be the prime determinant of school achievement, and we have no control over that situation. In the absence of any science that prescribes how to teach children, how can we be evaluated for our instruction?" These justifications, like most human rationalizations, are partly accurate, and the present accountability model does little to blunt their validity. Indeed, it aggravates weaknesses and in so doing provokes professional educators to resist evaluation more fully.

Another possible dysfunctional consequence of the present accountability system's failure is an even greater skepticism about education among legislators and other public officials. Because the technical model is not providing needed information, education is becoming increasingly vulnerable to simple political arguments. Its once privileged access to finances is jeopardized. Schools increasingly must compete with other public sector services for resources and the absence of performance data or cost effectiveness information hurts their cause.

In short, from the policymakers' viewpoint, public education gives the impression of being out of control. If the situation is not rectified, the possible outcomes are intervention and further diminution of professional autonomy, greater erosion of public confidence and consequent reduction in financial support, and a general undermining of this nation's long commitment to a high quality system of public education.

INDETERMINACY: WHAT TO DO WHEN THERE ARE NO ANSWERS

Present conditions prohibit implementation of a simplified cost benefit or performance budgeting model to assess school effectiveness and increase school productivity. There is too little agreement regarding expected school outcomes and the technology for measuring outcomes is too weak to be reliable. In addition, research findings to date do not permit detailed prescriptions regarding the instructional process or teacher training. In short, too little is known to enable a state or school district to install a conventional industrial-sector model of management and efficiency. Moreover, the persistent efforts of zealots, many of whom are well meaning, to enact and install a technical accountability model will probably prove counter-productive in the long run.

Aside from the usual plea for additional funds and time to conduct the necessary research on instructional techniques and school effects, what can be done? Given the present state of indeterminacy, are there any principles by which schools can be organized, instructional performances evaluated, and teachers recruited and trained to perform with added competence? The following pages will describe a proposed series of activities to cope with indeterminant conditions. However, it should be recognized from the outset that the system of reforms described is admittedly stop-gap. If greater agreement on the outcomes of schooling is reached and more reliable knowledge regarding instructional strategies is developed, a separate agenda of effectiveness reforms might be necessary.

A Digression Regarding Principles

In addition to coping with the indeterminacy described, a reform program directed at increasing school effectiveness also must be sensitive to several other criteria. Specifically, it must balance a series of state-level concerns with those of local-level clients, parents and students, and must seek an equilibrium between lay control and professional autonomy.

Balancing State and Local Interests. In general government decisionmaking discretion should rest with the smallest jurisdiction possible. Assuming a wide range of values and tastes throughout our population, individual preferences would most likely be maximized in the smaller governmental units of a multi-tiered federal hierarchy. For a decision to be elevated to a higher level, there must exist a compelling reason. Simply translated, this means that school decisions should take place, whenever possible, at the school site. This is where the greatest amount of interaction takes place between those who deliver instructional services and those intended to benefit from them. Also, judging from studies of the relationship between size of governmental jurisdiction and electoral participation, smaller units facilitate increased constituent expression of educational preferences.[33] School districts are presently the prime level for school governance decisions, and accommodation with political reality probably will demand that this condition persist for some time. Whether it be the school site or the school district, as many policy decisions as possible should be taken at the lowest level.

When examined closely, however, there are several compelling reasons that justify state intervention or state-level decisionmaking about schools. First, if left totally to their own discretion, lower-level decisionmaking units, whether they be families, schools, or school districts, might underinvest in schooling to the detriment of both the child and the larger society. In addition to the sufferings visited on the children themselves, their ignorance would be a handicap to the state. Such children might become economic burdens to the society requiring welfare support or added health care; they might be more likely than their well-schooled peers to eventuate as crime statistics; if drafted to perform military duties, they might endanger the lives of their companions; and so on for a long list of consequences of under-education. The point simply is that in a period of extraordinary social and economic interdependence, society must protect itself from the risk that a governmental subunit will shirk its schooling responsibilities.

A further consequence of an intolerably low local level of educational quality is the damage inflicted on the individual student. Usually both school officials and the child's parents are sufficiently concerned to see that each student learns in accord with his or her capabilities. However, the state must have a means to protect children in those exceptional instances where parents and local school officials tolerate school situations likely to be damaging—physically, psychically, etc.—to the child.

Beyond its concern for minimal standards of instructional quality and student learning, the state also has an interest in assuring the larger population that school resources are utilized in a legal and efficient manner. Even when generated from local property taxes, school funds are legally state revenues subject to state accounting standards. Moreover, since some portion of the revenues for almost every school district is generated outside its geographic boundaries, the state has an interest in seeing that these general funds are not "wasted" in financially extravagant or outrageously inefficient ways.

Balanced against these and other state concerns are the substantial views of local school clients that their voice be heard regarding school purposes and practices. If we had a society of extraordinary homogeneity, this might not be a concern. However, the United States represents a complicated mixture of values and tastes with regard to schooling. If such diversity is to be protected, whether it be the school district, school, classroom, or individual pupil, room must remain for choice.

Public Control and Professional Autonomy. In principle, client welfare is of paramount concern to professionals. Each client must be assessed separately and the optimum mix of services prescribed. In order to ensure client welfare, that "treatment" is appropriate and of the highest order, then the professional must be allowed substantial personal authority and discretion, subject only to review by peers. Laymen, presumably, would not embody sufficient expertise to assess whether or not an engineer, physician, lawyer, or pilot had performed correctly. In that education aspires to be a profession, teachers and other school practitioners argue that they should be permitted similar autonomy.

There are at least two circumstances that mitigate against unfettered professional autonomy for educators. First, unlike many professional services offered in the private sector, public schools have close to a monopoly. A dissatisfied parent or student has only a small margin for changing school districts, schools, or teachers. Thus, as with many other monopolies, there are reasonable grounds for regulation by the larger society.

A second reason for lay control over professional educators stems from the socially sensitive nature of the school's functions. Schools are commonly held responsible for transmitting values from one generation to the next. In order to maintain society and ensure social cohesion, the values handed down must be consistent with those held by the wider society. Consequently, the lay public must have within its power the authority—rewards and punishments—to accomplish this end. In short, to paraphrase Talleyrand, "Schooling is too important to be left to educators."

A proposed school evaluation scheme must strike a delicate balance between several competing forces. By necessity, such compromises are complicated; many adjustments are necessary to accommodate the numerous legitimate interests involved in the interplay between professionalism, lay control, state protection, and local autonomy. Obviously, such compromises contain components that are, at best, prickly to one interest or another. Nevertheless, we are sufficiently brazen to propose a strategy that may simultaneously enhance student learning, efficient use of public resources, public participation, and professionalism for educators.

A New Strategy for Enhancing School Productivity

In order to accomplish the purposes and remain within the constraints already described, a seven-point reform plan is proposed.* The seven components constitute a system-wide change, but each component is capable of standing on its own insofar as enhancing effectiveness. If the state should adopt all or any combination of components, then productivity would be elevated exponentially. Matters related to the evaluation of teachers are deliberately deleted from this discussion. Teachers are such a crucial element of schooling that a later section will be devoted to an analysis of the problems of educational personnel evaluation and proposals for reform.

School Site as Basic Unit of Management. State legislatures have traditionally seen fit to delegate much of their educational authority to local district boards of education. These local agencies have existed as governmental entities for more than a century and,

*The proceeding ideas are not the product of the author alone. They were developed by senior staff members of the New York State Education Commission, most notably Charles S. Benson, Will Riggan, Roger Hooker, Carl Jaffee, and the author. These ideas have also received widespread attention by the Florida state legislature and frequently are referred to as the "Florida Plan."

despite the fact that their numbers have dwindled dramatically over the last several decades, they exhibit no prospect of disappearing altogether. Furthermore, there probably are good practical and political reasons for their continuation.

However, there are drawbacks to using the district as the basic governmental building block for decisionmaking. The important contact between the practitioner and the client takes place, not at the district level, but at the school site. It is the teacher and principal, rather than central office personnel, who appear to be in the best position to make judgments about programs for students within their custody. It is to the local "school" that parents appear to accord their strongest allegiance.

One might reasonably inquire, however, "Why not use the classroom as the basic management unit?" In an earlier era, this may have been appropriate. Today, even at the elementary level, students are in contact with more than one teacher during the course of a school day or week. Team teaching is increasing and intensified use of specialists makes it difficult if not impossible to specify a group of students as being the exclusive responsibility of one instructor. This is even more true at the secondary level. Thus, because the classroom is too small and the district too large, the individual school seems the most reasonable unit for assigning primary managerial functions, and the force of these proposals hinges on this concept.

Parent Advisory Councils. In order to compensate for the overpopulation and resulting depersonalization of school districts, and to facilitate a better "fit" between local school programs and client tastes, the formation of a Parent Advisory Council (PAC) is recommended for all school sites in districts with more than 1,000 students.[34] The number of PAC members should be proportional to a school's enrollment. The following figures illustrate such a ratio scheme:

School Enrollment	PAC Membership
1-300	5
301-500	7
501-700	9
701-900	11
901-	13

Regardless of school size beyond 900 pupils, it is not recommended that Parent Advisory Councils extend further than thirteen members to maintain effective small-group interaction.

Who is eligible to serve and how are they selected? The manner in which individuals come to sit on a PAC is crucial. After having debated the many possible responses our answer is that only parents of children presently enrolled in the school should serve. (Citizens without children, obviously, have school-related interests. However, these interests are best expressed at the school district and state level.) Those eligible to serve might be nominated by a nonpartisan caucus[35] or through a petition arrangement in which any parent obtaining signatures from 50 or five percent of the parents in the school (whichever is least) would be placed on the ballot.

Although the electoral process never guarantees "true" representation, it seems better than any other procedure for choosing PAC members. Nominations by principals or district school board members are open to substantial criticisms of professional dominance, non-representativeness, and personal favoritism. Thus, as cumbersome and time-consuming as they are, elections are probably the best selection procedure. Terms of office should be two years with members permitted to serve no more than two terms. Terms should be staggered so as to provide continuity from year-to-year.

Parent Advisory Councils, as the label suggests, are advisory to the principal. Their most important function, not unlike their parent body—the district's board of education, is participation in the selection of the school's chief executive officer. The principal appears to be the single-most important component of a school's success. It is possible to have a capable principal and a bad school because other conditions are overwhelmingly dismal. However, it is extraordinarily rare that a good school have an incompetent principal. Even though there are very few incentives for the principal to manipulate in order to encourage good teaching, he or she appears to set the tone of a school, to light the spark of excitement that spurs staff and student body to excel. In short, if the public desires good schools and programs in keeping with client tastes, then local citizens must participate heavily in the selection of school principals.

PAC participation in principal selection can take place either from the ground up or by a "trickle down" process. In the former, the

PAC interviews and recommends three to five acceptable candidates to the district board and administration, and one or both of them makes the final choice. Conversely, the central administration or school board might select a number of acceptable candidates, and then permit the local school PAC to make the final choice. Whichever route is pursued, the principal should be placed on a three-to-five year contract with renewal subject to Parent Advisory Council approval.

Principal Power. The PAC's prime activity is to select and thereafter advise the local school principal on matters such as budget allocation, personnel policies, curriculum, and school discipline. On all these matters, the principal, working within the boundaries of state statute and overall school district policy, has the final word. The justification for principal power is an important component of the entire plan and should be made explicit. If a school system, or any other kind of large formal organizational endeavor, is to be accountable, responsive, sensitive, and whatever other adjective is in fashion, it is crucial that responsibility for success and failure be fixed as precisely as possible. To declare the school site the basic management unit and thereafter leave it ambiguous as to who is in charge is to add to the present confusion. Thus, once selected, the principal should be in charge.

But why accord so much authority to the principal? The answer is straightforward; if the principal is to be held responsible for the success or failure of a school, then he or she must be given the power to make changes. This is what is meant by principal power. The power is held in check by numerous legal constraints and the strengthened voice of teachers. The principal is also balanced, in at least one instance, by the authority of the PAC to terminate or renew contracts.

There are at least three important discretionary dimensions for principal decisionmaking: personnel, budget, and curriculum. In terms of personnel, a school principal might well receive hiring guidelines from the PAC, existing staff at a school site, and students above the ninth grade. However, consistent with state credentialing requirements, the principal should make the final employment decision. Presently, central office administrators recruit, interview, and then assign new teachers to schools. A principal may have an element of veto power, but even that is seldom formally assured. We believe strongly that the principal, with client and staff "advisors," should make employment decisions. This procedure is consistent with the axioms of accountability and principal power, and, in addition, there exists a modest amount of empirical evidence to buttress the idea's utility.[36]

In another dimension, principals should become chief budget officers for their schools. With the important exception of categorical funds for special programs of varying kinds, school monies should be distributed to each school in a district as a lump sum in accord with an equitable set of district-wide decision rules. Thereafter, a principal and advisors can determine, within state and district-established boundaries, the allocation of the funds. Under an ideal system, school administrators would determine the mix of courses, the mix of teachers at varying credential steps (see discussion on educational personnel), and how many teacher aides, tutors, and non-professional staff they wished to employ.

Phasing in a lump-sum school budgeting system takes a number of years because of built-in financial commitments to existing staff. However, as several school districts throughout the nation have dramatically demonstrated, a good-faith effort by parents, administrators, and teachers can place responsible budgetary discretion at a school site.

Curriculum decisions are also bounded by state code and whatever requirements a district board of education sees as necessary. Hopefully, these would be few in number. Aside from state requirements, there are powerful pressures from sources such as college entrance standards, national textbook publishers, test manufacturers, and federal program incentives to standardize the curriculum in our nation's schools.[37] Local boards of education need to withstand these pressures in order to preserve the small amount of program variation still possible at the school site. When such discretion permits a trade-off between methods of teaching or between different program offerings, the principal is the final authority. However, this set of decisions will almost inevitably be taken in conjunction with budget allocation decisions. Thus, the annual development of the school's lump-sum budget should be a time of intense participation by PAC members and school staff. Given the interests and powers of parents and teachers, the absence of substantial discussion with the PAC and teaching staff advisors would appear to be a form of folly leading almost inevitably to loss of one's administrative position.

Statewide Testing Program. To this point, the weight of our plan has resided with or favored local interests and intensified client participation. The state's interests have been acknowledged, but no mechanism for protecting these interests has been offered. One such mechanism is a system of statewide examinations intended to assess the degree of student achievement on at least two dimensions—reading and mathematics. If state legislatures desired, they might include other dimensions for testing, *e.g.*, music, science, literature, civics, foreign language, and history, but inclusion of the two prime areas of basic skills is almost an absolute necessity.

Despite the diversity of tastes for schooling and the general public inability to achieve consensus on specific school objectives, it is assumed there is widespread acceptance of reading and computing as minimal learning components for every child. Individuals may disagree on the relative significance of these skills, but it is difficult to identify a rational point of view which holds that they are of no importance. Consequently, it is highly probable that an annual statewide assessment of children's achievement on these two dimensions will be acceptable.

Other than to stipulate that the tests be criterion-referenced (described in an earlier section), it is not necessary to specify a single best method of establishing a statewide testing scheme. Nor is it necessary to test every child every year. By selecting a relatively small sample at each grade level from each school, it would be possible to assess the students' achievement gain. However, it is important that the sampling population be sufficient to generalize about each grade level at each school. To sample in larger aggregates would only tell us how a district or state is performing, and these units are too large to permit accurate identification of which pupils are learning and which are not.

Annual Performance Reports. Whereas the statewide testing program is intended to provide the state with an early-warning system regarding minimum levels of student achievement, the Annual Performance Report is intended primarily to enhance local client interests. The principal is primarily responsible for overseeing the production of this report, which is to appear once each year, probably in early spring. However, it should have sections reserved for exclusive use of the Parent Advisory Council, students (above the ninth grade), and staff. The report would be published in the local newspaper, posted prominently in the school, and, most importantly, sent home to the parents or guardian of each student. The report would be the primary printed instrument by which clients could assess the effectiveness of their local school.

Proliferation of reporting forms and data collection efforts has long been a frustrating fact of life in both the private and public sectors. Well-designed Annual Performance Reports should help reduce some of the burden. For the state, federal government, and local school district as well as for the individual school site, the performance report should be the primary data compilation instrument. The school district could aggregate the information it needed from school reports, and then pass them forward to the state. Rather than imposing yet an additional information function on local school personnel, the Annual Performance Report might well serve as the focus to consolidate all other such efforts.

The contents of an Annual Performance Report for an elementary school should include topical categories and items such as:

School Information
Name, location, enrollment, age of building, number of classrooms, number of specialized rooms, school site size, state of repair, amount spent on maintenance in the last year and last decade, library volumes, etc.

Staff Information
Number of staff by category, proportion in various license classifications, age, sex, ethnic background, experience, degree levels, etc.

Student Performance Information
Intellectual performance: all results of student performance in standardized tests should be reported in terms of state-established minimum standards. Relative performance of different schools in the district should also be provided. Other performance information might also be included: student turnover rate; absenteeism; library circulation; performance of past students at next level of schooling (junior high, high school, college); etc.

Areas of Strength
Here the school can describe what it considers its unique or noteworthy characteristics. The purpose is to encourage every school to have one or more areas of particular specialization and competence, or to espouse a particular educational philosophy, or employ a distinct methodology or approach. This section would inform parents about the tone or style of the school.

Areas for Improvement
This section would identify five areas in which a school needed improvement

and would outline its plans regarding them. These problem areas might in some schools change over the years, but in others remain the same as the schools mounted a long-term improvement project. This section should encourage schools to be self-critical, to establish specific goals and to report on subsequent progress.

Parent, Teacher, and Student Assessment of School Performance
Responsible parents, teachers, and students should be permitted an uncensored opportunity to assess school performance. This section would permit various school constituencies to express their opinions of school success or failure with respect to such matters as actual instruction, curriculum development, racial relations, student participation in decisionmaking, drug abuse, etc.[38]

School Site Budgeting. In order to provide school sites with the flexibility they need to match programs with client tastes, budgetary discretion must be accorded the school site. This is best accomplished through a system of lump-sum allocations to school sites based upon formal, districtwide decision rules. Presumably these would allocate an equal amount of money for every similarly-situated student in the district. This basic allocation would not include federal, state, or local categorical funds intended for specialized programs or populations (*e.g.,* handicapped children and ESEA Title I). The principal and advisors would then be free, within state and district budget guidelines, to determine the mix of items for which they wished to spend their funds.

There are two major components of budgeting: (1) budget development, which concerns itself with generating a resource allocation plan for some forthcoming time period that presumably reflects the objectives an organization desires to accomplish, and (2) fiscal accounting. Accounting is essentially a control function to ensure that the organization's activities are in keeping with the previously agreed-upon budget plan. To make budgets school-by-school and then not have accounting based on the same unit would be foolish. Some means must exist for assuring that each school site remains reasonably within the boundaries of its budget plan. Moreover, it makes no sense, in terms of economies of scale, to have each school act as a bursar. Actual purchasing of most materials, payment of bills, and accounting for dollars should remain a school district central office function. However, the district accounting office should keep its ledgers on a school-by-school basis. A rudimentary audit report should be included annually in a school's performance report.

In addition to revealing to school clients and staff alike how monies are being spent, school-by-school fiscal reporting is critical if we are ever to have a better understanding of the linkage between resources and school performance.[39]

Family Choice. Among a segment of educational policy analysts, the school voucher plan is attractive. The voucher concept would inject a substantial amount of the competitive market mechanism into what is frequently described as a monopoly—public schools. There are various voucher plan proposals; however, the primary aim of each of them is to give parents, or, above some age, students, the power to choose the type of school they prefer. A family would be provided with a voucher redeemable for services at a state-approved school. Some plans would permit vouchers to be redeemed by public, private, and sectarian schools; others would permit vouchers to be valid only for public schools.

Voucher plans have not been widely tried in lower education. They have been used extensively at the post-secondary level through the "GI Bill," government-supported schooling for veterans. The only systematic effort to assess the consequences of vouchers is still in progress at Alum Rock, California.[40] However, we reject the notion of a pure voucher scheme for two reasons. First, the possibility exists that a voucher plan would leave the state too exposed. Without an extraordinarily elaborate accountability mechanism, the state would have no way of ensuring its interests in minimal performance, social cohesion, and value transmission. Secondly, a judgment of a very different nature, vouchers presently appear to trigger such substantial opposition from almost all segments of the public school establishment that it is politically unlikely that this concept will be adopted.

Despite philosophic and, perhaps, political weaknesses, schooling might well benefit from an element of competition introduced through vouchers. Further, vouchers are a convenient mechanism for promoting greater choice for clients and stimulating greater diversity of offerings.

We advocate a "family choice" plan restricted to the public sector. Schools would be grouped into clusters of three or four, and small units created within larger schools (mini schools) would be counted as separate operational units. In each school a specified segment of the curriculum would be devoted to those areas with state-established minimal performance standards. However, outside these areas, each school within a cluster would be encouraged to adapt its courses and instructional style to the desires of its clients, establishing an instructional format, tone, and quality that are unique. This uniqueness would be determined by the principal, the staff, and (in high schools) the students, working in conjunction with the Parent Advisory Council. For example, some schools might emphasize a specialty such as vocational education, fine arts, mathematics, or ethnic studies. Some parents might desire a school setting employing open corridor or open classroom techniques; other parents might prefer a more structured and traditional school. In any event, decisions in such matters would involve the active participation of Parent Advisory Councils.

Once any plan is instituted, a careful record should be kept of family choices. If a clear-cut pattern emerged where one school or type of school was becoming very popular and another school or type of school less popular, the district board and administrative staff should identify the reasons and take appropriate action. This might mean opening more schools of the type frequently chosen, or allowing successful administrators (*i.e.,* those who operate popular schools) to manage another nearby school in a similar fashion. If a school were consistently avoided, the explanation might be found in the quality of the personnel, or simply in a diminished demand for that type or style of school. In the latter case, the school should be eliminated or combined with another type in a single school. If the fault rests with personnel, they should be transfered to a more appropriate setting.

The idea of a family choice plan is not particularly a radical idea. The mid-1970's "alternative school" movement provided parents with a choice of school in many districts. A somewhat more formalized version of such an idea presently exists in Minneapolis where preliminary evaluation by the National Institute of Education suggests remarkable parental satisfaction.[41]

Educators and Educational Productivity

The overwhelming proportion of school costs are attributable to teacher and administrator salaries. For example, in 1972-73 more than 60 percent ($26 billion) of total school expenditures were used to pay for instructional and administrative personnel.[42] If the past accomplishments of America's schools are to be sustained at reasonable costs, then instructional personnel must be encouraged to be even more productive. However, if left to the present system, there is little hope that such an objective will be achieved on any significant scale. Education everywhere is notoriously weak on numerous professional dimensions. For example, school systems are almost wholly inadequate in evaluating teaching, rewarding outstanding instructional performance, effectively utilizing highly specialized personnel, and encouraging employees to upgrade their skills.

If schooling is to be made more effective, then these weaknesses must be overcome. The set of proposals offered in this section* addresses these problems of professionalism and productivity. The reforms are highly interrelated and require substantial explanation of complicated matters such as teacher training, credentialing, promotion policies, and inservice training. However, the task of comprehending these suggestions is easier if the reader has at least a basic grasp of the manner in which public school evaluation and incentive systems presently operate.

The Present System of Educator Incentives

Teacher Recruitment and Preservice Training. Teacher training is subject to stylish fads. Periodically legislatures in various states require only a Bachelors degree; in other states at other times, graduate work may be necessary for a teaching credential (this seldom involves more than a year of study beyond the Bachelors level). Education majors usually are required to have a number of courses in various facets of pedagogy and a period of "practice teaching" ranging from one semester to two years, depending upon the institution and state involved. In all of this, schools or departments of education are usually permitted to establish their own admission and graduation standards. Relative to other professional schools, such standards are generally low. The result is that teachers, with some splendid exceptions, do not match the academic qualifications of individuals in professions such as law, engineering, medicine, or public administration.[43]

Credentialing. The body of knowledge and repertoire of skills one

---

*As with our earlier school-related reform proposals, ideas in this section have benefited from the author's experiences with the Fleischmann Commission.

is expected to master during teacher training is seldom made clear, but it is particularly vague in the area of practice teaching. The assignment of student teachers to their mentors in the field is haphazard at best and the supervision given a student teacher varies remarkably from day-to-day surveillance by an expert and experienced instructional craftsman to total—sink or swim—unsupervised freedom. In all of this, the state acts as something of a disinterested party or referee, seeing only that the credential candidate has the correct number of required courses recorded on his or her transcript. States delegate much of the determination of course content and supervision of credential candidates to schools of education.

Employment. After receiving a credential or teaching license, a teacher usually finds initial employment either in a rural area or in a central city school system. The obvious consequence is to burden such districts with an inequitable proportion of inexperienced teachers.[44] (A sustained period of economic duress and teacher surplus may alter this pattern; as of now, however, there is insufficient information to judge.) Once hired in such circumstances, the ambitious and upwardly mobile teacher sets for him or herself one or a combination of several goals, transfer to a "better" school or school district, tenure, and promotion.

Tenure. This status is frequently misunderstood. It is a legal classification noting that a teacher cannot be dismissed without "cause." Cause is typically defined as constituting incompetence or moral turpitude. Tenure status, in most states, is granted upon completion of three years of successful classroom teaching. During the three-year trial period, presumably the teacher can be dismissed simply as a consequence of an administrative decision. However, this is becoming more complicated as court cases and dismissal hearings increasingly assert that due process applies even in attempts to oust a probationary teacher, and a case must be made that the nontenured teacher's efforts were systematically evaluated and found wanting.

Evaluation. For practical purposes, little of the foregoing description matters. The overwhelming majority of teachers hired by school districts percolate upward through the system and are granted tenure, if not in the district where they are initially employed, then in their subsequent teaching position. Once granted tenure, the proportion of teachers dismissed for any reason is miniscule.

One might reasonably ask: "How can that be?" "Certainly there are some incompetent or immoral teachers." The obvious answer is "yes there are." However, the proportion of incompetent individuals is probably no greater among teachers than the proportion of incompetents in any other endeavor. And immorality, however defined, is probably lower for teachers than most occupational categories. But, given that some teachers do not perform their jobs well, why are they not dismissed? The problem is typically one of evaluation. How can you tell if a teacher is performing his or her job well? What yardstick should be used to measure? There are widely conflicting views on the qualities of good teachers, probably as many opinions of good and bad teaching exist as there are students. Administrators argue that, even when they know how to evaluate teachers, they are so belabored with paper work and other duties that they seldom have time to assess teachers' classroom performance. In the face of such overwhelming disagreement and confusion, and in the absence of glaring evidence to the contrary, the typical administrative judgment is that the teaching is adequate and the individual involved is promoted. Once promoted over the trial threshold to tenure, teacher dismissal becomes harder by many times over.

To be sure there are sporadic examples of teacher dismissals, but the majority are for physical abuse of students or in patently evident instances of teachers not being able to maintain order in their classrooms. Seldom are dismissals based on whether or not a teacher's instructional performance resulted in pupils not learning.

Migration. Studies of the life cycle of teachers demonstrate that they typically perceive their status as linked to the status of their students.[45] Thus a frequent pattern is to attempt to gain teaching jobs in middle-class, academically oriented schools. The effort to improve one's position may also involve a shift from elementary to secondary teaching. The latter with its greater emphasis on subject matter specialization usually leads to higher status and pay, and thus draws teachers from elementary ranks. The general outcome of such status concerns is that teachers try to migrate from rural areas to middle-class suburbs or from central city schools to schools in suburban districts or those on the periphery of the city district itself. This migration pattern is facilitated by employee organization contractual arrangements with school districts that usually render teacher transfers a function of seniority. Thus, those locations that are frequently perceived as the most desirable teaching locations are part of the reward system and professional prerogatives of senior teachers. Aside from a few dedicated professionals, this transfer phenomenon typically leaves schools with low-income or hard-to-teach youngsters staffed by the least experienced teachers.

Promotion and Pay. Getting ahead is as important to teachers as it is in most occupations. However, an educator's elevation to higher levels of pay is not linked to performance. The two primary determinants of a teacher's pay are number of years of experience and amount of schooling beyond the Bachelor's degree. Of the two, experience is typically rewarded more highly by school district salary schedules. There are automatic or built-in teacher pay increases that leave little room for administrator discretion or judgments regarding quality of performance. Why not? In the absence of acceptable objective measures, teachers fear that administrator judgments will be overly subjective and open to favoritism and scandal. The outcome has been a teacher pay and promotion system that is politically sanitized, chronologically automatic, and relatively insulated from any assessment of instructional performance.

Upward Mobility and Implicit Rewards. Even when a teacher achieves the top rungs of a district's salary schedule, the pay is not likely to be high in relation to top pay in similar occupations. Consequently, ambitious teachers are frequently provoked into altering their careers either by leaving education altogether or by striving for a school administrative position. The mobility pattern is demonstration teacher, subject matter or grade-level department chairman, Guidance Counselor, Vice Principal, Central Office Curriculum Supervisor or Director, Assistant Superintendent, and then Superintendent, State Education Department official, or college instructor. Each sequential step brings substantially higher pay or prestige. Thus, our educational system conveys its highest regards, financial and otherwise, to those who are furthest from children and classroom teaching. In short, if you want to be a success in education, get out of teaching.

In-service Training. Many occupations and professions depend heavily for success upon their employees keeping abreast of new developments. Education is no exception. The U.S. spends $4 to $5 billion dollars annually on in-service training of teachers. There are strong incentives for teachers to continue their education and training. The difficulty is that the state and local school districts have forfeited control of the training endeavor. In-service education is almost completely at the discretion of the individual teacher. In most instances, pay scales provide salary increments simply when higher college course credit plateaus have been achieved. The nature of the courses, the degree to which they are related to a teacher's instructional duties or subject matter specialization, and their ability to buttress weaknesses uncovered in a systematic performance evaluation are almost nil. In-service training or continued education could be vastly more effective if a means could be found for overcoming these weaknesses.

Summary. The present system of teacher recruitment, training, licensing, employment, evaluation, promotion, and compensation frequently discourages capable individuals from entering teaching as a career and acts as a disincentive to those already in teaching to the continued mastery of their professional tasks. Moreover, it is a personnel system that severely inhibits any form of effective supervision, supportive criticism, or leverage on change either by colleagues or administrators. Under such conditions it is no wonder that teachers frequently feel alienated, find it difficult to view themselves as professionals, are forced to moonlight at demeaning tasks, and are induced to leave challenging teaching situations and the classroom as soon as possible. In short, the personnel system is essentially out of control.

A New System

Many of the problems of teacher effectiveness are triggered by conditions beyond the boundaries of this chapter. For example, part of the problem of increasing teacher professionalism concerns the degree of autonomy or influence granted teachers to make instructional decisions and district policy generally. It is difficult to imagine, for example, that physicians would tolerate for very long the administrative subjugation from which teachers are only now beginning to emerge. Nevertheless, aside from the necessity of many basic reforms in school governance and school site size, there are some steps that can be taken now to encourage greater teacher effectiveness and promote professionalism in education.

Teacher Recruitment. During the Great Depression of the

1930's many individuals understandably were motivated to seek stable employment opportunities; public school teaching is generally agreed to be stable employment. As a consequence, America was able to attract at that time a most capable corps of teachers. Economic instability in the mid 1970's, when coupled with at least a temporary excess of licensed teachers, may offer a similar opportunity to elevate the overall quality of those entering teaching.[46] There are several useful steps that can be taken by teacher training institutions in this regard.

First, colleges and departments of education should elevate admission standards for teacher training programs. While making every effort to recruit training candidates from a broad ethnic spectrum, admission officials should scrutinize grade transcripts, Graduate Record Examination (GRE) scores, previous experience in teacher related activities, letters of recommendation, and other evidence of ability so as to accept only the most highly qualified potential teachers. If such a program is pursued effectively over the next several years, average scores of education students on the GRE and equivalent measures should equal or surpass those of students in other graduate departments such as social science, business, public administration, and engineering.

The U.S. presently employs approximately 2.5 million licensed teachers. Our population projections suggest that this situation is likely to remain stable at least for the next decade. In times of economic prosperity, there is approximately a 5-percent turnover rate in school district professional staff members due to career changes, promotions, retirements, deaths, etc. In periods of economic hardship, this rate drops. Using these figures, we estimate that the U.S. will need to employ approximately 125,000 new teachers each year until 1985.

It is difficult to obtain precise figures, but we estimate that there are at least one-half million individuals enrolled in teacher training programs in private and public institutions.[47] Some of these persons, of course, anticipate careers other than teaching. Whatever their plans, the number presently in training probably represents a misplaced investment of resources. To correct this situation, we recommend that teacher training institutions proportionally decrease the number of their students so that the national total approximates 250,000. At the least, state level policy should reduce the number of pre-service or entry level teacher training positions at state institutions. The resources saved by such reductions should be redistributed so as to increase the quality and intensity of instruction for teacher trainees in ways described below.

Pre-service Teacher Training. Both for elementary and secondary school personnel, teacher training should take place exclusively at the graduate level. Following completion of a Bachelor's degree an individual would be eligible to apply for admission to a department of education. The teacher training program would then occupy two years of graduate study. The successful candidate under these conditions should emerge with a Master of Arts degree in Teaching (MAT). For secondary teachers this would include a year of graduate work in a subject matter field. The expertise necessary to be a good teacher of history, English, foreign language, or any other subject specialization seldom is acquired during the undergraduate years. Public school students' respect for beginning teachers, and teachers' self-respect, would be substantially enhanced if subject matter competence were better assured.

Elementary teachers should be specializing also, primarily in the teaching of reading and mathematics. In addition, they need an intensive understanding of child development processes. Beyond their graduate year of specialization, both elementary and secondary teacher trainees should spend an additional year in courses in pedagogy and practice teaching with the trainee assuming gradually increasing levels of responsibility for a group of students. Practice teaching should take place not only under the tutelage of a supervisor from the collegiate training institution, but also under the auspices of a Master Teacher in the public school setting. (See the description of Master Teacher later in this chapter.) An important component of the two-year teacher training program would be the trainees' initial compilation of a Professional Portfolio to serve subsequently as the primary instrument for teacher evaluation.

Teacher Licensing. The State should move to revise its credentialing procedures in favor of four major categories: (1) Intern Teacher, (2) Classroom Teacher, (3) Special Teacher, and (4) Master Teacher. Each of these categories would represent added levels of training, experience, and competence. Moreover, transition from one level to the next would necessitate successful accomplishment of a number of evaluation procedures. Lastly, each successive credential category would be associated with significantly higher pay scales. In subsequent sections the evaluation and remuneration parts of this plan will be discussed. The different functions of each credential category are:

Intern Teacher. This credential category would be open to those individuals who successfully complete the two-year graduate program in teacher education. Success would, among other things, be gauged heavily by academic performance over the two years, and high ratings in the practice teaching component. Upon being awarded Intern Teacher status, an individual would be eligible for employment in a local school district, *but* would have to remain under the systematic supervision and criticism of a licensed Master Teacher for yet another two years. Presumably, Intern Teachers would carry the equivalent of what presently is defined as a 1/2 to 2/3 regular teaching load. They would be practicing and developing a repertoire of pedagogical techniques suitable to their instructional responsibilities. Also, the Intern Teacher would be planning and conducting simplified classroom research projects and continuing to accumulate materials useful for his or her professional portfolio.

Classroom Teacher. This credential category would be accessible to those individuals who successfully complete at least two years of internship teaching. After negotiating the evaluation process covering the transition from Intern Teacher, a teacher would be eligible for regular classroom instructional responsibilities at either the elementary or secondary level. Presumably this would be defined as a full teaching load. Because of the greater emphasis on professionalism and better pre-service preparation, the Classroom Teacher hopefully would also have responsibilities for conducting research and serving on personnel panels to evaluate fellow teachers and administrators.

Special Teacher. This credential category would be open to those who had amassed four years of successful teaching as a Classroom Teacher, had completed a minimum of one additional year of graduate study, and had passed State Teacher Licensing Commission procedures for this credential level. Special Teachers would be assigned to those instructional settings requiring added knowledge and expertise, for example, physically and mentally handicapped children and underachieving students in low-income rural or big city schools. Simply possessing Special Teacher training and credential would not suffice to draw the pay rate at this level, the individual must actually perform in a teaching assignment with a group of students designated as Special. These assignments probably would not be found in schools filled with "normal" children from comfortable economic circumstances.

Master Teacher. This category would be reserved for no more than 10 percent of all employed teachers in the state. To be accorded Master Teacher status, an individual would have to hold an earned doctorate, have successfully served as an Intern, Classroom, and Special Teacher, and passed the State Teacher Licensing Commission evaluation. Master Teachers would have instructional and supervisorial functions consisting primarily of overseeing the practice teaching of trainees and the work of Intern Teachers. Master Teachers, as the title implies, would represent the apex of instructional capability, control of a subject matter area or skill speciality, knowledge of pedagogical practices and how to conduct research about them, and a record of outstanding performance as a teacher. Master Teachers should be professionals in every sense of the word, and should enjoy the status, autonomy, and pay of a professional. Master Teachers should be on the same pay schedule as school principals in a local district.

Evaluation and Promotion. Evaluation procedures are at the heart of any system designed to improve teacher performance. Such procedures must satisfy at least the following criteria: (1) be based in substantial measure on valid and reliable information, (2) permit a degree of participation by the party to be evaluated, in at least the establishment of evaluation ground rules, (3) include judgment by ones' peers, and (4) provide feedback to the individual being evaluated. The following arrangements would satisfy these conditions:

State Teacher Licensing Commission. Primary responsibility for the establishment and supervision of teacher evaluation regulations should rest with a special state commission. This body would be authorized to assess eligibility for the four credential levels already described. (Progress through the various steps *within* any one credential category would be the primary responsibility of the local school district in which the teacher was employed.)

The licensing commission should be composed of ten members:

two representatives from teacher-training institutions, two Master Teachers, two superintendents, two local school board members, and two citizens. The six members in the first three categories should be appointed by the State Superintendent of Public Instruction with the approval of the State Board of Education; the four members in the last two categories should be appointed jointly by the governor and state legislature. The term of office for commission members should be no less than two years and no more than four. Terms should be staggered so as to assure continuity of experience among the membership. The commission should be provided with an annual appropriation by the legislature to cover operating expenses and the cost of a small staff.

The licensing commission would appoint, annually or biannually, regional review boards throughout the state that would take responsibility for assessing the qualifications of teachers applying for promotion from one credential category to another, *e.g.,* Intern to Classroom Teacher. Each board would be a microcosm of its parent containing a Master Teacher, college faculty member, superintendent, local school board member, and a citizen.

Evaluation Procedures. Upon achieving the prescribed years and other qualifications necessary for a particular credential category, a promotion candidate would apply to the State Teacher Licensing Commission to be evaluated. The application would be delegated to the appropriate regional review board. Each regional board would convene annually in the winter to review the candidates' professional portfolios (described below). The regional board would also have the prerogative of interviewing candidates, and talking with students, parents, teaching colleagues, and supervisors. The staff of the state commission would prepare the materials and schedule appropriate interviews for these regional board meetings.

The regional Board should communicate its decisions to the state commission by early spring of the same year; candidates would be informed of credential promotion decisions simultaneously. If a candidate desired to appeal a negative decision, he or she would do so directly to the state commission, which would have the right to reverse regional board judgments. A positive judgment would accord a candidate the appropriate credential and eligibility for any school district opening in the appropriate credential category. School districts would choose from the pool of those eligible. Upon attaining a job at a specific credential level, the teacher would then receive remuneration consistent with the initial entry step in that category. In other words, it would be possible to have a larger pool of eligible Special Teachers than there were Special Teaching positions. Only those actually employed in such positions would draw commensurate pay. This point is important to remember, particularly in the instance of Master Teachers because, by definition, only 10 percent of the State's public school instructors can assume such rank.

Professional Portfolio. It is crucial that a significantly greater share of teacher evaluation reside with teachers themselves. Toward this end we have already proposed that teachers be represented on the State Teacher Licensing Commission and its regional subunits. Beyond that, the individual teacher should begin to exercise initiative in the evaluation process by assembling basic evidence upon which district and state level evaluation would be based. The keystone of the individual teacher's record should be a professional portfolio consisting of items such as:

1. A description of and academic transcripts from an individual's undergraduate, graduate, and professional coursework;

2. A record of the scores on statewide tests of the students who have been in the teacher's charge (the need for a statewide testing program is discussed in the earlier section on systemwide accountability);

3. Questionnaires submitted each year to parents and, above the 8th grade, to students;

4. Video tape records of observations and special instructional activities of the teacher;

5. Letters of evaluation from the Master Teachers under whom one has taught over time, and from administrators and college supervisors;

6. Evidence of classroom research studies; and

7. Other items of the teacher's choosing that he or she believes illustrate instructional prowess.

These are the primary items for teacher evaluation. However, regional review boards and the state commission could collect additional information wherever they believed it would be of use.

Local School District's Role. Evaluation of teachers' performances clearly must take place more regularly than the periodic assessments conducted under State Teacher Licensing Commission auspices. Between the reviews for credential promotion purposes, local officials must assume evaluation responsibility. This should be done every two years and in a manner consistent with the state level procedures already described. One example would be a local district panel composed of a Master Teacher, principal, parent, and a student above the 8th grade. Again, the teacher's professional portfolio should serve as the primary basis of such an evaluation.

There should be at least two important outcomes stemming from such biennial local evaluation sessions. First, the individual teacher should be provided with feedback regarding his or her performance. This performance report, along with the state specified qualifications for credential promotion, should serve as the primary guideposts for teachers' in-service education efforts. Secondly, the results of the evaluation should determine the teacher's placement on the district salary schedule for the particular credential category involved.

In-service Education. The U.S. presently spends literally billions of dollars annually for upgrading teachers' skills. However, teachers' efforts on this dimension are not tied systematically to their instructional performance. Despite their strengths and weaknesses, teachers are free to take whatever summer or evening college courses they desire. In part this problem arises because the courses offered by teacher training institutions are too frequently not useful to teachers, but they have little choice but to enroll in what is available. In terms of salary schedule increments, it seldom matters; the local district will grant teachers pay increases almost regardless of what courses are taken. Consequently, we propose that salary schedule advances either be tied to the successful completion of courses consistent with the recommendations contained in a teacher's biennial local evaluation or else be clearly tied to credential advancement requirements.

In order to assure that college courses for teachers are as useful as possible, teacher organizations should form advisory panels to higher education teacher training departments to assist in determining offerings. If this proves unsatisfactory, school districts should give serious consideration to offering their own in-service education programs geared to local teacher needs. This appears to be a function ideally suited for intermediate level education units with their ability to hire instructors on a contractual basis.[48] Such in-service arrangements might possibly be more tightly geared to teacher improvement requirements and would provide teacher training institutions with badly needed competition.

Administrators and Teaching. Because promotion to central office and school site administrative positions now acts as a subtle incentive to attract capable individuals from classroom instruction, we have already advocated that ten percent of the state's teachers be recompensed at an annual rate equal to school principals. However, it probably will take more than this to reverse the present situation and restore dignity and added status to classroom instruction. Consequently, we strongly urge that at least 90 percent of all school administrators in local school districts be required to carry a minimum of one-fifth-time teaching load. This would save the state some money, but much more importantly, it would convey the idea that instruction is the *sina qua non* of schooling.

Prospects for Success

Given the obstacle course facing any endeavor to reform public education, particularly efforts directed at enhancing educational productivity, why should these proposals provide accountability when previous plans have fallen short? It is possible that our proposals will also succumb to professional opposition, political inertia, or intellectual challenge. Nevertheless, our intent has been to construct a judicious mix of existing analytic technology, market place economics, and political participation sufficient to facilitate adaption.

The absence of a widespread consensus regarding the purposes of schooling has led us to advocate a relatively small decisionmaking jurisdiction for deciding most educational goals. Though it is by no means certain that all the parents at a particular site will agree on the objectives of schooling, it is more probable that this relatively small unit can reach agreement than a larger jurisdiction such as a school district, county, or state. Certainly this will be the case if the element of family choice is included because parents would be more homogeneous with regard to tastes for schooling than is presently the case in most school systems. The expression of parent values by consumer action and the use of parent advisory councils should make it possible to reach agreement on purposes at each school. Moreover, diversity of opinion can be accommodated by having different types of schools.

The state is able to protect its interests because the school is a sufficiently integral unit to permit the identification of failure. By requiring statewide tests, public officials can isolate intolerably low levels of achievement in sufficient time to rectify the condition.

By establishing hierarchical categories on a professional ladder and offering economic and status rewards for each successive step, our accountability plan endeavors to restore performance incentives for teachers. An effort is made to enhance professional autonomy and pride by relying heavily on peer judgment in promotion decisions. Under these conditions teachers should gain a measure of direction over their professional destiny heretofore unavailable. Also, by permitting capable teachers to earn salaries comparable to school principals and by requiring administrators to assume at least a minimal teaching load, the possibility exists that instruction will regain the emphasis it must have if schools are to be made more productive.

These proposals are directed, over the long run, at increasing school efficiency. By deliberately encouraging diversity in educational styles and instructional modes, the hope is that "a thousand flowers will bloom." By the systematic collection of information regarding which "flowers" work and which do not, we can build a body of pedagogical science. Feedback about school effectiveness will stem from at least two sources—the statewide testing program and the school choices of families. One measure is relatively objective, the other subjective; both appear necessary to encompass the complicated aims of schooling. Moreover, in time, school-by-school budgeting and accounting will permit more rigorous cost-effectiveness analyses to take place than is currently possible.

Our accountability scheme does not rest on unsupportable assumptions regarding an educational knowledge base of technology. Instead, we pursue a centuries-old strategy for making decisions in the face of incomplete knowledge. We rely on a modified version of the market place, competition, and consumer choice. In the absence of widely accepted absolute standards by which to judge school performance, the consumer should be permitted to choose what best maximizes his or her tastes. Assuming that parents have the best interests of their children at heart, they will make school choices and PAC policies consistent with what they regard as good education.

Admittedly, all of this may appear complex and bulky. However, this is probably an inevitable consequence of a system that must balance complicated and potentially competing values such as lay control, professional autonomy, social cohesion, local choice, concern for private values, and prudent deployment of public funds. These values presently appear out of balance and the technical accountability model may be exacerbating the situation. Our hope is that an accountability model that acknowledges political reality and technical shortcomings, even if complicated, may restore equilibrium.

NOTES

1. The title of an address on public sector budget analysis given by Willian Gorham (then Assistant Secretary for Program Evaluation in the Department of Health, Education and Welfare, now Director of the Urban Institute) at the University of California at Berkeley in 1968.

2. *A Century of Public School Statistics*, and *Statistics of Trends in Education: 1962-63 to 1982-83*. Both published by the National Center for Educational Statistics, U.S. Office of Education, Department of Health, Education and Welfare, 1975.

3. *Ibid.*

4. *Ibid.*

5. For more information on the topic of the local property tax see Dick Netzer, *Economics of the Property Tax* (Washington, D.C.: Brookings Institution, 1966). A contemporary reanalysis of the property tax is provided in Henry J. Aaron, *A New View of Property Tax Incidence* (Washington, D.C.: The Brookings Institution, 1974).

6. A more detailed explanation of the increased interest of state level officials in education is provided in James W. Guthrie and Paula H. Skene, "The Escalation of Pedagogical Politics," *Phi Delta Kappan* 54(No. 6, February 1973), 386-99.

7. Another approach to controlling the growth of public expenditures generally, and school expenditures specifically, takes the form of strict spending limits. For example, in 1972, the California state legislature enacted Senate Bill 90, which prohibits school district expenditures from increasing annually by more than an amount equal to cost of living increases. Oregon has long had a similar revenue limit provision. Many other states attempt to meet the same problem, cost increases, by limiting the tax rate a local board of education can levy. Again in 1972, California voters were asked to vote on a statewide ballot measure which, if enacted, would have limited all state spending to a specified portion of the growth in statewide income. The measure failed.

8. See Michael W. Kirst, "The Rise and Fall of PPBS in California," *Phi Delta Kappan* 56(No. 8, April 1975), 535-38.

9. Educational Testing Service, *State Educational Assessment Programs, 1973 Revision* (Princeton, New Jersey: Educational Testing Service, 1973), 1.

10. For an exchange that nicely illustrates the controversy surrounding the

Michigan accountability effort, see Ernest R. House, Wendell Rivers, and Daniel Stufflebeam, "An Assessment of the Michigan Accountability System," *Phi Delta Kappan* 55(No. 10, June 1974), 663-69, and C. Philip Kearney, David L. Donovan, and Thomas H. Fisher, "In Defense of Michigan's Accountability Program," *Phi Delta Kappan* 56(No. 1, September 1974), 14-19.

11. Educational Testing Service, *Proceedings of the Conference on Educational Accountability* (Princeton, New Jersey: Educational Testing Service, 1973).

12. Aaron Wildavsky, "A Program of Accountability for Elementary Schools," *Phi Delta Kappan* 52(No. 4, December 1970), 212-16.

13. Annual Meeting Issue: Accountability '70, *Compact* 4(No. 5, October 1970); Issue on Accountability, *Phi Delta Kappan* 52(No. 4, December 1970).

14. The conference was organized in April of 1970 by Dr. Myron Lieberman of the City University of New York.

15. This equation is presented in Henry M. Levin, "Measuring Efficiency in Educational Production," *Public Finance Quarterly* 2(No. 1, January 1974), 3-24. Added criticism of the industrial accountability model is provided in a set of reviews on accountability books by Ernest R. House, "Accountability: An Essay Review of Three Books," *American Educational Research Journal* 11(No. 3, Summer 1974), 275-79.

16. Levin, *op. cit.*, 21-22.

17. For example, Aristotle once wrote: "At present opinion is divided about the subjects of education. All do not take the same view about what should be learned by the young, either with a view to plain goodness or with a view to the best life possible . . ." Ernest Barker, *The Politics of Aristotle* (Oxford, England: Oxford University Press, 1969), 333.

18. In fact, as a University of Chicago study amply demonstrated, there is also substantial geographic variation in publicly held expectations for schools. See Lawrence W. Downey, *The Task of Public Education* (Chicago: Midwest Administration Center, University of Chicago, 1960).

19. For an example of early differences of opinion regarding schooling, see Frederick Rudolph, *Essays on Education in the New Republic* (Cambridge: Harvard University Press, 1965).

20. Good statements of the so-called radical view of the function of American schools are provided in the following: Samuel Bowles, "Schooling and Inequality from Generation to Generation," *Journal of Political Economy* (May 1972, Supplement); David K. Cohen and Marvin Lazerson, "Education and the Corporate Order," *Socialist Revolution* (March/April 1972); Herbert Gintis, "A Radical Analysis of Welfare Economics and Individual Development," *Quarterly Journal of Economics* 86(No. 4, November 1972).

21. A concise general description of all types of testing is provided in *Tests and Testing* (McLean, Va.: National Council For the Advancement of Education, Winter 1974).

22. The technical details of the measurement problems contained in norm-referenced testing are described in Barbara Heyns, "Education, Evaluation, and the Metrics of Learning," a paper prepared for the American Sociological Association meetings held in Montreal in 1974.

23. An excellent description of the NAEP and a history of its early political difficulties is provided by Ralph W. Tyler, "National Assessment: A History and Sociology," in James W. Guthrie and Edward Wynne, *New Models For American Education* (Englewood Cliffs, N.J.: Prentice Hall, 1971), chap. 2.

24. James S. Coleman *et al., Equality of Educational Opportunity*. Office of Education, National Center for Educational Statistics, OE 38001 (Washington, D.C.: Government Printing Office, 1966).

25. The logical and technical weaknesses regarding the research procedures employed by social scientists to control for out-of-school influences on learning are well described in the following works: Glen G. Cain and Harold W. Watts, "Problems in Making Policy Inferences from the Coleman Report," *American Sociological Review* 35(No. 2, April 1970), 228-42; James S. Coleman, "Reply to Cain and Watts," *American Sociological Review* 35(No. 2, April 1970), 242-49; Eric A. Hanushek and John F. Kain, "On the Value of Equality of Educational Opportunity as a Guide to Public Policy," in Frederick Mosteller and Daniel P. Moynihan (eds.), *On Equality of Educational Opportunity* (New York: Vintage, 1972), 116-46; Robert E. Klitgaard, *Achievement Scores and Educational Objectives* (Santa Monica, Cal.: RAND, 1974) R-1217-NIE; Robert E. Klitgaard and G. Hall, *A Statistical Search for Unusually Effective Schools* (Santa Monica, Cal.: RAND, 1973) R-1210-CC/RC; Andrew C. Porter and Garry L. McDaniels, "A Reassessment of the Problems in Estimating School Effects," paper presented at the American Association for the Advancement of Science, March 1974.

26. Robert E. Klitgaard, *Improving Educational Evaluation in a Political Setting* (Santa Monica, Cal.: RAND, 1974), i.

27. See, for example, Committee on National Program Priorities, *The Power of Competency Based Teacher Education* (Boston: Allyn and Bacon Inc., 1972).

28. Alfred P. Wilson and William W. Curtis, "The States Mandate Performance-Based Teacher Education," *Phi Delta Kappan* 55(No. 1, September 1973), 76, 77.

29. Robert W. Heath and Mark A. Nielson, "The Research Basis For Performance-Based Teacher Education," *Review of Educational Research* 44(No. 4, Fall 1974), 463-84.

30. CBTE is also explained and criticized in substantial detail in Phyllis Hamilton, *Competency-Based Teacher Education* (Menlo Park, Cal.: Stanford Research Institute, 1973).

31. In a recent survey of teacher attitudes, 79 percent of those queried reported that, at least in theory, they were in agreement with the idea of accountability. The study, conducted by Thomas L. Good, *et al.*, is summarized in *Phi Delta Kappan* 56(No. 5, January 1975), 367-68.

32. *Releasing Standardized Achievement Test Scores*, published by Educational Research Service, Arlington, Virginia (as reported in *Education USA* 17(No. 18, December 30, 1974), 102).

33. For added information on the association between school district size and voter participation in bond and tax elections, see the forthcoming paper by W. Norton Grubb and Jack W. Osman, "The Causes of School Finance Inequalities: *Serrano* and the Case of California." A working paper of the

Childhood and Government Project, Boalt Hall, University of California, Berkeley.

34. The interaction of increased population and vastly reduced numbers of school districts has substantially diluted the representative nature of school boards. For example, each U.S. school board member now represents a constituency of approximately 3,000 citizens. The equivalent figure 50 years ago was 200 citizens. This phenomenon is explained in greater detail in James W. Guthrie, "Public Control of Public Schools: Can We Get It Back," *Public Affairs Report* 15(No. 3, June 1974), published by Institute of Governmental Studies, University of California, Berkeley.

35. The nonpartisan caucus is widely used throughout the midwest for generating school board candidates.

36. For example, in a 1971 study of a large metropolitan school district, Kittredge demonstrated that school sites at which the principal made personnel decisions experienced noticeably less staff turnover, absenteeism, requests for transfer, and filing of formal grievances. Michael H. Kittredge, *Teacher Placement Procedures and Organizational Effectiveness*, unpublished dissertation, U.C. Berkeley, 1972.

37. For a full explanation of the many forces acting to standardize our nation's school curriculum, see Roald F. Campbell and Robert A. Bunnell (eds.), *Nationalizing Influences on Secondary Education* (Chicago: University of Chicago Press, 1963).

38. *The Fleischmann Report on the Quality, Cost, and Financing of Elementary and Secondary Education in New York State.* Vol. III (New York: The Viking Press, 1973), 58-59.

39. For example, school-by-school accounting would permit us to escape from research flaws such as the Coleman Report exhibited on this dimension. In its assessment of school effects, the Coleman team used districtwide average per pupil expenditure figures. This is almost always a misleading number. For example, high schools generally spend half again more per pupil than elementary schools.

40. Daniel Weiler, Director, *A Public School Voucher Demonstration: The First Year at Alum Rock* (Santa Monica, Cal.: RAND, June 1974), R 1495/1-NIE, 2, 3, R-1495-NIE.

41. An interesting description of the Minneapolis family choice experiment is contained in the winter 1975 issue of *Information*, the quarterly newsletter of the National Institute of Education.

42. Derived from USOE, Statistics of Public Elementary and Secondary Day Schools (DHGW Publication No. (OE) 73-11402) Fall 1972.

43. Educational requirements for certification as a teacher are, at most, one year of graduate training, compared with three or more years for law, medicine and other professions. Also, mean GRE aptitude test scores for Education majors consistently are lower than for fields such as social science, physics, and natural science.

44. For added information on this topic, see James W. Guthrie, Douglas H. Penfield, and David N. Evans, "Geographic Distribution of Teaching Talent," *American Education Research Journal* 6(No. 4, November 1969), 645-59.

45. Howard S. Becker, "The Career of the Chicago Public School Teacher," *American Journal of Sociology* 57(March 1952), 470-77.

46. The teacher supply and demand situation is more complicated than appears at first glance. There is substantial discussion in educational circles and in the public media regarding the "teacher surplus" of the mid-1970's. However, it is not altogether clear that this is a permanent condition. As might reasonably be imagined, the NEA argues that if class sizes were what they ought to be, smaller, then the "excess" supply of teachers would be absorbed rapidly. A recent RAND Corporation study argues that the problem is more complicated. The RAND report demonstrates that there is a substantial lag time in matching teacher supply and demand. The production of teachers from the time of their recruitment into training programs until their availability for employment is anywhere from two to six years. Potential recruits do respond to their perception of the market for teacher services. Presently, potential teacher trainees are beginning to choose other occupational fields. Thus, the supply of trained teachers will soon be sharply reduced. If the U.S. population continues its downward path, there may be no future supply problem. However, if, after 1980, our present secondary school enrollment bulge opts to have families larger than two children, then the size of our population will again head upward. Under such circumstances, we are likely to need more teachers than are in the production pipeline. Because of the previously mentioned lag time in matching supply with demand, we may even experience a teacher shortage. See Stephen J. Carroll and Kenneth Ryder, Jr., *Analysis of the Educational Personnel System: Vol. V. The Supply of Elementary and Secondary Teachers* (Santa Monica, Cal.: RAND, 1974).

47. The RAND study, *ibid.*, contends that approximately 30 percent of all BAs are prepared to teach. Assuming 1.2 million BAs per year, we arrive at 360,000 per annum, times 4 years, equals almost 1.5 million.

48. Such intermediate units exist in most states already and are authorized to offer teacher training services. For example, New York has Boards of Cooperative Educational Services (BOCES), Oregon has Intermediate Education Districts (IED), and California has County Offices of Education.

SELECTED REFERENCES.

Barro, Stephen M., "An Approach to Developing Accountability Measures for the Public Schools," *Phi Delta Kappan* 52(No. 4, December 1970), 196-205.

Cunningham, Luvern L., "Our Accountability Problems," in Frank J. Sciara and Richard K. Jantz (eds.), *Accountability in American Education* (Boston: Allyn and Bacon, 1972), 78-91.

Department of Health, Education and Welfare, *Educational Accountability and Evaluation* (Washington, D.C.: Government Printing Office, 1972).

Dyer, Henry S., "The Measurement of Educational Opportunity," in Frederick Mosteller and Daniel Moynihan (eds.), *On Equality of Educational Opportunity* (New York: Random House, 1972), 513-37.

Dyer, Henry S., and E. Rosenthal, "An Overview of the Survey Findings," *State Educational Assessment Programs* (Princeton, N.J.: Educational Testing Service, 1971).

Educational Policy Research Center, *Accountability in Education* (Menlo Park, Cal.: Stanford Research Institute, 1972).

Hanson, Gordon P., *Accountability: A Bibliography* (Madison: Wisconsin Department of Public Instruction, 1973).

Hawthorne, Phyllis, *Legislation by the State: Accountability and Assessment in Education* (Madison: Wisconsin Department of Public Instruction, 1974).

Hawthorne, Phyllis, and Archie A. Buchmiller, *Characteristics of, and Proposed Models for, State Accountability Legislation* (Madison: Wisconsin Department of Public Instruction, 1973).

Lessinger, Leon M., "Issues and Insights into Accountability in Education," in James E. Bruno (ed.), *Emerging Issues in Education: Policy Implications for the Schools* (Lexington, Mass.: D.C. Heath & Co., 1972), 229-49.

Lessinger, Leon M., *et al.*, *Accountability: Systems Planning in Education* (Homewood, Ill.: Etc Pubns., 1973).

Sciara, Frank J., and Richard K. Jantz (eds.), *Accountability in American Education* (Boston: Allyn and Bacon, 1972), 78-91.

Wynne, Edward, *The Politics of School Accountability: Public Information About Public Schools* (Berkeley, Cal.: McCutchan Publishing Corporation, 1972).

11. Social Science and School Decentralization

DAVID W. O'SHEA

The major development in urban school district politics over the past decade has been the emergence of demands for greater responsiveness to parental preferences on the part of individual schools and even, at the extreme, the demand for local community control. Though initially the demands for community control were directed toward securing decentralization of educational governance, school district authorities typically have responded by decentralizing administration only, retaining control at the center over policy decisions regarding personnel, program, and budget.[1] Behind this outcome lies a continuing division between professional educators on the one hand and local control advocates among the public on the other. This division centers on the different perspectives each group brings to bear upon educational problems; perspectives that lead each group to propose solutions that conflict with the interests of the other.

The precipitating factor giving rise to the original calls for local control was the low average level of achievement and high dropout rates characterizing inner-city schools. Inevitably, social science research was looked to for solutions, but to date has found none, and offers little hope that either local control, as proposed by community people, or decentralized administration, as proposed by professional educators, actually will lead to increased learning in school. Low achievement, the research tells us, is not caused by schools but by the lower socioeconomic background that children bring to school with them, a factor schools cannot alter.

Given the failure of social science research to provide any solution to the low achievement problem, how does a school board make decisions regarding community control? If community control could be said to offer promise to rectify the low achievement problem, then there would exist powerful justification for its implementation. Yet in the absence of any evidence that community control will change current low achievement patterns, what basis is there for allowing parents to interfere with professional judgment in educational matters? Indeed, it can be argued that if the expertise and technology for solving the achievement problem do not exist at the district level, what reason is there to assume it exists at the school level or among parents?

Despite considerable challenge to the efficacy of decentralization posed by the research, pressure for structural reform continues. One reason for continued pressure is that, as with other social issues, educational policy is determined as much by normative as by empirical considerations. The same norms that find expression in community control demands have long been accepted as a basis for the highly decentralized pattern of educational governance characteristic of rural and suburban areas. Urban residents, especially minorities, have now begun to appeal to these same values in the belief that through local community control important outcomes of schooling, including academic achievement, can be improved, research notwithstanding. From this ideological perspective, community control is not simply an attempt to increase the effectiveness of education, but a challenge by minorities, especially blacks, to the very legitimacy of existing education. In other words, the demand for community control is an effort to create a different kind of education relevant to minority children and minority cultures. Research findings on school effectiveness, then, may have differing implications for decentralized governance than for decentralized administration, which seeks only to improve existing education while retaining centralized governance.

Moreover, even if achievement patterns cannot be altered, decentralization may produce other desirable outcomes that provide a basis for its adoption. Indeed, once initiated, decentralization tends to acquire a life of its own. Decentralized governance helps minority communities to use school resources for community development. From the point of view of professional educators, decentralized administration devolves more decisionmaking to the local schools, increasing their responsiveness to particular local needs, and, hopefully, generates increased public support for system maintenance. From the point of view of parents, both in minority and in majority white communities, the school-level advisory councils that commonly accompany administrative decentralization have opened up the possibility of these councils taking on broader functions, including parental participation in personnel selection and the determination of local school goals.

These trends, deriving from the original demands for community control, now find expression in the growing debate over the concept of school-site management. Ideally, school-site management combines elements of decentralized administration and decentralized governance, balancing the devolution of administrative decisionmaking to the school level with school staff accountability to elected representatives of the parental population. These several outcomes, other than improved student achievement, must be considered in evaluating the implications for decentralization of social science research findings on the achievement issue.

This chapter, then, examines the policy bases for decentralization, given the current lack of criteria for improving schooling outcomes. Discussion first turns to the bases upon which decisions have actually been made regarding both forms of decentralization, administrative and governmental. Having delineated the expectations held by proponents of each, decentralization is then evaluated in terms of its proven and potential outcomes.

PRESENT MODELS AND FUTURE POLICIES

Models of Decisionmaking

Policy outcomes from school district governance are influenced by the prevailing division of labor between school boards and their professional staffs, a division based on ideas promoted originally by the municipal reform movement in the late nineteenth century. Deficiencies of the then highly decentralized urban school systems helped fuel the reform efforts. In New York City, for example, as Ravitch[2] reports, the public schools of that era had poorly trained and low paid staffs that were dependent on political patronage for their appointments. Schools were characterized by severe discipline, rote teaching, and high dropout rates at the elementary level. Ironically in the context of recent developments, reformers such as Joseph Rice blamed the system's failures upon

the complexity and inefficiency of the decentralized system. The central problem, he thought, was that no one was accountable for errors. He proposed a radical reorganization, dividing the system's functions between an expert Board of Superintendents, which would have complete control of educational policies, and a central Board of Education, which would stick strictly to the system's business affairs.[3]

This division of labor between lay board and professional staff has become the prevailing model in American education. One consequence is the dominance of what Allison calls *organizational processes* in determining school district policies, at least within the limits permitted by state education codes.[4] However, while processes within the formal organizational structure of school districts are likely to be the major determinant of policy decisions, seldom are they the only processes at work. For purposes of a more comprehensive analysis, Allison argues that policymaking should be examined also from the perspectives of two other process models: *rational decisionmaking* by governing boards and *political bargaining* among the decisionmakers themselves.

A rational model assumes that the decisionmaking group's members act in unison to select from among alternative means the one most likely to facilitate attainment of agreed goals at minimum cost. Criteria of efficiency take precedence in guiding the decisionmakers' choice. Clearly, therefore, the rational model requires the availability of fairly complete knowledge regarding means-ends relationships. Unfortunately, the predictive validity of most theories about means to attain educational ends is very low. From this one has to conclude either that educational policymaking is largely irrational or that Allison adopts too restrictive a definition of rationality. Support for the latter conclusion comes from Mannheim's[5] discussion of the nature of rationality. He proposes two distinct types: functional and substantial. Where scientific knowledge regarding means-ends relationships is available, functional rationality becomes possible. The most typical expression of functional rationality occurs in decisions governing the organization of industrial production in which the functions that have to be performed in order to achieve a given outcome can be specified with great accuracy.

In the absence of tested knowledge, choice between the means available for attaining given ends generally is based upon plausible, or substantially rational, grounds. Mannheim defines substantial rationality as "an act of thought which reveals intelligent insight into the interrelations of events in a given situation."[6] Therefore, Allison's rational model should be divided between a functionally rational model and a substantially rational model. It is clear, for example, that arguments for and against decentralization, either of governance or of administration, are not based upon scientific evidence, but upon appeals to substantially rational positions, frequently rooted more in normative rather than in empirical considerations.

Apart from organizational processes and rational decisionmaking, Allison[7] proposes that political bargaining between members of the policymaking group is yet another process influencing the nature of policy outcomes. However, in urban school districts bargaining between board members on the basis of their interests is more likely to occur in the determination of policy regarding issues defined by school district staff as "political" rather than "educational." Consider, for example, the typical approaches to the contrasting issues of desegregation and community control. Professional educators commonly view desegregation as a political rather than an educational question, and therefore one that properly may be left to the board, or even the courts, to resolve.[8] Community control, however, represents a direct challenge to professional autonomy at the school level, and though the demand originates in the political arena, quickly it is redefined as an educational issue. Once so defined, community control is commonly accepted as an issue on which the board defers to the expertise of the professional staff. Legitimating this deference to professionals, or in effect to organizational processes in the determination of educational policies, is general public acceptance of the municipal reform movement's ideology. While the reformers argued that there is neither a Republican nor a Democratic solution to technical problems, but only a correct solution, they also proposed "the corporate board rather than the political forum"[9] as the correct model for school boards to emulate in making policy. Professional

expertise rather than public debate or the clash of interests was seen
as the appropriate basis for policy decisions. Public acceptance of
this approach, at least outside inner-city communities, underlies Zeigler and Jennings' finding, based upon data from more than eighty
school districts, that nowadays: "Although the school board has un-
contested formal authority over local educational systems, evidence . . . indicates that the leadership over educational policy rests
as much or more with the superintendent."[10] Reinforcing the influence of district superintendents, and the related dominance of
organizational processes in policy determination, is the "overpower-
ing force of professionalism, which by its nature asserts the right of
the professional to tell the client the appropriate course of action."[11]

Most educational policymaking at the school district level is structured by some combination of organizational processes and substantial rather than functional rationality. A problem is that substantially
rational arguments contain a heavy subjective component. The possible consequences of this subjectivity for policy proposals are obvious in the light of Mannheim's insight into the potential impact of
social environments upon the individual's interpretation of reality. In
this regard he writes:

> It could be shown in all cases that not only do fundamental orientations, eval-
> uations, and the content of ideas differ but that the manner of stating a prob-
> lem, the sort of approach made, and even the categories in which experiences are
> subsumed, collected, and ordered vary according to the social position of the
> observer.[12]

Minority group parents and professional educators bring different
perspectives to bear upon the achievement problem, which is so
prominent a characteristic of inner-city schools, and upon other educational issues, and therefore propose different solutions. Further, it
is evident that the solutions proposed are not divorced from the distinctive material and ideological interests of the parties involved. For
example, minority group advocates of local control typically view
the failure of schools serving their communities as one more mani-
festation of discrimination against minority students and their cultural traditions by the majority white population, who exercise ultimate control over the educational system. This analysis leads
logically to the plausible, or substantially rational, proposal that educational governance should be decentralized by placing parental

representatives in charge of the schools, and holding staffs account-able to these representatives for student performance.

However, an argument for community control premised on the prevalence of systemic discrimination predictably is unacceptable to most educators. From their perspective, the achievement problem is essentially a student problem, rooted in the economically disadvan-taged backgrounds of many inner-city children. The premise of dis-advantaged backgrounds allows educators to argue (with decreasing plausibility as the failure of most compensatory programs becomes increasingly evident) that schooling outcomes can be improved by: (1) greatly increased funding of the schools, and (2) decentraliza-tion of administrative decisionmaking in order that schools might adapt to the special needs of their particular student population. Most school administrators, who see community control as letting the passengers take over the ship, demand more power to the prin-cipal rather than to the parents.

The problem, of course, is that in the absence of tested knowledge regarding the impact of either decentralized administration or com-munity control, the efficacy of either approach as a means to im-proving student achievement cannot be determined. Therefore, the response adopted by a given district to community control demands is likely to depend on the extent to which community control advo-cates can mobilize public support to ensure that the issue of school-ing outcomes is dealt with not by organizational processes dominated by professional educators but by bargaining in the political arena. In this regard, it is interesting to note that in the few districts where some measure of community control, or decentralized governance, has been adopted, the relevant decisions were made not at the school district level, but in the highly partisan environment of the state legislature. This has been the experience common to New York City, Detroit, and Los Angeles, though in the latter case district officials were successful ultimately in persuading the Governor of California to veto the decentralization legislation adopted by both houses of the state legislature.[13]

At the state level, decisionmaking is structured most importantly, though certainly not exclusively, in accordance with the political bar-gaining model, with all the multiple interests competing, rather than being worked out within the administrative offices of the board of education. Professional groups and their organizations continue to play an important role in determining statewide educational policies, but minority group leaders, community organizations, civic leaders, labor unions, political parties, and many others also are actively lobbying. Such broadened involvement allows multiple perspectives upon educational problems, not simply the viewpoint of educators, to contribute toward policy decisions. Ultimately, of course, the effectiveness of whatever policies are adopted, either at the state or school district levels, is conditional on the extent to which they produce results that satisfy public expectations. To determine public expectations with regard to school district decentralization, we must analyze the factors underlying the demand for community control, or decentralized governance.

Governmental Decentralization

Minority Expectations. Demands for community control over local schools originated with leaders of the black community in New York City's East Harlem area in 1966. Precipitating the demand was the intersection of two factors, one empirical, the other normative. These were the educational failure of ghetto schools, and the emergence of a powerful commitment to racial identity, articulated in the call for black power.[14] Analysis of the educational failure of East Harlem schools from a black power, or "nationalist" perspective, led community leaders to the conclusion that institutionalized racism, albeit unconscious, was the major factor inhibiting student progress, thus provoking the call for community control. From the point of view of these leaders, final evidence of the racist character of the system in New York City came with school board insistence upon locating a new intermediate school, IS 201, in East Harlem where it would be impossible to have an integrated student body. This action of the Board of Education contradicted the Board's own policy commitment of 1964, that new schools were to be placed in locations that would allow for integration. Faced with this evidence of majority group rejection of integration, community leaders proposed that IS 201 be used for an experiment in community control. Behind this proposal, presented in written form by Preston Wilcox,[15] lay two assumptions. The first was that placing a local school under the direction of parental representatives, and holding staff accountable to these representatives for student outcomes, would be the most effective way to secure control over the organizational processes determining school level policies and to bring personnel attitudes and behaviors into line with parental preferences and values, thus establishing a basis for productive student-faculty inter-action. Special stress was placed on parental selection of the school principal to ensure a person who: "Instead of being committed to the elimination in his pupils of all that he feels is repulsive in their background and values, . . . would be committed to utilizing those values as a resource for education."[16]

The second assumption was that a parental committee controlling a local school could help the institution contribute to community development. Initially, the major possibilities envisioned were the involvement of students in community service and action programs, introduction of parents into the school as paraprofessionals, thus giving new career positions to neighborhood people while helping develop school-community relations, and the use of the school building for adult social activities in the evenings and on weekends.

Essentially, therefore, Wilcox's original proposal contained the key themes that continue to find expression in demands for community control in cities around the country that: schools be accountable to a parent committee to ensure that parental preferences determine educational policy; the parent committee control selection of the principal; and the school building and resources be available for community development. These proposals have evoked wide support not only in many minority communities but increasingly in the majority white population, as evidenced both by the emerging debate regarding school-site management and by actual experiments with parentally governed alternative public schools in several cities.

Majority Group Expectations. Community control has found support in the white population for negative reasons, such as avoidance of inter-school busing for purposes of desegregation, but a more durable and growing interest has a positive motivation based upon a tendency among parents to view publicly funded neighborhood schools as functional substitutes for private schools, the cultural ideal in terms of elementary and secondary education. While the very wealthy shop around to locate a private school that meets their preferences, most families have to use the public schools serving their own neighborhood. Unable to choose a school on the basis of its compatability with their expectations regarding personnel and program, the alternative is to work for expression of these preferences in the public school. As noted by the chairman of a recent district-wide citizens committee in Los Angeles, "few parents are ever completely happy about giving a child over to a formal system of education unless the parent is allowed to continue participation in the choices and processes which will shape the life of the child."[17] To structure such participation, parents in the white population are showing growing interest in the concept, advanced originally by minority group proponents of community control, of school level parent committees authorized to play a determinative role in principal selection, the setting of school goals, and the development of criteria for assessing progress toward goal implementation. Detailed proposals of this nature, referred to nowadays as school-site management, are included in the Fleischmann Commission Report[18] for New York State, and also in the report of the Governor's Citizens' Committee on Education[19] for the State of Florida, details of which are discussed later.

Reaction of Professional Educators. Proposals for community control, especially from minority communities, have not been enthusiastically received by the great majority of school administrators and teachers. From a professional perspective, the achievement problem has more complex roots than staff attitudes, and it is not likely to be solved by holding staff accountable for student learning. Further, experience with community control experiments in New York City (from 1967 through 1970) proved unhappy in terms of staff-community relationships. The removal of 19 teachers from the Ocean Hill-Brownsville experimental district, allegedly without due process, gave rise to a six-week strike by teachers in all the city schools in the fall of 1968. The dispute also led the president of the teachers' union, Albert Shanker,[20] to conclude that community control is no more than a veiled demand for the right to hire and fire staff on grounds of race.

Defensively, as noted previously, professional educators have responded to community control demands by proposing the alternative of administrative decentralization. An early example of this counterresponse is provided by the reaction of New York City's Council of Supervisory Associations to the original demand for community control. The school district's supervisors responded with the substantially rational argument that:

. . . a decentralized plan that negates central authority and establishes independent, autonomous school boards creates duplication, financial waste, and confusion and disrupts the entire school system, On the other hand, a decentralized school system without local school boards increases flexibility in terms of specific activities for individual schools and communities and also avoids conflict and confrontation.[21]

In practice, the actual decentralization plan adopted for New York City (and also for Detroit) represents a compromise between the somewhat conflicting alternatives of decentralized governance and decentralized administration.[22] In most cities, however, the issue has so far been resolved in favor of decentralized administration, though the stability of this solution remains in doubt.

Administrative Decentralization

Demand for community control originated in a minority community perspective that views the educational failure of ghetto schools as due in large part to the fact that "the operating philosophy of the existing system is too often manifested in a conscious or unconscious belittling of the values and life styles of its clientele."[23] To change this philosophy, and its accompanying discriminatory attitudes, minority proponents of community control argue that professional staffs should be accountable to parental representatives. This would allow ghetto institutions "to become what schools in more privileged areas already are, a reflection of local interests and resources, instead of a subtle rejection of them."[24] In an accepting environment, students are likely to find schooling a more positive, and productive, experience.

This approach, of course, is directly opposed to the perspectives on school failure typically held by professional educators. In their view, multiple factors account for the low average levels of achievement in inner-city schools. These factors include failure of parents to motivate children to learn; a social and physical environment outside of school that provides little opportunity, or encouragement, for study; untreated physical and emotional problems of many children; and a lack of sufficient authority for principals to adapt instructional programs to local needs. From the point of view of professionals, therefore, the solution lies in compensatory education coupled with increased discretionary authority for principals. Also, parental participation in an advisory role only is considered important to alert the school to community feelings and to harness community support. These alternative approaches of community persons and of professional educators are distinguished clearly in the report of the Task Force that developed the decentralization program for the Los Angeles school district.

> The debate over decentralization seems inevitably to devolve upon two basic points of view: that advocated by those who favor *local control*—basically political in orientation—and that advocated by those who favor *administrative decentralization*—oriented more to function and professionalism.[25]

Reflecting the dominance of norms of professionalism within the decisionmaking process, in response to pressure from the state legislature and from minority communities for increased community control, the Los Angeles school board adopted the alternative approach of administrative decentralization, dividing the district into twelve areas, extending the authority of local school principals, and mandating community advisory councils for each school. This administrative response, adopted now by many cities, takes on generalizable meaning in the light of Thompson's theory of organizations[26] as being systems that are constrained by norms of rationality to insulate their internal operations from potentially disruptive external influences, while at the same time being forced to remain open to their external environment in proportion to their dependence upon it for resource inputs, and the utilization of outputs. School districts, for example, generally depend upon electoral support for access to local property tax revenues. In order to buffer or "manage" the effects of such dependency, organizations develop specialized structures to span the boundary with their environment. Boundary-spanning is the process by which an organization receives inputs of information and resources from its environment and, conversely, exerts some measure of influence upon those persons who constitute the social dimension of that same environment.

Calls for community control signal a breakdown of the effectiveness of traditional school district boundary-spanning structures, such as elected governing boards and school level PTAs, and indicate serious erosion of public support for the system, due largely to parental dissatisfaction with the educational services provided by the schools. Restoration of support requires greatly increased responsiveness to the particular needs of students, and to preferences of parents, in the individual attendance areas. As pointed out in 1972 by the director of the Los Angeles school district's Decentralization Task Force, the importance of decentralization "is in encouraging local schools to become more individual, just as communities now are becoming more different."[27] However, whether administrative decentralization as typically implemented can, in fact, bring about sufficient change in the schools to satisfy parental expectations remains problematic.

A major difficulty, as Cibulka[28] notes in discussing school decentralization in Chicago, is that while administrators at the district level want improved boundary-spanning with the public, the means adopted especially school advisory councils conflict with the interests and day-to-day operational objectives of school principals. While elected community or parent councils offer promise of co-opting public support for the schools to the extent that councils have real authority over school level decisions, they pose the threat of winning parental support at the cost of breaking down what principals and their staffs legitimately regard as the necessary insulation of in-school instructional processes from the potentially disruptive impact of exposure to multiple, and most probably conflicting, community pressures. To protect schools from this danger, school district authorities typically emphasize the purely *advisory* character of community councils and stress that legal responsibility for the school rests with the principal alone. Principals, therefore, may ignore the advice proffered, a condition that limits parental interest and thus restricts the potential of councils to actually span the school-community divide. Ironically, principals are offered a rationale for ignoring parental opinion in the report of the Los Angeles school district task force that actually proposed the district's decentralization plan, including the mandatory school level advisory councils. Addressing the question of why private schools in general, and public schools in small affluent suburbs, appear to work well in comparison to the allegedly poor performance of public schools in the cities, the task force submitted that:

an important reason these schools appear to "work" better is that they are governed by local administrators who have considerable managerial power, managerial discretion, and managerial immunity to outside pressures (*including* parental pressures). Public school principals in the Los Angeles District compare favorably enough to these school principals. What they have too frequently lacked is any kind of real power to do a good job. Decentralization is one thing, democracy is another . . . .[29]

This restrictive approach among school administrators to parental involvement in school level decisions is demonstrated by Marmion's[30] study of principals in an urban school district as well as by Cibulka's Chicago report.[31] Not surprisingly, therefore, three years after the 1971 mandate for creation of school advisory councils in Los Angeles, a blue ribbon citizens' committee, instituted by the district superintendent to recommend city-wide educational goals, concluded that these councils have some serious inadequacies. The major difficulty identified by the committee, as the Los Angeles Times editorialized, is that the councils are:

advisory, and their effectiveness often depends on the willingness of school principals to cooperate. The citizens' committee wants to change that relationship by increasing "the number of matters in which the community will have decision-making or consultation involvement and decreasing the number of matters in which community involvement is advisory. . . ." In short, the committee would take some authority away from school principals and give it to the councils. The councils would have some responsibility for setting standards by which teachers are selected, and standards for the evaluation of the work of principals.[32]

The editorial then makes the point that the committee report "does not denigrate the role of the professional educator. It simply underscores the often-frustrated desire by parents to be more closely involved in the education of their children." Satisfaction of this parental desire in ways that also protect the legitimate interests of professional educators requires a merging of community and school system approaches to the decentralization issue. Present developments point to such an accommodation within the framework of proposals for school-site management.

Future Trends

In Detroit, a 1968 citizens' committee looking into the problem of developing better relations between high schools and their environing communities, recommended that most decisions should be made by the school principal. The committee believed that the principal "should be the one person who combines necessary decision-making with a clear grasp of the needs peculiar to a given neighborhood. He should be given the responsibility for relating the school to its environment; he should be given the authority to do it; he should be held accountable for the results."[33]

The question, of course, is accountable to whom? Community control advocates might be willing to go a long way toward giving principals more responsibility and authority if accountability was to representatives of the parents, rather than to administrative superiors. In fact, some parental intrusion into the administrative hierarchy is evident in Chicago where the Board of Education, responding to pressure from minority community leaders, has authorized a procedure allowing parents a large role in the selection of principals. When a vacancy occurs, the parent advisory committee at the school is asked to form a principal nominating committee containing representatives of the advisory committee, PTA, and any other school-related groups. On the basis of criteria approved by the Board in 1972, the nominating committee selects two candidates from among those applying for the opening, all of whom already have passed the district's qualifying exam. The Board and senior administrators finally determine which of the two nominees shall receive the position. The Chicago procedure comes close to the Fleischmann Commission's recommendation that every public school in New York State institute a Parent Advisory Council, "in order to foster and facilitate citizen involvement in the educational process,"[34] the most important function of which would be to participate in the selection of the school principal. Further, to ensure continued principal accountability to the parents, the Commission proposed that principal employment be based upon two-to-five-year contracts with renewal being dependent upon parental approval.

Control over the principal's appointment goes far toward establishing one of the basic conditions for effectively structuring school accountability to the parental community and is responsive, therefore, to a community perspective on educational problems. However, if principals are to be held accountable for schooling outcomes, they need more authority over school staff and operations than normally allowed. To meet this need, the Fleischmann Commission has proposed that paralleling the initiation of parental control over the appointment of principals, the latter should be given full authority over the selection of teachers and paraprofessionals, though in accord with criteria acceptable to the parents. If the principal is to be held accountable for schooling outcomes, clearly he must have the authority to select his own staff.

Extending the authority of the principal within the school, especially with regard to personnel selection, and giving the Parent Advisory Council authority over the principal, effects a balance between parental demands for some measure of control over school policies and the legitimate demand of administrators and teachers for professional autonomy. Also, this approach may resolve the problem of harnessing community support; a parent committee with real authority being, in principle at least, the most effective boundary-spanning structure.

Similar to the Fleischmann Commission proposals for the State of New York, suggestions for school level parent committees emerged from the Governor's Citizens' Committee on Education[35] for the State of Florida. However, in that state professional educators joined with school boards and PTA members to fight the issue of local parental control, not on the basis of whether structural changes should be introduced, but with regard to the more general and highly emotional normative question of "the extent of the state's role in education vis-a-vis the local school board's."[36] Consequently, rather than the state mandating parent committees with real authority, it has been left to the individual school districts to decide how much authority the parent committees will have. Confirming the conclusions reached earlier in this chapter with regard to the dominance of organizational processes in the determination of school district policies, the parent committees that have been created by school districts themselves in Florida actually have a strong advisory emphasis, paralleling those associated with administrative decentralization in northern cities. As with the latter, however, the Florida committees are likely to be just a beginning, with the initial wave of participants creating a base for more meaningful participation later.

The consequences of parental participation in school level governance and administration is the question that we turn to next, drawing on the still rather limited research for guidance. In low-income areas, the primary concern, of course, is the potential impact on average levels of student achievement of changes in the structure of school-community relations. For more affluent sectors of the population, the chief interest is likely to be parental desire to have a voice in policies governing the in-school experiences of their children.

SOCIAL SCIENCE RESEARCH AND
DECENTRALIZATION

Recent research on the effectiveness of schools raises substantial doubts as to the ability of any school policy to alter the patterns of student achievement. One might fairly ask, then, what policy justification exists to support demands for decentralization? How can it be justified in educational terms? If not, then what other desirable outcomes can be effectuated? To respond to these questions, we turn next to an examination of the consequences of decentralization for student achievement, community development, and public participation in educational decisionmaking.

Student Achievement and Other Student Outcomes

Social science research offers little guidance to policymakers concerned with improving school outcomes, especially achievement. The magnitude of the achievement problem is reflected in the fact that the national survey conducted by Coleman *et al.,*[37] showed that twelfth-grade students from the black, Puerto Rican, and Mexican-American sectors of the population performed at an average level three years behind their peers in the white population. The Coleman team found that the major determinant of this difference was the gap in socioeconomic status between white and minority students. Differences between schools in terms of their operating characteristics proved to have relatively little impact upon average learning outcomes. Characteristics studied included per pupil expenditure, teacher-pupil ratios, teacher quality, and physical facilities. An extensive review of published educational research conducted by Averch *et al.,*[38] reveals widespread agreement that how much students learn in school is directly related to their prior experiences out of school, and that schools, as presently organized, find these out-of-school factors virtually impossible to overcome.

Of course, advocates of community control take issue with this conclusion, typically taking heart from the Coleman Report findings regarding student attitudes. Of all the variables measured in the survey, three attitudes—student interest in school, self-concept, and sense of environmental control—show the strongest relation to achievement.[39] Given this finding, Berube[40] and Gittell[41] have advanced what the latter calls the domino theory of educational change. This theory makes the assumption that giving control over the school to the local community will lead to changes in staff, and in staff attitudes toward students. These changes in turn will create the condition for students to internalize greater self-respect, to take more interest in school, and to develop a greater sense of control over their own destiny. As a consequence, they are likely to perform better academically. Perhaps so, but while the Coleman data show a strong relationship between certain attitudes and achievement, they say nothing about how students acquire these attitudes. Unfortunately, the one major research study that does look into the effectiveness of formal schooling in forming student attitudes comes up with the typical conclusion that out-of-school factors again are crucial. This study, conducted by Greeley and Rossi,[42] used the parochial school system as, in effect, an experiment in attitudinal socialization. Analysis of their data led the authors to conclude that formal schooling can reinforce attitudes that students bring to the classroom, but cannot establish new attitudes in most students, thus challenging the credibility of the domino theory.[43]

The major implication of the research findings discussed thus far is that if one wishes to improve average student outcomes from schools, the longest way round may be the shortest way home. Investment in *community* rather than *educational* development ultimately might be the most effective route to take in providing conditions for solving the achievement problem. In fact Benson et al.,[43] have proposed dividing compensatory education funds between educational and community services; the educational funds would be based upon in-school achievement levels of students, while the community funds would be keyed to level of family income. So far, however, there is no indication that such a proposal will find much welcome from professional educators, and as noted earlier, they dominate generally within the decisionmaking processes of school district governance.

Two studies that specifically address the question of decentralization's impact on school effectiveness are those by Gittell and Zimet. Gittell evaluated the experimental community-controlled districts that existed in New York City from 1967 until being absorbed within the overall city-wide decentralization plan in 1970. Regarding schooling outcomes, the best that Gittell[44] could conclude was that while test results averaged across all schools in the city showed some downward movement over the three-year period, educational achievement in the experimental districts was not reduced. Further, some individual programs appeared to have worked well for some children. Clearly, however, the overall impact of local control upon student performance was disappointing. Given the atmosphere of political crisis within which the experimental districts maintained their tenuous existence, it can be argued that in a calmer setting the results may well have been better, though Zimet's[45] data are not especially encouraging in this regard.

Zimet's study focused upon one of the new community school districts in New York City—District 7 in South Bronx. For the 22 schools in this district, located in a largely black and Puerto Rican community, test scores remained remarkably constant from 1965 through 1972. Zimet's study ran from 1970-1972, two years after the system's governance was partially decentralized. Data for the city as a whole, one year after decentralization, showed that "predominantly white schools achieved above grade level and predominantly minority-group schools achieved below grade level."[46] On the basis of these and other data, the Fleischmann Commission concluded that "there are two public elementary school systems in the City of New York; one largely white, in which students learn how to read well, and the other largely black and Puerto Rican in which they do not."[47]

Data from other cities around the country continually repeat the same story, whether governance has been decentralized to some degree (as in New York City and Detroit) or whether change has been limited to administrative structures (as in Chicago and Los Angeles). These findings not only point to a lack of impact on student achievement by either form of decentralization, but also indicate the relative failure of compensatory education, which has been operating in various forms quite intensively in virtually all urban school systems since 1965.

The absence of a direct effect of decentralization upon average levels of student achievement may be a greater problem (in terms of policy justification) for decentralized administration than for decentralized governance. The idea behind decentralized administration is that principals and other school-level professionals have lacked the power and resources to do good jobs in raising low achievement patterns that are regarded as the result of student socioeconomic status.

The purpose of administrative decentralization, in other words, is to increase the effectiveness of existing education. The social science research does not leave one hopeful that mere decentralized administration will offset the learning deficiencies of poor and minority children.

By contrast, decentralized governance, where professionals are accountable to parents and community, offers somewhat more promise, and can at least be justified in terms of other desirable school and community outcomes. Hamilton, for example, argues that from the viewpoint of many blacks, community control is not simply an attempt to improve existing educational processes. Rather, the demand for community control, which originated in the deep alienation of minority communities from the existing system, is a challenge by minorities to the very legitimacy of traditional institutionalized schooling. Hamilton, expanding upon Wilcox's position cited earlier, takes the view that providing an effective education for minority students means more than improving verbal and math skills; it means creating a different kind of education, broader in concept than existing education and relevant to minority children and minority cultures.

> They [the experts] fail to understand that their criteria for "educational achievement" simply might not be relevant anymore. . . .
> The experts must understand that what is high on the liberal social scientist's agenda does not coincide with the agenda of many black people. *The experts are still focusing on the effectiveness of existing educational institutions. Many black people have moved to the evaluation of the legitimacy of these institutions.* . . .
> The focus has shifted: emphasis is now on viable ways to gain enough leverage to drastically revise a system. Black people, having moved to the stage of questioning the system's very legitimacy, are seeking ways to create a new system. (Emphasis added.)[48]

Hamilton's new system is a comprehensive family-community-school plan that is concerned with the whole family, not only with student outcomes of schooling but with other outcomes as well, such as greater public participation in decisionmaking and community socioeconomic development. Decentralized governance, by facilitating parental participation in educational decisions and by addressing itself to the socioeconomic deficiencies of the community, focuses on what researchers see as the primary cause of low achievement.

Community Development

Decentralized governance, by aiding community development, offers an opportunity to affect the major determinant of student performance, the socioeconomic status of the local school community. Indeed, facilitating the social and economic development of low-income communities may well be sufficient justification for the decentralization of educational governance.

Both in the original experimental districts in New York City and in the community district studied by Zimet, the main instrumentality for community development has been the availability of compensatory education funds that can be used to hire parents in paraprofessional roles. When Gittell conducted a community survey in Ocean Hill-Brownsville and asked parents to name the two most important things they wanted done in the schools, the top choices were reducing overcrowding and training neighborhood people as teacher's aides. In Gittell's opinion, the fact that parents held this view "could possibly reflect a wider function they are assigning to the schools—that of providing jobs for the community."[49] In fact, in the three experimental districts, more than 700 persons were employed in paraprofessional roles, confirming that: "Because the governing boards looked upon the districts in political and economic as well as in educational terms, they used every opportunity to facilitate the entry of minority group people into the system. This meant supporting programs which employed paid paraprofessionals."[50] Here, as in New York City's Community District 7, studied by Zimet, paraprofessionals were an important political plum.

In Community District 7, as in the other new districts in New York, the locally elected board has two major areas of final authority: the appointment of the district's superintendent and the allocation of compensatory education funds. In the years of Zimet's study (1970-1972), District 7 received about $7,000,000 in compensatory monies annually. With the help of these funds, approximately 500 persons were employed as paraprofessionals in the district's 22 schools. The Board also took every opportunity to add Puerto Rican and black professionals to the staffs of the schools.

While employment of local residents contributes in a rather obvious way to local economic development, the pattern of hiring in District 7 also strengthened the community political structure. In New York City, the poverty agencies have gained control of the screening and hiring of at least half of all paraprofessionals employed in schools with federal funds.[51] This practice is legitimated by the legal requirement that plans for the utilization of compensatory education funds under Title I of the Elementary and Secondary Education Act (ESEA) must be coordinated with other agencies serving the same target population. Control over the hiring of paraprofessionals reinforces the leadership position within the community of poverty agency officials, and also "contributes to the clout of community corporations vis-a-vis the Community School Board."[52] This clout allows community leaders not only to influence incumbent Board members, but also to determine who the incumbents will be. In 1970, of the nine persons elected to the Board of Community District 7, seven had the endorsement of one poverty agency, the South Bronx Corporation.[53] As these agencies have come to function for minority communities in much the same way that political clubs and parties served the needs of former white immigrants to the city, expansion of their ability to mobilize the population is an integral part of overall community development.

Community development is not only economic and political, but also cultural, as Greenstone and Peterson[54] emphasize. In this regard, Zimet discovered that in Community District 7, the issue that provoked the most intense interest at board meetings was the "recurrent demand by community members for an increase in the number of black and Puerto Rican teachers and supervisors."[55] Parents hoped that minority teachers would relate better to children of their own group, reinforcing rather than rejecting distinctive cultural traditions. Board meetings generally were well attended and were held at a different school each month in order to satisfy public demand for participation, which suggests a third theme in evaluating decentralization.

Public Participation in Educational Decisions

Apart from tangible outcomes, whether in the form of student achievement or the social and economic development of the local community, much of the contemporary discussion about the "quality" of American political life centers on the question of participation, and this is somewhat of an end in itself. Verba and Nie write: "Participation is not committed to any social goals but is a technique for setting goals, choosing priorities, and deciding what resources to commit to goal attainment."[56] In effect, to use Thompson's concept cited earlier, participation has come to be a major technique for spanning the boundary between public institutions and their environing communities. In this regard, therefore, it is especially interesting to find that after having studied decentralization in five major cities, LaNoue and Smith arrive at the conclusion that while decentralization has not generated mass participation in school affairs: "the participatory ethos remains the most powerful and appealing part of the decentralization ideology. Sometimes as a substitute for formal decentralization, sometimes in conjunction with it, advisory councils, paraprofessionals, community liaison workers—all manner of citizens—have come to be viewed as normal participants in school operations."[57]

However, as noted already, this participatory ethos causes problems for the stability of administrative decentralization. For participation to be a meaningful boundary-spanning technique, it has to give participants some measure of control, as Greenstone and Peterson[58] also conclude. Similarly, Verba and Nie quickly focus on the control objective, arguing that participation, in the context of democratic norms, is concerned with "acts that aim at *influencing* the government, either by affecting the *choice* of government personnel or by affecting the *choices made by* government personnel."[59] Other forms of participation, which are not necessarily democratic, they label as "ceremonial," or "support" oriented, and such forms are unlikely to maintain credibility with the public for very long.

CONCLUSION

The above discussion leads us to conclude that despite professional opposition, community-based pressure for more influence over school policies and programs appears likely to grow. While social science research on the problem of making schools educationally more effective so far has produced no knowledge useful for that purpose, public demand for improved schooling outcomes, and for participation by parents in school-level decisionmaking, has evoked a general restructuring of urban school district administration, school-community relations, and the beginnings of a movement toward decentralized governance.

The future pattern of decentralization is likely to incorporate structures that balance parental and school-level professional interests. Decentralized administration has a problematic outcome with regard to its major objective—the mobilization of parental support behind existing centralized structures of school district governance. Parents are likely to be dissatisfied with a purely advisory role, such as that allowed by the typical structure for harnessing parental support, the school-community advisory council. In fact, current developments suggest that over time school advisory councils will take on decisionmaking responsibilities, especially regarding personnel selection and school-level goals. At the same time, school administrators will be granted greater discretionary authority for policy implementation. This emerging pattern represents a reflection downward to the local school site of the existing structure of relations between elected lay persons and appointed administrators at the school district level. It is tension between lay persons and professionals, each guided by substantial rather than by functional rationality, that is helping to shape this future pattern of educational governance and administration, typically characterized as school-site management.

In summary, therefore, evaluation of decentralization yields the following conclusions:

1. Decentralization, whether of governance or administration, has yet to have an observable impact upon average levels of student achievement, although to be fair, decentralized governance has never been fully implemented or allowed to operate for a sufficient period of time to evaluate properly.

2. Decentralized governance has sounder policy justifications than decentralized administration in that the former may influence other important student outcomes, such as political socialization and student attitudes, and may hold some promise even in terms of student achievement.

3. Decentralized governance allows for exploitation of school resources for community development, especially resources available under compensatory education programs.

4. For all sectors of the population, the participatory ethos appears to be a major factor motivating continuing support for all forms of decentralization.

Thus, decentralization of school district governance, either by the formation of community sub-districts or by creating elected parent committees at the school level to which administrators would be accountable, as proposed originally by Wilcox[60], does offer policy incentives. Though apparently unable to help the achievement problem, at least in the short run, such restructuring facilitates utilization of school resources for community development in poverty areas, and for all sectors of the population offers the opportunity for more direct participation by parents in their children's schooling.

NOTES

1. A survey shows that 18 out of 21 school districts with enrollments of 100,000 or more students either had decentralized by 1973, or planned to do so, though invariably confining change to a restructuring of administration only. (Allan C. Ornstein, *Race and Politics in School-Community Organizations* [Pacific Palisades, Calif.: Goodyear Publishing Co., 1974], 5.) Among smaller districts, enrolling from 50,000 to 100,000 students, the proportion decentralized was lower than for the larger districts, but still high. Among 44 districts in this smaller category, 29 had decentralized, or planned to do so.

For a detailed discussion of the background to the emergence of demands for community control, and subsequent changes in school district governance and administration, see George R. LaNoue and Bruce L. R. Smith, *The Politics of School Decentralization* [Lexington, Mass.: D. C. Heath & Co., 1973] and Jay D. Scribner and David O'Shea, "Political Developments in Urban School Districts," in C. Wayne Gordon (ed.), *Uses of the Sociology of Education.* 73rd Yearbook of the National Society for the Study of Education [Chicago, Ill.: University of Chicago Press, 1974], chap. 13, 380-408.

2. Diane Ravitch, "Local Control in the New York Public Schools, 1842-1896," *Notes on Education* 6(January 1975), 1-5.

3. *Ibid.,* 4.

4. For a discussion of the utility of Allison's models of decisionmaking (Graham Allison, *Essence of Decision: Explaining the Cuban Missile Crisis* [Boston: Little, Brown, 1971]) for the analysis of school district governance, see Paul E. Peterson and Thomas Williams, "Models of Decision-Making," in Michael Kirst (ed.), *State, School and Politics* [Lexington, Mass.: D. C. Heath & Co., 1972], 149-68, and Paul E. Peterson, "Afterword: The Politics of School Decentralization," *Education and Urban Society* 7(No. 4, August 1975), 464-79.

5. Karl Mannheim, "Types of Rationality and Organized Insecurity," in C. Wright Mills (ed.), *Images of Man: The Classic Tradition in Sociological Thinking* (New York: George Braziller, Inc., 1960), chap. 18.

6. *Ibid.,* 508.

7. Allison, *op. cit.*

8. The differential response of school district superintendents and school boards to the demands of civil rights groups for school desegregation is described by Crain in his study of desegregation in eight cities (Robert L. Crain, *The Politics of School Desegregation* [New York: Doubleday, Anchor Books, 1969]). Crain describes the response of the superintendents as containing three elements:

(a) an insistence that the only morally correct position is strict non-discrimination (color-blindness) and that efforts to intentionally integrate schools are improper for this reason; (b) an insistence on a narrow definition of the function of the school which stresses "educational" rather than "social" values and hence sees integration as outside the school's province; and (c) an unwillingness to engage in serious discussion of the issue with lay persons, and an extreme defensiveness in the face of criticism. *Ibid.*, 144.

Discussing the experience of Los Angeles, Tim L. Mazzoni, Jr., in "Political Capability for Urban School Governance: An Analysis of the Los Angeles City School Board (1967-1969)," unpublished Ph.D. dissertation, Claremont Graduate School, Claremont, California, 1971 reports that the incumbent superintendent in the 1960's clearly "questioned the educational worth of desegregating schools; that he considered such demands to require 'a political judgment, not an educational one'; and, thus, that he felt no great responsibility to exercise positive leadership in respect to this issue" (211-12).

9. William L. Boyd, "School Board-Administrative Staff Relationships." Paper presented at the National School Board Association's Invitational Symposium, "School Board Research: Main Lines of Inquiry," Miami Beach, Florida, April 16-18, 1975, at page 6.

10. L. Harmon Zeigler and M. Kent Jennings, with the assistance of G. Wayne Peak, *Governing American Schools: Political Interaction in Local School Districts* (North Scituate, Mass.: Duxbury Press, 1974), 4.

11. *Ibid.*, 6.

12. Karl Mannheim, "The Prospect of Scientific Politics," in C. Wright Mills (ed.), *op. cit.*, 93.

13. For details of developments in Los Angeles, and action by the state legislature in California, see LaNoue and Smith, *op. cit.*, and also Scribner and O'Shea, *op. cit.*

14. A full description of events in East Harlem leading up to the call for community control is provided by LaNoue and Smith, *op. cit.* A shorter summary is provided by Scribner and O'Shea, *op. cit.*

15. Preston R. Wilcox, "The Controversy Over IS 201: One View and a Proposal," *The Urban Review* 1(No. 3, 1966), 12-16.

16. *Ibid.*, 13.

17. Los Angeles Unified School District, "Report of the District Goals Review Committee." Mimeo. October 22, 1974, ii.

18. *Fleischmann Report on the Quality, Cost, and Financing of Elementary and Secondary Education in New York State.* Vol. III. (New York: The Viking Press, 1973).

19. Governor's Citizens' Committee on Education, *Improving Education in Florida* (Tallahassee, Fla.: Office of the Governor, 1973).

20. Albert Shanker, "Cult of Localism," in Patricia C. Sexton (ed.), *School Policy and Issues in a Changing Society* (Boston: Allyn and Bacon, Inc., 1971), 213-23.

21. Ornstein, *op. cit.*, 53.

22. See Melvin Zimet, *Decentralization and School Effectiveness* (New York: Teachers College Press, 1973).

23. Wilcox, *op. cit.*, 15.

24. *Ibid.*

25. Los Angeles Unified School District, *Educational Renewal: A Decentralization Proposal for the Los Angeles Unified School District* (Los Angeles: The District, 1971), 26-27.

26. James D. Thompson, *Organizations in Action* (New York: McGraw Hill, Inc., 1967). For an insightful elaboration of Thompson's approach, and an example of its application in the context of school decentralization, see Mary T. Moore, "The Boundary-Spanning Role of the Urban School Principal," unpublished Ph.D. dissertation, School of Education, University of California, Los Angeles, 1975.

27. Los Angeles Unified School District, *Decentralization: One Year Later.* Report presented by the Decentralization Task Force to the Los Angeles Board of Education (May 1972), chap. VII, p and q.

28. James G. Cibulka, "School Decentralization in Chicago," *Education and Urban Society* 7(No. 4, August 1975), 412-38.

29. Los Angeles Unified School District, *Educational Renewal, op. cit.*, 28-30.

30. William H. Marmion, "The Relationship of School Principals' Characteristics to the Community Advisory Council Process," unpublished Ph.D. dissertation, Claremont Graduate School, Claremont, California, 1974.

31. Cibulka, *op. cit.*

32. *Los Angeles Times* (Editorial, November 21, 1974), Part II, 6.

33. William R. Grant, "Community Control vs. School Integration: The Case of Detroit," *The Public Interest* 66(Summer 1971), 62-71.

34. *Fleischmann Report, op. cit.*, 7.

35. Governor's Citizens' Committee on Education, *Improving Education in Florida, op. cit.*

36. Florida Senate Education Committee, "A Report on School Advisory Committees in Florida." Mimeo (August 12, 1974), 1.

37. James S. Coleman, *et al.*, *Equality of Educational Opportunity*, Office of Education, National Center for Educational Statistics, OE 38001 (Washington, D.C.: Government Printing Office, 1966). Hereafter cited as the Coleman Report.

38. Harvey A. Averch *et al.*, *How Effective is Schooling? A Critical Review and Synthesis of Research Findings* (Santa Monica, Calif.: RAND, 1972).

39. Coleman Report, 319.

40. Maurice R. Berube, "Achievement and Community Control," in Particia C. Sexton (ed.), *op. cit.*, 224-32.

41. Marilyn Gittell, *Demonstration for Social Change* (New York: Institute for Community Studies, Queens College of the City of New York, 1971).

42. Andrew M. Greeley and Peter H. Rossi, *The Education of Catholic Americans* (New York: Doubleday, Anchor Books, 1968).

43. Charles S. Benson *et al.*, *Planning for Educational Reform: Financial and Social Alternatives* (New York: Dodd, Mead & Co., 1974), 86-87.

44. Gittell, *op. cit.*, 137.

45. Zimet, *op. cit.*

46. *Fleischmann Report, op. cit.*, 145.

47. *Ibid.*, 151.

48. C. V. Hamilton, "Race and Education: A Search for Legitimacy," *Harvard Educational Review* 38(1968), 669-84.

49. Gittell, *op. cit.*, 61.

50. *Ibid.*, 95.

51. See Robert T. Simmelkjaer, "Anti-Poverty Interest Group Articulation and Mobilization for Community Control in New York City," unpublished Ph.D. dissertation, Teachers College, Columbia University, New York, 1972.

52. Zimet, *op. cit.*, 67.

53. See Simmelkjaer, *op. cit.*, 236.

54. David J. Greenstone and Paul E. Peterson, *Race and Authority in Urban Politics: Community Participation and the War on Poverty* (New York: Russell Sage, 1973).

55. Zimet, *op. cit.*, 137.

56. Sidney Verba and Norman H. Nie, *Participation in America: Political Democracy and Social Equality* (New York: Harper & Row, 1972), 4.

57. LaNoue and Smith, *op. cit.*, 230-31.

58. Greenstone and Peterson, *op. cit.*, 94.

59. Verba and Nie, *op. cit.*, 2.

60. Wilcox, *op. cit.*